JAMES

THE NIV
APPLICATION
COMMENTARY

From biblical text . . . to contemporary life

JAMES

THE NIV
APPLICATION
COMMENTARY

From biblical text . . . to contemporary life

DAVID P. NYSTROM

ZondervanPublishingHouse
Grand Rapids, Michigan

A Division of HarperCollins*Publishers*

The NIV Application Commentary: James
Copyright © 1997 by David Nystrom

Requests for information should be addressed to:

 Zondervan Publishing House
Grand Rapids, Michigan 49530

Library of Congress Cataloging-in-Publication Data

Nystrom, David P., 1959–
    James / David P. Nystrom.
       p . cm.—(NIV application commentary)
      Includes bibliographical references and index.
      ISBN: 0–310–49360–9
      1. Bible. N.T. James—Commentaries.   I. Title.   II. Series.
    BS 2785.3.N97 1997
    227'.91077—dc21   97–34172
                                                   CIP

This edition printed on acid-free paper and meets the American National Standards Institute Z39.48 standard.

All Scripture quotations, unless otherwise indicated, are taken from the *Holy Bible: New International Version*®. NIV®. Copyright © 1973, 1978, 1984 by International Bible Society. Used by permission of Zondervan Publishing House. All rights reserved.

All rights reserved. No part of this publication may be reproduced, stored in a retrieval system, or transmitted in any form or by any means—electronic, mechanical, photocopy, recording, or any other—except for brief quotations in printed reviews, without the prior permission of the publisher.

Printed in the United States of America

00 01 02 / ❖ DC / 10 9 8 7 6

Contents

The NIV Application Commentary Series

When complete, the NIV Application Commentary
will include the following volumes:

To see which titles are available,
visit our web site at http://www.zondervan.com

NIV Application Commentary
Series Introduction

THE NIV APPLICATION COMMENTARY SERIES is unique. Most commentaries help us make the journey from the twentieth century back to the first century. They enable us to cross the barriers of time, culture, language, and geography that separate us from the biblical world. Yet they only offer a one-way ticket to the past and assume that we can somehow make the return journey on our own. Once they have explained the *original meaning* of a book or passage, these commentaries give us little or no help in exploring its *contemporary significance*. The information they offer is valuable, but the job is only half done.

Recently, a few commentaries have included some contemporary application as *one* of their goals. Yet that application is often sketchy or moralistic, and some volumes sound more like printed sermons than commentaries.

The primary goal of The NIV Application Commentary Series is to help you with the difficult but vital task of bringing an ancient message into a modern context. The series not only focuses on application as a finished product but also helps you think through the *process* of moving from the original meaning of a passage to its contemporary significance. These are commentaries, not popular expositions. They are works of reference, not devotional literature.

The format of the series is designed to achieve the goals of the series. Each passage is treated in three sections: *Original Meaning*, *Bridging Contexts*, and *Contemporary Significance.*

THIS SECTION HELPS you understand the meaning of the biblical text in its first-century context. All of the elements of traditional exegesis—in concise form—are discussed here. These include the historical, literary, and cultural context of the passage. The authors discuss matters related to grammar and syntax, and the meaning of biblical words. They also seek to explore the main ideas of the passage and how the biblical author develops those ideas.[1]

---

1. Please note that when the authors discuss words in the original biblical languages, the series uses the general rather than the scholarly method of transliteration.

After reading this section, you will understand the problems, questions, and concerns of the *original audience* and how the biblical author addressed those issues. This understanding is foundational to any legitimate application of the text today.

THIS SECTION BUILDS a bridge between the world of the Bible and the world of today, between the original context and the contemporary context, by focusing on both the timely and timeless aspects of the text.

God's Word is *timely*. The authors of Scripture spoke to specific situations, problems, and questions. Paul warned the Galatians about the consequences of circumcision and the dangers of trying to be justified by law (Gal. 5:2–5). The author of Hebrews tried to convince his readers that Christ is superior to Moses, the Aaronic priests, and the Old Testament sacrifices. John urged his readers to "test the spirits" of those who taught a form of incipient Gnosticism (1 John 4:1–6). In each of these cases, the timely nature of Scripture enables us to hear God's Word in situations that were *concrete* rather than abstract.

Yet the timely nature of Scripture also creates problems. Our situations, difficulties, and questions are not always directly related to those faced by the people in the Bible. Therefore, God's word to them does not always seem relevant to us. For example, when was the last time someone urged you to be circumcised, claiming that it was a necessary part of justification? How many people today care whether Christ is superior to the Aaronic priests? And how can a "test" designed to expose incipient Gnosticism be of any value in a modern culture?

Fortunately, Scripture is not only timely but *timeless*. Just as God spoke to the original audience, so he still speaks to us through the pages of Scripture. Because we share a common humanity with the people of the Bible, we discover a *universal dimension* in the problems they faced and the solutions God gave them. The timeless nature of Scripture enables it to speak with power in every time and in every culture.

Those who fail to recognize that Scripture is both timely and timeless run into a host of problems. For example, those who are intimidated by timely books such as Hebrews or Galatians might avoid reading them because they seem meaningless today. At the other extreme, those who are convinced of the timeless nature of Scripture, but who fail to discern its timely element, may "wax eloquent" about the Melchizedekian priesthood to a sleeping congregation.

The purpose of this section, therefore, is to help you discern what is timeless in the timely pages of the New Testament—and what is not. For example, if Paul's primary concern is not circumcision (as he tells us in Gal. 5:6), what *is* he concerned about? If discussions about the Aaronic priesthood or Melchizedek seem irrelevant today, what is of abiding value in these passages? If people try to "test the spirits" today with a test designed for a specific first-century heresy, what other biblical test might be more appropriate?

Yet this section does not merely uncover that which is timeless in a passage but also helps you to see *how* it is uncovered. The author of the commentary seeks to take what is implicit in the text and make it explicit, to take a process that normally is intuitive and explain it in a logical, orderly fashion. How do we know that circumcision is not Paul's primary concern? What clues in the text or its context help us realize that Paul's real concern is at a deeper level?

Of course, those passages in which the historical distance between us and the original readers is greatest require a longer treatment. Conversely, those passages in which the historical distance is smaller or seemingly nonexistent require less attention.

One final clarification. Because this section prepares the way for discussing the contemporary significance of the passage, there is not always a sharp distinction or a clear break between this section and the one that follows. Yet when both sections are read together, you should have a strong sense of moving from the world of the Bible to the world of today.

 THIS SECTION ALLOWS the biblical message to speak with as much power today as it did when it was first written. How can you apply what you learned about Jerusalem, Ephesus, or Corinth to our present-day needs in Chicago, Los Angeles, or London? How can you take a message originally spoken in Greek and Aramaic and communicate it clearly in our own language? How can you take the eternal truths originally spoken in a different time and culture and apply them to the similar-yet-different needs of our culture?

In order to achieve these goals, this section gives you help in several key areas.

First, it helps you identify contemporary situations, problems, or questions that are truly comparable to those faced by the original audience. Because contemporary situations are seldom identical to those faced in the first century, you must seek situations that are analogous if your applications are to be relevant.

Second, this section explores a variety of contexts in which the passage might be applied today. You will look at personal applications, but you will also be encouraged to think beyond private concerns to the society and culture at large.

Third, this section will alert you to any problems or difficulties you might encounter in seeking to apply the passage. And if there are several legitimate ways to apply a passage (areas in which Christians disagree), the author will bring these to your attention and help you think through the issues involved.

In seeking to achieve these goals, the contributors to this series attempt to avoid two extremes. They avoid making such specific applications that the commentary might quickly become dated. They also avoid discussing the significance of the passage in such a general way that it fails to engage contemporary life and culture.

Above all, contributors to this series have made a diligent effort not to sound moralistic or preachy. The NIV Application Commentary Series does not seek to provide ready-made sermon materials but rather tools, ideas, and insights that will help you communicate God's Word with power. If we help you to achieve that goal, then we have fulfilled the purpose for this series.

The Editors

General Editor's Preface

WE SEE SO MANY INSTANCES these days of people saying they believe one thing but not acting in ways that support that belief or, worse, acting in ways that contradict that belief: public politicians talking about remorse but displaying little; private individuals making resolutions regarding what they eat, drink, and say and not following through; an all-time low in ethical behavior that can only be attributed to some kind of national moral "numbness" (to borrow a phrase from David Nystrom in the pages that follow). Belief and practice do not seem to go together in many people's minds. And they should be seen as a pair.

That's what makes James such an important letter, for it deals with precisely this problem. And it does so in a sophisticated way. James does not just say, "Practice what you preach," although that is part of the message. He gives reasons for what he says, and he shows subtle connections between faith, action, wisdom, and what you do in church on Sunday morning that really help sort out the disconnection between Christian faith and Christian living to which our culture seems so susceptible.

Why are we so susceptible? Neil Postman in his book *Amusing Ourselves to Death* claims that television has created in our culture a low information-action ratio. People are accustomed to learning good ideas, but not acting on them. That is the nature of the way we receive our information through public media. Unfortunately, too many sermons have followed this mode—in the understandable interest of good communication. Since Americans learn this way, let's teach and preach this way.

The book of James is a good antidote. It calls us to account for a high information-action ratio. As Nystrom expertly shows, James makes his argument using the following propositions:

(1) The Christian life is more than just intellectually assenting to some beliefs. It means acting in ways inspired by and consistent with those beliefs. It means developing a wise lifestyle that makes Christian practice more likely. And it means worshiping in ways that actually have a chance of being translated into action.

(2) There are observable pinch points where the disjunction between faith and practice most often shows up: in times of persecution and trial; whenever we open our mouths and speak with our tongue; in all of our ongoing relationships with other people; and in the perplexing matters that pertain to handling money.

(3) Clear benchmarks can be established that show us when we are doing it right.

Call them community busters. James lists at least three. (1) Our tongues can so easily reveal a discrepancy between faith and practice, particularly when we use it to talk about God's love in ways that display little love to our fellow human beings. (2) We can talk about treating everyone equally; but when it comes to practice, we so often, even in the church, show favoritism to the rich over the poor. Money is as dangerous a commodity as the tongue, according to James. We easily become inconsistent between what we say we believe and what we do where financial gain is part of the equation. (3) Truth can be taught arrogantly or with humility—the same truth, mind you! Yet it becomes "more true" when taught with personal humility and a desire for peace, and "less true" when taught with an arrogance born of a desire to manipulate. True wisdom comes only when our attitudes and practices match up with the content of what we say.

James is the quintessential New Testament book for our day and age where we see Christianity unfairly caricatured as either moral legalism or pure ethics. James says that Christianity is both, but it is neither if both are not present. Read it and see why.

Terry C. Muck

Author's Preface

THE BOOK OF JAMES is something of an oddity. James combines practical instructions with a rugged assurance independent of other voices in the New Testament choir. E. Thurneysen has said that "James preaches Jesus Christ, His cross and resurrection, the power of forgiveness and the obedience of faith, and nothing else; but he preaches this in his own peculiar way."[1] C. F. D. Moule writes that James "reflects a type of Christianity as different as can well be imagined from the Pauline or Johannine, yet one that confesses Jesus as Lord . . . believes in rebirth by God through the Gospel . . . and looks forward to a denouement. . . ."[2] It is a "timeless document," to borrow a phrase from J. A. T. Robinson,[3] and its clear ethical guidance and evident connection with the teaching of Jesus have made it a challenging favorite of Christians over the centuries. This combination I have found fascinating since I spent a term in seminary studying James. It offers us a picture of early Christians as they wrestled with the application of the life and teachings of Jesus in the concrete landscape of their own lives. It is a book that challenges, affirms, unsettles, and convicts, but one that will not be trivialized. Its message, I believe, needs to be heard today.

A project such as this cannot be completed without a significant amount of assistance from one's community of family and friends. I am grateful to North Park University for granting me a course reduction to allow time to complete this book. Among the many individuals who deserve mention I would like to extend warm thanks to editors Jack Kuhatschek and Terry Muck, each of whom made many useful suggestions and provided needed encouragement. Verlyn Verbrugge not only edited the manuscript but did so in a way that placed me deep in his debt. For this, and for his warm spirit, I thank him. My colleagues Scot McKnight and Sonia Bodi read the entire manuscript and at many points offered the benefit of their wise advice. I treasure their support and friendship. I am also grateful to professors Daniel de Roulet and Klyne Snodgrass of North Park for their warm interest. To my brother, Professor Bradley Nystrom, I also offer my thanks. He is a companion, friend, and in many ways a model for me. No litany of thanks would

---

1. Quoted by Ralph P. Martin, *New Testament Foundations: A Guide to Christian Students* (Grand Rapids: Eerdmans, 1978), 2:365.

2. C. F. D. Moule, *The Birth of the New Testament* (New York: Harper and Row, 1962), 166.

3. J. A. T. Robinson, *Redating the New Testament* (Philadelphia: Westminster, 1976), 118.

Author's Preface

be complete without mention of my friend and former teacher, Professor L.
D. Hurst, from whom I learned so much. Finally, I wish to thank my parents,
Paul and Aileen Nystrom, and my wife, Kristina. To them I dedicate this
volume.

David P. Nystrom
Summer, 1997

Abbreviations

ABD	*Anchor Bible Dictionary*
ANRW	*Aufstieg und Niedergang der römischen Welt*
BBR	*Bulletin for Biblical Research*
CBQ	*Catholic Biblical Quarterly*
DJG	*Dictionary of Jesus and the Gospels*
EvQ	*Evangelical Quarterly*
ExpTim	*Expository Times*
HNT	Handbuch zum Neuen Testament
HTR	*Harvard Theological Review*
ICC	International Critical Commentary
JB	Jerusalem Bible
JBL	*Journal of Biblical Literature*
JETS	*Journal of the Evangelical Theological Society*
LXX	Septuagint
NCBC	New Century Bible Commentary
Neot	*Neotestamentica*
NICGT	New International Commentary on the Greek Testament
NICNT	New International Commentary on the New Testament
NIDNTT	*New International Dictionary of New Testament Theology*
NIV	New International Version
NRSV	New Revised Standard Version
SJT	*Scottish Journal of Theology*
TDNT	*Theological Dictionary of the New Testament*
TNTC	Tyndale New Testament Commentary
WBC	Word Biblical Commentary
WTJ	*Westminster Theological Journal*
ZNW	*Zeitschrift für die neutestamentliche Wissenschaft*

Introduction

ON JANUARY 1, 1990, President Václav Havel[1] of Czechoslovakia addressed his nation. It had been a few weeks since his country peaceably ousted the Communist totalitarian government that had held power for forty years. Only two days before, Havel had been elected President by a parliament still dominated by Communists. Havel said:

> We live in a contaminated moral environment. . . . We learned not to believe in anything, to ignore each other, to care only for ourselves. Concepts such as love, friendship, compassion, humility, and forgiveness lost their depth and dimensions, and for many of us they came to represent only psychological peculiarities, or to resemble long-lost greetings from ancient times. . . . When I talk about contaminated moral atmosphere . . . I am talking about all of us. . . . Why do I say this? It would be quite unreasonable to understand the sad legacy of the last forty years as something alien, something bequeathed to us by some distant relative. On the contrary, we must accept this legacy as a sin we committed against ourselves.[2]

There are many points of similarity between this brief excerpt from Havel's speech and the letter of James. Havel writes from the heart, and like James his is a heart that has known adversity as well as joy. Both are keen observers of human nature. Both are vitally interested in the creation of true community, a community marked by mutual care and interdependent responsibility. In an era in which a sense of personal responsibility seems endangered, Havel calls it true. James also is unafraid to call sin by its true name, and like Havel he will not allow us to shirk responsibility for our own actions, or for the evil that occurs because of our inaction.

James wrote to a church beset by a number of problems. These problems included divisiveness, intolerance, favoritism, and the overpowering desire for wealth and status. Giving shape to and electrifying these problems were the

---

1. Havel is a playwright and essayist of no mean distinction. Under Communist rule he was an anti-totalitarian dissident, who made it his duty to combat evil armed with only the truth. In 1979 he was sentenced to four and a half years in prison as a result of his role in the human rights movement in Czechoslovakia. As President he has continued in the same vein, refusing to allow himself to be "packaged," like so many Western politicians.

2. Václav Havel, *The Art of the Impossible: Politics as Morality in Practice; Speeches and Writings, 1990–1996*, tr. Paul Wilson et al. (New York: Knopf, 1997), 3–4.

presence and popularity within the community of errant teaching that was vibrant enough to question the great commandment as expressed by Jesus and yet to maintain an influential place in the community. It was a teaching tailor-made for the time, for it allowed its followers to understand the church as one among many opportunities for social climbing and the exhibition of social snobbery.

This false teaching not only exacerbated these selfish and aberrant activities, but it also sanctioned them as acceptable and even exemplary. The danger of this false system is both obvious and lethal. Perhaps the most severe of these tensions divided the wealthy (and those who desired to be wealthy) from the poor in the community. Uppermost in James's mind is the creation of true Christian community out of the interpersonal rubble caused by the blasts of the teaching of self-interest.[3]

James combats this teaching and its effects with a frontal assault. He points out that the rich will be humbled and the poor exalted; that the poor are God's elect; that far from being a sign of divine displeasure, periods of adversity are used by God to purify and strengthen those whom he loves. James supports this approach by calling on Jewish notions of suffering, sin, poverty, and wisdom. He makes crystal clear his assertion that friendship with the world is enmity with God (4:4). Those who wish to have it both ways are the double-minded, and James warns them that this folly has unsavory and eternal consequences. To them he proffers the forgiveness of God if only they will repent.

James and His Letter

BY ALL ACCOUNTS James is something of an oddity among the books that comprise the New Testament. This letter is difficult to categorize and elicits a wide variety of descriptions. It is simple and straightforward, marked by unambiguous ethical teaching and authoritative pronouncement, but seems bereft of any sustained theological argument. These factors, in part, led Dibelius to conclude that James is a jumbled series of unrelated bits of teaching material, strung together in a largely haphazard form.[4] On the other

---

3. W. Dyrness, "Mercy Triumphs Over Justice: James 2:13 and the Theology of Faith and Works," *Themelios* 6 (1981): 11–16, argues that the idea of mercy binds the letter together, seen especially in the ethics of the community (as seen in 2:1–12) and in loving hospitality and welcome for those who are in need (as seen in 2:14–26). See also M. J. Townsend, "Christ, Community and Salvation in the Epistle of James," *EvQ* 53 (1981): 115–23, who makes the case by focusing on the use of the term "brother" and on the ethics of forgiveness, mercy, and grace as expressed in the letter.

4. Martin Dibelius, *James: A Commentary on the Epistle of James*, Hermeneia, reissued by H. Greeven, tr. M. A. Williams (Philadelphia: Fortress, 1976), 4, 6.

hand, Francis has argued that far from being a random collection of discon-
nected teachings, the letter of James is actually a carefully constructed document that conforms to established patterns.[5]

James is notoriously reticent to yield clues concerning the traditional
questions of authorship, date, and addressees. It claims to have been written
by James, but there are a number of persons named "James" in the New Testament. The letter is addressed to a generic audience ("to the twelve tribes
scattered among the nations," 1:1), not to a specific church, as are most of
Paul's letters. Nor is the body of the letter of much help in answering these
questions. The difficulties the letter attempts to solve, while onerous, are
likely to have afflicted numerous early Christian communities. Any attempt
to answer these questions is necessarily an adventure that requires a willingness to settle for uncertainty.

Nevertheless, several general observations can be made with no little
confidence. (1) It is clear that James can be placed within the context of the
earliest forms of Christianity. There is no shortage of evidence to support this
contention.

- There are numerous and striking parallels to the teachings of Jesus in
  the synoptic tradition, and apparently in a form more primitive than
  that which appears there. Perhaps the best example is 5:12, which
  closely resembles what Jesus said concerning oaths in Matthew 5:33–
  37. The Matthean text contains every element found in James 5:12,
  plus a number of others. This suggests that James had contact with an
  early source of the sayings of Jesus, perhaps the same source(s) that the
  synoptists (especially Matthew) had at their disposal.
- The many other parallels between James and the Synoptics all but
  cement this conclusion. These include: believers are to rejoice in trials (James 1:2; cf. Matt. 5:12); believers are called to be perfect/com-
  plete (James 1:4; cf. Matt. 5:48); believers are encouraged to ask God,
  for God loves to give (James 1:5; cf. Matt. 7:7); believers should expect
  testing and be prepared to endure it, after which they will receive a
  reward (James 1:12; cf. Matt. 24:13); believers are not to be angry
  (James 1:20; cf. Matt. 5:22); faith and action go together in such a way
  that actions are the proof of true faith (James 2:14; cf. Matt. 7:16–19);
  the poor are blessed (James 2:5; cf. Luke 6:20); the rich are warned
  (James 2:6–7; cf. Matt. 19:23–24); believers are not to slander (James
  4:11; cf. Matt. 5:22); believers are not to judge (James 4:12; cf. Matt.
  7:1); and finally, the humble are praised (James 3:13; cf. Matt. 5:3).

---

5. See Fred O. Francis, "The Form and Function of the Opening and Closing Paragraphs of James and I John," *ZNW* 61 (1970): 110–26.

- Beyond the merely aphoristic and terminological similarities lie deeper ones, such as a shared theology of prayer between James and Matthew.[6]
- Both James and Paul are concerned with the dynamic of faith and works, and while it is probably wrong to read James as a reaction against Paul, it is nonetheless evidence of the Christian environment of James, if not also a clue as to date.
- When James calls Jesus "glorious" in 2:1, it is hard not to see in this an acquaintance with a Christological trajectory that also surfaces in the Gospel of John.

In short, there is ample evidence that James belongs to the world of the earliest forms of the Christian faith.

(2) James is fully at home in the world of Judaism. While this book is unquestionably a Christian one, its roots in Judaism are virile and deep.

- The first letter of Peter is the close companion of James. But while 1 Peter uses Christ as its hero of endurance and faith, James chooses Old Testament models of faith, such as Abraham, Rahab, and Job.
- James's picture of God is consonant with the Jewish understanding of God. He knows that "there is one God" (2:19). He knows the importance of the terms "Almighty" (5:4) and "Father" (3:9) used in reference to God. He teaches that God is merciful (4:8), and that he desires purity and humility in his people (4:8, 10). He is aware that the world tends to work in ways that oppose God and his intentions (4:4). Finally, he knows that God desires to give (4:2).
- James is aware of other characteristic features of the beliefs of first-century Judaism. He knows the term *Gehenna*, and that it often served as a cipher for satanic power (3:6). He is aware of rabbinic theological and psychological anthropology, specifically the belief in the *yeṣarim*, the two impulses within each one of us (1:14): The "good impulse" (*yeṣer ha-tov*) is pure, while the "evil impulse" (*yeṣer ha-ra*) leads one to sin. James knows that within the Judaism of his day the poor had become associated with the righteous (2:5; 4:6). Finally, he knows about the perfect law, the law of the love of one's neighbor as found in Leviticus 19:18 (James 1:25; 2:11).[7]
- Furthermore, James frequently uses the Old Testament. He makes reference to what "Scripture says" (4:5) and even quotes the Old Testa-

---

6. R. M. Cooper, "Prayer, a Study in Matthew and James," *Encounter* 29 (1968): 268–77.

7. See L. T. Johnson, "The Use of Leviticus 19 in the Letter of James," *JBL* 101 (1982): 391–401, highlights the pervasive use of the "royal law" in James.

ment (4:6). His concern for widows and orphans (1:27) shows his familiarity with the prophetic notion of justice. Further, he refers to the great Old Testament heroes of the faith, such as Abraham (2:23), Rahab (2:25), the prophets (5:10), Job (5:11), and Elijah (5:17–18).

- Unlike Paul, James does not argue the Christian position against Jewish purity laws or food laws.

(3) But James also is familiar with the Hellenistic world. These factors all but guarantee that this book was written by someone familiar with broader Hellenistic culture.

- The letter is written in good and even fluid Greek, betraying a relatively wide vocabulary and skill (with rare lapses) in wordplays and figures of speech. On the other hand, the letter avoids both complex words and sentences that mark the highest Greek literature.
- The author knows and makes use of Hellenistic literary conventions (1:1–12).
- The letter also betrays an interest in Greek oral composition, as its use of alliteration and rhyme bear witness.
- A number of the metaphors in the book are drawn from the stock wisdom of the Hellenistic Mediterranean world and are alien to the Palestinian context.
- James uses more than sixty *hapax legomena*, and of these as many as thirteen are used for the first time by our author.[8]

Authorship and Date

SCHOLARS OFFER THREE basic options concerning authorship and date. (1) James is essentially a pre-Christian Jewish document, which at a later date came to bear a patina of Christian teaching after it was embraced by one of the infant Christian communities. According to champions of this position, the author and editor(s) are unknown. The Christological formulae found in 1:1 and 2:1 are seen as the chief Christian accretions. Supporters of this position consider the book's concern with adherence to the stipulations of the law as evidence of the Jewish origin of the letter. Further, the many features that betray the letter's comfort with the Old Testament and other typically Jewish themes are diverted to support this view. This position is becoming increasingly difficult to maintain.

(2) Others see the letter as composed of a different type of two-stage development. Martin, for example, surmises that the letter originated with

---

8. See Peter H. Davids, *The Epistle of James*, 58–59.

the teaching of James, the brother of Jesus, who was martyred by the high priest Ananus II in about A.D. 62. Then after the Jewish War of A.D. 66–70, the community of which James had been a part left Palestine and settled in Syria. There they refined the teachings of James and created a final product, the letter we know as James. The conflicts to which the letter bears witness (rich vs. poor, Sadducees vs. messianic priests, and Zealots vs. the rich) were already at work in the larger matrix of the Palestinian Jewish sociocultural landscape.[9]

A. S. Geyser has argued much the same point, claiming that the original document was a letter written by James, the Lord's brother, before the Jerusalem Council, most likely no later than A.D. 48.[10] The idea that behind this letter is a Zealot-inspired tension within the community is not without its supporters.[11] Davids[12] offers a sober and more modest proposal. He envisions that the early traditions that eventually wended their way into the letter began to circulate in the late 40s and were then edited just prior to the Jewish War. To him the conflicts that face us when reading the letter more likely reflect Palestinian conditions *before* the war. His claims are admirable for their restraint and correspondence to the available evidence.

(3) A third option is that James, the brother of the Lord, is the sole author of the letter. There are six (perhaps seven) persons named James in the New Testament: James the brother of Jude (Jude 1); James the father of Judas (Acts 1:12) not Iscariot; "James the younger" (Mark 15:40); James the son of Zebedee (3:16); James the son of Alphaeus (3:18); and James the brother of Jesus (Matt. 13:5; Gal. 1:19). If the letter of James was written by someone not found among these six, then we have seven figures named James in the New Testament.

However, there is no good reason to suppose that James the brother of Jesus is not our author. James the son of Zebedee is the only other serious candidate, but his early martyrdom (see Acts 12:2) seems to rule him out. Moreover, references to James in Paul (1 Cor. 9:5, 14; 15:7; Gal. 1:15–2:12) and Acts (15:13–21) make clear that James the brother of Jesus held a prominent place in early Palestinian Christianity.

The position is not unassailable, however. One of the difficulties is the paucity of references to James in the early church fathers relative to the other books in the New Testament canon. Origen (ca. 185–ca. 251) mentions the

---

9. Ralph P. Martin, *James*, lxvi–lxvii.

10. A. S. Geyser, "The Letter of James and the Social Condition of His Addressees," *Neot* 9 (1975): 7–24.

11. See M. J. Townsend, "James 4:1–4: A Warning Against Zealotry?" *ExpTim* 87 (1976): 211–13.

12. Davids, *The Epistle of James*, 28–34.

letter and claims that it was written by James. Eusebius (ca. 266–ca. 339) makes the same claim, notes that the letter of James was "read publicly in many churches," but adds that some in his own day doubted whether James wrote the letter that bears his name. Today the view that James the brother of Jesus wrote the letter in a form substantially as we have it is not popular, but it must be admitted that the evidence for later redaction on stylistic grounds, theological or otherwise, is at times not firm or, where it is apparently firm, uncertain.[13] In short, it seems likely that James the brother of Jesus did write the letter, or at the very least is the origin of the teaching it contains.[14]

The Teaching of James

JAMES OFFERS INSTRUCTION on a wide variety of issues, and those surveyed here are among the most significant. Each serves to assist the community and individuals within the community to understand the path to Christian maturity.

Suffering

IN MANY WAYS the theology of suffering is the starting point of the letter. This is the theme with which James begins, and it is also the theme that binds all the others together. James says that trials are often a challenge to the faith of the believer, and that when we waver, the trial becomes for us a temptation (1:12–15). Both the English terms *trial* and *temptation* are derived from the same Greek word, *peirasmos*. This indicates that what is at issue is not only the *condition* of the trial, but also the *attitude* of the one undergoing the trial. It is this matter of personal character and its development that is central to James. For this reason we should not give in to temptation, but rather should stand fast and even rejoice in trials, for they are opportunities that God uses to mold and shape as he wills, until we are "mature and complete, not lacking anything" (1:2–9). This theology of suffering undergirds his discussion of community dissent in chapter 2, as well as the suffering of the poor (4:13–5:12).

There is a rich Old Testament background to this theology of suffering. At times Judaism connected suffering to sin, as can be seen in the wisdom tradition. Proverbs, for example, argues that the righteous and diligent are

---

13. For instance, the tension between faith and works in James can be used to argue a late date because James is a polemic against Paul, or an early date, because James seems unaware of the Pauline position.

14. R. A. Rendall, *The Epistle of James and Judaic Christianity* (Cambridge: Cambridge Univ. Press, 1927), argues that the author is a Palestinian Jew thoroughly conversant with the Hellenistic Scriptures.

blessed, while the wicked and slothful suffer (see Prov. 10:1–6). Personal experience, however, taught the Hebrews that the righteous are often made to suffer, and that in fact it is precisely God's chosen servants whom he allows to suffer.

Job is a prime example. He is the archetypal wisdom figure. He is upright, and God has blessed him. Satan challenges God, claiming that the respect Job has for God is thin and fragile, and that the only reason Job fears God is the material property his pure life has earned from God. Job's friends believe that his affliction has been caused by sin. Note Eliphaz's comment to Job: "Consider now: Who, being innocent, has ever perished? Where were the upright ever destroyed? As I have observed, those who plow evil and those who sow trouble reap it" (Job 4:7–8). But by the end of the book Job has come to know better; he has come to know that life is not that simple and neat. His suffering has broadened his understanding of God and of himself.

The book of Daniel offers another variation on this theme. Daniel is righteous, and because of his steadfastness he endures suffering. So in Judaism suffering is often the lot of the righteous because at times the world persecutes the righteous because they are righteous; God can use suffering to purify and strengthen his people. Thus, suffering is, in a sense, a sign of God's activity in the life of the believer.

The church to which James wrote was experiencing adversity, and James sees this complex of trials as a cause for joy, because he discerns that God's purpose is purificatory. He knows that if they endure with patience, they will be both purified and approved (1:12). But there is another possibility. If like Israel in the desert they blame God or seek to blame others for this adversity, they will fail in the test. It will have become for them a temptation. They will have succumbed to the evil impulse (1:14).

There appear to be three major sources of adversity afflicting the community James is addressing. The first is the "evil impulse" within each person. James says that this is the cause of the selfish attitude that has led to the internal divisions within the church (4:1–6).

The second source of adversity involves money and status. The community was marked by the presence of individuals who desired recognition and status and who were not afraid to use the church to serve this end. This is what lies behind the injunction against showing favoritism in 2:1–4. But the church has also suffered from problems involving money. Some in the community were consumed with becoming wealthy, while others were used to the prerogatives that the wealthy arrogate to themselves. In either case, such persons ignored their responsibilities to others in the community (2:4; 4:13–5:6). In this way they stared unblinking at the prospect of God's condemnation but were so blind they failed to recognize it (1:10–11; 2:4; 4:16; 5:5–6, 9).

The third source of adversity is Satan. James introduces this character slowly and in a veiled fashion, but not because he judges Satan's role insignificant. Satan is the ultimate source for the false teaching that has recognized, united, and championed the various elements of the trials affecting the community.

Sin

CLOSELY RELATED TO the idea of suffering is James's notion of sin. There are two primary sources for evil that lead us to sin. (1) The first is external, and James makes it clear that this source is Satan. But he makes this point in a curious way, beginning with circumlocutionary references before identifying the devil in plain fashion. The first reference is to Gehenna (or "hell") in 3:6, which James says lights the consuming evil fire that is the tongue. The second reference is to "the demonic" (lit. trans.) in 3:15, by which James indicates the source of the "false wisdom" of the errant teachers, who have caused such trouble for the church. This is an expression of Satan and his minions working in concert with the "evil desire." Finally, James in 4:7 instructs Christians to "resist the devil."

Thus, James presents us a picture of the world that is dualistic, but only in a truncated and limited fashion. Satan is powerful, but when measured against the power of God, he is not a serious contender for ruler of the universe. God is so superior to Satan that the believer can resist Satan and he will flee (4:7). However, without vigilant attention the lure of Satan over the believer can be devastating in its effects. For this reason James implores his readers to "come near to God" (4:8). There are cosmic forces of good and evil at work in our world, but God is far more powerful than the devil.

(2) James knows that this talk of the devil carries the potential for a dangerous side effect. It could cause us to believe that we are not responsible for our sinful actions because Satan is the source of temptation. James will not allow us to deceive ourselves on this matter and so cowardly to shirk our responsibility. There is another source of temptation—the "evil desire" that is within each one of us. Here James is building on the Jewish idea of the *yeṣerim*. Hebrew theological and psychological anthropology posited the existence of two desires within each of us. The first is the good impulse, the *yeṣer ha-tov*; the other is the evil impulse, the *yeṣer ha-ra*.[15] The latter (Gk. *epithymia*, 1:14) is within us, as an integral component of the human condition. It impels us to evil all on its own, and therefore we are responsible for the evil we do.

---

15. See J. Marcus, "The Evil Inclination in the Epistle of James," *CBQ* 44 (1982): 606–21; Peter H. Davids, "Theological Perspectives on the Epistle of James," *JETS* 23 (1980): 97–103.

Paul likewise builds on this notion when in Romans 7:21–24 he speaks of "another law" at work within himself, one that prompts him to sin and evil. James wants us to know that ultimately we are responsible for our actions. In a fashion similar to Paul in Romans, James urges Christians to control this internal evil desire and live in such a way that faith and actions are in harmony. When we fail to see adversity as an opportunity for God to purify us and to see the test as a reason for joy, we prove ourselves in love with the world (4:4) and out of touch with God (4:3). Thus, we contribute to strife within the community by giving in to the desire to possess things; this is among the most acidic of forces undermining the health of the church (4:1–2).

Christology

JAMES DOES NOT develop a Christology for us; rather, when the need arises, he presses into service an assumed Christology.[16] For James Christ is "Judge" (5:9), several times "Lord," and perhaps even king (cf. 2:8). His use of the word "Lord" is particularly striking. Note how James

- declares himself a "servant of God and of the *Lord* Jesus Christ" (1:1)
- offers the claim that the *Lord* gives (1:7)
- describes "our" *Lord* as "glorious" (2:1)
- notes that we praise our *Lord* and Father (3:9)
- instructs that we should "humble" ourselves before the *Lord* (4:10) and that we should be concerned about the *Lord's* will (4:15)
- refers to "the *Lord* Almighty" (5:4)
- says that the *Lord* will return (5:7) and that his coming is near (5:9)
- reminds us that the prophets who "spoke in the name of the *Lord*" are examples of patience (5:10)
- claims that the *Lord* uses adversity to purify us and balances this with the contention that the *Lord* is full of compassion and mercy (5:11)
- reminds us that we should pray in the name of the *Lord* (5:14)
- finally, claims that the *Lord* will "raise" up the sick person (5:15).

Clearly James uses *kyrios* ("Lord") both in contradistinction to "God" and in ways that seem to equate the two. His reference to the "Lord Almighty" is in close juxtaposition to the claim that the Lord will return (5:4, 7). The phrase "God Almighty" (Heb. *'el šaddai*) is a common reference for God in the Old Testament. If "Lord Almighty" in 5:4 refers to God and "the Lord's coming" in 5:7 refers to the return of Christ (as it must), we have evidence of a high Christology.[17] Furthermore, James says that both God and "the Lord"

---

16. So Davids, *The Epistle of James*, 39.
17. See the discussion of this commentary, pp. 285–86.

give (1:5, 7), and that Christians are to come in humility to both God and to "the Lord" (4:8, 10). In short, James does not offer a developed Christology, but his assumed Christology is one that freely links the resurrected Jesus as Lord with God the Father.

More must be said, however. For James, Christ is not only the heavenly Lord, who will come as judge, but he is also the leader of the church. The members of the community belong to him (2:7), and the church continues to be guided by him. James is deeply interested in the moral application of the lordship of Christ in the concrete, pedestrian stuff of daily life. Note James's frequent quotation of and allusion to the teachings of Jesus. Indeed, it is not inaccurate to say that James represents not teaching about Jesus but the teaching of Jesus applied to a new situation.

The Poor Are Righteous

THE PIETY AND righteousness of the poor is a frequent theme in James (see 1:9–11, 27; 2:3–7, 15–16; 5:7–11). In the ancient world more than 90 percent of the population qualified as "poor." In Palestine, as everywhere else in the ancient Mediterranean, the few who had wealth exercised power over the many who did not. True, the Old Testament has examples of wealth as a sign of God's favor (e.g., Prov. 14:24: "The wealth of the wise is their crown, but the folly of fools yields folly"), but the exigencies of life taught the Hebrews that the righteous often suffer poverty. As a result of the national experience of exile and the admonitions of the great prophets, the poor came to be seen as "the righteous," because they had no other recourse than to rely on God. This is why "the LORD hears the needy" (Ps. 69:33). The poor were considered innocent sufferers, especially at the hands of the unfeeling rich (see James 5:4), and God is portrayed as the defender of these poor innocents and the champion of justice (James 1:27; cf. Amos 4:1; 5:11–12, 24).

The poor whom James knows of have been placed at the margins of society—widows and orphans, and those victimized by economic conditions as well as the dishonesty of their employers. The poor are the pious because they throw themselves on the mercy of God in the face of injustice. It is this inclination that James extols.

James has little good to say about the rich. But it is not so much the fact of their wealth that he finds odious, but rather the corrosive effect this wealth has had. Their wealth has dulled their spirits and minds so that they ignore the injunctions of the Old Testament concerning the care of the poor. They impudently claim the right to be above the command of Jesus to love the neighbor, and in so doing they have, in effect, made themselves "god." The possession of and desire for wealth has caused them to be in love with the world, to possess a divisive spirit as they seek social status, and to become hard-hearted toward others. To them James offers the serious warning: The Judge is at the door (5:9), their wealth is as transitory as the flower's bloom (1:11), and in fact it has already begun to become worthless (5:2–3). For the poor James manifests great compassion, and to the rich he counsels humble penitence.

Wisdom

THE IDEA OF wisdom is of key significance for James. Wisdom is not primarily of human derivation. Rather, true wisdom

- is a good gift from heaven that has the capacity to render us truly the children of God (1:17–18)
- is the gift of God through prayer that assists the Christian during times of trial and helps us understand why God allows adversity (1:5–8)
- is the source of a variety of Christian virtues that God desires to develop in the lives of believers (3:17)[18]
- serves as the pure counterpoint to the evil desire within us
- is linked to peace and health within the community (3:17), and to discernment with regard to healing (5:14–15).

In the Old Testament wisdom is closely linked to the work of the Holy Spirit. Isaiah 11:2, for instance, says, "The Spirit of the LORD will rest on him—the Spirit of wisdom and of understanding." The *locus classicus* of wisdom is, perhaps, the book of Proverbs, in which personified wisdom plays the roles normally assigned to the Spirit (Prov. 1:20–33; 8:1–36). Wisdom theology is creation theology, and this explains James's penchant for the themes of God's original intention (James 1:4; 2:7; 3:7). For Paul wisdom is linked to Christology, but James presents us with a wisdom pneumatology.

James's Relevance

APPLYING THE MESSAGE of James to our world is fraught with difficulties. James sounds themes that are familiar, but the details do not always bear close correspondence to our own age. He is vitally concerned with the poor, for example, but in his world the poor comprised more than 90 percent of the population. He writes to wealthy landowners who abused the trust and rights of their hired laborers, but there are few such "gentleman farmers" in

---

18. James says that heavenly wisdom is "pure," and that it is "peace-loving, considerate, submissive, full of mercy and good fruit, impartial and sincere" (3:17).

America today. These minor differences might make it easy for us to consider James only an interesting and perhaps even quaint letter of purely antiquarian interest, but we would do so at our peril. The message of this brief book is as sharp and needful today as ever. Perhaps our tendency to read its unequivocal ethical instruction as somehow distant reflects the accuracy of James's analysis of sin—the sins of his ancient brothers and sisters as well as our own.

James has some harsh words to say concerning wealth, and people in the Western world are among the wealthiest human beings ever to have lived. I am writing this on a notebook computer in my home, and I have another computer at the office. I am surrounded by furniture, and I have a nice car in the garage. What would James say to me about my use of wealth? The church needs to take seriously the ethic he has here outlined.

When James says that true religion is to care for widows and orphans, he is speaking with deadly seriousness. We need to have our eyes and our hearts open to the "widows and orphans" in our world. We have a responsibility to others and are called to use our wealth with that responsibility in mind. Like Jesus, James offers us a warning in the most stern terms at his command: Wealth can be acidic and lethal in its effects. Here is grist for careful thought, deep prayer, and courageous prophetic action.

James also extols the virtues of adversity. This is clearly an idea that is alien to our culture. We seem fascinated, even obsessed, with the elimination of even discomfort, let alone actual trials. But James calls us to eschew the patterns of thought that undergird and sustain our culture, and instead to pray for God's wisdom in order to discern the purpose he intends through trials. James exhorts us to encourage each other along the path of prayer, for prayer is the key to enduring trials.

James also provides for us a picture of sin. As a culture we are not too willing to admit to sin. In reviewing a number of public scandals, the *Wall Street Journal* commented:

> The United States has a drug problem and a high school sex problem and a welfare problem and an AIDS problem and a rape problem. None of this will go away until more people in positions of responsibility are willing to come forward and explain, in frankly moral terms, that some of the things people do nowadays are wrong.[19]

When we fail to recognize things we do as sins, we treat them as unimportant, minor, too weak to gain a hold on our lives, as if the Lord's Prayer read, "Forgive us our miscalculations as we forgive those who miscalculate

---

19. "The Joy of What?" *Wall Street Journal* (Dec. 12, 1991).

against us."[20] At other times we redefine sin in terms that sound more savory. We also confuse nature with behavior. "This is how I am," says the habitual sinner. "This is the way the world works," say the comfortable wealthy. We have begun to accept this sort of thinking as accurate. But James does not recognize that formula. His vocabulary is studded with terms like "moral filth" and "humble yourselves." To this false view he says that sin has the power to spring up within us, intertwine itself in the stuff of our lives, and finally cause death. He tells it like it is, and he wants us to understand the origin, progress, deceptive powers, and eternal consequences of sin.

James also calls us to true community. His heart yearns for the creation of true community in the church. Like the prophets of the Old Testament, he defines "true religion" with the vocabulary of the compassion of God: "Religion that God our Father accepts as pure and faultless is this: to look after orphans and widows in their distress and to keep oneself from being polluted by the world" (1:27). He envisions a Christian community composed of relationships of mutual care and mutual responsibility. The challenge for today includes not only the creation of such community within our local churches, but also of such a spirit among Christians worldwide.

A particular feature of the community concern of James is the elimination of factions based on wealth. This presents a serious challenge to the American evangelical church, for we segregate ourselves on the basis of wealth, status, and race. James calls us to seek ways to admit that these walls exist, then to practice humility before one another with the aim of mutual understanding, and finally to work together to eliminate these walls.

In the end, the letter of James is eminently practical. One challenge that faces us is to refrain from emasculating the practicality of the letter with either academic obfuscation or self-righteous reinterpretation. We need to allow James to make us uncomfortable, for his message bears eternal consequences.

---

20. See Cornelius Plantinga, *Not the Way It's Supposed to Be: A Breviary of Sin* (Grand Rapids: Eerdmans, 1995), xi.

Outline

Address and Greeting (1:1)
  I. **Building Christian Maturity (1:2–1:27)**
     A. Trials and Temptations (1:2–11)
     B. The Evil Desire (1:12–18)
     C. True Religion is Compassion in Action (1:19–27)
  II. **Building a Healthy Community (2:1–5:18)**
     A. The Effects of Sickness (2:1–26)
        1. Sin of Favoritism (2:1–13)
        2. Faith and Deeds (2:14–26)
     B. The Source of Sickness (3:1–18)
        1. Teachers and Tongues (3:1–12)
        2. True and False Wisdom (3:13–18)
     C. Symptoms and Antidote (4:1–5:18)
        1. Friendship with the World (4:1–10)
        2. Slander and the Desire for Money (4:11–17)
        3. The Corrosive Power of Wealth (5:1–6)
        4. Patience in the Face of Suffering (5:7–11)
        5. The Prayer of Faith (5:12–18)
Conclusion: **The Forgiveness of God (5:19–20)**

Annotated Bibliography

James B. Adamson. *The Epistle of James*. NICNT. Grand Rapids: Eerdmans, 1976. Adamson studied under both C. H. Dodd and C. F. D. Moule, and his commentary reflects the careful study expected of one with this pedigree. Adamson argues that the style, content, and structure of the letter reflect the teaching of Jesus as transmitted through James, his brother. The letter betrays not only the environment of Palestine, but also "the home bond between James and Jesus." This is a good commentary, but is beginning to feel dated.

Peter H. Davids. *The Epistle of James: A Commentary on the Greek Text*. NICGT. Grand Rapids: Eerdmans, 1982. This is a stimulating commentary, bristling with insights, particularly concerning the Jewish backgrounds relative to the thought of James. Davids argues that the letter reflects the conditions of Palestine before the Jewish War of A.D. 66–70. It was composed of homilies and maxims that originated with James, the brother of Jesus. He is less certain than most that James is trying to combat a Pauline or misunderstood Pauline position. Davids sees the letter organized around three great themes introduced in the double opening: rich and poor; tongue and speech; trials and wealth. While there is much to commend this view, we must admit that much of what Davids claims relates to the tongue in 3:1–4:12 is of a far more varied nature. Nonetheless, this is a splendid commentary.

Peter H. Davids. *James*. Good News Commentary. San Francisco: Harper & Row, 1983. A shorter, more popular commentary than his 1982 publication. Given its limitations, it is a fine work; if only one of Davids' commentaries can be chosen, the other is preferable.

D. E. Hiebert. *The Epistle of James: Tests of a Living Faith*. Chicago: Moody, 1979. Hiebert's fine commentary is intended for the student who does not know Greek but who is nonetheless serious. Hiebert sees James's chief emphasis as the testing of faith. He argues that the letter was written by James, the brother of Jesus, about A.D. 46.

Sophie Laws. *The Epistle of James*. Black's New Testament Commentaries. Peabody, Mass.: Hendrickson, 1980. While hardly brief (273 pages), this spare commentary conveys an enormous amount of helpful information and observations with a minimum of extraneous material. Laws argues for a relatively late date and pseudonymous authorship. She believes the letter was written from Rome and is reacting to a misunderstood Pauline position on the matter of faith and deeds. Laws provides no outline for the letter, following Dibelius in seeing it as a collection of ill-fitting units of material. She does argue for a theological basis upon which its rigorous ethical teaching rests, and sees a chief contrast between the doubleness of human beings and the singleness of God. In general this is an insightful and fair-minded resource.

Ralph P. Martin. *James.* WBC. Waco, Tex.: Word, 1988. This commentary from a distinguished scholar and former professor at Fuller Theological Seminary is richly knowledgeable and luxuriantly detailed. Martin is taken with the theory that James represents a tension involving the poor (with whom he has great sympathy) and the rich (whom he condemns); but James does not go far as to embrace the violent revolutionary plans of the Zealots. Martin has surveyed all of the relevant material and offers the benefit of his shrewd and balanced judgment. This is a first-class commentary.

C. L. Mitton. *The Epistle of James.* Grand Rapids: Eerdmans, 1966. This dated commentary is nonetheless able to yield worthwhile observations. Mitton points out that James has been subjected to dismissive treatment and seeks to rehabilitate the letter. He does so by pointing out connections between the teaching of James and that of Jesus, Paul, and even John. He also believes that the letter was written by James, the brother of Jesus, and for the benefit of Jewish Christian visitors to Jerusalem. Like others who wish to be responsible for the evidence in James that supports an early composition as well as that which supports a late composition, Mitton argues for a two-stage development.

J. A. Motyer. *The Message of James: The Test of Faith.* The Bible Speaks Today. Downers Grove, Ill.: InterVarsity, 1985. Motyer offers the intriguing observation that the control of the tongue is introduced in 1:26 and then expanded in 3:1–12, and the care of the needy is introduced in 1:27 and then expanded in 2:1–26, thus forming a chiastic structure. This is a serviceable commentary, but one that places too much emphasis on the role of biological metaphors in James.

Douglas J. Moo. *The Letter of James: An Introduction and Commentary.* TNTC. Grand Rapids: Eerdmans, 1985. This is a brief but helpful commentary based on the NIV text. Moo teaches at Trinity Evangelical Divinity School.

J. H. Ropes. *A Critical and Exegetical Commentary on the Epistle of St. James.* ICC. Edinburgh: T. & T. Clark, 1916. This commentary remains a good resource for investigations of the Greek text of James. Commentary on the argument and thematic content of James, already sparse, is now out of date. Ropes argues for late pseudonymous authorship.

E. M. Sidebottom. *James, Jude, 2 Peter*. NCBC. Grand Rapids: Eerdmans, 1982. This commentary by a well-known scholar takes the position that James was written in the context of the flood tide of Pauline Christianity. Sidebottom argues that James, the brother of Jesus, is responsible for the letter, and that it was written in the decade before the Jewish War of A.D. 66–70.

George M. Stulac. *James*. The IVP New Testament Commentary Series. Downers Grove, Ill.: InterVarsity, 1993. This recent effort by the pastor of Memorial Presbyterian Church in St. Louis is both fresh and helpful, although it is directed towards those who have not mastered Greek. The series is intended for use in the church by "pastors, Bible teachers, and small group leaders."

James 1:1

J AMES, A SERVANT of God and of the Lord Jesus Christ,
To the twelve tribes scattered among the nations:
Greetings.

THE FIRST CENTURY knew of many different kinds of letters.[1] In recent years scholars have spoken of two major categories: literary letters (those written with an eye to posterity and in general marked by a concern for style) and documentary or nonliterary letters.[2] Of course, a single letter might bear evidence of many "types" of letter writing.

In spite of this variety, the practice of letter writing was quite conservative, for conventions changed little over time.[3] Most letters from antiquity, and indeed most of the letters in the New Testament, can generally be seen as of a common type between individuals.[4] These follow an established formal pattern: first, the name of the sender; then the name of the recipient; a word of greeting, usually a blessing or the expression of a desire for good health; the body of the letter; and finally the closing. The usual practice in Greek was to employ the term *charein* ("greetings") as the word of greeting.[5] The typical form in Hebrew was *shalom* ("peace"), although among Greek-speaking Jews *charein* was common.[6]

---

1. The handbook attributed to Demetrius of Phalerum, known as *Epistolary Types*, lists twenty-one kinds of letters. This handbook seems to be concerned only with official letters written by persons in public service. See Stanley K. Stowers, "Letters (Greek and Latin)," *ABD* 4:290–93.

2. See John L. White, *Light From Ancient Letters* (Philadelphia: Fortress, 1986), 3.

3. The letters produced by the early Christians are remarkable in part because of their willingness to stray beyond these set parameters.

4. Other types include philosophical letters (which often contained moral exhortation) and instructional letters. Early Christian letters, including those in the New Testament, closely parallel these (see Stanley K. Stowers, "Letters [Greek and Latin]"). There are also the letters between friends and acquaintances, such as the letters of Cicero and those between Pliny and Emperor Trajan. These types generally avoid the more formal patterns.

5. Thousands of these letters are known and have been collected. A short sampling can be found in the recently reprinted volume by A. Deissmann, *Bible Studies* (Peabody, Mass.: Hendrickson, 1988), 22–25.

6. We can see examples of this general pattern in Acts and in the Pauline corpus. In Phil. 1:2 Paul writes "Grace and peace to you from God our Father and the Lord Jesus Christ." In

The book of James is also a letter, but of somewhat different character. It possesses a homiletical quality and reads much like a tract or a didactic essay. This is true for at least two reasons: (1) The letter begins an exposition of its themes almost immediately, with little or no evidence of personal sentiment; and (2) the audience is essentially undetermined. Like other examples in the New Testament, James has altered the standard formula by adding theologically important terms and by including in his opening a précis of the main themes of the letter.

The letter begins with a claim to be written by James. As we have seen,[7] there is no viable reason to doubt that James the brother of Jesus is the source for this letter. The author wishes to emphasize several points: While he does bear authority, in character this authority is that of service, and loyalty to Jesus Christ does not in any way diminish loyalty to God.

Servant. James refers to himself as a "servant" (*doulos*). There is little agreement among the commentators as to his intended meaning. Some[8] argue that James wants to distance himself from his readers by assuming the mantle of authority. Others[9] claim that James is interested in presenting himself as one among many brothers, with the emphasis on his authority colored by humility. Perhaps it is best to explore the full range of possibilities before determining the meaning of James's use of *doulos*.

(1) Slavery. *Doulos* was the common Greek term for "slave," although it could also be used for "servant."[10] Our understanding of this term is heavily and unfortunately colored by the American experience, a model that bears almost no resemblance to slavery in the Roman empire. This is true for at least two reasons. (a) Roman slavery had little if anything to do with race.

(b) Roman slavery was far more complex than its modern manifestations, having four major types. (i) The most egregious form was slavery in the mines, normally reserved for criminals or others judged to be enemies of the Roman state. Life expectancy was low, although in spite of this we do know of cases of Christian communities providing care for Christians condemned

---

Acts 15:23 we find the opening of the letter from the Jerusalem council to Gentile believers: "The apostles and elders, your brothers, To the Gentile believers in Antioch, Syria and Cilicia: Greetings."

7. See the Introduction, pp. 19–21.

8. See Ralph P. Martin, *James*, 4.

9. See Sophie Laws, *The Epistle of James*, 45–46; James Hardy Ropes, *The Epistle of St. James*, 118.

10. M. A. Beavis has recently argued that in the New Testament *doulos* means slave, not servant. See her article "Ancient Slavery As an Interpretive Context for the New Testament Servant Parables With Special Reference to the Unjust Steward (Luke 16:1–8)," *JBL* 111 (1992): 37–54.

to the mines.[11] (ii) Next was rural slavery. The agricultural manuals of Columella, Cato, and Varro describe unenviable conditions: Work could be performed in chain gangs,[12] family life existed at the whim of the owner, and rations could be cut to the bare minimum for slaves when they fell ill.[13] (iii) The type of slavery that the New Testament has most often in view is urban household slavery. Here conditions also varied, but we do know of cases where persons sold themselves into slavery,[14] counting on rewards of personal benefit. The new master provided food, shelter, and training in a skill. Many scholars believe that urban household slaves could expect manumission (a word referring to the process by which a slave was legally set free) after only a few years of service,[15] and some argue that it was nearly automatic at the age of thirty.[16] Manumission could be rendered under a variety of conditions, including the awarding of a sum of money to the freed person or even adoption by the master. This helps inform New Testament injunctions to slaves to "please" their masters,[17] and perhaps even to masters to "provide your

---

11. Eusebius in his *Ecclesiastical History* (4.23.10) relates that Dionysius, bishop of Corinth around A.D. 170, wrote a letter to Soter, the bishop of Rome. In it Dionysius commended the Roman church for its generosity in sending contributions to churches in many cities, thereby "relieving the poverty of the needy and ministering to the Christians in the mines."

12. Cato, *De Agri Cultura*, 56; Columella, *Rei Rusticae*, 1.3.12.

13. Cato, *De Agri Cultura*, 2.5.

14. See Philostratus, *Apollonius*, 8.7.12.; Dio Chrysostom, *Orations*, 15.22–23. Paul speaks against the practice in 1 Cor. 7:23. First Clement 55:2 asserts that some Christians have sold themselves into slavery in order to secure the ransom of other enslaved Christians: "We know of many among ourselves who have given themselves up to bonds, in order that they might ransom others. Many, too, have surrendered themselves to slavery, that with the price which they received for themselves, they might provide food for others."

15. See Susan Treggiari, *Roman Freedmen During the Late Republic* (Oxford: Clarendon, 1969), 12–20, 111–12, 255.

16. See G. Alföldy, *Noricum*, tr. E. Birley (London: Routledge and K. Paul, 1974), 129–31; idem, *The Social History of Rome*, tr. David Braund and Frank Pollock (Baltimore: Johns Hopkins Univ. Press, 1988), 135. Under Roman law the slave of a Roman citizen, when granted manumission, was often granted citizenship as well. In the first century such a condition was highly to be prized, and somewhat rare in the Roman provinces, as the surprise of the Philippian officials at Paul's claim to bear citizenship attests. A series of laws enacted under Augustus were intended to limit the number and the rights of manumitted slaves, presumably because Augustus feared that these *liberti* (freedpersons) would overrun the state.

17. See Eph. 6:5–8; Col. 3:22–25; 1 Tim. 6:1–2; Titus 2:9–11. In all of these passages the Greek term is a form of *doulos*. First Peter 2:18ff. contains similar teaching, but Peter uses the Greek term *oiketai*, a more specific term for household slave/servant. A letter from a freedman to his former owner in Egypt in 14 B.C. provides us with an interesting parallel. It reads "You know in your heart that I have behaved in a manner which is beyond reproach, wanting your goodwill, just as a slave wants to please in the interests of securing his freedom" (*Berliner Griechische Urkunden, Ägyptisch Urkinden aus Königlichen Museen zu Berlin*, 4.1141 [pp. 23–25]).

slaves with what is right and fair."[18] (iv) The final type of slavery was imperial slavery—slaves in the household of the emperor. Some of these held
positions of power and wealth second only to the emperor himself.[19]

(2) Old Testament. In the Old Testament the word "servant" (*'ebed*) is
sometimes used of Israel's great heroes of the faith, and as such it is a designation of honor. Solomon concluded his prayer of dedication for the temple by referring to Moses in this way: "For you singled them [Israel] out from
all the nations of the world to be your own inheritance, just as you declared
through your servant Moses" (1 Kings 8:53). Second Samuel 7 is a key chapter that recounts the promise of God to establish an everlasting Davidic
dynasty. The chapter describes how the Lord came to Nathan and said, "Go
and tell my servant David" (2 Sam. 7:5). In a similar fashion God describes
his prophets as "my servants" (Jer. 7:25).

Such passages demonstrate that in the Old Testament the term *servant* is
often used of persons who are placed in positions of authority because they
combine loyalty to God with humility before him. This is especially true of
the "servant songs" of Isaiah 42–53.[20] In summary, the Old Testament often
describes a person or persons selected by God to bear authority as "servants."
This designation indicates a humble willingness to be at God's disposal and
to live according to his principles.

It is probably beyond the range of certitude to say that James meant *doulos* only as a mark of authority over his readers, or only as a mark of solidar-
ity with them. A sober judgment is that he meant something like the early
church intended when, in its wisdom, it used the Latin phrase *nolo episcopari* as
the requirement for church office: "I do not wish to be a bishop." Only those
who did not desire personal power could be trusted with authority within

---

18. Col. 4:1; cf. Eph. 6:9.

19. Narcissus, the freedman of Emperor Claudius, amassed four hundred million sesterces
(HS400,000,000), one of the largest fortunes known during the early empire. Rendering
monetary figures from the ancient world (here sesterces) into modern equivalents is a notoriously dangerous and imprecise affair. It is best, perhaps, to offer parallels of monetary value
in terms of goods purchased. C. Nicolet ("Economy and Finance," *The Cambridge Ancient History*, eds. J. A. Crook, A. Lintott, E. Rawson [Cambridge: Cambridge Univ. Press, 1994],
10:631) estimates that the purchase price of an upper class house in Italy during the first
century B.C. would be HS4,000,000, or the equivalent of "four tonnes of silver." Ramsay Mac-
Mullen in his *Roman Social Relations, 50 B.C. to 284 A.D.* (New Haven, Conn.: Yale Univ. Press,
1974), 145, estimates the cost of building a temple at HS100,000; a theater at HS400,000;
and a library at HS500,000. MacMullen concludes that these figures support "the rather
unexpected possibility that a city's full architectural equipment might draw on the fortunes
of only a very few wealthy families, expended over a generation or so."

20. In the LXX *doulos* can also refer to all of Israel, not just to heroes and authorities (see
Deut. 32:36).

the church. Of course, this should not be confused with a strong sense of call. The issue here is integrity and purity of motive. James is a leader because God has placed him in that role, and he has recognized and accepted it; he is not a leader because he desires personal power. James, then, speaks as one with authority, but as one with the mind of Christ, the servant of all.

Lord and God. In this first verse James describes himself as a "servant of God and of the Lord Jesus Christ." This is an odd construction, found only here in the New Testament. Nor is it as clear as it might first appear. Some commentators have offered the following reading: "Servant of Jesus Christ, who is Lord and God." This is an intriguing hypothesis, one supported by a variety of admittedly tenuous points. Divine titles are linked elsewhere in James (1:27; 3:9). Moreover, this construction in Latin (*dominus et deus*) was accepted by Emperor Domitian (A.D. 81–96), a development even the Romans found both extraordinary and unsettling. They were used to granting divine status only upon the death of the emperor.[21] Domitian was no friend to the Christians, as he allowed fierce persecution of the early church. In Christian tradition he stands with Nero as a type of anti-Christ, and seems to be so held in the view of the writer of Revelation. Certainly his apparent claim to divine status reminded readers of the "man of lawlessness" in 2 Thessalonians 2.

The apotheosis (elevation to divine status) of the state in the person of the emperor disturbed both Jews and Christians, who together believed that only God deserved such unwavering loyalty. Both were labeled "atheists" by the Romans because they believed in only one God, not the many of Mediterranean paganism. Perhaps James used this formula to designate the one who truly is Lord and God.

Against this position, many hold that the theology of James is too simple to have been written as late as the reign of Domitian.[22] In any event it is still possible that James used this construction as a way of countering the claims of the Roman state. In sum, while "Jesus Christ, who is Lord and God" is a grammatical possibility, it is less likely than the traditional reading.

---

21. Vespasian is famous for his sardonic deathbed comment *Vae, puto deus fio* ("Alas, I think that I am becoming a god"). Vespasian grudgingly understood the need felt by the state to perpetuate the cult of emperor worship, but he harbored no illusions about his own status. Domitian, the son of Vespasian, took this address seriously, for he was a man of less ability, greater insecurity, and greater tyranny than his father.

22. This idea, that greater theological complexity necessarily goes hand in hand with chronological development, has attained the status of a nearly unquestioned axiom in New Testament studies. It is also a fallacy, as G. B. Caird pointed out ("The Development of the Doctrine of Christ in the New Testament," *Christ For Us Today*, ed. N. Pittenger [London: SCM, 1968], 66–80.). The Christology of Mark, for example, is "higher" (or more "divine" and less "human") than that of Luke, even though nearly all agree that Luke wrote later than Mark.

James's intent here is most likely the same as in Titus 1:1—to demonstrate that loyalty to Jesus Christ does not undermine loyalty to God; that, in fact, they are one and the same.[23] Balancing the divinity of Jesus Christ with monotheism was no small problem for early Christianity,[24] and the formula James uses constitutes a portion of his answer to this dilemma.

The twelve tribes. James addresses his letter to "the twelve tribes scattered among the nations." This construction is also unusual. The only parallel in the New Testament is 1 Peter 1:1. There are two main lines of interpretation available: The "twelve tribes" means Jews and/or Jewish Christians, or it refers to the multiracial church.

Those who posit the former view point out the following:

- This is an obvious way of referring to the Jewish nation (e.g., Acts 25:7).
- Parallels in Qumran literature and Haggadah intend ethnic distinctions.
- *Phyle* ("tribe"), when unmodified, must refer to historic Israel.[25]
- While the New Testament does use the term in reference to the church, it can use it to refer to ethnic Israel (e.g., Rev. 21:12).
- While a symbolic interpretation of the "twelve tribes" is possible, the addition "scattered among the nations" necessarily limits the referent to Jews, and probably to Jewish Christians,[26] although it is possible that James hopes that his letter will have success in attracting Jews to the new faith.

Against this is the view that the phrase in question should be viewed symbolically.

- If the "twelve tribes" must refer to ethnic Israel, then it is unclear how it can refer only to Jews who happen to be Christians. Logic demands that we either understand the term as referring only to all Jews, or else we understand the term symbolically.
- Others argue that while "the twelve tribes" clearly indicates ethnic/geographic Israel, the addition of "scattered among the nations" opens the possibility of a symbolic meaning,[27] since after the fall of the north-

---

23. Here the parallel to the Gospel of John is evident (e.g., John 14:10).

24. See G. B. Caird and L. D. Hurst, *New Testament Theology* (Oxford: Clarendon, 1994), 338–40.

25. Ralph P. Martin, *James*, 9, argues that the use of the phrase "the twelve tribes" would be meaningless in relationship to Luke 2:36 if the phrase meant "the multiracial church".

26. This is the line of thought taken by James Adamson, *The Epistle of James*, 49–50.

27. Sophie Laws, *The Epistle of James*, 47–49.

ern kingdom the ten tribes were "lost." The reconstitution of the twelve tribes of Israel belonged to the messianic hope, and the further parallel of these tribes understood as the pilgrimage people of God so closely parallels New Testament usage concerning the church that it is likely James has the multiracial church in view.

- "Twelve tribes" stands for the unity and integrity of the nation of Israel/people of God. The church, in the universal view of the New Testament, is the successor to Judaism in this regard. In the LXX and other Jewish literature, the phrase usually carries a genitive, the genitive of nearer definition, such as the "twelve tribes of Israel" (Ex. 24:4) or "the tribes of Jacob" (Sirach 48:10). The absence of a genitive of nearer definition here does open the way for a symbolic interpretation, especially since the New Testament ascribes to the church all of the ideal attributes of Judaism in relation to God

- The fact that Greek-speaking Jews in Jerusalem could employ a formula that approximated the traditional Hebrew greeting tends to imply an ethnically mixed audience as the intended recipients of the letter of James.[28]

What can be said by way of summary? James writes in the knowledge that he has been given authority in the church. But he also knows that this authority has the character and tenor of service: service to God and service to others. For this reason he calls the recipients of this letter "brothers." James addresses his letter to the multiracial church, but the native thought world of the letter is Judaism, the multiform Judaism of the first century, and more particularly messianic Judaism. Finally, James writes with a sensitivity to Jewish monotheism, but desires to make the case that loyalty is due to Jesus Christ, and that this loyalty does not endanger loyalty to God.

Bridging Contexts

JAMES 1:1 HAS several important issues for us to consider in bridging contexts. The first two concern the fashion in which we rightfully can render words employed in Scripture into our modern context. The third deals with the idea of service, a key idea in this verse. How can we faithfully bridge the gap between the cultural and theological content of that idea in the first century with our own definition of the term?

---

28. In 2 Macc. 1:1 the Jews in Jerusalem send greetings to Jews throughout the world with the formula *eirenen agathon*. If James had wished to restrict his message to Jews or even more narrowly to Jewish Christians, we might have expected him to use such a formula that approximates the traditional Hebrew greeting.

Slave, servant, and authority. We argued above that the word "slave" (*doulos*) needs to be understood not according to its contemporary English definition, but rather in light of the varieties of slave conditions within the Roman empire. But we also argued that in this particular case there is insufficient evidence to claim that James has only one particular image in mind. This may have seemed a cavalier and unwarranted conclusion. But we must remember that biblical writers thought in terms of concepts, to which any number of terms might point. They did not usually think in terms of words with static meanings. The idea of the selfless love of God, for instance, is deeply lodged in Scripture. Writers such and Anders Nygren[29] and C. S. Lewis[30] have pointed out that this notion is linked to the Greek verb *agapao*. But as James Barr has shown, both the LXX and the New Testament use the Greek verb *phileo*, usually understood as intending the idea of "brotherly love," interchangeably with *agapao* to convey the same idea.[31]

In a similar manner, a single word or expression can imply a variety of different meanings. Jesus, for example, filled the word *kyrios* ("Lord") with new meaning, so that in the New Testament it can imply either oppressor or servant-leader. In short, biblical terms are far more flexible than we often construe.

Furthermore, while we know a great deal about the ancient world, what we do know is far outweighed by what we do not. Sobriety, probity, and humility ought to characterize our conclusions.[32]

The twelve tribes. We also argued above that the phrase "the twelve tribes" most likely refers not to ethnic Israel, but to the new Israel, the multiracial church. There are certainly reputable scholars who have taken the opposite position. What is particularly important here is not so much the conclusion one comes to on this issue, but a principle of theological interpretation that can be of great help in creating a bridge to span the distance from the text to our own world. Some point out that the original meaning of "the

---

29. Anders Nygren, *Eros and Agape*, tr. P. S. Watson (Philadelphia: Westminster, 1953). Nygren understood that the idea of self-giving love was not intended every time some form of *agapao* appeared. But popular perception often took this view.

30. C. S. Lewis, *The Four Loves* (New York: Harcourt, Brace, 1960).

31. See James Barr, "Words for Love in Biblical Greek," *The Glory of Christ in the New Testament: Studies in Christology in Memory of George Bradford Caird*, eds. L. D. Hurst and N. T. Wright (Oxford: Clarendon, 1987), 3–18.

32. As Martin Hengel put it recently: "New Testament scholarship has always been in good part a *science of conjecture*. . . . This fact should make us more modest. . . . Too often there exists the danger of confusing what is precisely possible with what in fact is really probable. . . . We should not be ashamed to speak candidly of our great uncertainty" ("Tasks of New Testament Scholarship," *BBR* 6 [1996]: 75–76). Hengel here speaks of New Testament scholarship as an admittedly specialized branch of the discipline of ancient history.

twelve tribes" was restricted to ethnic Israel. This argument, that when we uncover the original meaning of a term, we uncover its meaning in a text, is called the etymological argument. It is widely held to be a sure route to truth, but it is often false. We should not be swayed uncritically by the siren song of original meaning.

While discovering the original meaning of a term may be satisfying and ultimately helpful, there is no necessary guarantee that in doing so we have discerned the meaning the author intended the term to bear *in a particular text*. Examples from Scripture abound. In the Old Testament the term *ger* ("stranger") was originally used as a self-reference by the Patriarchs (see Gen. 21:23; 23:4), because they wandered in a land not their own. Even the name Moses gave to his son, Gershom, reflects this idea. Once firmly established in the land, however, *ger* came to refer to non-Jews. The point is that a term means exactly what the author wishes it to mean, neither more nor less. Etymological concerns may be of service, but we should never allow them unthinkingly to govern our interpretation.

Authority and service. A major theme of this passage is the balance of authority with service. A stock component of the Roman *mythos* was precisely this. The Romans believed that their conquests were laid upon them by fate, that they had a civilizing mission to exert on the rest of the world.[33] Virgil put it well when he noted that it was the task of the Romans to "submit the whole world to the rule of law" (*totum sub leges mitteret orbem*).[34] The Romans believed that it was for the good of other peoples that they conquered. By some measures they were accurate. At times and in some places Rome could be a beneficent and generous master.[35] But the vast majority of

---

33. The Romans used the Greek word *oikoumene* (Latin: *oecumene*) to refer to the world, or more properly the inhabited world. This word, derived from *oikos*, the Greek word meaning "house," indicates the degree to which the Romans understood their "right" of patronage. Emperor Hadrian even constructed a sprawling palace complex at Tibur (modern Tivoli), in which was displayed *flora, fauna*, and replicas of buildings from around the world. The point, obviously, is that the entire world is the proper home of the Romans.

34. Virgil, *Aeneid*, 4.231. A similar notion is found in the Latin phrase *fiat iustia pereat mundus*, "Let justice be done even if the world perishes."

35. Three examples will suffice. (1) Under Emperor Trajan a policy was established whereby he lent money from his imperial treasury to Italian landowners, under the condition that they pay a 5 percent tax into a municipal chest, the revenue to be used to care for the children of needy families in that area. This practice is known as the alimentary institutions. (2) In the correspondence between Trajan and Pliny, we read of the concern of Trajan for mundane matters, such as a proper water supply for provincial municipalities. (3) Note the case of Emperor Tiberius. When given advice to raise taxes in the provinces, Tiberius replied that it is the part of a good shepherd to shear the flock, not skin it (Suetonius, *Tiberius*, 32).

those living under Roman rule did not know this experience. Most knew authority figures, rulers, and masters, whether Romans or provincial elites, only as oppressors.[36] Similarly, most slaves experienced their relationship with authority figures as less than desirable. Nor was the condition of urban household slavery a guarantee of well-being. Pliny tells us that some were severely mistreated.[37] In fact, the vast bulk of the population, women and men, slaves, peasants, and poor urbanites, who together composed more than 90 percent of the population, perceived authority as generally callous, indifferent, and demeaning.

Our world is not too dissimilar. We experience authority in a negative way, as it seems to us basically self-interested. The growing problem of violent, illegal, and misdirected anti-government groups is only one expression of this perception. In more mild forms we experience this dissociation every day. The evidence is there, from voter apathy to fear of the police to jokes about the Internal Revenue Service.

James here carves out a different picture. In his world and in ours the combination of authority with service, which he conveys by use of the term *doulos*, is rare. The close juxtaposition of the term *doulos* with the idea of service is intended to compel us to take notice. Familiarity with the idea and the phrase "servant leadership" may have jaded us. It is a notion as radical and as far reaching as virtually any in Scripture. Jesus calls us to live it out, not merely to pay it lip service. Failure to live it out is a form of double-mindedness.[38] The kingdom of God has upside down priorities. The wisdom of God is foolishness to the world, and the wisdom of the world is foolishness to God. Leadership, and especially leadership in the church, is to be undertaken only with a strong and sincere commitment to seek God's will and the manifestation of that will in the well-being of others. In making his case in this way, James sets out a pattern for church leadership.

---

36. Josephus tells us that the combination of Roman taxes and the temple tax "bled the country dry" (see his *Antiquities*, 17.304–8). Jewish farmers whose families were murdered by the Romans because they could not afford to pay their taxes turned to banditry and open rebellion because of the blunt edge of Roman rule. On banditry as a peasant movement in Palestine under Roman rule, see Gerd Theissen, *The Shadow of the Galilean* (Philadelphia: Fortress, 1987), 75ff.; S. Applebaum, "Judaea As a Roman Province: The Countryside As a Political and Economic Factor," *ANRW*, 2d series (Berlin: de Gruyter), 8:355–99.

37. Pliny, *Epistulae*, 3.14.

38. "Honesty," said Juvenal, "is praised and then left to shiver" (*probitas laudatur et alget*) (*Satires*, 1.74). Our lack of resolve to live the principles of servanthood is no less worthy of remark.

THE KEY ISSUES for James in 1:1 are the combination of authority and service and the notion of loyalty to God. What is the shape and texture of these two issues in our contemporary setting?

Servanthood and authority. James, like Paul in Philippians 2, issues a strong call for the basic character of the Christian life to be that of servanthood, after the model of Jesus himself. The witness of the Gospels is that Jesus was a Servant-Messiah.[39] The model of servanthood is to be lived out by those in leadership. James makes this clear when he combines images and themes of authority with comradeship and service in his opening salutation. Leadership in the church of Jesus Christ ought to be reserved for those who have no selfish agenda. The goals set and the practice used to achieve them must be marked by a servant attitude.

It is a sacred and terrible thing to be perceived as the agent of God. The potential for such power attracts charlatans. Recent exposés by journalists have catalogued cases in which "evangelists" have used the name of Jesus Christ to fleece the faithful and make themselves rich. I read recently of one case in which the recipient of a prayer letter responded (along with a ten dollar donation) with the request that the evangelist in question "stop exploiting suffering people with his arrogant self-deification." A week later came the reply. This special prayer request was offered up to God by the "evangelist" in question for three days and nights during a prayer vigil while in his special prayer chamber. He then had the audacity to ask for more money.[40]

But this power has a less obvious but potent seductive quality. Pastors and other church leaders are human. At times they abuse our trust, whether the matter is sexual sin, inappropriate financial dealings, or simply a tendency to self-importance. When I was in seminary, I knew of many students who said, "I love to preach," in a fashion that was cavalier or frivolous. As a pastor and professor I cannot say this. While I often feel the presence and the joy of the Lord while preaching, I am also keenly aware of the responsibility that the office and function place on me. No one prepares a lecture on Alexander the Great supposing that those awaiting its delivery hope God will speak to them through the lecture. But a good many saints so anticipate a sermon.

---

39. At Jesus' baptism the voice from heaven combined kingship (by quoting Ps. 2) with service (by quoting Isa. 42). The temptation accounts confirm that Jesus resolved to be a Servant-Messiah. Even Jesus' favorite self-designation, "Son of Man," points to this. The Son of Man in Dan. 7 is to be served, but Jesus attaches to the notion of the Son of Man the idea of servanthood: "The Son of Man did not come to be served, but to serve, and to give his life as a ransom for many" (Mark 10:45).

40. David G. Myers, *The Pursuit of Happiness: Who Is Happy—And Why* (New York: William Morrow and Company, 1992), 180–81.

There is another side to this matter. Most do not aspire to positions of Christian leadership wholly out of a desire for power. The vast majority love God and desire to see his kingdom progress in our world. One of the reasons those in leadership get into trouble is that we have set an incredibly high standard for ourselves. We often expect our pastors to preach as well as those we see on television, to counsel as well as a professional therapist, and to administrate as well as a CEO. It is a difficult and often lonely thing to be a pastor.

These high expectations often have two results. (1) Many gifted and godly people choose not to enter the ministry, having witnessed the pain endured by pastors and desiring not to be such obvious targets. (2) In the face of such expectations, many pastors choose the human response of ignoring the obvious. They may pretend that conditions are better than they are, or they refuse to admit that their skills are weak in certain areas. In so doing they gradually become distant from themselves and from others, because they do not feel able to be honest with the church, with themselves, or perhaps even with God. This is the opposite of the New Testament idea of community. The church is supposed to be a place where (in the proper contexts) we can be open and honest with each other, confident that we will receive encouragement, prayer, and even discipline in the proper admixture. Those in the pew bear a responsibility to those whom God has called to lead.

Servant leadership means first to resolve to accomplish what is God's will in the best interests of others. But it also means to carry out those endeavors in a fashion that relates to others the care and compassion of Jesus. In this way one does know joy—the joy that comes in giving oneself away.

Loyalty to God. A major theme for James in 1:1 is loyalty. But this is not blind loyalty. It is a loyalty that seeks to understand God, to grow into what God intends. In various ways James also makes the point that loyalty to Jesus Christ is not a threat to monotheism, that in fact loyalty to Jesus Christ and loyalty to God amount to the same thing.

This idea also carries with it an implied warning: Be vigilant and introspective concerning your own heart and mind. Loyalty to the government, to a particular political party or philosophy, to a particular religious expression, or to anything else besides God and the concomitant commitment to be humble before God always contains the potential for the seeds of idolatry to germinate and flourish. Many in the evangelical community, especially the "Christian Right," identify the United States with Christianity. While the United States can at times stand for what is moral and right, often it does not. To confuse loyalty to the state with loyalty to God is idolatry, the same idolatry to which the ancient Israelites fell prey. James here pushes us to consider the ways we unwisely grant elsewhere loyalty that rightfully pertains to God alone.

James 1:2-11

CONSIDER IT PURE joy, my brothers, whenever you face trials of many kinds, ³because you know that the testing of your faith develops perseverance. ⁴Perseverance must finish its work so that you may be mature and complete, not lacking anything. ⁵If any of you lacks wisdom, he should ask God, who gives generously to all without finding fault, and it will be given to him. ⁶But when he asks, he must believe and not doubt, because he who doubts is like a wave of the sea, blown and tossed by the wind. ⁷That man should not think he will receive anything from the Lord; ⁸he is a double-minded man, unstable in all he does.

⁹The brother in humble circumstances ought to take pride in his high position. ¹⁰But the one who is rich should take pride in his low position, because he will pass away like a wild flower. ¹¹For the sun rises with scorching heat and withers the plant; its blossom falls and its beauty is destroyed. In the same way, the rich man will fade away even while he goes about his business.

JAMES FOLLOWS HIS introduction and greeting with a passage pregnant with practical questions and answers rich in theological content. He makes his case here in two broad strokes. In the first (1:2–8) James addresses the question of trials: What is the source of misfortune? Why does God allow difficulties in our lives? How are we to respond to them? To these questions James answers that prayer, and specifically the wisdom of God, are the tools necessary to negotiate successfully the minefield of trials and the questions they spur in our minds. In the second broad stroke (1:9–11) James discusses poverty and wealth and the effects these conditions can have on spiritual life. He urges his readers to remember that wealth is fleeting and that God elevates the poor.

Trials (1:2–8)

JAMES MAKES HIS case that (1) testing ought to be received with joy, for it results in benefit, and that (2) wisdom is needed as the gift from God in order to perceive testing in this manner. In so doing the section begins to build the case that true religion is composed of the development of both individual character (1:2–18) and corporate character (1:19–2:26; that is, the church itself should stand for truth and spurn duplicity in both teaching and worship). The section also introduces some of the major themes of the letter— prayer, faith, and testing.

James 1:2–8 is a chain argument that is given structural unity by the use of verbal links (the words "greetings" [*chairein*] and "joy" [*charan*] in verses 1 and 2; "perseverance" in verses 3 and 4; "lack" in verses 4 and 5; "ask" in verses 5 and 6) and the placing of one idea over the other, aiming at the effect of strong moral exhortation (cf. also Rom. 5:3–5; 1 Peter 1:6–7). While there are some differences in these three passages,[1] all share the idea of *endurance*. It is possible that each depends on a common source, such as the teaching of Jesus.

Pure joy. In the phrase "pure joy," "pure" translates *pasan* ("whole, complete, utter"), thus heightening the effect of joy. Plato uses this word when in the *Laws* he has Clinias argue that it is unlikely that a man would willingly "plunge into the *utter* depths of depravity."[2] In the Apocrypha God is described as the one who is "gracious ... with *complete* favor" (2 Macc. 2:22). Paul in Colossians prays that the believers in Colosse will be filled with "*all* spiritual wisdom and understanding" (Col. 1:9–11). So the "joy" James speaks of here is a complete, overflowing joy. Although it seems strange, trials are to be occasions of such joy.

My brothers. With "my brothers" we revisit the question of addressees. Earlier we came to two conclusions: (1) James speaks with authority, but as one among peers; (2) James writes to the multiracial church. "My brothers" conveys warmth and comradeship, which agrees with our earlier conclusion. Two other factors cement the case. James makes no claim to apostolic authority,[3] and his use of *doulos* ("servant," v. 1) argues that he wishes to minimize the aura of authority.[4]

This leaves the question of the ethnic identification of his "brothers." The Hebrew *'ah* ("brother" = Greek *adelphos*) is used, for example, of fellow countrymen in Exodus 2:11 and 2 Maccabees 1:1. On the other hand, in antiquity pagan religions used "my brothers" to refer to fellow adherents of various ethnic backgrounds.[5] By far the most attested use of the term was within the early

---

1. Peter is more concerned with the test, which he values, while Paul and James agree that the virtues produced by the test are the most important issue.

2. *Laws* 646B.

3. Surely an odd *lacuna* if the writing is pseudonymous.

4. J. H. Ropes, *The Epistle of St. James*, 118, argues that Paul claims to be a servant only in Romans and Philippians, two occasions in which he wished to avoid claims of personal authority.

5. See G. Adolf Deissmann, *Bible Studies*, tr. Alexander Grieve (Peabody, Mass.: Hendrickson, 1988), 142.

church. Here "brothers" could be used of fellow Jews, as Paul sometimes did (e.g., Rom. 9:3), but the overwhelming use in the New Testament and early Christian literature is of fellow Christians in contradistinction to the world at large.

It is not at all unlikely that the pervasive use in the New Testament was the product of its use by Jesus (Matt. 23:8; Mark 3:35; Luke 22:32) and of the radically different definition he gave to community. Loyalty to God, not ethnic composition, was his clarion call. James teaches that Christians sometimes encounter trials because of this loyalty to God. That Jesus so radically redefined the composition of the people of God offers us assurance that the previous conclusion concerning the twelve tribes as symbolic of the church was accurate.

Encountering trials. Christians "encounter" trials. The Greek word used here (*peripipto*) suggests an unwelcome and unanticipated experience. Jesus uses the same term when he tells the story of the good Samaritan, as the man "fell into the hands of" robbers (Luke 10:30). There is no room here for the idea of seeking out trials as a way of "proving" faith to oneself or to others. The trials James assumes here are unexpected and, at least initially, unwelcome.

Given what we know of contemporary Jewish thought, the trials "of many kinds" probably arose from both external and internal sources. There is little doubt that a great variety is in view; they are multicolored, intricate, and diverse. This contrasts with the straightforward integrity of God (v. 5) and recalls the subtlety of Satan.

The Hebrew word that stands behind the Greek word "trials" (*peirasmos*) is *nasah*, which means to prove the quality or worth of someone or something through adversity. In tenor it is neutral. *Peirasmos* is linked to *peirates* ("attacker, pirate") and can mean both incitements to evil thoughts and actions and hardships that prove mettle.

Several points need to made here. (1) Testing can be linked to Satan. The New Testament sometimes refers to Satan as the attacker or the pirate (Matt. 4:3; 1 Cor. 7:5; 10:13; 1 Thess. 3:5; 1 Tim. 6:9). The incitement to do evil parallels a portion of the portfolio that Satan has arrogated to himself. (2) The testing is subtle and multiform, images that remind us of the description of the serpent in Genesis 3:1. (3) Jewish theological anthropology and psychology may stand behind this passage. In order to understand the thought of James here, a brief discussion of the biblical view of Satan is necessary (see comments in "Bridging Contexts" section).

There are also links to the Gospels here. Popular Jewish belief held that misfortune could be the result of either some internal fault or drive or some external force. The first is well illustrated in John 9:1–2. Passing the temple Jesus and his disciples spied a man born blind. In asking Jesus if the man or his parents sinned, the disciples expressed a popular belief that this man experienced misfortune as a result of sin. Regarding the second point, both the New

Testament and rabbinic tradition recognized that Satan can and does entice human beings to sin (cf. the temptation of Jesus, Matt. 4:1–11; Luke 4:1–13).

There are other links to Jesus as well. Trials are the common experience of humanity, including Jesus; that is, we face trials just as did Jesus (see Heb. 4:14–16). Furthermore, in Luke 6:22 Jesus calls us blessed when we are persecuted for the sake of the kingdom.

In summary, James drew upon not only the developing rabbinic tradition, but also upon the life and teaching of Jesus for his understanding of trials. They can be a part of the normal ebb and flow of life, they can result from the wiles of Satan, or (as we are about to see in 1:12–18) they can be allowed by God and even sent by God. No matter their source, James insists that we should respond not with anger or disappointment, but with utter joy.

To respond to difficulties with joy seems absurd. James knows this, and so in verse 3 he offers his answer to our natural question: Why should we rejoice in the face of trials? Trials have a purifying quality; they are the arena in which and the process through which something good develops. Here in James is a parallel to the Hebrew idea that testing can result in purification even if it is the result of a person's natural impulse to sin (*yeṣer ha-ra*).

Trials can have this effect as a result of the means of "testing" (*dokimion*). The root of this word means "approved character," so we can see the close link between the testing and its intended result. Judaism provides a rich background for understanding trials.[6] Psalm 66:10–12 speaks of God's testing his people like silver and then leading them to a spacious place. Proverbs 3:11–12 contains perhaps the classic statement of this idea: "My son, do not despise the LORD's discipline and do not resent his rebuke, because the LORD disciplines those he loves, as a father the son he delights in." In 2 Maccabees 6:12–17 we read about the calamities that befell the Jewish nation as the result of God's chastening resolve. James believes that these trials are evidence of God's mercy (James 1:16).

Endurance and perfection. The result of the testing of faith is "perseverance" or endurance (*hypomone*)—a highly prized trait. *Hypomone* is a new feature added to the character of a Christian in the crucible of testing. This word does not refer to a solitary and exceptional act of fortitude, but to a deeper component of character that manifests itself in various situations. It means active steadfastness, staying power, constancy, and a determination under adversity. But it is colored with the idea of hope,[7] which animates and enriches these other qualities.

---

6. See 4 Macc. 17:2–4.

7. See, for example, Ps. 71:4–5. In 4 Macc. 17:23 we read a slightly different twist: "It is unreasonable that those who are religious should not stand up against adversity."

Hypomone is also a means to an end. We should not be satisfied with constancy, as important as this virtue is, but we should let it grow to its fullest, in order to become "mature and complete, not lacking anything."[8] This idea of perfection has roots in the Old Testament and can be illustrated by two words with mutually implicatory meanings. The first word is *tamîm*, which means "blameless" or "innocent." It implies a character without defect and describes the person who lives in obedience to God. This term is used of Noah in Genesis 6:9 ("Noah was a righteous man, blameless among the people of his time"). The second word is *shalem*, "perfect, whole, single-minded." In the *Testament of Joseph* 2:4–7 the sufferings of Joseph are described, providing a parallel to the thought expressed in James.[9]

> For a short time he may stand aside in order to test the disposition of the soul. In ten testings he revealed to me that I was approved, and in all of them I persevered, because perseverance is a strong medicine and endurance provides many good things.

The point to notice here is that the reason for the test (James 1:2–4) is linked with the character of God (1:5–8), and God is the only one deserving of such trust.

The "complete" person is one whose character is fully formed according to Christian standards; it is not "perfection" according to some standard common to popular culture. Paul found many in the church in Corinth guilty of accepting the standards of their society, and he reminded them that the wisdom of God appears foolish to this world, just as the wisdom of this world is foolishness in the sight of God (1 Cor. 1:18–31).

"Mature" (*telios*) denotes "goal" or "rightful purpose." This is a key term for James; no New Testament book uses it more often. When it is used of character, it implies that God is a part of whatever process is involved in the formation of character. Its range of meaning extends to the fullest expression of character in the age to come.[10] It is also important to note that this is not some unachievable high standard[11]; rather, we can become persons of *integrity*, persons who are single-minded in their loyalty and devotion to God. It is the fully developed character of stable righteousness.

---

8. See parallels in Rom. 6:1–23 and Gal. 5:6.

9. See Pheme Perkins, *First and Second Peter, James and Jude* (Louisville: John Knox, 1995), 96.

10. Ralph P. Martin, *James*, 17.

11. For example, in James 3:2 being "perfect" is the ability to control the tongue. While admirable, this is hardly reserved only for those who are morally perfect or even morally superior.

The Gospels generally see maturity as the imitation of God, the development of the character traits of God within ourselves. At the conclusion of the Lukan beatitudes Jesus says:

> But love your enemies, do good to them, and lend to them without expecting to get anything back. Then your reward will be great, and you will be sons of the Most High, because he is kind to the ungrateful and the wicked. Be merciful, just as your Father is merciful. (Luke 6:35–36)

What stands behind this passage is what grammarians call the *"ben* [son] of" classification. To be a child of someone or something is to be like the thing to which one is compared. So James and John, who angered quickly, were called *"Sons of* Thunder" (Mark 3:17). Jesus calls us to nothing less than to be like God in terms of character.

God gives wisdom. At this point James moves from moral integrity to wisdom (*sophia*), whose only source is God.[12] While human beings are, at least in part, responsible for their moral development, wisdom comes only from God. In the New Testament generally, wisdom is allied to understanding God's purposes and plan and indicates a determination to live accordingly. We need wisdom to know how to cope with trials, for wisdom provides a clear view of our situation from God's perspective. With wisdom we perceive that what the world calls misfortune, whatever its source, is an opportunity for God to bring about his purpose. Wisdom as the gift of God logically leads to our asking for it. Here again we see verbal links to Jesus: "Ask and it will be given to you" (Matt. 7:7; Luke 11:9); "And I will do whatever you ask in my name, so that the Son may bring glory to the Father" (John 14:13).

Some commentators point out that in Luke 11:11–13 Jesus promises to give the Spirit, while in James the gift that comes from God is wisdom.[13] There is no essential conflict here, for Judaism had developed a rich theology of wisdom, often seeing it as personified: Lady Wisdom, who seeks to reveal herself to humanity (e.g., Prov. 1:20–21). The granting of wisdom from God, who alone is truly wise, is a complicated notion. The Jews understood wisdom not only as the mind and purposes of God, but also as the content of revealed truth. In John the Holy Spirit performs both functions. Jesus promised his disciples that the Holy Spirit would come, saying, "[He] will be in you" (John 14:17) and "will teach you all things and will remind you

---

12. The Old Testament has many references to God as the source of wisdom. Proverbs 2:6 says, "For the LORD gives wisdom, and from his mouth come knowledge and understanding."

13. Sophie Laws, *The Epistle of James*, 56.

of everything I have said to you" (14:26). For this reason it is better to speak of James's "wisdom pneumatology" rather than his "wisdom Christology."

James goes on to say that God gives generously without hesitation (v. 5). He contrasts God's single-hearted devotion and purpose to the varied and complex nature of the fraudulent schemes created by the evil one. God also gives "without finding fault" (*me oneidizontos*). The root word means "to utter insult" and carries an active tone. As in Jewish literature, one who gives without reproach knows that kindness and generosity are to be granted to the poor (see Sir. 18:15–18). Taken altogether, James conveys the notion that God's spontaneous generosity is unwavering, regardless of our previous record (see Luke 6:35).

Without doubt. Having discussed the character of God as the giver of what we need, James turns his attention to the matter of those who do not receive wisdom from God. He calls on us to ask without doubt, that is, without waffling back and forth. He employs the metaphor of a rudderless vessel in the midst of a wavy sea, buffeted by strong winds. It seems clear that these forces are linked to the human evil impulse, especially as this inclination not only allows the body to commit evil, but also impedes it when the mind and heart determine to do good. This echoes Ephesians 4:13–14, where Paul speaks of our maturation as Christians, until we are no longer children, tossed to and fro and carried about by every wind of doctrine.

Verse 6 offers the human side of prayer. Although Luther took a generally dim view of the letter of James, this verse he viewed with favor, as he wrote in his *Instructions for the Visitors of Parish Pastor:* "The Pastors should also instruct their people that prayer includes faith that God will hear us, as James writes in Jas. 1."[14] When a person asks from God, "he must believe and not doubt." God does not hesitate to give to us, although we sometimes hesitate to ask. The verb *aiteo* ("to ask") also appears in verse 5 in reference to prayer, and there some extraordinary things were said: God gives universally, his gift is beneficent, and it is given without regard to merit. Here, however, it is used of situations in which God does not give.

Verse 6 is therefore a difficult passage, and many of the attempts to explain it seem to make the meaning more opaque rather than more lucid. These difficulties revolve around the meaning and implications of "faith." Some suggest that prayer that is effective is prayer that is made with confidence and in full conviction, especially with a faith that manifests itself in works.[15] In contrast is the view that faith here means "confidence in prayer" and not

---

14. See *Luther's Works*, ed. Conrad Bergendoff (Philadelphia: Muhlenberg, 1958), 40:278–79.

15. Martin, *James*, 18–19.

"constancy in the Christian religion." It is a coming to God, believing that he is able to do a certain thing.[16]

There are strong objections to this second view. James has just laid down the idea of the universal generosity of God, and it is unclear how this can be rectified with the image of God's giving only to those with sufficient confidence that he is able to accomplish a certain task. Some argue that it is precisely this confidence that unleashed the healing powers of Jesus. This is a misconception.[17] Those who hold this position also believe that the doubter has no such confidence that he or she will be healed.[18] It is therefore more likely that James means a faith that manifests itself in action. The previous verses have made much of character and unwavering integrity, two themes that have to do with action. Further, in 2:22 James describes the faith of Abraham as one of faith and actions working together. So perhaps James is arguing that those who are growing in the will of the Father will receive even more from God, just as this growth allows more room for grace. This is essentially the thought in John 14:13—14.

The contrast here is with "doubt,"[19] and since doubt is a waffling back and forth, the result of doubt is inaction. The one who doubts wavers and is tossed to and fro as on a tempestuous sea. Honest intellectual doubts are

---

16. James Adamson, *The Epistle of James*, 57. Yet Adamson notes that in 1:3 faith does mean "constancy in the Christian religion."

17. The common view that Jesus could not heal unless there was sufficient faith in the heart of the one afflicted is easily unhorsed. No one, we may suppose, would argue that Lazarus, or the daughter of Jairus, or even anyone in attendance at either of these occasions, had faith for a resurrection. The often misunderstood *locus classicus* of this view is Mark 6:1–5, in which Mark tells us that in Nazareth Jesus "could not do any miracles there ... [because of] their lack of faith." Careful inspection of the text reveals that Jesus did heal people of afflictions, surely what we would consider a miracle. The problem is in the vocabulary employed by the New Testament, for the terms used most often (*thauma* ["wonder, miracle"], *semeion* ["sign"], and *semeia kai terata* ["signs and wonders"]) have a range of meaning far wider than our notion of "miracle." The aged Simeon considers the very presence of the baby Jesus a "sign" in Luke 2:34. Mark 6:1–5 is the only time one of these terms is used in reference to Jesus, who "marveled" (*ethaumazen*) at their unbelief. The point here is that miracles do not necessarily "cause" faith (see Luke 16:31); and so Jesus declines to perform them when he perceived that the result would be the wrong kind of belief, namely, a belief in Jesus the wonder-worker. This incorrect belief, perhaps a belief in their own vision of what the Messiah was to do and be, characterized the disciples who left Jesus in John 6:66. Jesus sought to create and nurture a different kind of belief, a belief in Jesus as God's agent, as the one who reveals the living God. A similar situation pertains in the case of the so-called "messianic secret."

18. In Mark 9:14–32 Jesus heals a boy with an evil spirit. In verse 24 the father of the boy exclaims "I do believe; help me overcome my unbelief!"

19. See Ropes, *The Epistle of St. James*, 140–41.

not in view here. After all, to doubt is human, as the Psalms attest. David, for example, gives voice to his doubts about the character and trustworthiness of God (cf. Ps. 96:1). In Psalm 6 he wonders aloud if God has rejected him, and he even attempts to force God into action by an obvious bribe. Yet in the midst of this honest doubt, David is reminded of all that God has done for him in the past, and he gains the hope necessary to continue. Faith here in James understands and has experienced the character of God, who gives freely and generously; because of this experience, such a person has confidence. Finally, prayer should be offered in integrity, it should be single-hearted, even as God has integrity and is single-hearted.

Double-minded and unstable. James next describes the one who doubts as double-minded (*dipsychos*). Behind this stands the Hebrew idea of being double-tongued or double-faced (e.g., Ps. 11:2). Deuteronomy 26:16 warns the Israelites against worshiping God with two hearts, and Psalm 12:2 speaks of the double heart: "Everyone lies to his neighbor; their flattering lips speak with deception [lit., heart to heart]." Such a heart contrasts sharply with God, who is single-hearted. James is speaking of someone who constantly changes allegiances and cultivates the patina of faith, wrongly thinking mechanistic action to be the heart of faith. James calls us to be people of character, whose faith manifests itself in action commensurate with what God has called us to be.

James touches upon an important biblical theme here: God is the one who means what he says, who always accomplishes his purpose: "So is my word that goes out from my mouth: It will not return to me empty, but will accomplish what I desire and achieve the purpose for which I sent it" (Isa. 55:11). His word is like a hammer that splinters rock (Jer. 23:29). The words of human beings, by contrast, often are only wind (Job 16:3); they cannot stand up (Isa. 8:10), and they fall to the ground (1 Sam. 3:19).

James has in mind not only simple confidence that God can answer, but has added to it a deeper commitment to live in the will of the Father, even if that aspiration is one at which we often fail. What is clearly excluded is the person for whom faith is a matter of little or no account, whose words are not commensurate with the heart, which is the wellspring of deeds (cf. Luke 6:43–44), because the heart is the *locus* of character.

The double-minded man is "unstable in all he does." This phrase denotes a person who is unsettled and not at rest. It reinforces the image of the one who doubts as "wavering." Being "unstable" is a quality that marks one's whole existence, not just spiritual life. It carries the idea of inclining this way and that, but never committing. Paul uses the noun form of this word to mean "disorder" (1 Cor. 14:33; 2 Cor. 12:20), and in Luke Jesus uses it to mean "revolutions" (Luke 21:9). This word is rare in Greek literature before James, but prevalent in Christian literature afterwards, speaking perhaps to the influence of James.

Poverty and Wealth (1:9–11)

JAMES NOW TURNS to the questions of poverty and wealth within the Christian community. It is worth remembering that the vision of Judaism encased within the Mosaic Law was of a society marked by a high degree of egalitarian concern. But the excesses of Solomon and his successors led the prophets to castigate the bloated rich for their lack of concern for the poor. In a similar fashion, the priestly aristocracy of the second temple period was known for its material excesses. This led to two popular conclusions. First, the poor were the pious, for they had supported Judas Maccabeus against the Hellenizing aristocracy in Jerusalem. Second, wealth tends to make its possessor double-minded, just as in the view of the poor the priestly aristocracy had sold out their religion and people in the interests of personal power.

James is intent upon playing off these two popular views: "The brother in humble circumstances ought to take pride in his high position. But the one who is rich should take pride in his low position. . . ." This verse is arresting, for it appears suddenly and seems to have little to do with what has come before. But upon further reflection the connections come into focus. (1) The conditions of poverty constitute another "trial," parallel to others already described by James. (2) The contrast between faith and double-mindedness seems to parallel that between humility and wealth.

New questions are introduced here: Are both the poor and the rich Christians? Is this poverty economic or spiritual? Why should each "take pride" or "exult"? What do "riches" reveal about us? The first question has occasioned the most debate. All agree that the poor brother is a member of the Christian community. But what about the rich man? He "boasts" in his riches. In this he was not alone. In a world without abundant opportunities for distinguishing oneself, the display of wealth was one of few available options.[20] As Plutarch said, "Most men think themselves robbed of their wealth if they are prevented from displaying it, and that display is made in the superfluities of life, not in the necessities of life."[21]

---

20. With the conquest of the Mediterranean basin Rome brought peace and Roman administration to the region. This resulted in a lack of opportunities for advancement through valor displayed in warfare or through political life. Cities and prominent families were forced to compete with their peers for fame through other avenues. We know of hundreds of cases of wealthy families that drove themselves pell-mell into bankruptcy in an effort to pay for public works, so that the fame of their names might be spread and last in perpetuity. Similarly, so few opportunities were available that Pliny complained to the Emperor Trajan that the cities of Asia Minor were ruining themselves economically by trying to outdo one another in the building of massive and elaborate public works. See Pliny, *Epistulae*, 10.39, and p. 39, note 19.

21. Plutarch, *Marcus Cato*, 18.3.

There are abundant reasons for seeing the rich man as a Christian. Grammatically, both the terms "brother" and "to take pride in" found in verse 9 are linked to "rich man" in verse 10. Furthermore, to suppose that the rich are not members of the Christian community seems unnecessarily to dissociate this section from the emphasis on "trials" with which the entire passage is stamped. If the rich are outside the Christian community, why should they even think about living according to Christian principles?[22]

Many commentators opt to believe that the rich man is not a member of the Christian community. The rich, in this view, are outside and see their wealth as worthy of boasting.[23] These scholars point out that the word *plousios* ("rich") is used in 2:7 exclusively of non-Christians. This means that "to take pride in" here must be ironic: The rich have had their day, and all they can look forward to is the eschatological judgment. This line of interpretation, it is claimed, complements James's teaching that the poor will be vindicated but the rich destroyed.[24]

But there is another way to understand the matter. The wealthy whom Amos dubbed "cows of Bashan" (Amos 4:1–3) were Israelites, and yet they received condemnation, because their actions were not consonant with their claim to be children of Abraham. Like the cows of Bashan it is possible that the "rich" in James includes wealthy members[25] of the Christian community whose pattern of life gave little or no evidence of Christian commitment, thereby disqualifying them from true membership.[26] This is one of the issues in 1 Corinthians 11, where the rich Christians, in emulation of Roman public feasts, sponsored a Eucharist marked by demarcations of social and economic status. They thus imposed Roman cultural values upon the church, values that presupposed the legitimacy of markers like status and wealth in determining worth in the eyes of the community. Rightfully, Paul responded with deep chagrin.

The humble should rejoice (1) because their poverty provides an arena for their faith to be tested and thus for endurance to grow, and (2) because

---

22. See the discussion of a similar case in James 4:4, in which the term "adulterous people" is used.

23. Martin (*James*, 23) is representative here.

24. Ibid., 25–26.

25. In 2 Thess. 3:6–14 Paul speaks against idleness and instructs the industrious to warn the idle and to shame them into action. Yet the idle should be treated not as an enemy, but as a brother. Here "a brother" stands in danger of losing membership because of his behavior. I believe we have here in James a parallel situation.

26. This is not a matter of Arminian or Reformed views of eternal security. Rather, the idea here is fully consonant with the words of John the Baptist (Matt. 3:9) that God could make children of Abraham out of the rocks strewn about. The question is one of loyalty manifesting itself in action.

they will be exalted, just as the prophets and Jesus had promised. These poor are poor both spiritually and materially. The ancient world knew almost nothing of what we would call a "middle-class." About 90 percent of the population of the Roman empire lived at or below what moderns would consider the poverty level. Except in select urban locations such as Corinth, social climbing in the Roman world was a virtual impossibility.[27] But they are poor spiritually as well, and here James taps into the rich theology of the poor in Judaism, where poverty and righteousness go hand in hand.

The rich man should glory in his abasement, not only because riches are transitory, but because they are an encumbrance. Trials will either relieve him of this encumbrance or force a shock of clarity. Trials, if properly understood through the gift of God's wisdom, will grant a new perspective, in which riches are seen for what they are. Riches have the capacity to dull our sight until we fail to see the image of God in those around us. They have the potential to woo us into an uncritical acceptance of the standards of the world as the rightful standards of the church.

The rich, like their riches, are fated for a transitory existence. They will pass away and wither in the scorching heat of the summer wind. The scorching wind has the power to wither flowers in a matter of minutes. The image is meant to convey both the suddenness of this discomfiture and the tenuous frailty of much that we deem secure. This is the lot of the rich, who refuse to see the world from God's perspective, for whom the pride of wealth plays the role of God, substituting itself for Yahweh.

Bridging Contexts

SATAN, EVIL, AND **trials**. James does not mention Satan in this passage, yet in the rabbinic theology upon which he draws, Satan was viewed as one of the sources of misfortune—a view Jesus shared. In our day we at times casually refer to Satan as the source of evil and mis-

---

27. The Roman economy simply did not allow it. Social climbing could be accomplished through three basic means, each of them rare. The first was a sterling career in the military. Vespasian, for instance, was an Italian peasant who rose to the rank of general, and then to the purple in the year of chaos following the death of Nero. As the empire grew older, this became more common. But statistically it remained the remarkable exception. The second route was that of citizenship and then wealth accrued by freedmen of Roman citizens. Trimalchio in the *Satyricon* of Petronius is such a one. There is considerable debate as to how widespread this practice was, yet its limit was the aim of a number of pieces of legislation instituted by Augustus. Finally, there were cities like Corinth. Corinth was destroyed by the Romans in 146 B.C. and recolonized by Julius Caesar in 44 B.C. He populated the city with army veterans and certain citizens of the city of Rome. As a result, there was no old aristocracy, and all could dream equally plausible dreams of achieving exalted social status.

fortune. Some movements (such as the Vineyard)[28] and certain writers[29] within modern evangelicalism offer a view of Satan's role in misfortune that at times seems foreign to the biblical material. It is therefore both proper and important briefly to discuss the biblical view of Satan if we are safely to bridge the gap between the biblical world and our own.

In the Old Testament Satan (from the Hebrew *šatan*, meaning "to accuse" or "to oppose") has a God-given appointment as the prosecuting attorney, a role he performs in Job 1–2 and Zechariah 3. While clearly interested in pursuing his own designs, he is still somewhat reticent to oppose God's authority. But in the New Testament, Satan is openly hostile to God and has gathered about himself minions, both natural and supernatural. In addition to his legal gown he has arrogated to himself both the mantle of tyrant and the disguise of *agent provocateur*. He is the strong man who, without legal right, has gained *de facto* control over the earth. When in the temptation narratives Satan offers to Jesus all the kingdoms of the earth, he has the power, but not the right, to do so.

Satan also incites us to sin. His usual path is one of stealth and deceit (cf. 2 Cor. 11:14), preying on our moral imperfections. He is especially successful when he masquerades as the good. He operates chiefly through institutions and structures, the "principalities and powers." Thus, Rome is described in Revelation as the consort of the beast, as a tool in Satan's hands. At the Crucifixion Satan's power was severely curtailed (John 12:31), but he is still dangerous.

Developments within Judaism—especially Jewish theological anthropology and psychology at Qumran and within the rabbinic tradition—form part of the background to James's thought here. In these contexts sin was beginning to be seen as the result of an impulse within each human being. This impulse was, therefore, natural and endemic to the human condition.

---

28. See John Wimber, *Power Evangelism* (San Francisco: Harper and Row, 1986). In this book Wimber, the founder of the Vineyard "Signs and Wonders" movement, argued that while the causes of disease may be "physical, psychological, or spiritual . . . Christians have power over disease. Christians in the first century saw disease as a work of Satan, a weapon of his demons, a way in which evil rules the world" (p. 97). In recent years the Vineyard has modified its view. See Wimber, "Signs, Wonders and Cancer" *Christianity Today* (Oct. 7, 1996), 49–51.

29. Frank Peretti is a good example here. Peretti's novels (the most famous being *This Present Darkness* [Westchester, Ill.: Crossway, 1986]) are wildly successful. They offer the metaphor of "spiritual warfare" as emblematic of the Christian life. This picture of the Christian life has been examined by Robert A. Guelich, the late Professor of New Testament at Fuller Theological Seminary, who finds Peretti's work interesting but offering a distorted picture of the biblical evidence. See Robert A. Guelich, "Spiritual Warfare: Jesus, Paul and Peretti," *PNEUMA: The Journal of the Society for Pentecostal Studies* 13 (Spring 1991): 33–64.

In some cases this impulse was undifferentiated and could be swayed to either good or evil. In other cases there were two impulses, the *yeṣer ha-ra* ("the evil impulse") and the *yeṣer ha-tov* ("the good impulse"). In later rabbinic literature these impulses are associated with various parts of the body, control the body, and act in ways inimical to the body.[30] Paul's idea of the struggle with the flesh outlined in Romans is drawn from this background.

In some contexts within Judaism the *yeṣer ha-ra* was virtually identified with Satan; in others the evil impulse is receptive to Satan, a ready and fertile field, prepared for him to plant his foul seeds. The remedy is not the excision of the impulse, but the addition of a pure force stronger than that of Satan in order to limit the evil impulse or even to direct it toward the good.[31] At times this wholesome force was described as wisdom, at others as the Spirit of God.

Concurrent with these developments were others that saw sin as externalized. Here Satan and God were viewed as in conflict and competition over human beings. In this view Satan hopes to lead people away from God and then to cause them to suffer. Paul, like James, is aware of these developments. In his view Satan has a part in leading people astray (2 Cor. 2:11), and Paul knows of the evil impulse (Rom. 7:13–23) and of its pure counterpart, the Holy Spirit (8:1–17).[32]

Wisdom. As was true in ancient Palestine, our culture associates wisdom with age and experience. But as the grandfather figures used to promote investment firms demonstrate, we often apply wisdom to personal "success" and financial health. One key to interpreting this passage correctly is to avoid understanding "wisdom" by our own standards. James draws upon the

---

30. In the Babylonian Talmud, *Nedarim* 32b, we read that the body is composed of 248 parts, and that Satan has seductive powers over humankind for 364 days a year, the only exception being the Day of Atonement. The *Midrash Rabbah* to Eccl. 9:14–15 claims that "the evil impulse" is like the powerful king of 9:14, besieging the body as the powerful king besieges the city. "The good impulse" is like the poor man of 9:15—poor because not all possess it, and of those who do many do not obey it. *Aboth Rabbi Nathan* 16 claims that the *yeṣer ha-ra* is thirteen years older than the *yeṣer ha-tov*, because it begins to develop in the womb. The *yeṣer ha-ra* is also "king over his two hundred and forty eight limbs. When he goes off to some good deed, all his limbs begin to drag. For the evil impulse within man is monarch over his two hundred forty eight limbs, while the good impulse is like a captive in prison." The evil impulse lies at the opening of the heart, and it is the evil impulse that even as infants drives us to harm others, and even ourselves.

31. Perhaps this idea stands behind Paul's thought in 1 Cor. 2:6–8, where the principalities and powers unknowingly cause their own destruction by crucifying the "Lord of glory."

32. For this entire matter see Peter H. Davids, *The Epistle of James*, 36–38; and W. D. Davies, *Paul and Rabbinic Judaism* (Philadelphia: Fortress Press, 1980), 20–35.

richness of the Jewish wisdom tradition in three passages: 1:5—8; 1:16—18; and 3:13—18.

Wisdom has three main functions for James: (1) It produces the virtues of the Christian life; (2) it grants what is needed to stand in the test and therefore aids in being made "perfect"; and (3) it leads to life, as opposed to "desire" (*epithymía*), which leads to death.[33] For James wisdom is initially God's gift to the Christian. In the Old Testament, wisdom can be searched out, but in James it is granted as the result of prayer. Furthermore, in James wisdom has practical application, as it results in a series of virtues (humility, perseverance, patience) that have the effect of preserving community.

James also contrasts the wisdom of God with the wisdom of the world. Heavenly wisdom grants to those who suffer the ability to make sense of life's injustices and difficulties, or failing understanding, still to have trust in God. The wisdom of the world, by contrast, teaches us that what we perceive to be trials and misfortunes are to be avoided. From this point it is a minor step to the erroneous conclusion that trials are proof that God does not care or that he is unable to act. James warns against these in 1:12—16.

Trials. Closely allied to wisdom, of course, are trials. As we have seen, they can result from Satan, they can be allowed by or sent by God, or they can be a normal part of the ebb and flow of life. There are four pitfalls to be avoided when considering trials. (1) We must not see trials as a sign of our election, so that we seek out trials in an effort to prove election to ourselves or others. James will have none of this. To him, God can use trials to develop character, but any attempt to seek out trials must be seen as fulfilling some self-interested need. Such an attempt effectively negates the possibility of character development, although it does proclaim the need for it.

(2) We must not see trials as necessarily the tool of Satan. Many in the name of Christ claim that sickness and infirmity are signs of sin or of satanic attack, or both. The Bible makes it clear that sickness can be the result of sin or of Satan. But the Bible also makes it clear that this is not necessarily the case. God sometimes uses infirmity for his purpose, as in the case of Paul's thorn in the flesh (2 Cor. 12:7—10) or of the man born blind (John 9:1—2). Not all sickness or infirmity is an attack against God and his people. We do a disservice to others when we teach this, as we load them with unnecessary guilt.

(3) Poverty, James says, can be a *locus* for trials in and through which our character can be shaped and molded. There is a rich theological heritage within Judaism linking poverty with spirituality, for the poor feel most keenly the universal human need for God. Recently at a conference I spoke with a man who works with the homeless in Portland, Oregon. In the suburbs, he

---

33. See Davids, *James*, 54—55.

said, it is a struggle to convince people that they need to be forgiven, but it is easy to convince people that God loves them. But with the homeless in the city, he said, the situation is reversed. The homeless already know that they need God and that they need to be forgiven. What is difficult, he said, is convincing them that God loves them, for many have never known this on a human level. Poverty, he said, not only allows people to see their need for God with keen clarity, it also contributes to their being shaped by God.

(4) James should not be construed here as advocating a nonchalant attitude toward the poor on the part of the wealthy, supposing that this status is somehow "good" for them. Nor does the passage allow for a pessimistic resignation to that status. James—and indeed the entirety of the New Testament—issues a call to community obligation. Christians who have the ability should put forth a responsible effort, in the interests of the greater good, to help the poor (see, e.g., 2 Thess. 3:6–14). No matter what the situation, those of us with resources are called upon to use them wisely and generously.

Authentic humanity. In this passage James deals with a variety of issues that touch upon the human condition. He knows that in our human frailty, we are prone to waver. Yet he also knows that we have been called to perfect completion. The New Testament speaks of this completeness in a variety of ways, making the point that Jesus has led the way. Hebrews calls Jesus "the author and perfecter of our faith" (Heb. 12:2). Paul refers to Jesus as the second or last Adam (1 Cor. 15:45). Jesus in John referred to his crucifixion by saying, "But I, when I am lifted up from the earth, will draw all men to myself" (John 12:32).

All three authors point to a central truth: Jesus overturns the sin of Adam, he completes what Adam left undone, and he therefore lives a fully human existence. The theological implications of this idea are varied, and in our text James has left them scattered about like the raw materials for a construction project. In the next section some of these implications will be addressed. In order to do justice to these issues that James has left disparate, we must briefly explore something of the biblical notion of humanness.

James speaks here of our wavering and duplicity, as well as our rightful purpose of "perfection." This tension pierces right to the heart of what it means to be human. We commonly think of this issue in terms of two categories: We are human; God is divine. We speak of Jesus as both human and divine, and when searching the Gospels for aspects of his humanness we point to his being thirsty and fatigued (John 4), or to his weeping at the grave of Lazarus (John 11). But it is quite possible that the Bible knows a different picture, a three-part image—one composed of divine, fully or ideally human, and subhuman components.

When God created humankind, he made us in his very image. But as a result of the Fall, we endure a quality of existence that is less than God intended. It is, if you will, subhuman. That is why Psalm 8, the first commentary on Genesis 1:26–27, can speak of humanity as just a little lower than God himself (Ps. 8:5),[34] because it speaks of human beings as God originally intended them, to be in close and constant communion with him. In James we find this tension—between who we are and who God calls us to be. As human beings we are frail, we fail, and we need God's grace, care, and forgiveness. But we are called to become authentically human. Ours is not a religion of works, but it does involve a call to action. God, who ushers this clarion call to be like Christ, is also a God who forgives, for he understands our pain and our frailty.

Doubt. One of the elements of authentic humanity about which James is concerned is doubt. We must understand James correctly on this point. While modern Christians often think of doubt as something to be avoided, the Bible knows the healthy and even helpful effects of honest doubt. We must bridge this gap in order to see that the doubt James want us to avoid is not honest doubt, but doubt that leads to temptation.

Human beings, according to James, experience a full range of emotion, including doubt, anger, and pain. In this James has much in common with the Psalms, for in these ancient hymns of faith the holy and the mundane are mixed. The Psalms deal honestly with human emotion. Sometimes the psalmist expresses anger at other human beings, even though he has tried to reign in his emotions and his tongue:

> I said, "I will watch my ways
> > and keep my tongue from sin;
> I will put a muzzle on my mouth
> > as long as the wicked are in my presence."
> But when I was silent and still,
> > not even saying anything good,
> > my anguish increased.
> My heart grew hot within me,
> > and as I meditated, the fire burned. (Ps. 39:1–3)

Nor is the anger of the psalmist directed only to persons. Often it is directed to God, for it seems as if the Lord has allowed the wicked to flourish. Where is justice? Where is fairness? Therefore the psalmist, with bile on the tongue and pain in the heart, asks, "O Lord, how long will you look on?"

---

34. The NIV, like many translations, uses "than the heavenly beings." This tradition is derived from the LXX, which chose to translate the Hebrew word for God with "angels."

(Ps. 35:17), and, "How long, O LORD? Will you forget me forever?" (13:1). In the press of life we, like the psalmist, often wonder where God is, whether he really cares, and why he waits. As a pastor I have seen the pain of a couple mourning the death of an eleven-month-old daughter. I have seen a family grieve over a nineteen-year-old woman killed by a drunk driver while on her way to church. I know firsthand the pain of couples who yearn for children they will never have. Such people know the pain of random, senseless loss. They know what it is like to cry out to God in despair and even in doubt.

Honest human doubt drives us to remember all that God has done in the past and therefore to remember the steadfast, trustworthy character of God (cf. Ps. 77:7–12). While at times our lives offer sorrow so profound that we question God, ultimately we know his character and his touch of compassion. As Kathleen Norris has put it, our faith has an "earthy honesty"[35] that allows us to pierce through the lie of false spirituality and holy talk, to see that we must be honest with our human frailty before we are holy, not the other way around. God knows us and meets us in the frailty, weakness, and dirtiness of the human condition. To pretend that our lives are otherwise is to lie to ourselves and to God. Like David we must be brought to the place where we can say to God, "My sin is always before me" (Ps. 51:3). We can do it with joy and confidence because we know the character of God. He has proven himself to be a God who forgives, who can turn sin into something good, who can turn weeping into joy.

We must understand the distinction implicit in the passage between honest doubt and duplicity. The sort of doubt James castigates is active duplicity, either conscious or sub-conscious. Duplicity makes claims or states resolve, but it cannot or will not follow through. Active doubt, double-minded doubt, can range from the extraordinary to the mundane, from the religious charlatan masquerading as an honest television preacher, to the faithful churchgoer with a heart devoid of compassion. Whenever God's name is invoked to sanction personal power, prejudice, economic stratification, or a national political policy, we have most likely strayed into the dangerous territory of the double-minded.

Prayer is needed because it opens our minds to the wisdom and will of God, which, as the Scriptures remind us, often comes as a surprise, casting its searchlight and exposing the mixed motives at work in our human frailty. James desires an honest heart that sometimes fails but has resolve to follow in God's path.

---

35. Kathleen Norris, "Why the Psalms Scare Us," *Christianity Today* (July 15, 1996), 21.

IT WAS ONCE the well-attested conclusion of scholars that James has no discernible theology.[36] This judgment has been challenged in more recent years, although it is true that the theology of James is not as readily apparent as that of other New Testament books. In any event, this is a theologically pregnant passage, with a great deal to say to our impatient, self-satisfied world. James here deals with tough, real world questions. Why do we suffer difficulties? Why does a good God allow suffering? What is the nature of faith? The answers that James provides teach us that God is a generous and lavish giver, even to the undeserving. James also points out that God desires the development of character within us.

There is a tension here, or a balance, depending on one's perspective. God loves and forgives us, but he also desires us to mature and grow. This development follows an often hard road, but it is a road that must be followed with tenacity and resolve. God grants what we need to sustain our journey, if only we will ask, and ask with a single-hearted devotion that, while it sometimes falters, is essentially true to itself.

In this passage James deals with diverse theological themes that do not easily cohere. One way of binding them into a meaningful whole is to envision the call to perfection as the unifying theme, with the others as component parts. In this way we can imagine four threads, each composed of various strands, which together bring strength and coherence to the composite whole. These four major threads are: the false wisdom of this world; the nature of prayer, for James tells us that prayer is the route to our true calling; the character of God's wisdom; and authentic humanity, which is our rightful purpose.

The wisdom of our world. The wisdom of our world is a false wisdom, offering counterfeit joy and bogus priorities. Ultimately, all are found wanting. It is immediately apparent that James speaks of wisdom and the joy it brings in a fashion almost unrecognizable to citizens of the modern world. Our world seduces us with its candidates for keys to a happy life.

David Myers, in his book *The Pursuit of Happiness*, neatly exposes these lies. He points out, for instance, that increasing wealth does not in any way add to a person's self-perception of joy or happiness.[37] In fact, the level of perceived joy, Myers found, is essentially the same regardless of age, gender, race, education, location, or even the presence of a tragic disability.[38] In some cases, in

---

36. Martin Dibelius in his 1921 commentary denied the possibility of writing on the theological themes in James.

37. David G. Myers, *The Pursuit of Happiness: Who Is Happy—And Why* (New York: William Morrow, 1992), 31–46.

38. Ibid., 177.

fact, superfluity actually serves to diminish perceived happiness. In 1991, for example, Barry Bonds of the Pittsburgh Pirates baseball team was offered $2.3 million, instead of the $3.2 million he asked for. Bonds said, "There's nothing Barry Bonds can do to please Pittsburgh. I'm so sad all the time."[39]

In an article in *Life* magazine, Christopher Whipple quotes Chris Evert Lloyd's recounting of her married life: "We play tennis, we go to a movie, we watch TV, but I keep saying, 'John, there has to be more.'"[40] At the time Chris was at or near the height of her fame and success. In the liner notes to her enormously successful CD *Pieces of You*,[41] the popular singing artist Jewel Kilcher includes a poem entitled "Faith Poem." It speaks more of unfaith, of a longing for goodness and coherence without its discovery.

> I don't know how to do anything. ... I look in the mirror and I see filth. ... Why is the soil of incompetence beneath my nails? ... This pen is scrawny and hardly seems able to ink out or erase this plague that infests my Generation, This Giant, This Ogre, This Beast, This Death that assumes a million faces, that borrows my own.

Our world seeks joy, but as David Myers has catalogued,[42] the wisdom of this world does not allow us to find it. Jesus recognized this when in John 12:25 he said, "The man who loves his life will lose it, while the man who hates his life in this world will keep it for eternal life."

James is speaking of a different kind of wisdom and a different kind of joy—a joy that understands sacrifice in the present for the attainment of the good, a joy that is the result of a deep sense of being in the presence and the will of God. If we are to understand James properly, we must dismiss modern notions of joy and happiness, linked as they are to immediate gratification and full satiety. It is a joy that is found fundamentally beyond the self. It is found in a sensitivity to and humility before God, and in service to others. It is for this reason that James castigates the rich (1:10) and the double-minded (1:7), for each has sought joy through various types of self-interested endeavor.

As unlikely as it sounds, fulfillment is often found in the midst of difficulty. Dr. Paul Carlson, a medical missionary, was martyred in 1956 by Simba nationalists in the Belgian Congo. On his body was found his New Testament. It contained a message dated the day before he died. He had written one word: "Peace."[43] Hillel said, "To begin with oneself, but not to end with

---

39. Peter King, "Bawl Players," *Sports Illustrated* (March 18, 1991), 14–17.

40. Christopher Whipple, "Chrissie," *Life* (June 1986), 64–72.

41. Jewel Kilcher, *Pieces of You*, Atlantic Recording Company, 1994.

42. I am indebted to Myers, *The Pursuit of Happiness*, for much in this section.

43. Susan Bergman, "Faith Unto Death: In the Shadow of the Martyrs," *Christianity Today* (August 12, 1996), 24.

---

oneself; to start with oneself, but not to aim at oneself; to comprehend oneself, but not to be preoccupied with oneself."[44] Jesus said, "Happy are those who realize that they are spiritually poor."[45] To be spiritually poor is to recognize one's need for God. It is in the midst of the challenging journey to meet God and be what he intends that joy is to be found. As Cyprian Norwid said, "To be what is called happy, one should have (1) something to live on, (2) something to live for, (3) something to die for."[46]

In calling on the theology of wisdom, James reminds us of the radically different character of the Christian life and experience in comparison to the world around us. But this is not a call to some morbid fascination with tragedy. It is rather a plea to seek God's face when life seems darkest. This is true because tragedy has the ability to impel us to disbelief when we view it on the world's terms, but tragedy also has the potential to draw us to God.[47]

Lee Atwater, the campaign manager for George Bush in the 1988 United States Presidential campaign, was a great success by the standards of the world. But after he was diagnosed with cancer of the brain, he began to reflect upon his life in terms that spoke of his desire earlier to have eschewed the wisdom of the world:

> The 80's were about acquiring—acquiring wealth, power, prestige. I know. I acquired more wealth, power and prestige than most. But you can acquire all you want and still feel empty. What power wouldn't I trade for a little more time with my family? What price wouldn't I pay for an evening with my friends? It took a deadly illness to put me eye to eye with that truth, but it is a truth that the country, caught up in its ruthless ambitions and moral decay, can learn on my dime. I don't know who will lead us through the 90's, but they must be made to speak to this spiritual vacuum at the heart of American society, this tumor of the soul.[48]

Without knowing it, Lee Atwater was echoing the thought of James. What human beings desperately need is the wisdom of God. Without God and his wisdom we are doomed to experience this tumor of the soul. Trials force us

---

44. This citation is found in Martin Buber, *The Way of Man* (New York: Citadel Press, 1963), 63.

45. The NIV renders it, "Blessed are the poor in spirit."

46. Quoted in Wladyslaw Tatarkiewicz, *Analysis of Happiness* (Dortrecht: Martinus Nijhoff, 1976), 176.

47. Myers, 184, writes: "Persons of faith who encounter tragedy are statistically more likely to view the tragedy as spurring them on to some greater good."

48. Lee Atwater and Todd Brewster, "Lee Atwater's Last Campaign," *Life* (February 1991), 67.

to the place where we ask God for this wisdom, and this wisdom allows us to endure the trial until we are complete. This is *not* the wisdom of the world.

Prayer for wisdom. James calls us to contemplation when he invites us to ask God for wisdom, especially during trials. This is to walk the middle course between irrational optimism and a worldly pessimism that betrays a lack of trust in God. Irrational optimism can be marked by a failure adequately to understand oneself, a failure adequately to understand one's situation, and a belief that what we consider comfortable is precisely what God considers best for us. Neither irrational optimism nor worldly pessimism takes seriously God or ourselves.

The wisdom of the cross, in the minds of the great medieval Christian thinkers, has the ability to hold two things together: a recognition of the power of evil without allowing the presence of evil to so fixate us that we forget the sovereignty of God. Gregory the Great, when counseling a friend undergoing trial, related that before he was crucified Jesus told his captors "This is your hour, and the power of darkness."[49] But Gregory also reminded his friend that Easter morning was already appearing on the horizon.

James links wisdom with the prayer of request. The Christian tradition contains a rich theology of prayer, with many different definitions offered. In his book *Prayer*, Olle Hallesby says that prayer is opening the door and allowing God to flood our lives.

> To pray is to let Jesus into our hearts. ... It is not our prayer which moves the Lord Jesus. It is Jesus who moves us to pray. He knocks. Our prayers are always a result of Jesus knocking at our heart's doors. This throws light upon the old prophetic passages: "Before they call, I will answer; and while they are yet speaking, I will hear" (Isaiah 65:24). ... To pray is nothing more involved than to let Jesus into our needs. To pray is to give Jesus permission to employ His powers in the alleviation of our distress. To pray is to let Jesus glorify His name in the midst of our needs. ... To pray is nothing more than to open the door, giving Jesus access to our needs and permitting Him to exercise His own power in dealing with them.[50]

Psalm 62 echoes this same thought: "My soul finds rest in God alone." Worship, someone once told me, is the position from which God becomes visible. We must find that place and make our home there.

The wisdom of God. The wisdom of God allows us to understand trials, and it drives us to perceive our responsibility to one another. Maria Skobtsova

---

49. Gregory the Great, *Epistles*, 6.2.
50. Olle Hallesby, *Prayer*, tr. C. J. Carlsen (Minneapolis: Augsburg, 1931), 11–13.

was a prisoner at the Nazi concentration camp called Ravensbrück. In the
midst of this unimaginable horror, it would have been easy and even normal
for her to despair. Yet the wisdom of God granted to her the ability to see
her situation not as misfortune, but as opportunity. She wrote: "I am Thy
message, Lord. Throw me, like a blazing torch into the night, so that all
may see and understand what it means to be Thy disciple."[51]

With wisdom through prayer comes an appreciation for the timing of
God. Peter Abelard wrote: "By faith which we have concerning Christ, love
is increased in us, through the conviction that God in Christ has united our
nature to himself and that by suffering in that nature he has demonstrated to
us the supreme love of which he speaks."[52] Abelard argued that the cross has
the power to bring about true repentance in sinners, to change our hearts of
stone into hearts of flesh, hearts of compassion, and hearts that desire ever
more to know and be known by God. In trials we ask for wisdom in prayer,
and trials push us to contemplate Scripture, to pray, and to seek God's face.
In so doing we become more like God himself, as his love wells up within
us more and more. This requires and fosters patience.

Contemplation helps us to realize that God is the author of every good
thing. Like Maria Skobtsova, we realize that God's definition of that good
thing might be very different than ours. Contemplation allows us to discern
the truly important and to reorder our priorities accordingly. A victim of
breast cancer put it this way:

> You take a long look at your life and realize that many things that
> you thought were important before are totally insignificant. That's
> probably been the major change in my life. What you do is put things
> in perspective. You find out that things like relationships are really
> the most important things you have—the people you know and your
> family—everything else is just way down the line. It's strange that it
> takes something so serious to make you realize that.[53]

Contemplation and prayer also fire within us a heart of compassion for
others. When viewing trials from a divine perspective, we are freed from the
shackles of self-centeredness that our world so often expresses. Pete Incav-
iglia, a player for the Texas Rangers baseball team, said: "People think we
make $3 million or $4 million a year. They don't realize that most of us only
make $500,000."[54] Such self-interest is shattered by contemplation. Instead,

51. Bergman, "Faith Unto Death," 22.
52. Peter Abelard, *Commentary on Romans* (on Rom. 8:32).
53. Myers, *The Pursuit of Happiness*, 49–50.
54. *Life* (January 1991), 23.

God's vision of the world floods our hearts and minds, and we recognize in others not only a treasure in the sight of God, but the manifestation of God's grace for us. We are called to be and receive this grace one from another, without regard to worldly considerations of wealth or privilege.

This is a particularly hard lesson for us to learn. We are taught individual responsibility and rugged independence, as if these were natural characteristics, and even biblical. In point of fact, these have more to do with the hallmarks of the Enlightenment than with the teaching of Jesus. This dangerous conflation of cultural values with Christian practice is one of the least recognized and most virulently inimical issues besetting the church. The acclaimed University of California sociologist Robert Bellah says that what is missing in our culture is a sense of connectedness—to each other and to some greater cause.[55]

James lived among and wrote to persons who knew poverty and hardship unimaginable to us. We must not so emphasize the spiritual element of these concerns that the concrete expression that James intended is lost. We must let these ideas speak for themselves and then seek to use them as a mirror for our own situation. All that we have—our health, our education, our wealth— these are gifts from God. We have a *sacred* responsibility to use them wisely.

When James discusses the rich and poor brothers, his intent is to call us to the practice of community. One of the hallmarks of biblical community is a deep practical concern for others. The concern of James might very well be based upon the teaching of Jesus. When in Matthew Jesus spoke of the Son of Man coming in glory, he spoke of the surprise of many who would find that their conduct disqualified them from true membership. The righteous, Jesus said, were those who gave to others the cup of cool water, who took from their own resources and clothed the needy. James knew of rich "brothers," but true brotherhood treats others as precious in the sight of God. Jesus considers our treatment of others our treatment of him (Matt. 25:31–46).

Nor should we fall victim to the arrogant assumption that those of us with material prosperity always play the role of beneficent giver. The model of Jesus and the teaching of James is that both rich and poor have much to give to and learn from the other. We bear a responsibility to give and to receive the touch of the hands of Jesus to and from those around us.

Authentic humanity. James calls us to perfection. But the idea of perfection is not one with which we are comfortable. It reminds many of us of unhappy childhood experiences in which we were unable to earn the praise of a parent or authority that we so desperately desired. This is not, how-

---

55. See Robert Bellah, et al., *Habits of the Heart* (Berkeley: Univ. of California Press, 1985), viii, 277–81.

ever, the notion of perfection James has in view. Kathleen Norris has learned this: "I have lately realized that what went wrong for me in my Christian upbringing is centered in the belief that one had to be dressed up, both outwardly and inwardly, to meet God."[56] That is why she so appreciates the Psalms, for they "demand engagement, they ask you to read them with your whole self ... through all the moods and conditions of life, and while you may feel awful, you sing anyway. To your surprise, you find that the psalms do not deny your true feelings but allow you to reflect on them, right in front of God and everyone."

A friend recently told me about a Catholic priest who ministers to women who have had abortions. He tells them that abortion is a terrible sin, but an equally terrible sin is not allowing God to forgive you if you have had an abortion. God, he tells them, wants them to come to him, for he loves them deeply. Honesty before God does not keep us from God; rather, it allows us to know him and to be known by him. It is the first step on the path that leads to our union with him, as Abelard noted. It is a path marked by trials and prayer, and it leads to perfection. For James perfection is tied to honesty, to honest appraisal of oneself before God and others. It is a singleness of heart and a patient resolve to know God and the character of integrity.

James teaches that on the road to authentic humanity life and death are paired. Jesus in Matthew 16:24–25 said: "If anyone would come after me, he must deny himself and take up his cross and follow me. For whoever wants to save his life will lose it, but whoever loses his life for me will find it." James echoes this teaching in his discussion of trials and wealth. To grow into Christian maturity is to lay down the wisdom of the world with its standards of success and joy, and to take up the imitation of Christ. In his *Murder in the Cathedral* T. S. Eliot envisioned the final Christmas sermon of Archbishop Thomas Becket: "The true martyr is he who has become the instrument of God, who has lost his will in the will of God, not lost it but found it, for he has found freedom in submission to God."

---

56. Norris, "Why the Psalms Scare Us," 20.

James 1:12-18

BLESSED IS THE man who perseveres under trial, because when he has stood the test, he will receive the crown of life that God has promised to those who love him. ¹³When tempted, no one should say, "God is tempting me." For God cannot be tempted by evil, nor does he tempt anyone; ¹⁴but each one is tempted when, by his own evil desire, he is dragged away and enticed. ¹⁵Then, after desire has conceived, it gives birth to sin; and sin, when it is full-grown, gives birth to death.

¹⁶Don't be deceived, my dear brothers. ¹⁷Every good and perfect gift is from above, coming down from the Father of the heavenly lights, who does not change like shifting shadows. ¹⁸He chose to give us birth through the word of truth, that we might be a kind of firstfruits of all he created.

Original Meaning

THIS PASSAGE IS filled with images of an extraordinarily vivid quality. The unwary are dragged off with violent intent reserved for prey caught in the hunter's snare. God the Father is the picture of stability in the midst of this danger, immutable and good. James uses this finely drawn imagery to signal to his readers the gravity of the situation they face. The unsuspecting are, after all, the ones attracted to the false lure with the hidden barb. His chief purposes are to argue that God is not to blame for our failure to stand firm in the test, and to point out that human beings bear responsibility for their actions; we cannot rightfully blame God, for he is the author of every good gift.

The passage proceeds in three strokes. (1) In the first (v. 12), James offers a summary of what he has already taught, namely, that Christians should persevere when they encounter trials. He then introduces a new element, that of future reward. Christians have the hope of true life, the "crown of life," which God has promised to those who stand firm. We should therefore be loyal to him and so prove our love for him. (2) James then turns his attention to correcting the errant beliefs of his readers (vv. 13–15). God is not the source of temptation, and true evil is ascribing to God such evil intent. Instead, we are the ones responsible for giving in to temptation, as we follow the evil desire within us—a path that leads to sin and death. (3) Finally, James relates to his readers the true character of God and the true destiny of human beings (vv. 16–18). God is the ultimate source of good in the universe, and he never changes. He has chosen us to be allied to him and his purpose. God wants us to choose him, and in so doing to choose life. Unfortunately, we often in purposeful ignorance reject God and choose death.

The Crown of Life (1:12)

SOME SEE THIS verse as belonging with the previous passage, and indeed it serves as a bridge between 1:1–11 and 1:13–18. But because James provides what many believe is the second element of a double letter opening (the first being 1:2), the break should be here.[1] The letter begins with an episto-lary introduction (1:1), followed by the initial opening of the letter, in which James presents the themes of trials, wisdom, and wealth (1:2–11). This sec-ond opening revisits and expands these themes, but it begins with the ideas of blessing and the crown of life.

James has pressed into service a standard of the theology of Judaism, the idea that people faithful to God are called "blessed." In the Prophets[2] and the wisdom tradition[3] many are called blessed: those who have the wisdom to see that through difficulty God forges character; those who seek God's forgive-ness; those who do justice. James reminds his readers of these theological tenets and uses them as a springboard for his new line of thought in verses 13–18, for in this palette are to be found God's gracious giving and forgiving nature, the nature and purpose of trials, and the formation of godly character.

It seems clear that the Psalms, and more broadly the wisdom tradition, comprise important elements of the background fabric to James.[4] As in the wisdom tradition, the word "blessed" has both present and future connota-tions, for the one who perseveres is qualified to be called "blessed," and the reward is the "crown [*stephanos*] of life."[5] In the Bible and in ancient Mediter-ranean culture, a "crown" was usually understood as the victor's crown,[6] an

---

1. See Fred O. Francis, "The Form and Function of the Opening and Closing Paragraphs of James and 1 John," *ZNW* 61 (1971): 110–26. Francis demonstrates that many literary and ordinary letters from the Hellenistic period contain a double opening, which usually includes the use of parallel terms that link the two openings. The double opening also introduces the key themes that provide the structure of the letter and inform its content.

2. For example, Isa. 30:18; 56:2; Jer. 8:32, 34.

3. For example, Job 5:17; Ps. 32:1; 42:1; 94:12.

4. This is not to say that James *is* an example of wisdom literature, however, as older com-mentaries often held.

5. The term "crown of life" is rare in Scripture (it is also found in Rev. 2:10), but it does have parallels: the "crown of glory that will never fade away" in 1 Peter 5:4; or the verbal form "[you have] crowned him [man/the son of man = humanity] with glory and honor" in Ps. 8:5.

6. The image of the wreath of wild olive granted to victors at Olympus springs to mind.

ornament of honor,[7] or the royal crown.[8] In the Bible all three types of crowns convey the ideas of reward and honor. In 1 Corinthians 9:24—25 Paul speaks of the crown as eternal life, which he compares to the perishable crown worn by victors at the games.[9] In Philippians 4:1 he speaks of believers as his "joy and crown." Finally, Sirach 6:31 speaks of wisdom in terms of a glorious robe and a crown of gladness.

The reference to wisdom in Sirach 6:31 is tantalizing, for according to James wisdom is needed to understand trials properly and so to gain the "crown of life." James does not imply a competition that eliminates all but the victor[10] or a royal power that serves itself with scant regard to the interests of others. Instead, the crown is the mark of honor *and the behavior* that leads to eternal life. That is, the "crown of life" is eternal life, and in this age it is a life lived in the will of God as his faithful and loyal servant.

In calling Christians who endure "blessed" (*makarios*), James is saying that Christians *belong* to God, for he has adopted us. We are a part of his family and life. Like true children, we are to be like him.[11] Part of the meaning of blessing is tied to our being "mature and complete" (1:4), which is a foretaste of our reward, fully realized in the age to come. This idea includes intimacy with God and participation with him in accomplishing his purpose. This is why so much of James is devoted to the practical components of living the Christian life. To become God's agent is simultaneously to live in communion with God and to be about God's purpose.

James then adds that this crown of life is what "God has promised to those who love him." As his children, Christians are to stand fast, as do all who truly love God, in order to receive our inheritance. Here the theme of loyalty to God and of turning from lesser and therefore potentially dangerous and false loyalties is present. The faithful are those who stand the test, for real love for God manifests itself in action. James is here faithfully following the teaching of Jesus (see Matt. 25:31—46).

Temptations and Their Source (1:13–15)

WHEN MISFORTUNE STRIKES, we tend to look for something or someone else to blame. Tragedy is often random and mindless: An infant is killed by a

---

7. This is the idea in Prov. 1:9, where the father bids the son to listen to his instructions, for "they will be a garland to grace your head and a chain to adorn your neck."

8. Another possibility is the crown of flowers worn on festive occasions, such as weddings.

9. See also 2 Tim. 4:8 and 1 Peter 5:4.

10. So Paul in 1 Cor. 9:24—25 contrasts the games, in which only one can win, with the life of spiritual endeavor, in which all can prove victorious.

11. See Luke 6:35—36, in which Jesus says that if we are merciful as God is merciful, we will be called "sons of the Most High."

stray bullet fired in a drive-by shooting; an airliner crashes, killing hundreds; a young woman dies in an automobile accident, the victim of a drunk driver. Senseless tragedy leaves us feeling numb, powerless, and uncertain. These are the sorts of situations that arise on the horizon of our text; thus, James turns his attention from those who endure and pass the test (v. 12) to those about to abandon the effort.[12]

It is common for humans to attribute difficulties or evil to Satan, or to God, or to the whims of fate. Homer has Zeus complain: "It is incredible how easily human beings blame the gods and believe us to be the source of their troubles, when it is their own wickedness and stupidity that brings upon them sorrows more severe than any which Destiny would assign."[13] Proverbs 19:3 makes the point well: "A man's own folly ruins his life, yet his heart rages against the LORD." When confronted by God in the Garden of Eden, Adam pleads innocence and blames Eve (Gen. 3:12–13). Eve in turn blames the serpent, and by extension God the creator. Neither takes responsibility for his or her actions. How human they are, and how quickly they prove themselves willing to place their relationship to each other and to God in jeopardy in the name of self-interest!

To this James offers a trenchant response: "When tempted, no one should say, 'God is tempting me.'" James offers two reasons for this. God cannot be tempted by evil, nor does he tempt anyone. God has nothing to do with temptation; and when we falsely accuse him or seek to force him to prove himself, we are guilty of trying to tempt God. It is not unlikely that James was reminded of the temptation narratives, in which Jesus quoted Deuteronomy 6:16 in response to Satan: "Do not put the Lord your God to the test" (Matt. 4:7; Luke 4:12).

James knows the origin of temptation. It is not God, nor is it Satan and Satan alone. It is instead a personal desire born of self-interest that renders us susceptible to the evil inclination and therefore, at times, to the wiles of the evil one. We may wrongly seek to blame others, Satan, or even God, but ultimately we are morally responsible. The key term here is *epithymia*, which means "desire." In the New Testament *epithymia* generally carries a negative meaning, such as "lust," "selfish ambition," or "evil desire."[14]

---

12. While James does not offer a full blown theodicy (an attempt to reconcile the presence of evil with the belief in a good God), it is not unlikely that he has in mind the theology of the book of Job.

13. Homer, *Odyssey*, 1.32–34.

14. In Matt. 5:28 Jesus speaks of "lust"; Paul in 2 Tim. 3:6 speaks of those who are swayed by "evil desires"; and Peter in 2 Peter 1:4 speaks of escaping the corruption caused by "evil desires."

Unlike the case in 1:2–8, here *peirasmos* ("temptation, trial") is clearly restricted in origin to the internal, to its source lodged within us. This source is the "evil desire," and James must be thinking again of the *yeṣer ha-ra*.[15] According to him, we are "dragged away" and "enticed" by evil desire. The expressions have their home in the realms of hunting and fishing. The fact that they appear in an odd order ("dragged off" is placed before "enticed") is best explained by the predilection of the Old Testament to mesh images of snares and nets. So in Ecclesiastes 9:12 we read, "As fish are caught in a cruel net, or birds taken in a snare, so men are trapped by evil times that fall unexpectedly upon them."

In other words, this verse contains two similar images, not a succession of action within one image. The first pictures the violent action of capture that follows setting a lure, and second the attractive bait that draws an unsuspecting victim. The extraordinary vividness of these images shows how dangerous James believes the evil impulse to be. Evil desire within us acts as both the attractive bait and as the lure. The evil desire is our own, and a bent to be attracted to it is equally our own responsibility. This deep character inclination explains the actions of the double-minded person in 1:6–8 and the wealthy person in 1:10.

James employs a biological/biographical image to describe a nearly inexorable devolution. When desire is conceived through our active encouragement, it gives birth to sin, which then matures, leading ultimately to death. James uses the verb form *apotelestheisa* (from *apoteleo*), which means "to bring to completion," "to achieve its goal." So *apotelestheisa* serves as the dark mirror image to "perfect" in 1:4.[16]

It is important to note that James has in mind the *nurture* of this desire. When tragedy strikes, it is natural for us to inquire of God, but we should not allow this natural desire to grow into sin. In the depths of his despair, for example, Job said, "Though he slay me, yet will I hope in him" (Job 13:15). Here is combined the very human tendency to cry out to God, but it is a cry in the context of trust. Too often, however, that tendency runs its own course within us.

James provides us with many contrasts here: double-mindedness and single-mindedness; complete in sin and complete in spiritual maturity; doubt and faith; death and true life. By the use of these parallels he makes his case that individuals are accountable, and that it is wrong to see difficult circumstance

---

15. See pp. 18, 23–24, 56–58, above. It is interesting to note that the variety of rabbinic views concerning the *yeṣerim* (sometimes it is undifferentiated, sometimes clearly evil, and sometimes clearly pure) parallels the intended ambiguity of James's use of *peirasmos*.

16. It should not be assumed that *apoteleo* must bear a negative sense. Jesus uses the word of himself in Luke 13:32: "[I will] heal [*apoteleo*] people . . . ! will reach my goal" (*teleoumai*, which literally means, "I am perfected").

as the result of a God who can do evil or of a God who wishes to do good but does not have the power to aid those in distress. Once again it is our attitude, our spiritual discernment, that makes the difference. James wants us to know that sin, when mature, is a fixed habit. If we are not wary, we can become trained in evil, which is a sobering thought.

The Father of Lights (1:16–18)

As a CAPSTONE to his argument that God does not tempt anyone, James offers a brilliant picture of the character of God: He is "the Father of the heavenly lights." James then contrasts the development of the desire to sin (which leads to death) with its positive correlate: birth "through the word of truth," which leads to becoming the "firstfruits of all he created." At this point the traditional wisdom picture of two ways—the way of life and of wisdom on the one hand, and the way of death and foolishness on the other[17]—can no longer be doubted as part of James's framework of reference. Self-interest opens wide the maw of death, to which the evil impulse within seeks to entice us. It expresses itself in a variety of forms, including the unbridled tongue. The way of heavenly wisdom, by contrast, leads to the good fruits of 3:17, and to life.

Since God does not send temptation, the implied question is, "What is it that God does send?" James answers that God gives good gifts, as we have already seen in his gift of wisdom (1:5). There is a rich Old Testament background for this idea. Psalm 94:12 tells us that the discipline of God is a good gift,[18] and Deuteronomy 26:11 speaks of Israelites and aliens together enjoying "all the good things" the Lord has given them. The latter text is particularly significant, as it appears in the context of the firstfruits, a theme James is about to introduce. It seems certain that James, like Deuteronomy, links the ideas of "good gifts" and "firstfruits" intentionally. Perhaps he wants to call to our minds the church as the new Israel, the true people of God.

In creating the phrase "Father of lights," James has combined two pairs of important theological ideas. The first is that God is the Father of the universe and that he has power over the heavenly luminaries as their creator (Gen. 1:14 –18; Ps. 136:7; Jer. 31:35); both concepts recall the creation account. The second pair is the notion of God as Father and of God as light.

---

17. The picture of the "two ways" is clear in the book of Proverbs, which offers us two examples of wise behavior (the wise man, the good wife/wise woman), and two examples of negative behavior (the foolish man, the wicked woman). Similarly, Jesus speaks of two ways or "two gates": the one broad and easy, which leads to destruction; and the small and narrow one, which leads to life and requires diligence in order successfully to navigate its approach and passage (see Matt. 7:13–14; Luke 13:24–30).

18. See also Num. 10:29; Josh. 21:45; Ps. 85:12.

James further describes God as one "who does not change like shifting shadows." God is light, and in him there is no shadow. God is also the creator of the heavenly luminaries, which do shift like shadows. The terms used here are technical terms denoting the movements of the heavenlies. In other words, unlike the planets and the stars, which shift and waver, there is no change in God. As Father, God is ultimately reliable. He does not change, whether in the specific (he is always and will always be the one who gives good things) or the general (God is unchangeable and good).

Clearly James is offering a contrast with astral images, if not with astrological religion itself. Some commentators[19] argue that James is actually countering a belief in astral religion and the occult, which lodged in the stars the power to decide human destiny. If such a specific belief was present among his readers, it would be a clear case of divided loyalty.

There is, however, no need to postulate an active belief in a full-blown astral system. True, James's readers were apparently seeking to absolve themselves of personal responsibility by claiming they were caught in the unpredictable hands of fate. Perhaps they were influenced by the belief of the ancients that caprice, or fate, directed human lives. Mere chance, for example, determined who was born wealthy and who was born a slave. The preeminent deity during this period was *Tyche* (Latin, *Fortuna*), the goddess Fortune or Chance. In a speech given in Pergamum in January, A.D. 167, Aelius Aristides discussed the greatness of cities in Asia Minor:

> It should be remembered that all of these goods ... for example the beauty of the public buildings, the magnitude of the temple precincts, the fair locations ... everything which pertains to its subject, should be said to belong to fortune which gives and again takes away each of these, whenever it wishes.[20]

Marcus Cornelius Fronto, the teacher, friend, and writing companion of Marcus Aurelius, put it this way: "Who is there that does not know that reason is merely a term for human judgment, while Fortuna is a Goddess and the chief of Goddesses?"[21] The Romans believed that fortune had granted to them the task of ruling the world. In such a milieu it is easy to see how persons wishing to blame someone or something else might obviate themselves

---

19. Notably Ralph P. Martin, *James*, 31–32, 39–42.

20. Aelius Aristides, *Orations*, 23.30.

21. The correspondence of Marcus Cornelius Fronto has come to us in fragmentary form, and no standard ordering is yet in force. This quotation, taken from paragraph 7 of a letter from Fronto to Marcus Aurelius dated A.D. 143, may be found on page 89 of the first volume of the Loeb edition of Fronto's correspondence.

of responsibility through the claim that their misfortune was the product of capricious chance. But such a belief does not imply an astral religion.

To cement his point, James points out that God made the heavenly bodies, as if to say that what some call fate is not really fate, for God made and controls the symbols of fate. James even claims that God purposefully intended the creation of both the heavens and of humankind, in order to heighten the contrast between God and a recourse to a general belief in fate that held humankind in its mindless changeable grip.

James's point, then, is that ultimately God controls all of the things to which we wrongfully attribute power, whether we do so from ignorance or to avoid responsibility. God supervises and controls political forces, economic forces, Satan, Fate, and the stars. Perhaps James is contrasting God as Father of the heavenly lights with the pretenders to his throne, the forces of the political order, which are mere shadows, unstable and unreliable.

In place of the idea that the destiny of those who follow their evil desire is death, James offers for consideration an alternate path: God, he tells us, has given birth to us. The past tense here probably refers to God's creative power and recalls that God made us for himself. While there is an inexorable element to the chain of events that ends in death, the rightful fate of humankind is to be counted among the firstfruits. This was God's desire in creating us.

Usually three options are offered for understanding James's phrase, "he chose to give us birth": that James has general creation in view; or that he has the creation of Israel, God's son, in mind (cf. Hos. 11:1: "When Israel was a child I loved him, and out of Egypt I called my son"); or that he is referring to Christian converts, who are "reborn." Given the intentional ambiguity of this phrase, it seems most prudent to assume that James was happy to allow his readers to draw upon the rich variety of all three streams, although it is obvious that in the New Testament the third tends wholly to swallow the second.

The agent God used in giving birth to us is "the word of truth." Here is an obvious similarity to John's Gospel, if not a direct link. "Truth" (*aletheia*) is one of the great themes of John's Gospel, and the "word" (*logos*) dominates its prologue (John 1:1–18). That Gospel even claims that "grace and truth came through Jesus Christ" (1:17). In the Old Testament the "word of God" is nearly personified, acting as a characteristic of God himself. The dominant background here is most likely the continuing action of the spoken word of God at creation, the word that accomplishes the purpose of God (Isa. 55:11). The word of God is God's plan revealing itself and moving to completion. That God chose to give us birth through the word of truth combines images James has already drawn: that God's word is an active force and that God desires us to be his active cooperatives in accomplishing his purpose.

The term "firstfruits" is used in a number of different ways in the Old Testament. Sometimes, for example, it means certain offerings of Israel; but it can also refer to Israel itself, emblematic of the elect nation whose purpose it is to be a "light for the Gentiles" (Isa. 42:6) and through whom "all peoples on earth will be blessed" (Gen. 12:3). Here, then, James calls "firstfruits" all who are loyal to God, all who develop into what God calls us to be. Paul can speak of Christian converts as "firstfruits" (Rom. 16:5; 1 Cor. 16:15), and of the risen Christ as the firstfruits of many brothers and sisters (1 Cor. 15:20).

The teaching of James 1:12—18 might be summed up this way: Since you were created by God with the full potential for truth and life, avail yourself of it and do not foolishly squander it or trade it for the false lure. If you stand firm in the midst of trial, if you do not capitulate to the evil desire to blame God and thus engage in sin, you will receive the crown of life in the age to come and its foretaste in the present. Remember that God is trustworthy and wholly good, and this will sustain you in the midst of any difficulty.

Bridging Contexts

WE ARE IN danger of making three potential false steps in interpreting this passage. The first has to do with the difference between "trial" and "temptation," since the same Greek word (*peirasmos*) means both. The second involves difficulties and how we view them. The third concerns the promised reward to which the text bears witness.

Trials and temptations. In 1:2—12 the NIV renders *peirasmos* with the English word "trial." This word group occurs in 1:13 three times as a verb and once as an adverb; here the NIV translates *peirasmos* as "temptation." This change is not the result of convenient caprice on the part of the translators of the NIV. James himself makes the distinction. In 1:2—11 "trials" are something to be endured, whereas in 1:13—14 "temptations" are something to be avoided. This is an example of polysemy, or multiple meanings of terms.

Here again the flexibility of the New Testament authors in the matter of words and their meanings is in evidence. We are not unfamiliar with this phenomenon. In English the word "sanction" bears two meanings that are opposed to each other. "Sanction" can mean "to approve," as in, "The professor gave her sanction for a group project to aid refugee children." But it can also intend disapproval, usually by way of penalty, as in, "Trade sanctions were leveled against them." With respect to James 1, particular "trials" or "temptations" may have different origins, but to human eyes, difficulties, no matter their origin, are troublesome. The other factor involved is how we respond to difficulties and what this response reveals about us. A "trial" to one person may well be the arena of "temptation" for another.

This double meaning of *peirasmos* implies the need for spiritual discernment. It is the lot of human beings to encounter difficult situations. When we perceive them as opportunities for the growth of character and spiritual maturity, they are to be endured. But often we give in to the temptation to blame someone or something else. This, James says, we should avoid, because each of us bears responsibility for allowing temptation to grow in us. God may be the author of trials by which he intends to strengthen us, but he is not to blame if we misconstrue them as temptations that lead to sin.

The difference between *peirasmos* in 1:2–12 and in 1:13–14 is that in the latter, the individual in view is willing to disobey God, to attribute to God evil intent. So James emphasizes that God is not actively involved in the sending of temptation; in fact, God never tempts anyone. What makes a "test" a "temptation" is not that God has put us in such a position, but rather that we willingly disobey God by seeing misfortune as his attempt to entice us to deny him. It takes spiritual discernment to see in difficulties the possibility of growth. Those who do not are more vulnerable to the lure of the evil desire within them.

A failure to understand these distinctions can lead to any number of problems. Some will see James as making no sense at all. They read it as if James says both "God tests and tempts" and "God neither tests nor tempts." This sort of simple reading has led many to the erroneous and sad conclusion that the Bible cannot be trusted, that it is "full of holes." Others will see the passage as presenting various contradictory views of God. How can God be the giver of good gifts, but also the source of evil? But this is not what James believes or teaches. This stumbling block must be identified and then avoided.

Sin, evil, misfortune, and temptation. The second potential misstep that this passage brings to view involves the relationship between the problems of sin, evil, misfortune, and temptation. In fact, there are more than a few difficulties to be found under this heading. James denies that God has anything to do with evil or temptation. One of the problems here is that we tend to blur what the Bible separates; this is one reason why we often fail to distinguish between "trial" and "misfortune," which we then blame on God.

This is especially true because tragedy and misfortune so often appear random and senseless. In the summer of 1995 a family was traveling from Chicago to Milwaukee. A portion of the brake system of a semi-truck became loose, bounced on the pavement, struck the gas tank of the family's vehicle, and caused a horrible fire. Several of their children died. Events like this foster both nervous and very human questions of ourselves as well as of God and his character.

When something unfortunate happens, we casually call it "bad" or "evil," because that is the way it appears to us. It is a problem or a tragedy that cuts to the heart. In practice we tend to define "good" the same way we think God does, and that God wants only "good things" for us. We also demand to know the answer to any misfortune immediately. But patience is needed, for time is a potent tool in God's hands. The stumbling block here is that in our arrogance and ignorance, we demand the right to define what "good" is. God's definition is often different from ours. So we need wisdom and insight from him in order to see difficulties for what they are.

This notion of the human perception of misfortune, destruction, and oppression is often tied to God's patience and restorative intent when his people disobeyed.[22] Similarly, when Paul says that he has "handed over to Satan" Hymenaeus and Alexander, that they may learn not to blaspheme (1 Tim. 1:20), he has the same restorative idea in view. Just as in James, there is no question of God's tempting the people to sin.

We may fail to distinguish between trials, temptations, and the difficulties or misfortunes with which we associate them. In fact, we usually see them as "evils" in some sense of the word. James did not see them in this fashion. He would have us work on separating the various ideas that our culture often binds together, that is, distinguishing between "trials," "temptations," "misfortune," and "evil."

The modern world affords few such clear-cut cases of Christians encountering "difficulties" beyond those our brothers and sisters have endured under Communist rule. Recently I attended an international theological conference. While there I had occasion to speak to a man who lives in Slovakia, a part of the formerly Communist Czechoslovakia. He had suffered under Communist rule because of his faith. But it was his opinion that while it was difficult to be a Christian under Communism, it has become more difficult without it. "At least under Communism," he said, "we had a clear perception of the enemy. Today the enemy is not so clear, and with increasing affluence, jealousy has reared its ugly head. Looking back I realize that we had opportunities under Communist rule that now seem closed to us."

While I have no wish to minimize the horrors of totalitarian regimes, his words left an indelible mark on me. In a situation I would be tempted to view as wholly evil, he could perceive signs of good. It takes spiritual discernment to see rays of hope in the midst of darkness.

Reward. A third potential misstep has to do with the idea of reward as an inducement for faith and behavior. If we stand the trial, James says, God will

---

22. Among many similar passages see 1 Kings 14:10; 2 Kings 22:16; Isa. 24:6; 34:5; 43:28; Jer. 6:19; 11:8; 35:17; 39:16; Mal. 4:6.

reward us with the promised "crown of life." Particularly in the Protestant tradition we are most comfortable with "salvation as a free gift." To us the idea of a reward for living the Christian life seems distastefully like a bribe offered by God.

We must distance ourselves from our modern idea of "bribe" and recognize that the New Testament is comfortable with *its* idea of reward. In 1 Corinthians 9:24–27 Paul employs the metaphor of a race to illustrate the Christian life, and he concludes with a startling statement: "I beat my body and make it my slave so that after I have preached to others, I myself might not be disqualified for the prize." In Philippians 3:14 he speaks of pressing on to the goal and prize for which God has called him heavenward in Christ Jesus. Even Jesus spoke of reward: "Rejoice and be glad, because great is your reward in heaven, for in the same way they persecuted the prophets who were before you" (Matt. 5:12). The New Testament idea of reward is not akin to our notion of a bribe. Rather, it is a reminder of the dignity, gravity, and integrity of the calling of God to which we have responded. It is an appeal to our pure inclination and a reminder of the example of the saints who have gone before.

JAMES'S IMAGE OF a lure that tempts us to fall from the truth aptly captures the practical application of many of the significant theological issues that he brings to our attention. We will discuss several such lures, each of which is manifest in potent and varied ways in contemporary culture.

(1) Because of the ability of sin to mask itself, a lure may appear harmless and innocent to our eyes, but in reality it has dire consequences. Take, for example, the powerful lure of success, especially if we can dress it in spiritual clothing. There is no denying that the rise of contemporary Christian music has met a great need in our culture. But Steve Moser, a veteran of the contemporary Christian music scene, recently expressed real concerns about the industry. In the beginning, he believes, contemporary Christian music "was a genuine outpouring of God's Spirit." But Moser has lately seen changes that disturb him, changes that were concurrent with, but not wholly the result of, the purchase of Christian record labels by secular companies.

> I look at the majority of the [Christian] music I hear today and I think it's virtually meaningless. ... We've created the opportunity for business to happen ... [and] now we're obligated to put something out. ... The bottom line is "if it is commercially viable, produce it." ... I would

probably be more inclined to call the industry "*commercial* Christian music," rather than "contemporary Christian music."[23]

Moser here points out an effective lure: "success" in terms of the definition offered by our culture. Certainly, we think, if God is in this enterprise, then we will be successful. The members of the "prosperity" wing of American Protestantism would, of course, agree. The problem is that God's priorities are his own, and when on occasion those priorities and "success" do overlap (such as in the "success" of Billy Graham), we should not mistake the one for the other. Sometimes God calls people to labor in vain, in fields that to our eyes appear barren. To such fields, for example, God called Jeremiah. Without God's wisdom we might assume that the "lying prophets" who opposed Jeremiah were in fact God's true agents (Jer. 23:9–24). Many of the contemporaries of Jeremiah made this mistake, to their ruin.

Scottie Smith, the pastor of the Christ Community Church of Franklin, Tennessee, the church home of many of the "stars" of the Christian music industry, knows this lure first-hand. He writes, "Celebrity-ism ... feeds the very things against which the Scriptures warn us."[24] Success and acclaim easily crowd out the servant model the Bible places before us. This is one of the oldest of sins, the sin of pride. The fact that it is well known and yet continues to claim many victims is a testimony to the power and tenacity of sin and to the success of the hidden lure.

The last two decades have seen a spate of prominent Christian leaders and preachers caught in sins like adultery and embezzlement, sometimes in an embarrassingly public fashion. These people did not begin with an agenda that included such sins. But they allowed themselves to nurture the lie that they deserved "comfort," even if from an illicit source. They cultivated the lie that they were above the standards of a biblical lifestyle or that they could safely dally with sin. They must have told themselves that this dalliance was harmless. But quickly it grew until it had the capacity to devour them. I know a pastor who cultivated an unwise relationship with his secretary. Although he was finally dismissed by his church board, he continues to see her, often in public. There are many sad consequences to this story, not the least of which is that the ability of this church to witness to its community has been dealt a severe blow.

(2) Another lure is the current popular belief that there is no evil impulse within us. When James discusses the evil inclination, moderns have a tough time believing him. Our age does not like to face the fact that humans have a tremendous capacity for evil. Contrary to all evidence, we seem intent on

---

23. Stan Moser, "We Have Created a Monster," *Christianity Today* (May 20, 1996), 26–27.
24. Scottie Smith, "Shepherding the Stars," *Christianity Today* (May 20, 1996), 28.

forcing ourselves to believe that human beings are essentially good and that the universe is a kind of nonspecific storehouse of safety and support.

We must take seriously the evil impulse and try to make it intelligible to our world. This is no easy task. The naive and happy New Age optimism of the actress Shirley MacLaine is one example. Another is the burgeoning popular belief in angels as friendly guardians, cut off from any biblical basis. These beliefs may make us feel better, but such beliefs in no way change what *is*. James teaches us what is: There are forces in us and around us that are opposed to God, and within us exists a bent to oppose God, to hide from God, to disobey. We may not like the fact that we have the capacity to sin. We may not like bearing responsibility for our actions. But however much we may wish it were not so, our wishing cannot change what is. And so James discusses this capacity for sin within us, because he does not want us to fool ourselves.

Some months ago I was teaching an introduction to the Bible course to a group of adults, many of whom had little or no previous exposure to the Bible. During our discussion of Romans, one student suddenly asked, "Are you telling us that the Bible teaches that human beings can be evil? Because I do not believe it is true!" I responded that the Bible does teach that human beings have the capacity for evil, and I offered that I thought human experience does too. How else can one explain apartheid, the horrors of the Nazi regime, the Stalinist terror, or economic exploitation here in the United States. He responded that he knew about these things, but that he still chose to believe that human beings were essentially without the capacity for evil.

James, on the other hand, knows that we possess a tremendous capacity to fool ourselves and to believe certain things simply because we wish to believe them, even against overwhelming evidence. Our task as Christians is to point out James's insistence that there is a powerful capacity for sin and evil within human beings, and that he is right. Only if we understand this will we recognize the grave danger we are in; to treat this capacity lightly, or even worse, to fail to recognize it,[25] makes us all the more susceptible to the temptation to dally in what appears to be an "innocent" sin. When we do this, we place our feet on the path that leads to sin and ultimately to death.

(3) The third lure dangled before us is the belief that sin is not really sin, so that it does not need to be taken seriously. Like Paul we need to see that there is something irrational about our behaviors in comparison with our commitments: "I do not understand what I do. For what I want to do I do not do, but what I hate I do" (Rom. 7:15). Our response should be humbly

---

25. In his *Screwtape Letters* C. S. Lewis points out that the enemy tries to keep us from recognizing his existence.

to ask God for forgiveness for our sins and to pray for his assurance and assistance in negotiating the shoals of life. We are going to sin, but the crucial issue is how we respond to our sin. We will be tempted to blame God, but James wants us to come before God and ask for help. Like David we should pray, "Wash away all my iniquity and cleanse me from my sin. . . . Create in me a pure heart, O God, and renew a steadfast spirit within me" (Ps. 51:2, 10).

Unfortunately, we do not take seriously enough the corrosive power of sin within us. When Jesus spoke of the thought of adultery as the same as the act itself (see Matt. 5:27–28), he had in mind something similar to what James teaches here. Actions are the result of character, but actions can also shape character. This is what James means when he said that desire gives birth to sin, and then sin leads to death.

Because sin is so fertile and so prone to masking its true character, we must be vigilant concerning the lures that our own evil inclination puts forward to engage our attention, imagination, and action. Lures are not effective if they appear obvious; they are only effective if they appear as something they are not, or at least as relatively harmless. Satan will not be effective if the temptations offered to us are so outlandish that we never will pursue them. But if Satan can get us to expend all of our energy and time doing good things, so that the best things remain undone, he has won a marginal victory, and he may in fact have placed our feet on the road to ruin.

Jeremiah knew this. God's people had rejected the Lord and followed the patterns of life practiced by their neighbors. While maintaining a belief that they were God's people, they had rejected his standards. They fooled themselves into thinking that they could remain his people, in spite of their lack of compassion for one another. In Jeremiah 7:4–8 their falsehood is catalogued as God speaks to them:

> Do not trust in deceptive words and say, "This is the temple of the LORD, the temple of the LORD, the temple of the LORD!" If you really change your ways and your actions and deal with each other justly, if you do not oppress the alien, the fatherless or the widow and do not shed innocent blood in this place, and if you do not follow other gods to your own harm, then I will let you live in this place, in the land I gave your forefathers for ever and ever. But look, you are trusting in deceptive words that are worthless.

The people of Judah had fooled themselves into thinking that the presence of the temple alone would protect them. But on its own it had no power. Their failure to live lives of compassion and justice in the image of God would result in their punishment. It was Jeremiah's sad task to warn them.

I am reminded of a story I recently heard about a pastor who carries placards outside funeral homes during the funerals of victims of AIDS. The placards read, "God hates fags." While the evangelical community is in my judgment correct in teaching that God does not condone homosexual practice, it is also true that at times in our certainty that we understand God, we act in ways that are contrary to his purpose. We are not so different from those who trusted in the temple and missed the heart of God. Our certitude allows us to fall prey to the hidden lure.

James also offers a warning. While he specifically mentions the sin of accusing God of being the author of temptation, clearly other sins are in view in his outline of the development of sin. James wants us to know that there are no harmless sins. Following our own evil inclination to ascribe evil to God starts our feet on a path that suddenly leads to death, for the seeds of sin quickly grow strong, often without our awareness of it. Largely this is because sin operates by stealth and thus soon does not even appear as sin to our eyes. In 1968 Richard Nixon accepted the nomination of his party to run for the office of President of the United States. In his acceptance speech he said, "Let us begin by committing ourselves to the truth, to see it as it is, and to tell it like it is, to find the truth, to speak the truth, to live the truth." Nine years later[26] CBS News reported Nixon taking a different slant: "When a President does it, then it is not illegal."

It is even possible that what we call "compassion" can lead to sin. Thomas C. Oden, professor of theology and ethics at Drew University, notes that in this age of absolute relativism and pluralism, heresy has taken on a new face. It used to be, says Oden, that a heretic had an "excessive regard for his own 'truth.'" But the "current error does not proclaim a better truth, but that all truths are equal and none is superior. . . . The modern relativist may be every bit as willful [as the old-time heretic] in considering all truths 'valid.'"[27]

Many Protestant denominations and individual Christians in practice jettison any notion of right and wrong in the interests of this pluralistic "compassion." The Episcopal Church reluctantly began a trial of one of its bishops on charges of heresy, specifically because the bishop in question ordained a practicing homosexual. The matter of the acceptability of Christian homosexual practice ought to be settled on the basis of the teaching of Scripture, not out of some vague notion of "compassionate concern." Issues such as these require us to walk the razor's edge along the mountain heights, with dangerous cliffs to either side. We must not stray too far to the left, lest we

---

26. May 19, 1977, well after his resignation from the office of the presidency.

27. Thomas C. Oden, "Why We Believe in Heresy," *Christianity Today* (March 4, 1996), 12–13.

fall from biblical teaching and call sin a harmless preoccupation. But we cannot afford to stray too far to the right, living in the fiction that in condemning both the sin and the sinner, we have somehow still "loved" the sinner and so fall from the biblical mandate of compassion. We are all fallen and need the understanding grace that is carried forth in the hands of Jesus. But we need his direction and model of a life lived with integrity before the Scriptures. For this reason Jesus could say, "Go now and leave your life of sin" (John 8:11). To this James would add a reminder to beware of the deceptive power of sin.

(4) A final lure that besets moderns is the desire to attribute to God evil intent and to blame him for misfortune. In making a distinction between the two definitions of *peirasmos* and adding the flat statement, "Don't be deceived" (1:16), James clearly teaches the need for spiritual discernment. Such discernment allows one to distinguish between "trials" and "temptations." But it also prevents one from questioning the character of God. The stumbling block that James wants us to avoid here is the tendency to ask the human question: "Why did God do that?" and so to blame God.

One of the characters in David Guterson's award-winning novel *Snow Falling on Cedars* is Ishmael Chambers. Ishmael lost an arm in the U.S. assault of the island of Tarawa in the Pacific during World War II; but he lost his capacity for warmth and joy when the war separated him from his childhood love, a young Japanese-American woman named Hatsue. In the midst of his emptiness he said to his mother, "I'm unhappy. . . . Tell me what to do." Her response included a firm faith in God. When confronted by the faith of his mother, Ishmael replies, "There were guys who prayed at Tarawa. . . . They still got killed, Mother. Just like the guys who didn't pray. It didn't matter either way."[28]

This is a typical modern response. When confronted by the horrible randomness of misfortune, whether the deaths of a mother and her children at the hands of a drunk driver, or the more garden-variety difficulty of a flat tire, we resort to four possible conclusions: (a) God does not exist; or (b) God is evil; or (c) God is powerless to help; or (d) God does not care. None of these is worthy of our worship, so we choose to believe that God is of no consequence.

As we have seen, human beings wish so much for a world in which people (including themselves) and forces are basically good that they will themselves to believe it regardless of the evidence. This simplistic worldview is also used to buttress the position that doubts God's existence, because it defines "good" from a human point of view. If anything that we perceive as "bad" hap-

28. David Guterson, *Snow Falling On Cedars* (New York: Vintage Books, 1995), 347.

pens, then we call into question the character of God. What is often at work here is our desperate and selfish inclination to avoid responsibility.

In late twentieth-century America, stories illustrative of this predilection abound. A thief in the process of robbing a home severely injured himself. He then had the audacity to sue the owner of the home for damages—and won the case! Or the Menendez brothers, whose defense for the brutal shotgun killing of their parents was that they had endured years of child abuse. Or Richard Allen Davis, the habitual criminal who murdered Polly Klaas, whose defense was that he had a difficult childhood. Certainly life is unfair. But this does not mean that we do not bear responsibility for our actions. It seems as if no one is accountable for his or her own actions anymore. More and more our culture claims that someone or something else is at fault.

But James calls us to learn spiritual discernment, to judge with right judgment, so that we will be able to see difficulties as opportunities for spiritual growth rather than suppose that in them is evidence that God does not care. How is this accomplished? And what does it look like?

The words of the great Oxford scholar G. B. Caird are helpful here. In his *New Testament Theology* Caird wrote:

> To follow Jesus or to follow his example turns out to be, as popular tradition has held, the higher road, that particular morality which the gospel imposes on the Christian. But such morality does not consist in conformity to any stereotyped pattern; it consists rather in learning from Jesus an attitude of mind which comprises sensitivity to the presence of God and to the will of God which is the only authority, a constant submission of personal interest to the pursuit of that will in the well-being of others, and a confidence that, whatever the immediate consequences may appear to be, the outcome can safely be left in God's hands.[29]

To follow Jesus is to learn an attitude of mind and heart that is sensitive to the will and presence of God. As we saw above, God seeks us out, and he waits for our attention and for our hearts to be turned to him. The first step is the simple but profound one of opening the door to God in prayer, of asking God to be at work in our minds and hearts, and to change us into his image. "For the Christian," says Richard J. Foster, "heaven is not the goal, it is the destination. The goal is that 'Christ be *formed* in you.'"[30]

---

29. G. B. Caird and L. D. Hurst, *New Testament Theology* (Oxford: Clarendon, 1994), 203.
30. Richard J. Foster, "Becoming Like Christ," *Christianity Today* (Feb. 5, 1996), 27.

James 1:19–27

MY DEAR BROTHERS, take note of this: Everyone should be quick to listen, slow to speak and slow to become angry, ²⁰for man's anger does not bring about the righteous life that God desires. ²¹Therefore, get rid of all moral filth and the evil that is so prevalent and humbly accept the word planted in you, which can save you.

²²Do not merely listen to the word, and so deceive yourselves. Do what it says. ²³Anyone who listens to the word but does not do what it says is like a man who looks at his face in a mirror ²⁴and, after looking at himself, goes away and immediately forgets what he looks like. ²⁵But the man who looks intently into the perfect law that gives freedom, and continues to do this, not forgetting what he has heard, but doing it—he will be blessed in what he does.

²⁶If anyone considers himself religious and yet does not keep a tight rein on his tongue, he deceives himself and his religion is worthless. ²⁷Religion that God our Father accepts as pure and faultless is this: to look after orphans and widows in their distress and to keep oneself from being polluted by the world.

Original Meaning	THESE CONCLUDING VERSES of James 1 present a diverse range of material, much of it common wisdom, which is here rooted in a theological context. While there is no rigorous logical devel-

opment in this passage, James does present us with a number of associated ideas that together illustrate the link between "faith" and "practice." His central purpose is to issue a call for the observance of a faith that practices, rather than a mere formal profession of faith. In this James echoes the thought of the great prophets.[1] He urges adherence to "the perfect law that gives freedom" (1:25), a phrase that constitutes one of the thorniest interpretive

---

1. Isaiah, Jeremiah, Amos, and the others argued that the practice of the cult without a moral standard that linked devotion to God with practical care for others was worthless. One of the classic expressions of this idea is found in Micah 6:8: "What does the LORD require of you? To act justly and to love mercy and to walk humbly with your God."

problems in the New Testament. What we can say is this: James not only calls us to positive action but also to eliminate immorality. He knows that mere intellectual assent is often accompanied by an anemic will in matters of morality. In making this case James teaches a central paradox of the faith: God's gift to us also lays upon us the responsibility of moral behavior.

This passage unfolds in three movements: In verses 19–21, James argues that to receive the word with humility is better than speaking in anger; next, he teaches us that simply hearing the word is without value unless it results in action (vv. 22–25); and the last two verses provide a transition from doing to the question of "pure religion" by citing a number of specific examples that add flesh and sinew to the general points made in the second movement. True religion is not merely "works," but a humble receptivity to God's word so that it can develop deep roots within us, shaping our character until the natural result is the sort of good works that James extols.

Receive the Word in Humility, Speak Without Anger (1:19–21)

FROM THE WORD of God (1:18) James turns his attention to human words, and in so doing presages chapter 3, wherein he will argue that the gift of God's wisdom influences how Christians speak. Believers should concentrate on listening with humility and meekness, rather than speaking in anger.

Immediately we are faced with something of a dilemma. The opening verb, "take note of this" (*iste*), can be either indicative or imperative. Martin[2] takes it as an imperative and so holds that this phrase should go with verse 18, serving as a concluding exhortation to that passage. I am rather inclined to agree with other commentators[3] who agree with Martin that the verb is in the imperative mood, but who see it introducing the thoughts to follow. These thoughts are expressed in terms of a proverb: "Everyone should be quick to listen, slow to speak and slow to become angry."

The idea is nearly universal. Certainly the ancient Greeks knew of it. Dio Chrysostom said, "I for my part should prefer to praise you for being slow to speak, and even more that you are self-controlled enough to keep silent."[4] But the saying in James is of a Palestinian context, seeing that the Greek *pas anthropos* ("everyone") is a Semitism, a rendering of Hebrew *kol 'adam*. More typically Greek would use the simple *pantes* ("all"). We think also of Proverbs 29:20: "Do you see a man who speaks in haste? There is more hope for a fool than

---

2. Ralph P. Martin, *James*, 38, 41.
3. E.g., Peter H. Davids, *The Epistle of James*, 91.
4. Dio Chrysostom, *Orations*, 32.2.

for him."[5] James may also have in mind a saying of Jesus: "But I tell you that men will have to give account on the day of judgment for every careless word they have spoken" (Matt. 12:36). A rich parallel is found in *Pirke Aboth* 5:12:

> There are four types of disciples: swift to hear and swift to lose—his gain is canceled by his loss; slow to hear and slow to lose—his loss is canceled by his gain; swift to hear and slow to lose—this is a happy lot; slow to hear and swift to lose—this is an evil lot.

Of course, to find parallels to the original meaning of a term is not necessarily to have discerned the meaning of a text. Some insist that James here is asking his audience to listen to their teachers.[6] While this interpretation has an innate appeal to preachers and teachers, we can hardly be certain that a meaning this narrowly focused is true to the historical picture. What is certain is that the passage finds its home in the Jewish wisdom tradition, which placed a premium on measured speech and studious listening. Yet the powerful appeal to community unity in chapter 3 makes it possible that a part of the thought here is a plea to peaceful coexistence—being slow to say rash and angry words to others within the Christian community.

It is enormously helpful to know the problems confronting the readers of James. While many of the specifics are lost to us, in 2:1–13; 3:1–4:12 James makes clear a number of the significant ones. The church had become divided over many issues. Some sought to use the church as a means to display wealth and to exercise power. Others taught a doctrine of fellowship that denied the centrality of the command to love one's neighbor. Still others had shown obvious favoritism to the wealthy. Beyond these, however, the text hardly requires extraordinary imaginative powers to envision concrete examples in contemporary church life.

James then turns his attention to two examples that illustrate his point: human anger and the righteous life that God desires. In verse 20 James seems to confirm our suspicion that in the background is to be found a concern with the character of Christian community, for he says that human anger does not produce the righteousness of God; therefore, we should be slow to anger.[7] In choosing this rendering the NIV has, perhaps, placed too soft a garment on the phrase. James uses the word *ergazetai*, and so the phrase should be translated "for *the practice* of human anger does not bring about the righteous

---

5. See also Prov. 13:3; 15:1; Eccl. 7:9; Sir. 1:22; 4:29; Ps. of Sol. 16:10; and many others.

6. James Adamson, *The Epistle of James*, 78.

7. In this verse James uses the word *aner* instead of the more typical *anthropos* for generic humanity. Although *aner* bears the dictionary definition of "man" as opposed to "woman," at this juncture James uses it in the interests of stylistic variety (cf. also 1:8, 12).

life that God desires." James seems to have no particular type of anger in view, but puts before us the proposition that anger is deleterious to the righteousness God desires of us.

It is possible, however, that James is instructing us to be slow to assume the mantle of righteous indignation, because in so doing we implicitly claim to speak for God. Such anger certainly has a rightful place, but should only be summoned after careful and diligent exercise of prayer and thought. In either the general or specific case, James's words concerning slowness to speak are well taken. Although the phrase "man's anger" is generic, it is more likely that James also has in mind the specific anger of the individual that provides concrete form for the general assertion.

In claiming that anger is undesirable James again offers an observation with parallels in Hellenistic and Jewish literature.[8] More to the point, a related teaching is found on the lips of Jesus, who saw other paths to righteousness: "Blessed are those who hunger and thirst for righteousness, for they will be filled. ... Blessed are those who are persecuted because of righteousness, for theirs is the kingdom of heaven" (Matt. 5:6, 10).[9] Human anger, which is the product of a retarded willingness to listen, is at odds with God's righteousness.

The chief question here concerns the meaning of *dikaiosynen theou* (lit., "the righteousness of God"). (1) It can refer to righteousness as an aspect of the character of God. Since God is righteous and he does not indulge in anger, neither should we. (2) It can mean "God's righteous standard." Because God expects us to be above anger, he demands this righteousness of us. (3) It can mean "the righteousness that God gives," that he grants to us. We cannot practice intemperate anger and suppose that we will receive this righteousness, for such activity disqualifies us. (4) It can mean "eschatological righteousness," that God is the one who will settle accounts.

This last option enjoys the benefit of a powerful advocate in 5:6–9, for we are told there not to grumble against each other, but instead to wait for the righteous judgment of God when the Lord comes.[10] But the second option is an equally potent candidate, championed by 3:8–12, where Christians are warned against cursing their fellows believers. Both of these are probably in James's mind, and in both cases the same may be said: Outbursts of anger do not produce the kind of righteous behavior God desires to see

---

8. Prov. 15:1 springs to mind: "A gentle answer turns away wrath, but a harsh word stirs up anger."

9. See also Matt. 5:20; 6:33.

10. This has a parallel in Paul: Christians are not to exact retribution, for that belongs to God alone: "Do not take revenge, my friends, but leave room for God's wrath, for it is written: 'It is mine to avenge; I will repay,' says the Lord" (Rom. 12:19).

in our lives. Thus, we might better paraphrase the sentence, "Righteous action does not spring from anger."

But there is more to it. In verse 21 James speaks in more expansive terms of this life of righteousness. By opening with "therefore" (*dio*, which can also be rendered "according to this principle") James makes it clear that he is concluding this line of thought. This conclusion opens with a brief catena of behaviors that should not characterize the life of a Christian. The first involves both restraint and renunciation: Christians should "get rid of" (NIV) or "strip off" certain behaviors. Originally this word was used of clothing, and the image of preparation for baptism springs to mind.[11] Perhaps James wishes to remind us of the powerful passage in Zechariah 3, where Joshua the high priest, a symbol for God's people, has his dirty robes removed and is given clean robes, a symbol of God's forgiveness. The verb "get rid of" (*apotithemi*) introduces similar lists of vices in Ephesians 4:25 and 1 Peter 2:1. It can also be used of washing dirt from the body, as in 1 Peter 3:21. The word carries with it the idea of total conversion, a complete change of life pattern.

James instructs us to remove "moral filth" (*rhyparia*) and "evil" (*kakia*). *Rhyparía* means dirt, filth, greediness, and moral uncleanness; *kakia*, when linked with the word "prevalent" (*perisseia*), has the connotation of an abnormal growth of wickedness or even malice. Since this noun can also mean "excess" or "surplus," some see James warning against only a superfluity of moral filth and evil (cf. NEB, "the malice that hurries to excess"). This is an odd rendering, for clearly James wants no vulgarity, moral filth, or evil to be present within the Christian community. These terms are among the strongest he has at his command and imply not only general moral evil, but also a premeditated evil intent. Laws ably and helpfully translates the phrase, "all vulgarity and the great mass of malice."[12] The meaning is clear: Christians must turn not only from anger, but from evil and malice, whether random or premeditated.

But turning from evil is not enough. James also places before us an alternative path: "Humbly accept the word planted in you, which can save you." This attitude of humility characterizes the one who has "converted." It is no longer a life of evil and wickedness, but one marked by calm and concern for others. Our attitude is to be one of humility, recognizing God's wisdom relative to our own poor resources in this regard. The way to salvation is to be found in meek listening to God's word. This posture is necessary if we are to

---

11. In Rom. 6:3–4 Paul speaks of new life in Christ as baptism: "Don't you know that all of us who were baptized into Christ Jesus were baptized into his death? . . . in order that . . . we too may live a new life." This image of dying to the old self was symbolized by the removal of dirty clothes—"stripping off" the old life.

12. Sophie Laws, *The Epistle of James*, 81.

"accept the word planted in" us. Humility is significant not only because the attitude is necessary in order to allow the word to flourish, but also because it is the essential attribute of the poor, those without resources who are dear to the heart of God.

What we are to receive or accept with humility is the word "planted in you." This "word" must be equivalent to the "word of truth" of 1:18, although here it is the true word spoken or read, for 1:22 enjoins us to "listen to the word." The term the NIV renders as "planted" can mean either something intrinsically possessed or something added. There has been no little debate concerning which is the best nuance. It is often pointed out that it is logically impossible to accept what one already has. But we should remember that James is concerned with the practical matters of moral teaching, not with intricacies of the logic of metaphysics. Most likely he intends both nuances. As members of the fallen human race we need to have this word of God planted in us and to nurture it so that its roots grow deep and strong. But as members of a race originally intended to be in close communion with God, this word has a rightful place within us. It is not an alien agent; rather, its implantation is like the rightful return of something needful but long lost. It is necessarily a constituent element of that "perfect humanity" of which James spoke in 1:4.

The NIV chooses to translate *sosai tas psuchas hymon* as "save you," where the Greek reads (lit.) "save your souls." "Soul" refers not to the Greek idea of the "higher" or more ethereal elements of the human person, but rather our whole beings. God's word has the power to save us. We must remember that the New Testament presents a triple pattern of salvation: We *have been saved* through the death and resurrection of Jesus Christ (Rom. 8:24–25); we *are being saved* (1 Cor. 1:18); and we *will be saved* (Rom. 8:21–23). This triple pattern helps us understand the shades of meaning that attend to "planted," as it presents us with an image of growth and development. The word of truth has saved us. We are to nurture it, for it is a motive force in the process of saving us. The result of this process is that we will achieve ultimate salvation.

There is a significant parallel to these thoughts in 1 Peter 1:23–2:2. Both passages discuss birth by the word of God, call for a rejection of *kakia*, and include advice to receive and nurture the word. This nurturing, of course, implies behavior and therefore codes of conduct; in short, the law. James will argue that the word involves the law, but he here stresses that the law does not control the word, nor are they identical. While James is often castigated for concentrating on works, we should note how at this critical juncture he carefully highlights the saving power of God's word, which when it grows strong within us creates Christian character that results in righteous action.

Hearing Without Doing Is Worthless (1:22–25)

"DO WHAT [THE law] says" is a Semitism, as the Jews often spoke of doing the law in these terms—most often as "to practice Torah" (cf. Deut. 28:58). In Exodus 24:3 we read, "When Moses went and told the people all the LORD's words and laws, they responded with one voice, 'Everything the LORD has said we will do.'" Jesus himself contributed to this tradition: "Everyone who hears these words of mine and puts them into practice is like a wise man who built his house on the rock" (Matt. 7:24). While both Judaism and Jesus understood holiness to be tied to this "doing the word," their radically different definitions of "holiness" led them in divergent directions. For Jesus, the center of God's character is his compassion and mercy, as expressed in the twin dictum, "'Love the Lord your God with all your heart and with all your soul and with all your mind,' and, 'Love your neighbor as yourself'" (Luke 10:27). For his contemporaries "holiness" had to do with purity and therefore with separation from "the world."

Both views of holiness require a life of action. James makes this point with the present imperative "do" (*ginesthe*), which has the force of "continue to do." We must continue to grow in carrying out the commands laid on us by our hearing of God's word. This hearing is most naturally the public reading of the Scriptures in the context of worship.[13] But hearing alone is insufficient. To hear and not to take action is to lie to oneself. Having introduced the idea of eschatological judgment, James's warning here takes on grave consequences.

In verses 23–24 James turns his attention to a negative example in the form of a proverb: The person who hears without acting is like a man who looks in a mirror and then forgets what he looks like. James's point is that the image in the mirror, whether the product of a furtive glance or an adoring gaze, quickly dissipates; whatever impression forms in the mind and heart while looking in a mirror is temporary. James may be thinking of an accurate self-appraisal, one that shows us areas that need attention. But he may also have in mind the image of true humanity (cf. 1:4), humanity as God intended, which in our mind's eye we glimpse when the Word is read, but a vision that soon evaporates and is replaced by more base desires that the world is intent on displaying before us.

Verse 25 offers a positive example, but this verse is perhaps the thorniest theological problem in the entire book. The person who looks into "the perfect law that gives freedom" and then does not forget but acts upon this vision is blessed. The phrase "perfect law that gives freedom" has precedents in the Old Testament. The psalmist declared, for example, "The law of the

---

13. It is the word used in Rev. 1:3: "Blessed is the one who reads the words of this prophecy, and blessed are those who hear it and take to heart what is written in it. . . ."

LORD is perfect, reviving the soul" (Ps. 19:7). For James "perfect law" and "word" are related, for each describes a pattern of life conduct. So "the word planted in you" (1:21) and "perfect law" are found in such close association that one implies the other.

This law is the law of freedom. In Paul freedom is most often *from* the Jewish law, but not always. Paul can say that "through Christ Jesus the law of the Spirit of life set me free from the law of sin and death" (Rom. 8:2). It is therefore dangerous to assume that "law" in Paul is always used to imply the negative. In a similar manner, James defines law in such a way that it grants freedom from self-interest and immorality, allowing the Christian to grow into what God intends. It is not unlikely that James is here reflecting the words of Jesus relative to the law. Jesus did not overturn the law of Moses; rather, he pierced to the heart of its intention, and in so doing elevated the law.[14]

Like Jesus, James does not have in mind a new law, but rather the fuller expression or more perfect distillation of the Jewish law. For the Christian this law is still the will of God, but a more refined apprehension of that will. This is a law for which a purer cannot be imagined. The perfect law, the word implanted and allowed to take root, is, then, the very teaching of Jesus.[15] Stephen Carter says that law has only two functions: It makes you do what you do not want to do, and it prevents you from doing what you want to do.[16] This is essentially the problem with Mosaic Law in the eyes of Jesus, James, and Paul. It is rigid, somewhat inflexible, and most significantly, *external*. It has little or no power to animate the heart.

In piercing to the heart of the law Jesus touched on the intentions and attitudes that undergird the law. Rules, such as law codes, are based on principles, and principles arise from some foundational beliefs. For Jesus the foundation is the creative act of God. Implicit in this act are principles concerning life that directed Jesus to adopt a more severe stance than the Mosaic Law concerning divorce (learn to love and forgive one another; see Matt. 5:27–32), as well as a more permissive stance than the Sabbath law (see Luke 6:1–11; John 5:1–30).

Furthermore, there is also the person who forgets what he has heard and in so doing misses the blessing. This blessing may be a promise for the future,

---

14. On this matter see G. B. Caird and L. D. Hurst, *New Testament Theology* (Oxford: Clarendon, 1994), 385–93.

15. It is not inopportune to note that in early Christian literature the doctrine of Christianity was frequently spoken of as a "law." But as with James and the Prophets, this law has the power to change hearts. See Barnabas 2:6 and Justin Martyr's first *Apology*, 1.43.

16. Michael Cromatie, "How We Muddle Our Morals," *Books and Culture: A Christian Review* (May/June 1996), 14.

as James has already presented the idea of reward, or it may be a natural part of obedience to the law. James could easily have had both definitions in mind.

Pure Religion (1:26–27)

TWO TIES LINK this section to what has gone before. (1) Verse 26 highlights the sin of rash speech, the theme that opened the passage (v. 19). (2) Here is provided an extension of the idea "not only hearing but doing good," in that worship is described as worthless without actions impelled by a godly character. In both this and the previous section self-deception plays a significant role. The practice of "pure religion" is described here as the control of speech, acts of charity, and resisting temptation.

A person who considers herself religious but cannot keep a tight rein on the tongue is only deceiving herself. The word "religious" (*threskos*) appears only here in the New Testament, though its root word (the noun *threskia*) is found elsewhere in the New Testament. It can refer to both the inner and outer qualities of worship; generally, however (as here), it points to external ceremonies. Paul uses it to refer to the worship of angels (Col. 2:18).

It is not clear what specific practices James has in mind, but like the prophets of old he claims that any religious practice that cannot influence the heart and therefore actions is worthless.[17] The tongue James compares to an animal that must be guided by an iron bit placed in its mouth (cf. 3:4), for so we must interpret *chalinagogeo* ("keep a tight rein on"), found only here in the New Testament. The idea, however, can be found in the Old Testament: "Keep your tongue from evil and your lips from speaking lies" (Ps. 34:13). The more specific metaphor (but not the precise language) is also to be found in the Old Testament: "I said, 'I will watch my ways and keep my tongue from sin; I will put a muzzle on my mouth as long as the wicked are in my presence'" (Ps. 39:1). James implies not only that rash speech has the ability to put one's faith in question, but a "religion" that results in such behavior has insufficient ability to shape the heart and is therefore worthless or futile (*mataios*).

Given the thematic character of James 3 and 4, James may also have in mind the specific example of certain "teachers" whose rash and angry words were sowing discord in the community. In any case, a person whose "religion" is like this is deceived, because it has no power over ethical behavior, as the

---

17. Amos argues that worth of worship was contingent upon moral behavior: "You who turn justice into bitterness and cast righteousness to the ground.... You hate the one who reproves in court and despise him who tells the truth. You trample on the poor and force him to give you grain.... I hate, I despise your religious feasts; I cannot stand your assemblies. Even though you bring me burnt offerings and grain offerings, I will not accept them.... Let justice roll on like a river, righteousness like a never-failing stream!" (Amos 5:7, 10–11, 21–22, 24).

case of the rash tongue demonstrates. It is a faith so useless before God that is can be considered no faith at all (see 2:20, 26). James uses the word *kardia* (lit., "heart") to stand for the self, the center of one's being and the locus of one's thoughts. Such a "religion" has no power over human hearts, for it does not allow God to be at work in us.

James then defines pure "religion" (*threskeia*) that God our Father accepts: to look after orphans and widows and to keep oneself unpolluted by the world. James continues his homage to the themes of justice and compassion as emblematic of pure religion by choosing a common idea found in the Prophets: God has special concern for the widows and orphans, as these are emblematic of all groups open to exploitation. Note that James has already discussed the issue of the wealthy brother and will do so again. People at the margins of the social, economic, and legal landscape are always open to exploitation and thereby suffer "distress." This distress can be the condition of poverty; if so, we are reminded that for the poor brother of 1:9 poverty is itself a test. James may also have in mind specific conditions of distress that the poor in the Christian community are facing, and he is offering them encouragement and exhortation.

In any event, God claims to be the protector of such people: "He defends the cause of the fatherless and the widow, and loves the alien, giving him food and clothing" (Deut. 10:18). Furthermore, in the Old Testament God enlists our participation with him: "Stop doing wrong, learn to do right! Seek justice, encourage the oppressed. Defend the cause of the fatherless, plead the case of the widow" (Isa. 1:16–17). In short, we are to be like God. It is not without significance that James designates God as "Father" here.

The second example of "pure religion" is to "keep oneself from being polluted by the world." In the New Testament the term "world" (*kosmos*) is extraordinarily flexible. It can mean the created universe, humankind, humankind in need of God's salvation, human-ordered society, or the world order as corrupted and evil, in rebellion against God. Here James uses the word in this last sense—the world as a place of evil and danger. But we should not miss the important point that he does not teach removal from the world. Rather, he stresses living in the world, but doing so with intelligence and forethought in order to keep one's life, one's reputation, and one's faith pure and secure. For James true faith enters the surrounding culture but remains free from the evil to be found there.

As Laws points out,[18] we are perhaps seeing James as typically Jewish here. "Religion" is directed to God the Father, not to Jesus the exalted Lord; and the exigencies of practical piety are expressed in terms that traditionally connote separation (*pure* and *faultless*). However, the specifically Christian

---

18. Laws, *The Epistle of James*, 91.

message here is powerful and should not be overlooked in our haste to define the world as evil. For Judaism the holiness of God was guarded from pollution. In the mind and life of Jesus, however, the holiness of God was robust and strong enough to stride into the mire and muck of human existence. It had a purifying force, able to cleanse the world. James's point is that we also are to be purifying agents in the world, but being mindful to prevent ourselves from being sullied. In this he is a faithful follower of Jesus.

WE MUST UNDERSTAND two key ideas in this passage if we intend safely to carry the message of James from the first century to our own. (1) The first concerns the question of law, and more specifically what James calls the "perfect law." This also involves his notion of the word, and more broadly the supposed tension between Paul and James relative to the matter of faith and works. We soon will see that in spite of his reputation, James presents a compelling case for the primacy of faith. (2) The idea of the necessity of justice also calls for careful discussion. There are many within the contemporary church who are quick to assume the mantle of prophet and speak with righteous and even splenetic anger, yet James cautions us to avoid this behavior. How can we balance the thought of James with current conditions?

The law. One of the most intriguing issues in New Testament theology is the relationship between the grace of God and the demands of the law. The two are often seen as opposites, whether the dynamic is expressed in terms of "faith versus works" or "word versus law." In speaking of "the implanted word" and "the perfect law," James places us squarely in the middle of this issue. Our attention will focus on the law in order to demonstrate that James defines "law" and "word" so that the two are not in opposition, but rather are complementary.

It can hardly be doubted that the contemporary Protestant tradition is colored by a healthy skepticism of "law." We are taught that the Jews of the first century kept the law in order to earn the favor of God, and that with the death and resurrection of Jesus we are free from the law. While it no longer seems likely that this picture of first-century Judaism is accurate,[19] there is

---

19. In recent years this view has been overturned. In a series of important works, but most significantly his *Paul and Palestinian Judaism* (Philadelphia: Fortress, 1977), E. P. Sanders has shown that first-century Jews kept the law not to earn salvation, but as a way of expressing the fact of their salvation. Simply being Jewish meant that they were within the sphere of God's grace. That Sanders is right can be seen in the attack against this view leveled by both John the Baptist (Matt. 3:9) and Jesus (John 8:31–41). In both cases the claim of eth-

some scriptural support for a negative view of "the law." After all, Paul claims that Jesus Christ set him free from the "law of sin and death" (Rom. 8:2), and John claims that "the law was given through Moses; grace and truth came through Jesus Christ" (John 1:17).

But the picture often drawn of grace versus the law is a too facile reading of Scripture. Paul says many good things about the law, as even a cursory reading of Romans 2–10 demonstrates. Nor is Jesus free of controversy in this matter. In Matthew 5:18–19, for example, Jesus speaks as a legalist, claiming that not the smallest letter, not the least stroke of a pen, not the least of the commandments will pass away. Yet this complex of statements is in stark variance with his activity throughout the rest of the Gospel. Similarly in Luke, we encounter a rapid series of teachings about the law. In Luke 16:16 we learn that the law has passed away; in verse 17 we learn that the law can never pass away; and verse 18 enjoins us to an obedience of the law that goes beyond that of the Pharisees. In order to understand what James means by "the perfect law," we must penetrate the understanding of Jesus on the law.

In Jesus' teaching on the law two items are firmly lodged: (1) The cardinal principles or intentions of the law take precedence over literalistic and niggling adherence to the law; and (2) while concentration on outward acts is not wrong, to concentrate on actions alone opens us to the danger of mistaking the good for the best. For this reason Jesus emphasizes the matter of the heart and of human character. All of this is enshrined by James in his heavy emphasis on "the word" in this passage. The word within us is living, growing, vital, and flexible. It has the power to woo us into compliance with God's will, which is the purpose of the law.

This, in fact, is the cornerstone of the teaching of Jesus on the law. The law is a guide, not an impediment. The law is good in that it is a channel that directs us to living out the intention of God. It is *a* means, not *the* purpose. On its own it has little if any power to change hearts. For Jesus strict observance to the letter of the law is not radical obedience. Jesus taught a higher standard of ethical obedience than can be enforced by any law. He taught an ethic that flows from hearts in tune with God's heart. James points to the same idea with his phrase "the perfect law that gives freedom." We might almost call this a "law of the heart," a growing and innate sense of God's purpose and pleasure in a given situation.

The Pharisees attacked Jesus for fraternizing with the common "polluted" people. In response Jesus told the crowds to beware the leaven of the Pharisees (Mark 11:15), for they were concerned with outward pollution but

---

nicity is shown to be insufficient. Instead, it is actions that arise from the heart which demonstrate that "stones" can be "children of Abraham."

ignored its source, the heart out of step with God's heart. The activity of Jesus caused the Pharisees and others to regard him as a figure guilty of creating scandal. He purposely broke the Sabbath (2:23–3:6); he claimed the right to forgive sins (2:1–12); he willingly and even gleefully associated with unsavory company (2:13–17). In so doing he expressed his right to pass judgment on not only the Pharisaic law, but on Judaism itself.

These differences stem from divergent conceptions of God and of his holiness. For the Pharisees holiness was fragile, easily polluted, and in need of protection. In the main[20] their view of God was of a legislator whose laws required scrupulous observance in order to protect this holiness. For Jesus the holiness of God was essentially his compassion and his mercy. This robust compassion had the power to render clean the unclean, as the encounter of Jesus with the hemorrhaging woman demonstrates (Luke 8:40–56). His picture of God was of a loving Father whose earnest wish was to welcome his rebellious children home. In fairness to the contemporaries of Jesus we must note a saying attributed to Simeon the Just, a high priest who lived approximately 200 B.C.: "By three things is the world sustained: by the Law, by the [Temple–] service, and by deeds of loving kindness."[21] The Judaism in which Jesus was raised understood the need for hearts to be remade, as opposed to slavish adherence to the form of the law.[22]

Jesus' dispute, then, was not so much with the law as such, but with what he considered a skewed understanding of the law, a tendency to view the law as an end and not the means for some greater good. Only in this way can we understand Matthew 5:17: "Do not think that I have come to abolish the Law or the Prophets; I have not come to abolish them but to fulfill them." For Jesus, then, "the law" was not what his contemporaries meant, but was a more accurate representation of God's character in the concrete and was therefore a joy, not a burden. James agrees. By emphasizing the implantation of the word *prior* to his discussion of behavior, he (like Jesus) presents this "perfect law" or

---

20. Sanders argues, quite rightly, that there was great variety to be found within the Pharisaic tradition. Many Pharisees found themselves in general agreement with Jesus concerning the law, as the Gospels attest.

21. Mishnah *Aboth*, 1:2. This translation is found in Herbert Danby, *The Mishnah Translated From the Hebrew With Introduction and Brief Explanatory Notes* (Oxford: Oxford Univ. Press, 1933).

22. Hans Conzelmann, in his *An Outline of the Theology of the New Testament*, tr. J. Bowden (New York: Harper and Row, 1969), in consideration of the Jewish law writes, "The question is: can obedience be achieved by legalistic casuistry at all? What is sought after is not just formal fulfillment, but the correspondence of my will with the will of God" (p. 21). He further writes (p. 226) that a "distinction must be made between the aim of the law which God pursued in the dispensation of the law, and the use made of the law by men. The law reveals the will of God. But it cannot by itself bring about fulfillment—it is 'weak.'"

"law of the heart" in descriptive terms. This is a picture of life in the kingdom of God.

Neither Jesus nor James are chary, however, of pointing out that the *commands* of God must be followed. These commands are, in the main, components of the foundation and principles of God's revelation: love for the neighbor, forgiveness, the preservation of life, and abstinence from idolatry and from sexual immorality. These are so closely illustrative of God's character that there appears to be no room for flexibility. Paul, for instance, can countenance differing opinions on the resurrection (1 Cor. 15), yet deals summarily with pagan practice (10:14–22) and with sexual immorality (5:1–5).

Like James we should understand Jesus' teaching on the law as directed toward the intention of the law. The word planted within our hearts allows us to live toward the goal of the law. This implies the next complex of issues to be discussed, the care given to widows and orphans.

Widows and orphans; compassion and justice. James is bold enough to claim that the definition of pure religion is, in part, "to look after orphans and widows." The intensity of the Hebrew idea is foreign to us and needs to be given voice if we are properly to understand James. In ancient Israel the cult involved sacrifices as a means of honoring God. Yet the prophets offered attacks, at times savage and violent, against sacrifices, for they proved unable to shape character. Even Samuel once said, "Does the LORD delight in burnt offerings and sacrifices as much as in obeying the voice of the LORD? To obey is better than to sacrifice . . ." (1 Sam. 15:22). Later prophets, such as Amos and Jeremiah, went even further, arguing that the actual worth of worship was contingent upon moral behavior. To live a life of injustice, one bereft of compassion, was to make worship worthless.

The pervasive nature of this idea is lodged even in Proverbs: "He who oppresses the poor shows contempt for their Maker, but whoever is kind to the needy honors God" (Prov. 14:31). Tied to this idea are two Hebrew terms that do not easily translate into English. The first is *mišpat*,[23] the root of which, *špt*, has a range of meanings, including "rule, judge, warn, deliver, vindicate." *Mišpat* is most often used to refer to the restoration of a condition of harmony, wholeness, and equity, a condition otherwise referred to by the Hebrew word *šalom*. It is normally reserved for the description of a mode of action. The second word is *ṣedaqah*,[24] which conveys the notions of right order in general, of right order before God, and of justice. *Ṣedaqah* tends to emphasize the quality or character of a person that results in righteous acts. But the two are inextricably related. Thus Amos 5:24 declares, "Let justice roll on like a river,

---

23. See Temba L. J. Mafico, "Just, Justice," *ABD*, 3:1127–29.
24. See J. J. Scullion, "Righteousness (OT)," *ABD*, 5:724–36.

righteousness like a never-failing stream," implying that *mišpat* and *sedaqah* are virtual synonyms.

We have already seen that the Psalms form a vital and vibrant portion of the background to James, and they are of significance here as well. They posit the view that God has established and is the guardian of justice. Psalm 97:2 reads, "Righteousness and justice are the foundation of his throne." Psalm 99:4 claims that God "loves justice" and has "established equity." God is the one who guarantees and administers justice as a feature of his holiness. As judge, God is called upon to redress wrongs, as in the Jephthah story (Judg. 11:27).

God also expects human beings to be involved in the maintenance of justice, and for this reason he requires more than piety; he requires a heart and actions of justice and righteousness.[25] In Jeremiah 9:23–24 we read:

> Let not the wise man boast of his wisdom
>   or the strong man boast of his strength
>   or the rich man boast of his riches,
> but let him who boasts boast about this:
>   that he understands and knows me,
> that I am the LORD, who exercised kindness,
>   justice and righteousness on earth,
>   for in these I delight.[26]

We would be remiss if we failed to note the quality of relationship conveyed in the verbs "understand" and "know." This is no mere affectation or the aping of behavior. This reflects action that springs from the core of one's being. So the judges in ancient Israel were to mirror the holiness of God in their actions (Ex. 18:21). The central thrust of the justice of God is to create an egalitarian society in regard to basic human rights (Ps. 113:7–9).

Since human society tends to withdraw from such a community vision, both God and his appointed judges were to have a special concern for the poor and oppressed, here spoken of by the emblematic phrase "orphans and widows." We can therefore see several themes within James converging. Like the judges of old, Christians are to mirror God's character, as James says when he calls us to perfect humanity. We are also to observe more than outward piety. Finally, we are to protect and care for the poor and oppressed. This last constitutes a challenge that Christians in developed countries will dismiss only at their peril.

---

25. Isa. 5:7 depicts God as one who searches in Israel for justice (*mišpat*) but finds only bloodshed (*mišpah*), who looks for righteousness (*sedaqah*) but finds only distress (*se'aqah*).
26. See also Ps. 51:4–7, 10; Amos 5:21–23.

JAMES HAS INTRODUCED a wide variety of issues here, but four form an umbrella broad enough to cover all. (1) We are often guilty of intemperate speech, whether it is an outburst of anger or premeditated gossip. (2) More and more, it seems, we are sure that we have been wronged and assume the posture of righteous anger, confident that God is on our side. (3) Certainly contemporary culture exposes us to moral filth, a situation that requires careful introspection. (4) We desperately need to remember the image we see when we peer into the mirror of God's Word.

Intemperate speech. When James says that we should be slow to speak, he has placed his finger on a problem that can have devastating effects. Just as he argues that we should protect the dignity of the poor through material generosity, he also insists that we need to protect the dignity of others in the realms of public and private discourse. The idea here includes impassioned spontaneous speech as well as calculated intemperate speech, such as gossip. While as children we may have chanted "Sticks and stones may break my bones, but words will never hurt me," the ditty is actually an exercise in whistling in the dark. Words have great power to both wound and heal.

Recently a student sought me out in my office. Over the course of a hour she cried tears of intense pain as she related to me a story. Along with her mother she had visited her aunt, who spoke of her own daughter in glowing terms. She wished, the aunt said, that she could have another daughter just like the first. But the mother of the student in my office responded in a way that devastated her daughter. "I wish," she said, "that my daughter had never been born." Such speech is destructive of not only the target, but eventually also of the speaker. Our speech has the power to encourage and nourish life, or to snuff it out. Which shall we choose?

In his wonderful and spare novel *All the Pretty Horses*, Cormac McCarthy tells the story of John Grady Cole. As a young man he travels to Mexico with two friends, each of them hoping to escape a childhood in Texas marked by largely unknown disappointments. While there, John Grady Cole gains employment on a cattle ranch and earns the respect and trust of the owner, Don Héctor Rocha y Villareal. He also falls in love with Alejandra, the daughter of Don Héctor. Doña Alfonsa, the grandaunt of Alejandra, becomes worried about this relationship and invites John Grady Cole into conversation. At one point she speaks to the question of reputation and gossip:

> You see that I cannot help but be sympathetic to Alejandra. Even at her worst. But I wont [sic] have her unhappy. I wont [sic] have her spoken ill of. Or gossiped about. I know what that is. She thinks that she can toss her head and dismiss everything. In an ideal world the gossip of

the idle would be of no consequence. But I have seen the consequences in the real world and they can be very grave indeed.[27]

Gossip can have real and tragic consequences. We all know the sting of being made the subject of gossip, and we all have participated in the spread of gossip. The saying is that familiarity breeds contempt, but we ought to say that familiarity often causes us to ignore the obvious. Perhaps this problem and its solution can be thrown into sharper relief by looking at a form of gossip that is not so obvious. The last few decades have been tumultuous for local congregations. Among the many issues that make it clear that our culture is becoming increasingly unstable is the startling rise in the frequency of clergy misconduct.

There are few issues that can so powerfully and quickly devastate a church. I know of a church that recently weathered two very different storms of this type over a short span of time. First the senior pastor resigned while admitting to moral failing. The suddenness of his announcement left the church reeling. He is a tremendously gifted preacher, well loved by many in the congregation. But many felt betrayed by him, and still others directed their anger to the denomination that ordained him. Shortly thereafter the associate pastor was ordered to observe a six-month hiatus from ministry, at the conclusion of which came a resignation. The close proximity of these two shattering events caused many in the church to question the action of the board in the latter situation. Speculation ran fast and free among the congregation as people tried to make sense of these events. In the wake of unsubstantiated rumor, many in the congregation demanded that the board reveal the rationale for the decision to ask the associate pastor to resign.

I wonder if these people had thought through their request. Did they really wish to force the board to defend such a severe action? What if the reason had to do with moral failure on the part of the associate pastor? Would this revelation be in the best interest of their "friend," the pastor in question? I doubt it. We sometimes excuse our gossip by claiming that we have a right to know some bit of information about someone else or by claiming that details have to be known in order to make wise decisions. Frequently this is a subterfuge. A simple but effective set of rules is this: Could the sharing of this information have the effect of harming someone? Is there any possibility that my motivation for sharing this information is less than pure? If the answer to either is yes, then perhaps the matter should not be pursued.

When is righteous anger justified? James also counsels against the presumption of righteous anger. This is particularly appropriate teaching and per-

---

27. Cormac McCarthy, *All the Pretty Horses* (New York: Vintage, 1992), 136.

haps among the most difficult to imagine as applicable to oneself. Our world is awash in injustice. There is no denying it. Many in North America have suffered beyond what one might reasonably expect. Women and minorities have been and continue to be oppressed and discriminated against in our society and in our churches. Other groups have faced similar disenfranchisement. Many who consider themselves on the margins of the broader American culture or the specifically Christian culture wish to voice their right to have justice done. In recent years this has been true of homosexuals, pro-life groups, pro-choice groups, AIDS patients, marijuana smokers, the gun control lobby, smoker's rights groups, women, minorities, and even white males. Each of these at times consider themselves to be worthy of a display of righteous indignation. Yet James cautions a slow and deliberate approach. When is righteous anger justified?

Perhaps the best answer is to investigate biblical patterns, especially that of the prophets. The prophets certainly expressed righteous anger. Amos could hardly be considered a promising candidate for the "James" award for temperate speech.

> Hear this word, you cows of Bashan on Mount Samaria,
>   you women who oppress the poor and crush the needy
>   and say to your husbands, "Bring us some drinks!"
> The Sovereign LORD has sworn by his holiness:
>   "The time will surely come
> when you will be taken away with hooks,
>   the last of you with fishhooks.
> You will each go straight out
>   through breaks in the wall. . . . (Amos 4:1–3)

Amos in his righteous anger proclaims God's judgment waiting to fall on the unfeeling rich, who have turned their backs on the poor and who by inaction have crushed the needy. How can we reconcile this prophetic tirade with the call in James to avoid the presumption of righteous anger?

The first factor to notice is that the prophets were *called*. Almost invariably they, like Moses, initially resisted the call of God. Jeremiah, for instance, wanted nothing more than to be excused from his duties.[28] In contrast, James is speaking to our *desire* to vent, our *predilection* to glory in self-righteous anger. We observe this on a daily basis. Children protest their right for exclusive use

---

28. The meaning of his name is ambiguous, but it could mean "the LORD throws," perhaps implying that God has thrown him into a hostile situation. Jeremiah's life was not pleasant, but was one of distress and anguish. "Alas, my mother, that you gave me birth, a man with whom the whole land strives and contends! I have neither lent nor borrowed, yet everyone curses me" (Jer. 15:10).

of a toy. Motorists angrily gesture at each other as they dispute the right-of-way. Politicians defend their case while besmirching their fellows. Nor is the church immune. Perhaps one of the most important and problematic examples concerns the role of women in the church. While many denominations ordain women, there is no doubt that the stories of women clergy are generally less than ideal. Many have experienced skepticism and even hostility from their brothers and sisters, whether in the pew or in denominational headquarters. Here is a problem that needs to be addressed.

Yet James advocates slowness of speech. This, it seems to me, is wise advice. A constant complaint does little to assuage the situation, and in most cases it actually has the effect of hardening the positions held by those in the opposition. Walter Brueggemann, in his splendid and challenging book *The Prophetic Imagination*, says that a prophet must do more than criticize. A prophet must also "energize" by offering an alternative vision that is marked by biblical hope.[29] James, I think, would counsel us to curb our desire to vent, to proclaim ourselves right. He would ask us to wait, to spend some time in prayer and thought, before arrogating to ourselves the role of God's messenger. This is not to say that righteous anger is not justified. It is to counsel a wise response that is the fruit of careful thought. An angry response nullifies the benefits of a position of moral authority.

A second factor is that the prophets reserved their harshest and most strident tones for times of imminent danger. It was the great danger to Jerusalem that made Jeremiah hold a pot over his head and declare that God will "smash this nation and this city just as this potter's jar is smashed" (Jer. 19:11). It was the imminent destruction of the northern kingdom that made Amos utter such brutal words to the women of wealth in Samaria. But even in the midst of such danger, there was held out to them, like to those drowning, a lifeline: "Seek good, not evil, that you may live. . . . Hate evil, love good; maintain justice in the courts. Perhaps the LORD God Almighty will have mercy on the remnant of Joseph" (Amos 5:14–15).

A third factor is that the righteous anger of the prophets was directed at injustices that others were experiencing, not at injustice that they personally experienced. Note the prophet Jeremiah, for example. He complained bitterly to the Lord about the abusive situation he experienced at the hands of his enemies, but he never "damned" the false prophets or the nation of Judah for the way they were treating him, only for their sins and their disobedience to God's law. Note too the example of Jesus, who preached against those who mistreated the poor and the oppressed; but when he himself was treated with gross injustice, "no deceit was found in his mouth" (1 Peter 2:22; cf. Isa.

---

29. Walter Brueggemann, *The Prophetic Imagination* (Philadelphia: Fortress, 1978), 67–79.

53:9). Moreover, when injustice comes our way, the apostle Paul instructs us to be willing to be wronged rather than to lash out in tirades of anger and perhaps even to launch lawsuits against others (1 Cor. 6:7—8).

Self-myopia manifests itself in our lives, especially in regard to our susceptibility to the "lure of the world." We generally view this phrase in terms of obvious temptations, but it is more often the subtle and unnoticed error that is most dangerous. Human beings have a tremendous capacity to be silent as they observe the pain of others. When the news footage of the modern-day concentration camps and ethnic cleansing of Bosnia first graced our television screens, Americans were outraged. A year later the latest editions of those images held little power over us as we switched the channel to the sports report. How can we be so callous?[30] As unsavory as it is to realize, we quickly become jaded to even the most outrageous evil.[31]

Brueggemann points out that this tendency to numbness is in the interests of authorities and institutions, particularly governments.[32] The 1996 United States presidential race saw serious allegations leveled against Bill Clinton, the incumbent. On election night it was reported by CBS News that over 60 percent of Americans felt that President Clinton had lied about the scandal known as Whitewater. Yet an equally high percentage claimed that character issues were unimportant in their choice.[33] The American public

---

30. The obverse is true as well. As St. Augustine noted in his *City of God* (14.15–16), the pursuit of earthly pleasures only serves to make us jaded to these "pleasures," requiring an ever more elevated experience to achieve the same effect.

31. In a famous experiment Stanley Milgram assigned to a number of volunteer subjects the role of "teacher" and explained that they would participate in an experiment testing the effect of electric shock on learning. In reality, it was an experiment testing responses to authority. The "teachers" were introduced to the "student" (actually an actor) and were then shown bogus electronic equipment that appeared authentic, including a shock switch and dial marked from 15 volts (labeled "mild shock") to 300 volts (labeled "intense shock") to 450 volts (marked "Danger: Severe Shock"). Each time the "student" answered a question incorrectly, the "teachers" were expected to administer a higher level of shock. If necessary, a researcher in a lab coat instructed the "teacher" to continue increasing the voltage. At the level of 120 volts the "student" shouted in pain, at 150 volts the "student" demanded to be released from the experiment, and at 270 volts he screamed in agony. After 330 volts the "student" exhibited dead silence. Well over half of the "teachers" willingly turned the dial to 300 volts, and more than 30 percent continued to turn the dial all the way to 450 volts. While Milgram's experiment tested conformity, it also revealed the disturbingly high human capacity for insensitivity. The experiment is described in John J. Macionis, *Sociology*, 6th ed. (Upper Saddle River, N.J.: Prentice–Hall, 1997), 178.

32. Brueggemann, *The Prophetic Imagination*, 46.

33. It is emblematic of the random inconsistency of this phenomenon that the public reacted in some outrage to Senator Bob Packwood's steadfast refusal to admit that he had sexually harassed female staffers for years, even though sixteen women made such charges

has become numb to the fact that character in large part determines policy and the integrity of that policy. We have become numb to the fact that actions spring from character: "No good tree bears bad fruit, nor does a bad tree bear good fruit" (Luke 6:43). This numbness allows the political order to behave as it will, with diminishing concern for integrity.

Most of us were filled with admiration for the protests in Tiananmen Square in 1989, and the image of a brave solitary man blocking a line of tanks is fixed in our minds. Yet the decision of the United States government to continue to extend to China "most favored nation" trading status stands as mute witness to the interests of institutions to encourage numbness in the population. We easily become numb to injustice. Oppression of the powerless needs to be pointed out, and in whatever terms necessary. But not every situation is such a crisis. James would have us choose words that are in fact appropriate to the issue.

Unpolluted and free of moral filth. There is no shortage of candidates for a list of American vices that qualify as "moral filth." Alcohol, drugs, laziness, pornography, abuse, hedonism, premarital sex, adultery, lying, and cheating are but a tithe of the candidates. In response, many Americans and American politicians have championed "family values." Apart from being a vague slogan, there are several problems with this position. Not the least of these is that the Bible is concerned with both personal and corporate morality. In fact, our tendency to see personal morality and corporate morality as wholly separate subsets of morality is itself a problem. These two are mutually interpenetrating on a number of levels.

In his marvelous book *Not the Way It's Supposed to Be: A Breviary of Sin*, Cornelius Plantinga devotes his attention to the distinctions between crime, sin, and evil. His hypothetical example involves Jim Bob, a white man in the American South in the late nineteenth century. While clearly evil, Plantinga points out that some might not believe that Jim Bob's racist views can be called "sinful," because Jim Bob (presumably) had no choice but to adopt the values of his family and his local culture. But the crucial point comes later. In Plantinga's words:

> What Jim Bob's racism shows us is that moral evil is social and structural as well as personal: it comprises a vast historical and cultural matrix that includes traditions, old patterns of relationship and behavior, atmospheres of expectation, social habits.[34]

in 1992. The closest Packwood came to an apology was to claim that he never meant to make anyone feel uncomfortable, and that he must have been drunk during these episodes and was therefore somehow "innocent" of purposeful wrongdoing.

34. Cornelius Plantinga Jr., *Not the Way It's Supposed to Be: A Breviary of Sin* (Grand Rapids: Eerdmans, 1995), 23—27.

This point is especially telling because we often see structural evil as outside of ourselves, as something in which we are not involved, as something perpetrated upon our world by institutions, corporations, or governments. Plantinga demonstrates that structural evil is this and more. It includes assumed attitudes and patterns that allow institutions, corporations, and governments to act as if certain evil actions are not evil, or that doing evil is worth the risk, because whatever punishment might be in store is far less severe than the gain to be had. When corporations are fined only $100,000 for excessive pollution of the environment, our values are revealed. How effective a deterrent is a $1,000 fine imposed on a professional basketball player who earns in excess of $5,000,000 a year?[35] When Roberto Alomar of the Baltimore Orioles baseball team can spit in the face of an umpire at the close of the season and still be allowed to play in the playoffs, something deeper and sick is revealed about the values of our society.[36]

James implores us to hold up to the mirror of God's Word not only our personal lives, but also the attitudes, tendencies, and assumptions of our culture as well. Failure to do so, or to do so only halfheartedly, places us at great risk. Slavery in the American South was defended on biblical grounds, but not legitimately. Is it not reasonable to assume that there are parallel features in contemporary American life?

Thus, personal evil is linked to structural evil. It is easy to proclaim that abortion is a sin, but until we as Christians understand our responsibility to the unmarried mother living in poverty, we cannot claim the righteousness of God. While many Christians claim that the poor alone are responsible for their condition, we must face the fact that this is a decidedly *American* opinion, based on a decidedly *American* value; it does not reflect the values of the Bible. Here is a case in which the lure of the world is at work. James plainly teaches that we are to care for the poor. Some might claim that he intended such generosity only for others within the Christian community, but the teaching of the Old Testament concerning care for the alien and of Jesus concerning the neighbor weighs heavily to the other side.

Julian the Apostate, emperor of Rome from A.D. 361–363, was the nephew of Constantine the Great. His immediate family was murdered in dynastic struggles, and his uncle forced the young Julian to learn Christian doctrine as a child. This left him with a lifelong hatred of Christianity. In spite of

---

35. See Phil Taylor, "Bad Actors," *Sports Illustrated* (January 30, 1995), 18–23. Taylor describes the case of Derrick Coleman, who during the 1994–1995 season earned $7.5 million with the New Jersey Nets and refused to comply with the team dress code while traveling. In anticipation of the fines he knew he would incur, he smugly presented his coach with a blank check.

36. Tim Kurkjian, "Public Enemy No. 1," *Sports Illustrated* (October 14, 1996), 28–35.

this, he conceded that the Christians (he always referred to them as "Galileans," in order to point out the obscure origin of the faith) were marked by great generosity. "It is disgraceful that, when no Jew ever has to beg, and the impious Galileans support not only their own poor but ours as well, everyone can see that our own people do not receive aid from us."[37] There is no doubt that James would have us avoid moral filth that is personal. But he leaves precious little room for us to claim that corporate responsibility is not included.

But there is another reason James counsels the avoidance of moral filth. In 1:15 he exposed us to the idea that sin can grow and flourish as the corrosive mirror image of spiritual growth. Indeed, one of the curious paradoxical truths about sin is that while it pollutes and destroys, it also propagates itself. One lie often leads to another; children of abusive alcoholics often marry people who become abusive alcoholics; persons with AIDS at times knowingly spread the disease. A former student of mine is the child of divorced parents, and he found himself trapped because his feuding parents manipulated him so that no matter what he did, he could please only one of them at a time. While he found the behavior of his parents distressing, it also produced in him the same tendency to manipulation. Sin gives rise to sin. To treat it as trivial is wholly to misunderstand the teaching of James.

Look into the mirror of God's Word. James provides for us the picture of the mirror of the Word; he instructs us to gaze at this mirror and then to remember the image. But we are quite adept at forgetting that image. We commonly deceive ourselves in a variety of ways. The great psychologist Carl Rogers believed that most people "despise themselves, regard themselves as worthless and unlovable."[38] While it is certainly true that many people suffer the crippling effects of an unrealistically low self-esteem, research seems to support the conclusion opposite to that offered by Rogers: Most people view themselves far more positively than reason would allow.

Often this takes the form of a fairly benign and healthy optimism. Neil Weinstein, a researcher at Rutgers University, has discovered that college students rate themselves far more likely than their peers to get a good job, own a house, and make a good living, and far less likely than their peers to get cancer, get divorces, or be fired.[39] In survey after survey at least 90 percent of busi-

---

37. Julian the Apostate, *Letters*, 22.430.

38. Carl R. Rogers, "Reinhold Niebuhr's *The Self and the Dramas of History*: A Criticism," *Pastoral Psychology*, 9 (1958): 15–17; quoted in David G. Meyers, *The Pursuit of Happiness: Who Is Happy—And Why* (New York: William Morrow, 1992), 110.

39. See Meyers, *The Pursuit of Happiness*, 27. Meyers has drawn upon a number of articles published by Weinstein.

ness managers and college professors rate their performance as superior to that of their peers. In Australia 86 percent of people rate their job performance as above average, while only 1 percent rate theirs as below average.[40]

At times, however, our ability to lie to ourselves becomes corrosive of others. Some years ago a friend of mine revealed that he felt persecuted at work. Apart from the disease I feel with his appropriation of the term "persecuted" to refer to an employment situation (we live in a world rife with human rights abuses, after all), I cannot help but think he deluded himself. His superiors at work decided to convene a committee to determine strategies that might strengthen this office. This investigation he viewed as proof of "persecution." Yet at the initial meeting my friend was made secretary of this committee, and his supporter and supervisor was named chairperson. When I pointed out to him that this hardly seemed evidence of a secret strategy bent on persecuting him, my friend laughed and replied, "Now that I think about it, you are right. I guess I was not seeing things clearly." His inability to see the situation with clarity placed him in danger of unfairly maligning others.

Of course such myopia is endemic to the human situation. We find ourselves tainted by original sin; we possess a bent and tendency to evil. Saint Augustine said that until we are redeemed in Christ, we are not free to do right.[41] This has been described by the memorable phrase *non posse non peccare,* "not able not to sin." Even the best of us carry good and evil as partners within. Thomas Jefferson, whose elegiac words "all men are created equal" stand as among the finest ever penned on human dignity, was a slave owner. Martin Luther, the great exponent of the grace of God, was an anti-Semite. The list of respected pastors who break their marriage vows and in so doing break trust with their families and congregations grows longer every day. We are myopic.

James pleads with us to spend time in introspection, in a careful and accurate gaze in the mirror of the Word, before we sally forth into the world to offer our ill-considered opinions in the name of Christ. Failure to do so can, at times, result in behavior that is unchristian and has the potential to harm others.

---

40. Ibid., 110–11.
41. Augustine, *Enchiridion,* 30.

James 2:1–13

M Y BROTHERS, AS believers in our glorious Lord Jesus
Christ, don't show favoritism. ²Suppose a man
comes into your meeting wearing a gold ring and
fine clothes, and a poor man in shabby clothes also comes in.
³If you show special attention to the man wearing fine clothes
and say, "Here's a good seat for you," but say to the poor man,
"You stand there" or "Sit on the floor by my feet," ⁴have you
not discriminated among yourselves and become judges with
evil thoughts?

⁵Listen, my dear brothers: Has not God chosen those who
are poor in the eyes of the world to be rich in faith and to
inherit the kingdom he promised those who love him? ⁶But
you have insulted the poor. Is it not the rich who are exploiting you? Are they not the ones who are dragging you into
court? ⁷Are they not the ones who are slandering the noble
name of him to whom you belong?

⁸If you really keep the royal law found in Scripture, "Love
your neighbor as yourself," you are doing right. ⁹But if you
show favoritism, you sin and are convicted by the law as law-
breakers. ¹⁰For whoever keeps the whole law and yet stumbles
at just one point is guilty of breaking all of it. ¹¹For he who
said, "Do not commit adultery," also said, "Do not murder." If
you do not commit adultery but do commit murder, you have
become a lawbreaker.

¹²Speak and act as those who are going to be judged by the
law that gives freedom, ¹³because judgment without mercy
will be shown to anyone who has not been merciful. Mercy
triumphs over judgment!

Original Meaning

THE FIRST CHAPTER of James is in some ways an
extended multilayered introduction to the entire
letter. With this completed, James now turns his
attention to a detailed discussion of one of the
major themes already placed on the table, that of wealth and charity. Here
he issues a warning against showing favoritism to the wealthy and display-

ing a belittling attitude toward the poor. Such favoritism mirrored the standards of the surrounding culture and ignored the essentially egalitarian tone of the Christian gospel. It is an obvious example of the failure to "keep oneself from being polluted by the world" (1:27).

In issuing this warning James builds on what has already been said (1:9–11) and constructs a foundation for the strong teaching found in James 4 and 5. Two possible settings are usually held up as the chief options for the occasion of this teaching: (1) James has in mind a public worship service in which the church has been guilty of currying favor with the wealthy in the broader community;[1] or (2) he has in mind a church court, and his warning is against finding in favor of the wealthy simply because their fine clothes and other accouterments of wealth have left a positive impression.[2] Any decision here rests largely on the interpretation of verse 6: "Are they [the rich] not the ones who are dragging you into court?"

The section is also marked by the diatribe form. This rhetorical/literary device is marked by the creation of an "opponent," who engages the author in a question and answer dialogue; in most cases the positions are exaggerated for clarity and drama. But in the diatribe form we are also to recognize actual situations—in this case, a concrete situation in the church. James may not be quoting any specific individual, but all in the church would recognize a general description of numerous specific situations in the life of their own community.

Finally, there is a clear association with the Matthean Gospel tradition. Like Jesus in Matthew, James pronounces a blessing on the poor (Matt. 5:3; James 2:5), issues a warning to the wealthy (Matt. 19:23–24; James 2:6–7), and warns against judging instead of showing mercy (Matt. 6:14–15; James 2:13). All of this speaks to an awareness on the part of James to the Jesus tradition. Further, the form in which James presents this material indicates that he had access to it at a very early date.

The general theme of 2:1–13 is that favoritism is not to be allowed in the Christian community, for it is antithetical to the gospel. The thought of James here is carried forward by three points. (1) James employs the image of a public service of the church, in which there is a temptation to relate to visitors or newcomers based on their dress (2:1–4). This adherence to the standards of the culture is unacceptable, says James. He defends his position on two grounds, which form the second and third points of this section. (2) Verses 5–7 form an intriguing argument from experience, in which

---

1. Among many who opt for this line of interpretation, see James Adamson, *The Epistle of James*, 105–6.
2. See Peter H. Davids, *The Epistle of James*, 105–10; Ralph P. Martin, *James*, 57–59.

James points out that the church is attempting to ape the standards of the very culture that oppresses it; such an attempt is inherently foolhardy. (3) In verses 8–13, James defends his position by way of a biblical argument.

No Favoritism Based on Appearance (2:1–4)

JAMES BEGINS WITH his typical warm address, "My brothers." He is about to combat an attitude and assumption that glorified the public expression of hierarchy and spawned displays of favoritism in the church. By addressing his readers in this manner, he eschews reference to his own high status and instead makes himself one of them. The object of his concern is "favoritism" (*prosopolempsia*). The root of this idea is tied to the Hebrew term *nasa' panim*, which means "lifting up the face." The phrase thus has its origin in the Old Testament, particularly the LXX,[3] and has overtones of the unjust favoritism granted to the powerful at the expense of others, often on the part of evil judges (see Ps. 82:2; Prov. 18:5; Mal. 2:9). As Laws notes, this is an attitude completely uncharacteristic of God.[4]

Whether in church, in the hearing of a legal case, or in some unknown context, the recipients of this letter had shown favoritism to those displaying the accouterments of wealth. If we may take 2:14–26 as linked to this passage,[5] it seems likely that this Christian community had accepted the mere profession of faith as sufficient not only for entrance, but also for the maintenance of a position of good standing. As he warned earlier, James argues that the true Christian life consists of a growing awareness of the word planted within and a concomitant change in life decisions. James urges a faith that is more than a mere profession—one that results in deeds. The particular expression of the position in view here is a double error: (1) to think one can win favor by a display of wealth, and (2) to allow oneself to be impressed by such a display. Both are examples of folly.

The genitive phrase *tes doxes* ("our glory/glorious") poses an interesting problem. The structure is marked by an unwieldy series of genitives. The phrase may be translated "faith in the glory of our Lord Jesus Christ"; "faith in our Lord of glory, Jesus Christ" (so the KJV and ASV); "faith in our Lord Jesus Christ, the Glory"[6]; the interesting suggestion of Adamson, "faith in the Lord

---

3. James H. Ropes, *The Epistle of St. James*, 185.

4. Sophie Laws, *The Epistle of James*, 93.

5. A strong case in favor is made by C. Burchard, "Zu Jakobus 2,14–26," *ZNW* 71 (1980): 28–30.

6. This position is championed by Sophie Laws, *The Epistle of James*, 95–97, who argues, quite rightly, that the intent of James is to show that Jesus is a theophany, a "manifestation of the presence of God."

Jesus Christ, our Glory"[7]; or the simplest solution, "faith in our glorious Lord Jesus Christ." The NIV prudently has chosen this last option. In any event it seems clear that in this rare case of Christology in the book of James, Jesus Christ is identified with the *Shekinah*, the visible manifestation of the divine. James believes that in Jesus God is revealed.

Furthermore, Jesus is the object of faith. There is clearly more than a meager gospel here, for Jesus Christ, the very manifestation of God's glory, chose to identify with the poor and the outcasts. On the strength of that model and memory James urges his readers to avoid favoritism, just as did our Lord. In this manner James continues his discussion of the proper way to treat the poor, which he began in 1:27 with his discussion of the widow and the orphan.

James gives a practical illustration[8] of this favoritism in the guise of a question (vv. 2–4). The situation posits the image of two guests at a church meeting. The first is obviously wealthy and not reticent to display that wealth. As in the parable of the prodigal son, the ring is a symbol of wealth and status.[9] The second guest is adorned in the garb of the poor. The two men enter the "meeting." Here another controversy surfaces, for instead of the more usual term *ekklesia*, James here presses into service the term *synagoge*.[10] If James intends "church" here, it is the only such use of the term in the entire New Testament. It is not unreasonable, however, to suppose that an author as idiosyncratic as ours may very well have used the term in this way.

James does not use the word *plousios* ("rich"), which he employed in chapter 1. Instead he merely describes the gold ring and the fine clothing worn

---

7. Adamson, *The Epistle of James*, 102–4. Adamson's argument is impressive, and his solution ought to be considered.

8. The first two words of verse 2 (*ean gar*), which the NIV renders "suppose," could also be translated "for example" or "to illustrate." There is no clear reason to believe that this is merely a hypothetical situation. James is most likely referring to an actual situation in the life of the community.

9. See Luke 15:22. It is probably too optimistic to suggest that the ring here signifies a member of the equestrian order, and this may account for the attempt of Laws to shy away from this position after seeming to endorse it (see her *The Epistle of James*, 98–99). It is not, however, out of the question. Of the 731 inscriptions of Diaspora Judaism found in Italy, seven or perhaps eight refer to "God-fearers," and one of these is a Roman of equestrian rank. See K. G. Kuhn and H. Stegemann, "Proselyten," Paulys *Real-Encyclopädie der classischen Alterthumswissenschaft*—Supplement IX, 1248–83.

10. Adamson (*The Epistle of James*, 105) sees this as evidence of an early date for James, and he may very well be right. However, it should be noted that later Christian writers could use "synagoge" to refer to Christian meetings (for example, Ignatius, *Letter to Polycarp*, 4.2). He further argues that the person greeting the newcomers may be a Christian version of the Jewish *hazzan*, the usher in the synagogue. Adamson envisions an early Christian-Jewish synagogue service as the setting, perhaps in Galilee.

by the individual. Davids suggests that this is a cicumlocutionary device for referring to wealthy Christians, and he apparently believes that the use of *plousios* in verses 5 and 6 refers to rich non-Christians.[11] The poor man (*ptochos*) is dressed in shabby (*rhyparos*) clothes.[12] What little we know of ancient mercantilism suggests that all but the wealthy wore homemade clothing. There is no reason to doubt that this was the case in Palestine. One of the clearest markers of status in the Roman world was attire.

According to verse 3, the man with the symbols of wealth is ushered to a fine seat, while the poor person is ordered to stand, or to sit, at the feet of the usher. As Martin points out,[13] the wealthy person must be a Christian, as the proper fashion to treat pagans would hardly have occasioned such division. The point is that it makes no sense to show favoritism to wealthy Christians just because of their wealth. After all, it is wealth and status that grants to non-Christians the ability to oppress the church. It makes no sense for Christians to show favoritism based solely on factors that on other occasions are used to exploit Christians.

Davids points out that the two people are unfamiliar with the meeting, or they would have no need to be directed to these positions.[14] He finds the solution of W. B. Ward satisfying, specifically that the situation in view is a church-court modeled on that of the Jewish synagogue's *bet-din*.[15] While this is an intriguing thesis, there is hardly enough evidence to support it.

In verse 4 James asks: "Have you not discriminated among yourselves and become judges with evil thoughts?" If his readers grant the wealthy man a place of privilege but the poor man a mongrel seat, James insinuates that they are guilty of being an evil judge. This last charge confirms our view of *prosopolempsia* in 2:1. Ward[16] quotes the Babylonian Talmud, *Shebuoth* 31a, as a parallel, "How do we know that, if two come to court, one clothed in rags and the other in fine raiment worth a hundred manehs, they should say to him, 'Either dress like him, or dress like you'?" From the *Midrash Raboth* Ward quotes R. Ishmael,[17] "If before a judge two men appear for judgment, one rich and the another poor, the judge should say to the rich man, 'Either dress in the same manner as he is dressed, or clothe him as you are clothed.'" Nor is abuse only the result of conscious resolve or clear action. The abuse of the

---

11. Davids, *The Epistle of James*, 108.

12. This is the same term used in Zech. 3:3–4 to describe the filthy clothes worn by Joshua the high priest, symbolic of the sin of the people.

13. Martin, *James*, 61.

14. Davids, *The Epistle of James*, 109.

15. W. B. Ward, "Partiality in the Assembly: James 2:2–4," *HTR* (62, 1969): 87–97.

16. Ibid., 89–90.

17. Ibid., 89.

poor can be passive and may be seen in the total lack of regard the wealthy show to them. In the Roman world the poor were faceless nothings in the eyes of the wealthy.

James's question in verse 4 implies that the known and accepted norm within the Christian community was egalitarian. As the Bridging Contexts section will make clear, such an ethic stands in stark contrast with the surrounding culture. Given the fact that James is soon to refer to Leviticus 19:18, it is possible, as Laws argues,[18] that James has in mind Leviticus 19:15: "Do not pervert justice; do not show partiality to the poor or favoritism to the great, but judge your neighbor fairly." But to insist on such a fine point is neither prudent nor necessary. The Old Testament affords no shortage of passages with a similar message.

It also seems likely that the discrimination within the church here refers to an acceptance of cultural standards by some, but a rejection of those standards by another group in the church in favor of the egalitarian social norms of the gospel. James has already used the term "double-minded" in 1:7 to describe the individual with the divided mind, where it referred to someone who could not decide between trust in God and trust in the world. Here he applies the same idea to the entire church, and James uses it here for the same reasons. It is easy to see that poor church members would sense common cause with other poor people who were harassed by those with wealth and power. The powerful and wealthy in the first century were accustomed to special treatment—precisely the sort of favoritism that James here decries.[19] It was not without merit that Jesus spoke of the difficulty of a rich man entering the kingdom of heaven (Matt. 19:23).

The Wisdom of Experience Is Against Favoritism (2:5–7)

AS WAS THE case in 1:16, 19, James links strong teaching and harsh words with the term *agapetoi* ("beloved"). Ever the pastor, James conveys a stern message with the timbre and tones of gentle tenderness. James buttresses his case by employing an experiential argument. "Listen, my dear brothers: Has not God chosen those who are poor in the eyes of the world to be rich in faith and to inherit the kingdom he promised those who love him?" This question balances others concerning the wealthy (vv. 6–7) and seems to suggest a diatribe style.

---

18. Laws, *The Epistle of James*, 102.

19. Cicero made his name through the successful prosecution of Verres, a former governor of Sicily who, as was common, extorted money from his subjects. Only the overpowering talent of Cicero led to the unusual outcome, the verdict of guilty. See Cicero, *Verrine Orations*.

In choosing this line of attack James draws upon the Jesus tradition, developing a case not dissimilar to that used by Paul in 1 Corinthians 1. In Luke 6:20[20] Jesus proclaims, "Blessed are you who are poor, for yours is the kingdom of God," and Paul declares that the wisdom of God appears as foolishness when seen through the lens of the wisdom of the world (1 Cor. 1:18–29). Furthermore, standing prominently in the background is the Hebrew belief that the poor were especially dear to God. The phraseology of James also draws on belief in God's choosing of certain persons and peoples. God chose Israel (Deut. 4:37), and he chose the Gentiles to be the mission field for Paul (Acts 15:7). According to James, God has chosen for himself the poor.

The word James uses for "poor" (*ptochos*) had by the late first century acquired the sense of the poor who put their trust in God and not in (the hope for) material wealth. Ernst Bammel quotes R. Akiba as having said, "Beautiful is the poverty of the daughter of Jacob like a red necklace on the neck of a white horse."[21] Bammel notes that the term had come to posses a range of closely related meanings, such as "the righteous who possess authentic faith," "the objects of God's actions," and persons who were almost God's "comrades as he is about his task."[22] Thus, for James the contrast is stronger than simply between rich and poor; it has to do with those who trust in God and with those whose trust in God is mixed with a trust in the standards of the world—standards that seem perpetually hostile to him and his designs.

The phrase "to be rich in faith" indicates that these poor, unlike the rich, not only have "true riches" here in this life, but also eschatological riches in that theirs is the kingdom. James makes explicit what Luke leaves implicit in Luke 6:20: He lays out for us the proposition that it is not poverty alone that issues forth in this inheritance, but rather the faith that poverty germinates. The grammar and vocabulary clearly describe that group in the church that, like the individual of undivided mind in chapter 1, will receive the crown of life promised to those who love God. James thus links the poor in the church with the poor in chapter 1 and with the poor in general, some of whom when visiting the Christian community experienced the same shabby treatment they received in the world at large. For James this is a tragedy.[23]

In spite of the principles outlined by Jesus (and Paul), which James expects his readers to have known, the community has "insulted" the poor (2:6). The

---

issue is not so much the treatment given the wealthy person, nor is there any hint that James believes membership in the church should be reserved for the materially poor. The issue is the uneven quality of the treatment, especially since it falls along the same status lines as was current in Roman culture. The word for "insulted" is derived from *atimao*, a term used for oppressing the poor in the LXX (Prov. 14:21).

This insult is rendered all the more unbelievable in that by favoring the rich, some in the church are favoring the very class of people who seek to harm the church, for it is the wealthy and powerful who drag Christians to court (v. 6) and slander the name of Christ (v. 7). James levels three accusations at the wealthy: oppression, legal persecution, and blasphemy. While almost all commentators wish to see the wealthy who "drag" Christians into court as outside the church, there are several reasons for preferring a different view. Martin's comment that the fashion in which pagans are to be treated would hardly launch such divisive energies is well taken. Further, note James's frequent use of "my brothers." Finally, the close association of the three charges seems to point to the identification of the wealthy as Christians. There are problems with this view, as the discussion of Ropes[24] concerning the use of the word "blasphemy" demonstrates. However, if we allow "the wealthy" to stand for the rich both inside and outside of the church, then the objections are largely silenced.

The passage is replete with forensic imagery, which explains the predilection of some to see the context for this favoritism as a church court. However, the rich Old Testament background of favoritism "in the gate" (i.e., in legal disputes) seems fully able to account for its use here. More serious is the inference that the wealthy within the broader community were bringing Christians to court. The grammar seems to support three possible interpretations: (1) Christians are dragged into court precisely because they are Christians, and those bringing suit thereby slander the name of Christ; (2) the fact that some Christians are in court, perhaps because they owe wealthy people money, is a cause for the population at large to slander the name of Christ; or (3) if the situation is wealthy Christians bringing suit against poor Christians, this has caused slander to be attached to the name of Christ.

While this last option parallels the thought of 1 Corinthians 6:1–11, it is the least likely grammatically. Either of the first two options is possible. The wealthy, Christian and non-Christian alike, were presumably bringing suit against the poor within the church. Normally in Roman provincial administration the state did not bring charges. Instead, the state relied on citizens

---

24. Ropes, *The Epistle of St. James*, 196.

to bring charges. Such a person was designated by the term *delator*.[25] Some wish to place the writing of James in the context of the reign of Domitian and thereby to assume that Christians were being persecuted precisely because of their faith in Jesus. While this is possible, it is not necessary.

Roman jurisprudence on the local level countenanced the bringing of lawsuits at any time, as Acts and probably Philippians attest. Simply to be brought to trial for any reason (debt, wages, etc.) then, as well as now, was more than a minor inconvenience, and James implies in verse 7 that whatever the charge, at least part of the reason had to do with the faith of the poor. Even if the charges were not in any sense motivated by the faith of the poor, one motivation would have to be the protection of the wealth and status of the rich, which is itself contrary to the gospel. James's point is that to curry favor with anyone simply because of their wealth is fundamentally to misunderstand the gospel and to do injury to the faith.

"Are [the rich] not the ones who are slandering the noble name of him to whom you belong?" (v. 7). The "noble name" must, of course, refer to Christ. In the LXX "the name" was a periphrastic way of referring to God (Deut. 28:10; Isa. 43:7).[26] But for Christians the name of Jesus was substituted.[27] Thus in Acts 2:38 Peter says, "Repent and be baptized, every one of you, in the name of Jesus Christ for the forgiveness of your sins." If indeed James is a document of early composition, the fact that it so clearly substitutes the name of Jesus for God is a strong argument that Christian teaching assumed a high Christology at an early date. Given the little Christology that James affords, it is striking that both here and in the ascription of "glory" to Jesus Christ in 2:1 we have statements of high Christology.

---

25. In A.D. 109/110 Pliny the younger was appointed by his friend, Emperor Trajan, to be his personal legate to the province of Bithynia-Pontus (northern Turkey today). Pliny and Trajan carried on a lively correspondence concerning many different matters of interest to the state. Some of these letters have to do with Christianity, and two of these (Pliny, *Epistulae*, 96—97) are of concern here. In the first Pliny describes Christians and their practices and requests advice on how to handle the matter legally. Trajan responds that Christians should be left alone, unless someone else has brought a charge against them. "You have done well, my dear Pliny, in the examination of those charged with being Christians. . . . These people are not to be hunted out, but if they are brought before you and the charge can be proven, they are to be punished."

26. Scot McKnight (forthcoming) argues that "the Name" was how Jesus referred to God.

27. Hermas, *Similitudes*, 8.1.1; 8.6.4; 9.12.4. This last is particularly significant, because it claims that the name of the "son of God" must be received in order to enter the kingdom of God.

Scripture Is Against Showing Favoritism (2:8–13)

THE THIRD PIECE of James's argument in this section is to show that Scripture does not condone the showing of favoritism. In contrast to the behavior he has just decried, James holds up the "royal law" found in Scripture: "Love your neighbor as yourself" (v. 8). If you follow this, he says, "you are doing right." Like Jesus (Matt. 22:37–40), James argues that obedience to the love commandment of Leviticus 19:18 meets the spirit of the entire Old Testament legal corpus. The use of "love" in the future tense (*agapeseis*) colors the phrase as indicative of James's hope, a command for future action. Showing a favoritism that discriminates against the poor places a person alongside those who slander the name of God. This is teaching fully in step with the prophetic tradition in the Old Testament.[28]

James makes a distinction between the Old Testament law (which he refers to by the simple word *nomos*) and the specifically Christian understanding of Old Testament law, which he marks by a qualifier, such as "the perfect law that gives freedom" (1:25) or "the royal law" (here in 2:8). C. H. Dodd[29] has collected a number of examples of the phrase *basilikos nomos* ("royal law") employed by Greek political thinkers, each of which refers to a law given by a king. This, of course, appeals to adherents of faith in Messiah Jesus. The beauty of this law is that it takes seriously both law and mercy, both sin and grace. God does not excuse us from our sin, but he does forgive us (Rom. 1:20; 2:1). To excuse is to claim that the offending party is not in fact guilty of the offense or to deny the seriousness of the offense. To forgive grants full weight both to guilt and to its seriousness, but it nullifies the guilt.

James goes on to argue that showing favoritism is itself sin, and this behavior convicts one of breaking the royal law (v. 9). His expression "you show favoritism" (*prosopolempteite*) links this verse with 2:1, where the noun form (*prosopolempsia*) appears, and in so doing grants unity to the entire passage. That James regards this sin of favoritism so seriously stands in stark counterpoint with the apparent lack of concern with which the Christian community viewed it. It is possible that the typical view of Hellenistic Judaism with regard to what was central (piety, philanthropy, and righteousness) is here condemned by James as off the mark. The depth of his chagrin and the power of his attack prefigures his later claim (2:11; 4:11–12; 5:5–6) that

---

28. Isaiah 3:14–15 says, "The LORD enters into judgment against the elders and leaders of his people: 'It is you who have ruined my vineyard; the plunder from the poor is in your houses. What do you mean by crushing my people and grinding the faces of the poor?' declares the Lord, the LORD Almighty" (see also 1:16; Amos 5:7; 6:12).

29. C. H. Dodd, *The Bible and the Greeks* (London: Hodder, 1935), 39.

those endorsing practices based on a view that belittles the need to adhere to Leviticus 19:18 are guilty of antinomianism.

In verse 10 James again echoes the timbre of Jesus' teachings when he says that to stumble at just one point of the law is to be guilty in all points. In the teaching of Jesus some parts of the law were of greater import than others, as his teaching on divorce makes clear.[30] In regard to his own understanding of morality (as opposed to the Old Testament law), Jesus held a view similar to James. In Matthew 5:28 Jesus says, for example, "But I tell you that anyone who looks at a woman lustfully has already committed adultery with her in his heart." The point here is that the injunction to love the neighbor as yourself is total: Christians cannot pick and choose who is to be the neighbor or when they are to follow this law.

"For he who said, 'Do not commit adultery,' also said, 'Do not murder.' If you do not commit adultery but do commit murder, you have become a lawbreaker" (v. 11). In what may seem as an odd pairing, James says that to commit murder but not adultery is the same as breaking the entire corpus. These two were not chosen haphazardly, for both represent core issues relative to ethical behavior, specifically the honor we bestow to other human beings. Murder is a clear case of dishonoring the victim, but adultery is as well, because it demonstrates in unmistakable ways that personal gratification is more important than spouse or children or family. It is for these reasons that these two sins are present in the Ten Commandments.

It is possible, of course, that James is speaking directly to the community of Christians to which he was writing, in that both murder and adultery were known there. But it should also be noted that Jesus associated the attitude of discrimination against the poor with murder, and that the Old Testament refers to a failure to adhere to God and his teachings as adultery (Hos. 1). His point seems that this discrimination, which at least some in the church are viewing lightly, or even positively, James equates with the most horrific of sins of which he is aware.

James thus links profession and action (see v. 12). His appeal to judgment is not foreign to the thought of the New Testament. Here is a strong reminder of the true center of the Christian life—the perfect law that is planted within us. It is in actions of self-sacrifice and love for others that the mettle of our faith is demonstrated. In a long passage (Matt. 25:31–46) Jesus makes the claim that the efficacy of faith is demonstrated in acts of mercy (providing for the hungry, the thirsty, the stranger, the ill-clad, the sick, and

---

30. As Wolfhart Pannenberg has shown (Wolfhart Pannenberg, "Revelation and Homosexual Practice," *Christianity Today* (Nov. 11, 1996), 35, 37), Jesus argues that the original intent of God revealed in the Creation accounts take precedence over Mosaic Law.

the prisoner). For both Jesus and James, in other words, the law that is the fulcrum of judgment is the law of love for one's neighbor.

In verse 13 James continues to follow in the Jesus tradition by arguing that for those who do not show mercy, no mercy will be shown. The Old Testament affirms that God is merciful (Ex. 34:5–6) and that people should, therefore, also show mercy to one another (Hos. 6:6). This was a hallmark of the teaching of Jesus (Matt. 5:7; Luke 6:36). A merciful attitude is one of the evidences that a person truly is alive in Christ.

Few commentators argue that the judgment here is eschatological—that is, that one case of showing favoritism condemns the perpetrator to eternal damnation. This seems hardly the point. Rather, James is pointing to the danger of allowing this attitude to grow within both the individual and the church, because if its growth is not retarded and reversed, this attitude will result in a basic thrust of character and will come to dominate future decisions, which will, in fact, affect one's eschatological judgment. It is this total failure to live out the implications of the faith that James sees as evidence of no faith at all—faith without works is dead.

It is significant that James ends on a message of hope: "Mercy triumphs over judgment." God in his mercy forgives even those who have been guilty of such discrimination—and the mercy that an individual shows has the power to grow strong both in the individual and in the ones shown mercy.

Bridging Contexts

WHEN JAMES SPEAKS of "the rich," "the poor," and "favoritism," he is speaking the parlance of social and economic markers. It is a language with which we are familiar. But therein lies a quagmire, a peril to be avoided. For in spite of apparent similarities, the world of James was different from our own in a number of fundamental ways, three of which are: (1) social standing was not nearly as often a function of wealth as it is in our world; (2) there was almost no possibility of social or economic climbing in James's world; (3) the social and economic pyramid in the Roman empire was incredibly steep, with virtually no middle class as we understand that term. Perhaps 8 percent of the population had wealth, another 2 percent were gaining it, and the remaining 90 percent lived in conditions that we might describe as poor. Seneca wrote, "Consider, at the outset, how great a majority are the poor."[31] Before we can move with confidence to application, we must know something of the values and standards of the social world of the Roman empire. A discussion of this social world will constitute the sole focus of this section.

---

31. Seneca, *De Consolatione ad Helviam*, 12.1.

In our world, social status is most often a function of wealth while other factors, such as education and social level at birth, play a secondary role.[32] My brother, sister, and I were the first generation in my family history to attend college. My sister is a surgical nurse, and my brother and I both hold doctoral degrees. In the eyes of our world we advanced "up the ladder," even though our grandparents never finished elementary school. I never cease to be amazed at the reactions of people to me when I am introduced as "Dr. David Nystrom" as opposed to "David Nystrom." Education matters in our culture. My grandmother worked as a domestic, and my grandfathers were blue-collar laborers. Such "social climbing" is not at all remarkable in our world, but it was virtually unheard of in the first century.

The social and economic culture of the Roman empire was marked by a far higher degree of rigidity than is ours. When one speaks of "standing" in the Roman empire, there are three classifications to consider: class, *ordo*, and status. Of these three "class" is the least helpful. In general, sociologists use the term to refer to income level,[33] and Marx used it to speak of the relation of the worker to the means of production.[34] Such a definition is inappropriate to the Roman world, for wealth did not guarantee social status.

Regarding social order (*ordines*), there were three: *ordo senatorius, ordo equester, and ordo decurionum.* (1) The senatorial order consisted of members of the oldest noble Roman families, and their wealth was concentrated in land and agricultural production. Entrance to this order was based on both birth and wealth, with a minimum set by Augustus at one million sesterces. This was the equivalent of 250,000 times the average day's wage of a laborer.

(2) Entrance to the equestrian order was based solely on wealth, with the minimum set at 400,000 sesterces. Equestrians made their fortunes as merchants, bankers, and entrepreneurs, as well as through consortiums that took government contracts to build roads, supply armies, and collect taxes.

In general the members of the *ordo senatorius* had little regard for the equestrians, and they despised everyone else. By the third century B.C. the senate passed legislation making it illegal for senators to engage in commerce, motivated in part by their desire to distance themselves from the equestrians. But as Ramsay MacMullen has demonstrated, the members of these two groups had much in common, for the total number whose income placed them in

---

32. An exception here is race. The United States remains a cultural context in which, as Cornel West has said, race matters.

33. See the discussion of G. E. M. de Ste. Croix, *The Class Struggle in the Ancient Greek World* (London: Duckworth, 1981), 31–69.

34. Among many other references see Karl Marx, *The Eighteenth Brumaire of Louis Bonaparte, VII,* in which Marx claims that economic conditions are chief in defining a class.

the two highest *ordines* amounted to no more than one-tenth of one percent of the population.[35]

To the other 99.9 percent of the empire, an equestrian was a person of uncommon prestige. In the eyes of a senator an equestrian represented "new money," without the niceties that a senatorial upbringing guaranteed. But then senators could afford to claim that money was not a significant factor in determining status. They already had it! To everyone else, money was king. Juvenal wrote:

> Let money carry the day, let the sacred office be given to one who came but yesterday with white feet[36] into our city. For no god is held in such high reverence among us as wealth, even though you, evil money, have no temple of your own as yet.[37]

Juvenal here reveals both a firm belief in the sacred nature of social stratification and the love of money that had, in his view, challenged that stratification. When viewed from below, money was a marker of social prestige in the Roman world. When viewed from above, it was of little value.

(3) The *ordo decurionum* consisted of the local elite, and here wealth was more important than birth. In this order, as with the senators, wealth tended to take the form of land, so in a given city a few families dominated the decurionate over the years.[38] Perhaps as much as 2 percent of the population of the empire was to be found here.

Alongside these official *ordines* was the informal *ordo Augustales*. This *ordo* consisted of persons who for various reasons of birth or status were prevented from entrance into the decurionate. Most were freedmen (former slaves) who had become somewhat well-to-do. This order, while lacking official status, emulated the decurionate in terms of titles and function. Allowing for women and children, this left some 90 percent of the population outside these categories.

The final social category is what we might call "status." In the Roman world of James "status" was determined by a complex miasma of factors. Age, status at birth, birthplace, gender, wealth, citizenship, military career, and occupation were the most significant factors in determining one's status. In general, rural

---

35. Ramsay MacMullen, *Roman Social Relations 50 B.C. to A.D. 284* (New Haven, Conn.: Yale Univ. Press, 1974), 88–89. MacMullen estimates that the equestrians accounted for less than a tenth of one percent of the total population of the empire, and senators for two-thousandths of one percent of the population.

36. The feet of slaves were marked with white chalk before they were to be sold.

37. Juvenal, *Satires*, 1.110–14.

38. See Michael Woloch, "Four Leading Families in Roman Athens," *Historia* 18 (1969): 503–12.

people were viewed as boorish (cf. John 1:46, where Nathaniel offers his opinion on the tiny Galilean hamlet of Nazareth: "Nazareth! Can anything good come from there?"), provincials were viewed less favorably than persons living in Rome, new money was less appealing than old money, the freeborn were considered better than the freed.[39] Of course, perspective mattered a great deal. To an impoverished member of the urban poor, a wealthy freedman was more enviable than a member of a senatorial family that had lost its fortune.[40]

With the book of James we enter the world of Roman provinces. The local decurions, whose wealth most likely paled beside that of Roman senators, were nonetheless persons of great power and prestige in their own community, and they would have been viewed that way by the church located there. Cities normally had a cadre of 100 decurions,[41] and from this group a number were selected each year to hold different city offices. Competition for the decurionate was fierce.[42] Membership afforded special forensic treatment, but there were special demands too.[43] This class, for example, was expected to provide the corn supply for the city, to pay for the construction of public projects such as buildings and roads, and to maintain public order.

When elected to serve in a public office, such men[44] were expected to pay a fee, designated by the term *summae honorariae*. This amount, like the minimum amount necessary to qualify for the decurionate, varied with the office in question and the population of the city.[45] These and other wealthy persons also paid for public works projects out of their own pockets (e.g., building of temples, public baths, paving of streets, and the city tax bill). Such voluntary payments were generally known as *munera*. A third type of payment were the *sportula*, a term that seems originally to have designated the daily payment a patron made to his clients.[46] Other kinds of *sportulae* included cash

---

39. Martial (*Epigrams*, 3.33) even went so far as to say that sexual relations with a free woman were to be preferred to those with a former slave, and these were to be preferred to those with a slave.

40. But not to other senators. Juvenal tells us of a wealthy *libertus*, the owner of five shops, who feels he is regarded as nothing compared to a senator, now destitute, forced into tending sheep (*Satires*, 1.102—6).

41. See R. Duncan-Jones, *The Economy of the Roman Empire* (Cambridge: Cambridge Univ. Press, 1982), 286—87. In the east the number was more fluid, ranging from 30 to 500.

42. See Dio Chrysostom, *Orationes*, 40.13—14.

43. See A. H. M. Jones, *The Greek City* (Oxford: Clarendon, 1949), 180; P. Garnsey, *Social Status and Legal Privilege in the Roman Empire* (Oxford: Clarendon, 1970), 84, 224—25.

44. There are a few cases of women serving on a local *decurionate*, but only in very small towns. This has led to speculation that women were allowed this honor only as a last resort.

45. See Pliny, *Epistulae*, 10, 112—13.

46. Martial, *Epigrams*, 10.116; relates that it was common for patrons in Rome to pay their clients about six sesterces a day, the rough equivalent of the figure necessary for an aver-

gifts at marriages, coming-of-age ceremonies, and other public functions. Another significant example was the public feast. It was not uncommon for a wealthy person to hold a public feast for the entire city, though the quality and amount of the food received, as well as when the meal was received, depended on social status.

The epigraphic evidence from Italy records some 277 *sportula* rates and reveals clear discrimination in favor of the powerful. Decurions received twelve sesterces, the *Augustales* eight sesterces, and ordinary citizens four sesterces. In most cases women were excluded, and in cases in which they were present, they generally received less than the men.[47] It is not unlikely that this accounts for the aberrant Eucharist practices against which Paul spoke in 1 Corinthians 11:17–22, as well as the flagrant displays of favoritism and toadyism decried by James.

One might very well ask, "What could have induced these people to pay for so much?" The answer is glory and honor. Before the establishment of the *pax Romana*, glory and honor could be won on the battlefield or through the arena of local politics. But with the establishment of Roman rule in the East, these chief routes to favorable reputation were sealed off. There were no armed conflicts to speak of, and virtually all significant political decisions were made in Rome. The result was a tightly restricted field of options, the surest being to spend money, with the proviso that a plaque or similar device would reveal the name of the generous benefactor for all to read, and for years to come.

The sociology of the Roman empire, particularly as experienced by urbanites, served this need. It was marked by a complex web of patronage systems and of the support of benefactors. Recipients (the "clients") of the largesse of benefactors were expected to demonstrate their dependence on and thankfulness to their "patrons" by public displays that often included flattery. Persons of modest wealth might engage in only private munificence, binding to themselves a group of former slaves[48] and freedmen. The wealthiest engaged in public munificence. They paved streets, built public buildings, sponsored political campaigns,[49] or even manumitted large numbers of slaves, all in the hope that glory would be brought to their

---

age meal. The term originally designated the basket in which patrons would place gifts for the clients.

47. See the tables on pp. 184–86 of R. Duncan-Jones, *The Economy of the Roman Empire*.

48. Upon manumission former slaves normally became the clients of their former masters.

49. Ramsay MacMullen, *Roman Social Relations 50 B.C. to A.D. 284*, 125, quotes a political slogan preserved in Pompeii: "The united street neighbors urge the election of So and So for magistrate. He will provide a four-pair gladiatorial show." Election to an office brought status and the opportunity for its further enhancement.

names.[50] Those whose birth precluded membership in the local decurionate, such as the *Augustales,* behaved similarly. Many families throughout
the empire spent themselves into poverty in just this way. Plutarch[51] has
given us this explanation:

> Most men think themselves robbed of their wealth if they are pre-
> vented from displaying it, and that display of it is made in the super-
> fluities of life, not in the necessities of life.

Nor was this phenomenon restricted to individuals. Cities vied with one
another over titles[52] and the magnificence of public works. In Bithynia-Pontus
Pliny found city after city mired in public debt because of the number and
enormity of extravagant but poorly executed public building programs.[53]
Juvenal said that *Pecunia* (the love of money) was a goddess. But she was a vas-
sal, a minion in the service of another goddess, *Philotomia* (the love of status).

In our world love of money and love of status are equally powerful and
pernicious lures. Americans dig themselves deeper and deeper into credit
card debt every year, and there are ever higher numbers of bankruptcies
filed. We spend our money on wants that we take to be needs: a flashier car,
a swimming pool, new designer clothes. Advertisements tell us to purchase
automobiles, houses, and even toilet paper with an eye to impressing others.
This trend has even infected the church. There is a line where excellence in
church architecture, facilities, and programming becomes excessive opulence, which closes the door of the church to some, who are made to feel
unwelcome, while those on the fortunate side of the social spectrum feel at
home. This line is different in every area and requires a sensitive heart to discern the wisdom of God.

For the vast majority of the population of the Roman empire who could
not seek glory by these avenues, there were other options. Trade associations
and private clubs (*collegia*) were established, bearing extravagant names: the
Universal Sacred Consistory of Linen Weavers, the Most August Work-

---

50. During his reign Augustus felt compelled to pass legislation limiting the number of
slaves one could manumit (the *Lex Fufia Caninia* of 2 B.C.), the minimum age (set at 20 by
the *Lex Aelia Sentia* of A.D. 4), and the favorable conditions under which slaves were manumitted (the *Lex Iunia* of A.D. 19).

51. Plutarch, *Marcus Cato,* 18.3.

52. In the middle decades of the second century A.D., Smyrna and Pergamum lusted after
the title "First and Greatest Metropolis of Asia," which had historically been used of Ephesus. The Emperor Antoninus confirmed the right of Ephesus to the title, and Pergamum
had to be content with "Metropolis of Asia and the first city to be Twice Temple-Warden"
(Ramsay MacMullen, *Enemies of the Roman Order* [Cambridge: Harvard Univ. Press, 1966], 186;
D. Magie, *Roman Rule in Asia Minor* [Princeton: Princeton Univ. Press, 1950], 1496, n. 18).

53. See, for example, Pliny, *Epistulae,* 10, 39.

Center of Wool-Washers, the Holy College of Dyers, the Sacred Craft of Linen-Workers.[54] These associations were organized along the lines of municipal administrations, with offices bearing titles that mimicked those of city offices.[55] Membership in such an association allowed a chance to experience the semblance of power and prestige, a feeling heightened by the exalted but meaningless nomenclature adopted.[56]

Frequently persons of wealth who had no other avenue for its display became the patron or patroness of a civic or religious *collegium*. Women in particular chose this route. It is not unlikely that many of the women we encounter in the New Testament fit this pattern.[57] To the Roman world, the Christian church was but another of these *collegia*, another avenue that afforded the wealthy an opportunity to demonstrate their superiority over others. Such a person would expect to be accorded the greatest respect during the meetings of the group.

The pervasive nature of this hunger for prestige is difficult to overemphasize. Cicero said, "Rank must be maintained." Four centuries later in the provincial city of Antioch the same sentiment was expressed by Libanus: "Whatever one's rank, it must be maintained."[58] Everyone knew their place. The Roman fascination with ossified social status helps to explain the desire to make clear one's own superiority, and this desire is mirrored in James 2:1—13. This was a society with few positions of real authority and an insatiable thirst for the sense of power.

The legal and literary sources for the period speak of the difference between the *honestiores* and the *humiliores*, "the great" and "the humble." In the first category were found the members of the three leading *ordines*. Everyone else, with the rare exceptions of those who had made money, considered themselves *humiliores*. Sallust has left for us a typical example: "In every city those who are poor envy the best citizens."[59] Aelius Aristides praised Rome for this distinction:

> But the following is easily the most worthy of consideration and admiration in your government, the magnanimity of your conception, because there is nothing else like it. For you have divided into two parts

---

54. See Ramsay MacMullen, *Roman Social Relations* 50 B.C. to A.D. 284, 76.

55. A. H. M. Jones, *The Roman Economy*, ed. P. A. Brunt (Oxford: Blackwell, 1974), 44.

56. In a similar fashion, Fred Flintstone and Barney Rubble, in the television cartoon *The Flintstones*, gained a measure of self-respect through membership in the Sacred Order of the Water Buffalo.

57. Such as Joanna and Susanna (Luke 8:3), and Chloe (1 Cor. 1:11).

58. Cicero, *Pro Cnaeo Plancio*, 15; Libanus, *Orationes*, 48.31. Pliny agreed, speaking of the need to "preserve the distinctions between classes" (*Epistulae*, 9.5).

59. Sallust, *Bella Catalinae*, 37.4.

all the men in your empire—with this expression I have indicated the entire inhabited world—and everywhere you have made citizens all those who are the more accomplished, noble and powerful people, even if they retain their native ways, while the rest you have made the subjects and the governed.[60]

This was reinforced by another important feature of life in the Roman world, the static nature of the economy that made social climbing almost impossible. There were exceptions, as we have seen already in the cases of the equestrians in Rome, but there were also exceptions within the provinces.[61] One sterling example was Corinth, destroyed by the Romans in 146 B.C., but repopulated with Roman citizens by Julius Caesar in 44 B.C. This meant that there was no old elite in Corinth, so it was ripe for social climbing. But these cases are the extraordinary. Barely 2 percent of the population found social climbing a possibility. In a local urban center, then, the elite consisted of members of the families of wealth and those fortunate enough to be engaged in local or provincial commerce. It was not unusual for freedmen to engage in commerce, and their status at birth precluded them from being ascribed honor by the freeborn wealthy. Such persons were perfect candidates to become the benefactors of a religious *collegia*.

It is often asserted today that the New Testament world was an "honor and shame" society, and this is no doubt a helpful (but limited) insight. "Honor," as defined by the cultural anthropologist Bruce Malina, is the value of a person in his or her own eyes, plus the value of that person in the social group.[62] Malina defines "honor" by three boundary markers, "power, sexual status, and religion, and where they come together, what they mark off, is something called *honor*."[63] "Power" is the ability to control the behavior of others; "sexual status" is the set of duties regarding behavior expected of men and women; "religion" is the "attitude and behavior one is expected to follow relative to those who control one's existence."[64] Honor is the socially proper behavior in the area where these three boundary markers intersect.

Honor could be gained in two ways: It could be ascribed (as through inheritance), or it could be acquired. Those considering themselves "noble,"

---

60. Aelius Aristides, *Orationes*, 26.59.

61. The family of Plancia Magna established themselves as a leading family in Perge within a century of moving there. See M. T. Boatwright, "Plancia Magna of Perge: Women's Roles and Status in Roman Asia Minor," *Women's History and Ancient History*, ed. S. Pomeroy (Chapel Hill, N.C.: Univ. of North Carolina Press, 1991), 249–72.

62. Bruce Malina, *The New Testament World: Insights From Cultural Anthropology* (Atlanta: John Knox, 1984), 27.

63. Ibid., 26.

64. Ibid., 26–27.

or aspiring to that status, would be vitally interested in ways to enhance the clarity of social stratification. They would seek groups in which, relative to others, they had "high status," and they would seek to highlight the potency of those status markers. For such persons, a local Christian church might appear a prime field for cultivation, an opportunity for people to consider themselves among the *honestiores*.

In a variety of ways our culture is reminiscent of that known by James. Both cultures are sick and dangerous: sick because they tend towards extreme self-aggrandizement, and dangerous because the church seems all too willing to fall prey to culture. The fascination with wealth and status is all too prominent in America. Our cultural heroes include the wealthy by virtue of talent or accident, such as Donald Trump, Ross Perot, Michael Jordan, Bette Middler, and Demi Moore. The advertising industry glorifies wealth in the pursuit of products from automobiles to disinfectants.

This fascination is also prominent in American evangelicalism. I spoke recently at a church that in its eighty-year history had relocated four times, from the urban center to ever newer suburbs. Today the church owns a beautiful ten-acre facility, complete with sanctuary, gym, kitchen, Christian education space, and a generous surrounding lawn. The church is further surrounded by homes worth half a million dollars, sporting Cadillac, BMW, and Lexus automobiles, many of which were to be found in the parking lot the Sunday I preached. On that Sunday the chairperson announced a capital fund drive the church was about to launch. While he was at the lectern, I could not help noticing (nor, I doubt, could anyone else) the enormous diamond ring he wore. Everything about this gentleman said "money."

Money is not inherently evil, of course; but if it is used as a measure of personal worth, either consciously or unconsciously, then we have fallen prey to the standards of our culture. In ways subtle and obvious we do crave status and wealth. We are also overly impressed by other markers of social standing, such as attire, profession, and even social polish. James would warn us against the subtle power these cultural markers may have over the Christian community.

These differences in the cultural patterns of the first century and our own will affect the way we read the three broad points James has outlined (the display of favoritism based on status, the attempt to ape the standards of the surrounding culture, and the biblical argument). Our world provides far more opportunities for achieving status and influence than did James's world. This means that a proper investigation of the contemporary significance of the passage must include our culture to uncover the many and various ways it grants status to individuals and to groups. What James has to say concerning the wealthy should be read as applying to this more diverse group in our own culture. In addition, the church of James's society was tempted to embrace certain cultural patterns—some of them obvious, some more subtle. The contemporary church falls prey to the same tendency, but of course the cultural patterns in our century are not necessarily the same as those faced by James. A proper discussion of the contemporary significance of this passage seeks to discern some of the dangers inherent in our culture that the church today, like the church of James's day, might be tempted to embrace.

JAMES HAS PRESENTED us with a picture of a church under the influence of the surrounding culture. In emulation of the prevailing Roman social norms the church was beginning to be marked by favoritism and social stratification. Some in the church seemed blissfully unaware of the danger. Others, perhaps, saw the problem, but did not understand its full gravity. To them James has outlined a holistic ethic: to stumble at one point of the law is to break all of it. This is the message that must be applied to the contemporary situation. In the pursuit of this task the following discussion will focus on four points: (1) Our culture is sick and dangerous. (2) Our culture is dangerous and debilitating in ways we do not always expect or realize. (3) The problem of favoritism, which had nearly crippled the church of James, is apparent in our own churches. (4) Like James we must pursue a holistic model of church life.

Our culture is sick and dangerous. As noted in the previous section, the Roman world that James knew was marked by largely ossified social stratification, combined with a social system in which the poor bestowed honor on the wealthy through public displays. The Roman historian Livy (59 B.C.– A.D. 17) commented on this development: "Wealth has made us greedy, and self-indulgence has brought us, through every form of sensual excess, to be, if I may so put it, in love with death both individual and collective."[65] It is a description that many Americans might find chillingly familiar.[66] In his famous 1978 commencement address at Harvard University, Alexander Solzhenitsyn charged that the West, by eliminating God and therefore the sense of accountability and purpose that follows from that belief, had chosen materialism, godlessness, and shallow attempts at freedom and happiness. Any attempt to return to greatness, he said, must begin with the recognition that

---

65. Livy, *History of Rome*, 1.1.

66. I am not here arguing that the decline of Rome in some fashion parallels contemporary America. Rome survived for nearly half a millennia after people like Livy began to speak of its decline.

human life and human nature are at their core spiritual, and therefore human beings have a responsibility to God and to others.

One among a spate of books that catalogues the moral decline in America is *Why America Needs Religion*.[67] A striking feature of the book is that its author, Guenter Lewy, professor emeritus of political science at the University of Massachusetts, is an agnostic. He claims to have begun the book with the intention of refuting the thesis that the decline in the American moral climate can be traced to the modern rejection of theological values, even the rejection of God. But, he says, a "funny thing happened on the way to the completion of this book, which I envisaged as a defense of secular humanism and ethical relativism. Positions which I had always supported turned out to be, on new reflection, far less convincing than I had assumed."[68] Instead, he found himself agreeing with positions and commentators that he had long dismissed.

Lewy continues to believe that moral arrogance and intolerance are to be avoided, but he is far less sanguine about the ability of moral relativism to produce a healthy society. Lewy calls for cooperation between Christians and non-Christians in this task, citing Vatican II, the Protestant theologian Paul Ramsay, the evangelical theologian Carl F. H. Henry, and Robert Bork as others who have issued similar calls.[69] He remains a nontheist, but his call for ethical reform is warmly supportive of the heart of Christian ethical teaching.

> I continue to question the claim pressed by many Christian theologians that they have a hold on moral Truth, yet I find myself in agreement with not a few of their moral positions. . . . The urgent task for believers and nonbelievers alike, I submit, is to replenish the moral capital that was accumulated over many centuries from a unique stock of religious and ethical teachings, a fund of treasure that we have been depleting of late at an alarming rate.[70]

In 2:1–13 James issues an unmistakably strong call to avoid certain aspects of Roman culture, particularly those aspects that supported social and economic stratification. It is vital to note that he is not universal in this condemnation of culture. What he opposes is the spirit of the age, a spirit of self-interest. Likewise, there is much that is dangerous and sick in our culture. But evangelicals should not be too quick to condemn all of culture. There is

---

67. Guenter Lewy, *Why America Needs Religion: Secular Modernity and Its Consequences* (Grand Rapids: Eerdmans, 1996).
68. Ibid., ix–x.
69. Ibid., 141–42.
70. Ibid., xii.

much that is worthwhile and much that can be redeemed. It is easy to issue blanket condemnations of American culture. But such actions and attitudes all too often seal us off from the world James calls us to engage as God's ambassadors. Yet our culture can and does find its way into the church, and some of these intrusions are inimical to its life and health. We may be strong and clear in our opposition to abortion or drug abuse, we may be vocal about the case for prayer in the public schools, but we can also be blind to the subtle ways our culture can shape our churches into an image that is not the image of Christ.

Sometimes cultural influence is not what we expect. Our culture influences us in ways that we neither recognize nor expect. In an article entitled "Hope Dreams," Amy Sherman reviewed a number of books that take as their subject "the other America," that is, life in the urban ghetto.[71] In ways that I find fascinating her article throws a spotlight on facets of culture that we often do not recognize. One of the books she reviewed is *The Ville*, by Greg Donaldson. The book describes what Amy Sherman calls,

> the truncation engendered by the ghetto: the reduction of "being" to "having." This triumph of consumerism emerges in large part from the dominance of television. "The teenagers [in Brownsville] are under-educated in most things," Donaldson says, "but they are connoisseurs of pop culture, ready receptacles for the jingles and scattershot imagery of television. Their speech is drenched in the verbal flotsam of television shows. The police are called Five-O's after Hawaii Five-O. . . . Brand names tyrannize the classrooms; prestige cars are worshiped."
>
> On the street, being a person of "substance" is defined, ironically, as having a certain appearance or image.

In his pursuit of the "appearance" of substance, one young man spent the first $75 he earned in a new job on a beeper, so he could look like a drug dealer. Drug dealers, he believes, are people of "substance" because they have money, women, and material goods. Donaldson calls them "props" and notes that in this corner of America the "props," the incidentals, have become the markers and symbols of "substance," even though there is no "substance" underneath. The young men Donaldson introduces us to call themselves "LoLifes," after the Ralph Lauren Polo shirts they wear as uniforms. They literally believe that "clothes make the man." Donaldson writes, "[The] LoLifes are more an outlaw consumer group than a gang. . . . The young black men of Brownsville indict society by their total belief in it. They trust what they have been told about

---

71. Amy Sherman, "Hope Dreams," *Books and Culture: A Christian Review* (May/June 1996), 3, 31–33.

image, status, competition, hierarchy, and the primacy of self-gratification. Their faith is lethal, mostly to themselves."[72] Donaldson also takes us to prison, where a member of the LoLifes is stripped of his Polo shirt identity, and in our discomfort we are left to conclude that there is little substance to the man.

Sherman wisely comments that the rest of America shares this belief in consumerism, but its heinous debilitating effects are rendered less obvious by the wealth of opportunities not available to persons in the ghetto. Is affluent evangelical America immune to this disease? Sadly, no. Evangelical Christianity is itself portrayed in consumerist terms. "God wants only the best for you. ... Church should make you feel good," says Tammy Faye (Bakker) Messner on the television show *Politically Incorrect*.[73] At what point do the megachurches that dot the American Protestant landscape sell out the gospel in their effort to provide a comfortable, nonthreatening, and familiar environment to the corporate types and aging yuppies that are often their target audience? At what point should our conscience bother us when we see the church chairperson drive off in a BMW or Jaguar?

Such examples of material culture are not inherently evil, as long as there is authentic substance underneath—in this case, spiritual substance. Otherwise, these are just the "props" of our culture. Have wealth and professional accomplishment superseded the exercise of the spiritual disciplines as the prerequisite for leadership in our churches? Several of my friends in the Christian college environment think so. When church architecture consciously mimics the architectural styles of the suburban corporate headquarters of high-tech companies, we have, perhaps, already capitulated. We may draw converts, but unless we combine the beneficial skills of worldly competence with spiritual maturity, the question of precisely to what we have converted people is open. It is possible that Generation X churches, with their passion for "authenticity" in contradistinction to the clear professionalism and color-coordinated outfits that mark Baby Boom churches, may indeed have a point.[74] Of course, Generation X culture has its own pitfalls to avoid.

Many who criticize evangelical corporate flattery are testimony to the eroding effects of our surrounding culture in other ways. The creeping effects of an ideology of antiseptic political and moral relativism can be seen, for example, in those who, without critical biblical reflection, have bought the "I was born this way" argument relative to homosexual practice. Born of a desire to be "nice" and to exercise Christian compassion, they fail to see that the broader application of that principle nullifies all sin. Many men, after all,

---

72. Ibid., 31.
73. Douglas L. Leblanc, "The Mars Hill of Television," *Books and Culture: A Christian Review* (November/December 1996), 14.
74. Steve Rabey, "Pastor X," *Christianity Today* (Nov. 11, 1996), 40, 43.

are "born" with a bent to promiscuity. This internal drive is what Paul calls the "old nature" or the "natural man" (*psychikos*), and what James calls the "evil impulse." Such a person is under the control of the law of sin in the flesh.[75] The New Testament recognizes that it is "natural," but it never argues that "natural" is therefore "right." It is not compassion to treat what the Bible calls sin as something less than what it is.

Nor should we expect biblical truth to be warmly endorsed by our culture. Such truth is not applauded; rather, it is vilified and rejected, as was Jesus. The body of Christ is called to serve our world, not to condemn it (cf. 1 Cor. 5:12—13; James 4:12). The evangelical church has currently fixed its attention on the issue of homosexuality. Justice demands that we recognize inappropriate desires and actions of the heterosexual community along with those of the homosexual community. They are equal in scope and of a piece with each other. We must confront and demonstrate profound concern about our own sin before we condemn the sin of others. In fact, this recognition of our own sinfulness allows us both to recognize sin for what it is and to speak of and confront it with compassion. People with AIDS are the lepers of our day; they need errands run, good meals served, and simple human companionship. Here is an opportunity for the church to walk in the footsteps of its Lord. But the gnawing effects of our surrounding culture become dangerous when we begin to show favoritism or to make decisions based on cultural standards of honor and acceptability.

The peril of favoritism. Our culture influences the evangelical church in a variety of ways that mirror the fashion in which James's church was influenced by his culture. One of the most obvious is the showing of favoritism, embracing certain expectations based on various markers. These markers become solidified in our minds, forming expectations of others that are sealed off from the possibility of change.

The 1957 film *An Affair To Remember,* starring Cary Grant and Deborah Kerr, is a favorite of many. It contains a scene representative of American culture in mid-century, which can be viewed only with discomfort and embarrassment today. The scene involves a number of children of various ethnic groups performing in a combined choir and orchestra. At one point the singing is interrupted, and the only two African-American children on screen move to center stage and perform a tap dance number. There is a proud history to tap, and African-Americans have traditionally been among its most skilled practitioners. But the scene in question is disturbing because the African-American children were present only to fulfill a role that our culture

---

75. See G. B. Caird and L. D. Hurst, *New Testament Theology* (Oxford: Clarendon, 1994), 99—100.

expected. There were no African-American violin players or vocal soloists. Our culture has taught us how to show favoritism. Markers we learn from childhood indicate one's station on the scale of respect—such as profession, "social polish," clothing, and wealth.

(1) *Profession.* In America there are clearly defined roles and professions that, we think, deserve greater respect than others. When I was twenty-seven years old, I was asked by an evangelical leader to attend the annual meeting of the ministers of his denomination. After one evening session a group of fifty of us were invited to join one of the denominational administrators in his suite for a time of conversation. Several hotel employees were present, wearing their hotel uniforms and serving coffee, soft drinks, and cookies. In situations like this I feel ill at ease and usually opt for an activity to keep me busy. I noticed that there were not enough hotel employees to cover all of the tasks in the room, because the soft drinks were handled in a self-serve fashion. So I began to pour soft drinks into glasses for the guests.

I suppose in my suit I may have appeared as the supervisor of the crew of hotel workers in the room. One distinguished-looking guest approached and I served him. He treated me in the brusque, inhuman fashion that anyone who has worked in the service sector knows all too well. I attempted to engage him in conversation, but with a dismissive glance he simply walked away. Soon after we were called to order and formed a large circle in order to begin the time of discussion. Along with a few others, I arranged my chair behind the circle and found myself sitting directly behind the gentleman whom I had served. Commenting upon the sermon we had heard a few minutes before, our host then said, "Let us begin by hearing the opinion of our resident New Testament specialist." At this point he turned and looked at me. The gentleman in front of me turned, and when he realized that I was the New Testament specialist in question, his visage fell and his skin paled. Afterward he approached me and without reference to our earlier noninterchange spoke in tones that were kind and flattering.

The entire scene left a bad taste in my mouth. What had changed? I was still the same person, wearing the same clothes, with the same foibles and frailties and hopes as before. It was simply that he had misjudged my "status" as our culture defines it. In his mind, a "New Testament specialist" is to be accorded more honor than the employee of a hotel.

Lord Acton, the man who said that "power tends to corrupt, and absolute power tends to corrupt absolutely," also said, "There is no worse heresy than that the office sanctifies the holder of it."[76] We far too easily ascribe or withhold honor, respect, or even simple human kindness merely on the basis of

---

76. Lord Acton in a letter to Creighton, April 4, 1887.

profession. How quickly and easily we have forgotten that each human being we encounter is equally deserving of our kindest attention, for each one is made in the image of God.

(2) *Anonymity and "social polish."* In James's world the poor were often put at economic and social risk by the wealthy, who were not even aware of them. There is a scene in the movie *Casablanca* in which Ugarte, the character played by Peter Lorre, speaks to Rick, played by Humphrey Bogart. "You despise me, don't you, Rick?" "I probably would," replies Rick, "if I gave you any thought." The peasant farmers on large estates owned by absentee landlords would understand this statement. So too would millions of people to whom our culture ascribes little value.

Several years ago I was a college pastor in the San Francisco Bay area, and our group was composed of people of college age in the working world, community college students, and a few students at Stanford University. Needless to say, it was an interesting mix. Our leadership team reflected this variety. It was an impressive group, blessed with real talent. But in many ways the most interesting person, and I think the clear leader of the team, was a young man named Frank. Frank had had a rough life. His father was out of the picture, and his mother, along with her series of boyfriends, lived with Frank and his brother. Frank dropped out of high school in order to get a job and support his family. His lack of social polish reflected this. Frank's conversational English was peppered with expressions like "I tooken it" and "he done it," as if his goal was to impress upon the listener his lack of social polish. Everything about him spoke of low expectations by the standards of our world: his speech, his clothes, his manner. But Frank was blessed by God with a tender heart, great insight, and leadership ability. Quickly he established himself as the leader of our leadership team; when he spoke, even the Stanford students listened with care. By all appearances Frank was a candidate for anonymity according to the standards of our world. How many other persons does the church ignore, simply because of our assumptions?

(3) *Attire.* On the CBS news show *Coast to Coast*[77] a reporter decided to embark upon an unorthodox experiment. On a bright, sunny day he rode his bicycle around Tucson, Arizona, looking for people. He found them everywhere—sitting and reading, waiting for friends, drinking coffee at a sidewalk cafe. He rode his bicycle up to these strangers, dismounted, and asked if they would watch his bicycle for a few minutes until he returned. When they agreed, he would depart, as if on some errand. Within minutes one of his comrades, posing as a thief, would take the bike and try to ride away. Each of the scenarios was caught on video tape.

---

77. January 15, 1997.

The reporter noted that it has become commonplace in America to bemoan the fact that "nobody wants to get involved anymore." There is a mountain of evidence to support this view, but the reporter wanted to test the veracity of this assumption. He wondered if there were not other Americans who would get involved. He chose to trust women and teenagers, a security guard (who watched the thief ride away with a calm and studied indifference), shirtless young men, and an army officer. Most people reacted immediately, putting themselves at potential risk in order to protect the property of a stranger. He even decided to trust a homeless couple, resting along with their dog on a blanket at the edge of a city park. The face of the woman showed the signs of prolonged exposure to the sun and elements. The man wore a soiled T-shirt and raggedy jeans. The reporter wondered how this couple would react. To his surprise and even to his shame, the homeless couple quickly and valiantly protected his property. When he interviewed them afterward, they observed that other people rarely if ever trusted them because of their appearance and situation. However, the wife said, "We are honest, trustworthy people." They proved it. But how many of us would bother to give them the opportunity even to do that?

(4) *Wealth.* Ministry takes money. Salaries, facilities, insurance, church vans—all of this requires a tremendous amount of money. A friend of mine once told me about his wise senior pastor, who once reminded the fiery youth pastor that some of the wealthy folks in the congregation, whom the youth pastor had criticized for their lifestyle (expensive cars, expansive homes), were the same people who made his ministry possible. They had bought the youth groups a van, covered the $3,000 shortfall incurred by the mission trip to Mexico, and were the anonymous donors who regularly contributed to a fund so the children of disadvantaged circumstances in the community could go on the $400 ski trip the youth group sponsored.

Wealth is the clearest marker of social status in our culture. Compared to the first century, our age offers of variety of options for its display. The automobiles we drive tell others how wealthy we are and what we think about ourselves.[78] Our attire often broadcasts the name of fashion designers, both figuratively and literally. Where we choose to live is supposed to be revelatory of our status. My wife and I live in the neighborhood of North Park University, where I am a professor. The school lies on the borderline between the "good" neighborhoods (to the north) and the "bad" neighborhoods (to the south). When we moved in, people at church asked us where we lived. When told our address the typical response was a startled, "South of Foster

---

78. I drive a used Volvo wagon. I am relatively certain that I do not want to think about what this choice says about the owner.

Avenue?" We had not chosen wisely, according the wisdom of status in our neighborhood.

James is not against wealth, but he is against the church becoming an arena for the display of wealth used to enhance status. Naming church facilities after the donor or other such displays would make James nervous, if not angry. His teaching is fully commensurate with that of Jesus in Matthew 6:2—4:

> So when you give to the needy, do not announce it with trumpets, as the hypocrites do in the synagogues and on the streets, to be honored by men. I tell you the truth, they have received their reward in full. But when you give to the needy, do not let your left hand know what your right hand is doing, so that your giving may be in secret. Then your Father, who sees what is done in secret, will reward you.

A holistic model of church life. In myriad forms the church either apes the surrounding culture or is unaware that in ways subtle and insidious the not-so-irenic manifestations of our culture have impressed their stamp on our church life. Livy and Solzhenitsyn each described their cultures, and in terms that were quite similar: godless, materialistic, self-indulgent, greedy, given to sensual excess. One of the most profound of these influences, perhaps, is isolation and the loss of a sense of true Christian community. Nouwen, McNeill, and Morrison write,

> Many very generous Christians find themselves increasingly tired and dispirited not so much because the work is hard or the success slight, but because they feel isolated, unsupported, and left alone. People who say, "I wonder if anyone cares what I am doing. I wonder if my superior, my friends at home, or the people who sent me ever think about me, ever pray for me, ever consider me part of their lives," are in real spiritual danger. We are able to do many hard things, tolerate many conflicts, overcome many obstacles, and persevere under many pressures, but when we no longer experience ourselves as part of a caring, supporting, praying community, we quickly lose faith. This is because faith in God's compassionate presence can never be separated from experiencing God's presence in the community to which we belong. The crises in the lives of many caring Christians today are closely associated with deep feelings of not belonging. Without a sense of being sent by a caring community, a compassionate life cannot last long and quickly degenerates into a life marked by numbness and anger. This is not simply a psychological observation, but a theological truth, because apart from a vital rela-

tionship with a caring community a vital relationship with Christ is not possible.[79]

James faced a situation in which the self-indulgent attitude of some in his congregation threatened to create not a community of compassion, but one of social stratification and privilege. He wrote to reestablish the necessary conditions for a community of compassion, which he called "the law that gives freedom" (2:12). But just as there were threats to James's congregation, there are threats to ours.

An African-American friend of mine frequently laughs at and occasionally with me about how "nice" white churches are. We are so worried about being "nice," about the appearance of health and correctness, she says, that we frequently are out of touch with the truth of our own private and corporate lives. When she speaks this way, I am often uncomfortable. Sometimes I even argue with her. But in my heart I know that most of the time she is right. I am not arguing for full public disclosure of every bit of dirty laundry, but something is amiss if the marital troubles of a pastor are kept from church leadership until it is announced that the couple has filed for divorce. Is there no trust in those leaders? All too frequently tensions among the staff result in the dismissal of one of the pastors in a quick and largely silent manner. Such situations are "difficult," "delicate," and "unseemly" and therefore better handled quietly, but with little if any opportunity for the body to be a part of a process of healing.

How can the body pray for and support its members in such a climate? How are those leaders, or the body as a whole, expected to view their role and the value in which they are held? Like our broader culture, we do not deal well with conflict. Often we hide it, hoping it will "just get better." Sometimes it does, but sometimes it does not. Would it not be better if the body were praying for and with the couple in question? Would it not be healthier if broader pools of support were available? But our culture tells us to hide such issues. One of the characters on the popular television sitcom *Friends* was worried that he was losing his girlfriend to another man. As he began to verbalize his concerns, another character interrupted with this advice, "Don't! Keep it inside! Never express your true feelings!"[80]

It has been my experience that predominantly white evangelical churches do not deal with conflict very well. Sometimes this involves issues of family life, an area our culture generally considers off-limits to others. One of my close friends from seminary served on a church staff that saw a prominent

---

79. Henri J. M. Nouwen, Donald P. NcNeill, and Douglas A. Morrison, *Compassion: A Reflection on the Christian Life* (New York: Image Doubleday, 1983), 61.
80. January 16, 1997.

couple in the church go through a divorce. Both the husband and wife were popular and respected in the church, and as is often the case, there was enough blame for the failure of the marriage to go around. My friend watched as the husband garnered support for himself within the church, subtly besmirching the reputation of his wife. His wife, for various reasons, passively allowed him to continue. In large measure the staff and church leadership simply stood by.

In our culture these are private matters. But should they be in the church? We have moved beyond the day when we safely can hide behind our naiveté. There are too many cases of physical abuse of spouses, of sexual abuse of children in our churches and among our parishioners. James stood for the proposition that the mere profession of faith was not enough to maintain membership in the Christian community. Faith is about the transformation of the inner life, and therefore also about "deeds." "Speak and act," he said, "as those who are going to be judged by the law that gives freedom" (v. 12).

In his review of the movie *The First Wives Club*, Michael G. Maudlin relates how his wife, a psychologist, at times comes home from work angry:[81]

> Nine times out of ten times what prompts her fury is a divorce case. The husband is hiding the assets, and his wife has no clue as to what they actually own. Or he has cheated on his wife and now wants half her pension. Or the wife wants to fight for a just settlement but is afraid her husband will beat her or even kill her. Or she simply doesn't know how she will raise three children and meet expenses while her husband gets to live out the dreams of a second adolescence.
>
> Karen has heard it all. . . . [She] seethes with frustration at her relative impotence. She is on the wife's side, but everyone else, it seems, is on the husband's: the lawyers, the judges, the government, and, tragically, the church. . . .
>
> My wife was once surprised by the candid and unguarded comment of a pastor: "Women who go through divorce often become so much more alive, more interesting than they were before." Karen and I have noticed this disturbing phenomenon, uncomfortable because it complicates the simple formula "Divorce is bad." . . .
>
> In *Gender and Grace*, psychologist Mary Stuart Van Leeuwen puts forth the intriguing theory that men and women experience the Fall differently. She speculates that men's sinful propensity is to objectify people and treat them as means to an end. Women, on the other hand, have a propensity to give away too much responsibility for the sake of a relationship. . . .

---

81. Michael G. Maudlin, "Female Fury Fuels Box-Office Frenzy," *Books and Culture: A Christian Review* (January/February 1997), 7.

The church has begun to mobilize against divorce, but ... *First Wives* reveals another step we must take: promoting models of marriage that allow women to thrive and grow without having to divorce.

Maudlin has put his finger on a disturbing truth: Our churches are not always places of sanctuary. I am not convinced that Mary Stuart Van Leeuwen is right when she speculates that men and women experience the Fall differently, but I do know that the church needs to ask if the perpetuation of a stereotypical role for women is cultural or biblical. Can the church be an agent of healing in situations like the one Maudlin has isolated? Can the church be an arena in which women, children, and men thrive and grow spiritually, emotionally, and intellectually? Can the church be a place where we substitute "nice" American behavior for honesty that is linked to compassion?

Henri Nouwen thinks so. In *Compassion*,[82] he claims that the "message which comes to us in the New Testament is that the compassionate life is a life together." This is what James is striving for in arguing against favoritism and in favor of "the law that gives freedom" (v. 12). While compassion is an individual trait, it is also essentially communal in nature. As such the Christian community is the antidote for the isolation that is the flip side of the self-indulgence of which Livy spoke. In community our lives become compassionate because of the way we live and work together. Willingly we place ourselves next to each other, and in working and sharing together we learn to trust each other and to be vulnerable to each other.

Part of what the modern church has lost and which we would do well to recapture is the intimacy and interdependence of the early church. James himself is a model of honesty in this regard. He cared enough about the members of the church to offer rebuke, but he did so wearing the mantle of brother, not of judge or superior. Far too often church order is maintained through a system that reflects that of our culture. We would do well to remember the humble spirit that caused James to claim the title "brother."

Surprisingly, church growth theory may be of help here. It can be marked by a pragmatic concern that at times seems to overlook biblical teaching. But many church growth theorists argue that in order to be healthy, large and growing churches need to ensure that each person is a part of a "congregation," a subset of the larger church. These "congregations" should be no more than 100 people so that intimacy, accountability, and honesty can thrive. George Hunter, in his *The Contagious Congregation*, argues strongly that churches must create opportunities for members to "be known."[83]

---

82. Nouwen, NcNeill, and Morrison, *Compassion*, 49-61.

83. George Hunter, *The Contagious Congregation: Frontiers in Evangelism and Church Growth* (Nashville: Abingdon, 1979), 149.

My wife, Kristina, and I live in the city of Chicago. We feel safe in our neighborhood, even though gang graffiti can be found and has appeared once or twice on our back door. There are a myriad problems in this urban landscape. Some churches have attempted to remedy the situation through a "goods-based" ministry of mercy, such as a food bank or a soup kitchen.[84] Others focus their energies on political action. These are good, admirable pursuits. But they easily fall prey to the peril of antiseptic liberalism. Neither of these broad approaches necessarily involves the members of the church in close contact with their neighbors, the very persons whom they want to help. Especially when associated with churches sporting a more liberal theology, these efforts presuppose a willingness to locate sin in institutions and structures, not in individuals. This thinking makes the fatal mistake of failing to recognize that structures are shaped and given direction by people. It also does a great disservice to the very people they are trying to help, because the implicit message is that there is nothing in them that needs reforming.

Most evangelical churches, by contrast, tend to see the individual in need of only reformation. By focusing almost exclusively on the spiritual needs of persons, we fail to comprehend the massive mutually implicatory web of problems that constitute the reality faced by a poor person in the city. In each of these cases is lodged a message, largely hidden from our eyes but abundantly clear to those we wish to "help" in our desire to serve Jesus. In each scenario, we play the role of Jesus, offering healing or a compassionate touch. Yet without realizing it, we have staked a claim to have high status and unconsciously adopt an attitude of superiority to these people. We do not allow them to be the touch of Jesus in our lives (cf. Matt. 25:31–46). It is possible that we need that touch as much or more as others need our help.

In Chicago the Lawndale Community Church has taken on this tough challenge,[85] and done so with no small degree of success through a multi-faceted community development program.[86] This church addresses the material needs of the community head on, challenging drug addicts and drug dealers to renounce their lifestyle as corrosive of their community, speaking for sexual abstinence, and teaching biblical principles for living. Its members are active in working for reform of the school system, the legal system, and the social service system. But it is equally passionate about the need for the lost to come to Christ. This is a church that has taken the words of James seriously. It has understood that there are Christians in the city, brothers and sis-

---

84. Sherman, "Hope Dreams," 33.
85. See the book written by Wayne Gordon and Randall Frame on the Lawndale Community Church, *Real Hope in Chicago* (Grand Rapids: Zondervan, 1995).
86. Ibid., 31–33.

ters who are part of a community that needs our help and in which God can reveal himself in new ways to the more affluent brothers and sisters. But by remaining insulated, whether in the suburbs or in "nice" white urban churches, we fail to recognize the face of Christ in the face of the city. This alien world allows us to keep our distance and therefore to show favoritism.

James has said that Jesus Christ is the *Shekinah* of God. His call is to avoid favoritism and to live by the law that gives freedom. Jesus, the very glory of God, modeled such a life. James faithfully has preserved this model and this call. Let us be found faithful.

James 2:14-26

W

HAT GOOD IS it, my brothers, if a man claims to have faith but has no deeds? Can such faith save him? [15]Suppose a brother or sister is without clothes and daily food. [16]If one of you says to him, "Go, I wish you well; keep warm and well fed," but does nothing about his physical needs, what good is it? [17]In the same way, faith by itself, if it is not accompanied by action, is dead.

[18]But someone will say, "You have faith; I have deeds."

Show me your faith without deeds, and I will show you my faith by what I do. [19]You believe that there is one God. Good! Even the demons believe that—and shudder.

[20]You foolish man, do you want evidence that faith without deeds is useless? [21]Was not our ancestor Abraham considered righteous for what he did when he offered his son Isaac on the altar? [22]You see that his faith and his actions were working together, and his faith was made complete by what he did. [23]And the scripture was fulfilled that says, "Abraham believed God, and it was credited to him as righteousness," and he was called God's friend. [24]You see that a person is justified by what he does and not by faith alone.

[25]In the same way, was not even Rahab the prostitute considered righteous for what she did when she gave lodging to the spies and sent them off in a different direction? [26]As the body without the spirit is dead, so faith without deeds is dead.

Original
Meaning

AT THE OUTSET of chapter 2 James expressed faith in "our glorious Lord Jesus Christ," in order to encourage his readers to pursue a life of integrity relative to faith. In this section he is at pains to clarify the nature and boundaries of that faith. A "faith" that consists of mere assent to doctrine, or perhaps of even the simple utterance of a doctrinal statement, is no faith at all. It is dead, unable to achieve salvation. In contrast, James offers for consideration as true faith one that demonstrates itself in deeds; as examples of this faith he cites Abraham and Rahab.

This passage offers three vexing problems. (1) What is the connection, if any, between this section and the preceding one (2:1–13)? It further clarifies the nature of true faith. Moreover, it provides specific examples of the failure of the community to show respect to the poor, thereby demonstrating the lack of practical faith. Finally, verses 15–16 are reminiscent of 2:3, in which James says that favoritism shown to the wealthy is unacceptable.

(2) The next problem is even more difficult, arising because James here follows his opening statement with a diatribe form of argument (in which the position of an imaginary opponent is presented and engaged by the author). Where precisely does the position of the "opponent" end, and where does James begin to mount his own argument? Verse 18 is the locus of much debate and of strenuous, even tortured exegesis.

(3) The most difficult problem comes into view with 2:24: "You see that a person is justified by what he does and not by faith alone." This is perhaps the most discussed verse in the entire book of James, for it seems to contradict Paul's view of deeds and faith as expressed in Romans 3:28. A discussion of this problem is reserved for the Bridging Contexts section.

The passage can easily be divided into four sections. Verses 14–17 are concerned with the case of the poor Christian who receives only words of encouragement from the church. In the eyes of James, this "help" is worthless. The second section (2:18–20) is a rational argument that is difficult to follow, the point of which is that while some claim the existence of a "true faith" apart from deeds, such a faith is not true, but dead and useless. The third (2:21–24) and fourth (2:25–26) sections are two biblical arguments supporting the position of James.

The Poor Christian Brother or Sister (2:14–17)

JAMES NOW TURNS from the contrast between judgment and mercy to the contrast between faith and deeds. He offers an example of a response to a sister or brother in need in order to argue that true faith is proven by a willingness to step forward and offer concrete assistance.

The passage opens with two rhetorical questions: What good is faith without deeds? Can such a faith issue forth in salvation? The phrase "What good is it" (*ti to ophelos*) marks the start of a form of style that is modeled on the diatribe. James introduces the players in the diatribe: the author and the fictional "someone" (*tis*) who represents the position James opposes. While this "someone" is fictional, the position as stated clearly represents an errant position actually held in the church. James has set his sights on this errant belief. It is likely that he has in mind the false teachers to which he refers in chapter 3.

The issue is not new in this letter, seeing that it was introduced in chapter 1. Can authentic faith find expression in a confession of right doctrine alone? Can authentic faith be expressed merely as sentiment that never reaches the point of action? Or is it by necessity a faith that goes beyond these to include practical action? The thrust of James's argument here (the use of *ti to ophelos* in verses 14 and 16 suggest that the expression serves as a bracket; i.e., verses 14–16 consist of a position that some within the church hold but James rejects) is that such a faith is without profit and without advantage; it does not issue forth in eternal life.

The use of the phrase "my brothers" in both 2:1 and 2:14 indicates that the people described in 2:1–13 are guilty of holding to a faith that will not issue forth in eternal life. In other words, the issue is not only moral, it is also soteriological (related to salvation). Both Paul and James see faith as a confidence in God's saving act along with the effect of that act in the lives of the followers of Jesus Christ. Neither Paul nor James see faith as the mere assertion of doctrine. The NIV rightly translates *erga* here as "deeds" and not "works," even though it translates this word as "works" in Romans 11:6. Much needless headache and heartache has resulted from a misunderstanding of this term. Paul often employs *erga* to mean "works of the law"; for James *erga* means "deeds of Christian righteousness," a practice that Paul would both expect and demand. The Bridging Contexts section will have more to say on this.

The "faith" in view in the second question of verse 14 is workless faith, not faith per se. James is loathe even to dignify this position with the term "faith." The use of *sosai* ("save") demonstrates that once again the soteriological sense is in view. Here is another clear link to 2:1–13, for this thought makes sense of 2:13. Those who show partiality to the rich at the expense of the poor are performing deeds not of faith, but of the wisdom and standards of Roman culture. Faith without deeds will not only not issue forth in salvation, but it also has nothing concrete to offer to the poor and the needy, for it is essentially self-interested.

Such a position is not unique to James. According to Luke 3:7–14, John the Baptist argued that deeds must accompany true faith. Moreover, after claiming that faith and deeds go together ("a good tree cannot bear bad fruit, and a bad tree cannot bear good fruit"), Jesus in strong terms warned that many who call him "Lord" will not enter the kingdom of heaven (Matt. 7:15–23).

James then offers an illustration from the life of the church. He envisions a situation in which church members fail to display even the most basic forms of charity to one another. The fact that this situation is pictured within the community makes it plausible that the "wealthy" of 2:1–13 includes some within the community. With "brother or sister" James may have in mind a married couple, or he may consciously mention a woman in order to highlight the contrast with Roman culture.¹ In any event, here is a clear case of ill-clad members of the community.

The example is stylized and so obvious that the point cannot be missed. Both the conditions of being ill-clothed and hungry are the stuff of stock phrases, having numerous Old Testament parallels (Job 24:7; Isa. 58:7). From this self-evident general example James will build his case. If the poorly clothed person of 2:2 is a visitor, James may here be reminding his readers of the parable of the Good Samaritan—they are to care for not only their own, but also others who are needy. They are not only without the necessary clothing, but also without the proper food.

Having given a hypothetical example of crystal clarity, James surprises his readers with a response that seems unbelievable (v. 16). Who could respond to such a clear need in so deficient a manner, so obviously motivated by an empty heart! Yet for James the position of his opponents in the church is equally shocking and unbelievable, even though it does not seem so obvious to the church. The verse presents a series of verbs in the imperative: "Go, be well, get warm, be well fed." James refers to a group of empty greetings or blessings: "Go in peace! Be well! Good luck!" The serious charge that he offers here is one of offering empty words with a failure to meet the basic human needs of others, perhaps even to become jaded to such needs.

James goes on to say that faith without deeds is dead (*nekra*). By this he means, of course, that such a faith fails to accomplish the aim of true faith. That kind of faith may have a type of power, but it is not the power proper to faith.² As Ropes notes, the contrast is not so much between faith and deeds (although this stands in the background) but between dead, useless faith and living faith.³ Faith alone without works is as dead as a body without breath. Deeds are not something extra to be added to faith; they are a

---

1. The wealthy within Roman society would often host a feast for the citizens of a town or city. These are known as *sportulae* feasts, from the Latin which refers to a basket in which patrons would place the gifts given to their clients. The idea was that the display of such wealth and munificence brought honor, fame, and prestige. While we know of some of these feasts that included women, the vast majority did not. See Petronius, *Satyricon*, 45, 71; R. Duncan-Jones, *The Economy of the Roman Empire* (Cambridge: Cambridge Univ. Press, 1974), 184–86. Such feasts and other cash distributions were weighted in favor of the wealthy and powerful. Since the point was the honor and status of the donor, it was more important to impress the wealthy and the powerful. See Steven E. Ostrow, "Augustales Along the Bay of Naples," *Historia* 35 (1985): 71.

2. It is striking that James appears to grant even less efficacy to this "faith" than the "faith" of the demons (2:19). This opens the possibility that some who hold and teach this position do not believe at all, but merely are using the church as an opportunity for status, much like the *collegia*. However, this is highly speculative.

3. James H. Ropes, *The Epistle of St. James*, 207.

necessary constituent part of faith. Without deeds faith is not really true faith—it is only a shadow, a shade, an impostor of true faith.

True Faith, Dead Faith (2:18–20)

JAMES NOW OFFERS a rational argument in order to show that while there may be a type of "faith" that does not issue forth in deeds, such faith is dead; it has no saving power. True faith, he insists, always changes the heart and therefore results in acts of mercy and compassion.

"But someone will say, 'You have faith; I have deeds.' Show me your faith without deeds, and I will show you my faith by what I do" (v. 18). Here is a bold challenge, one that has the tone to make many evangelicals nervous.[4] There is also a serious grammatical difficulty here. Clearly with verse 18 the diatribe style is in play, but where does this end? Who is the "someone" who is quoted? There are five basic options.

1. An ally to James is introduced at this juncture, and the ally engages in dialogue on behalf of James; James resumes speaking in verse 19.
2. The speaker in verse 18 is an opponent of James, and James resumes speaking in verse 19. Even though this option is not without its difficulties, it seems to be the best one, particularly in modified form.
3. Verse 18 is comprised of an imaginary dialogue between two fictive persons.
4. James resumes speaking midway through verse 18, "Show me your faith without deeds."
5. The opponent of James is the speaker through verse 19, and James resumes speaking in verse 20.

The first option is championed by James Adamson,[5] among others. This position posits the introduction of an ally to James, a supporter of his position. If it is an ally of James, most of the grammatical difficulties are settled, and "you" refers to the believer of "faith without deeds," and the "I" refers to the ally of James. To resolve the grammatical difficulties so neatly is no mean accomplishment. James 2:17–18 then reads, "Faith without deeds is dead. But if someone who believes that faith without deeds is dead says, 'You have faith, I (you admit) have deeds,' show me your so-called 'faith' apart from deeds (I know you cannot), and I will show you my faith by what I do." The problem with this interpretation is that the verse begins with an adversarial term *alla* ("but"). There is no apparent parallel for *alla* introducing anything

---

4. See the fine treatment of this problem by Scot McKnight, "James 2:18a: The Unidentifiable Interlocutor," *WTJ* 52 (1990): 355–64.

5. James B. Adamson, *The Epistle of James*, 124–25.

but the opposing position; it seems unlikely that James would provide the only exception known to us. In addition, it is difficult to discern what James would gain through the use of such a device. In short, it is grammatically possible, but unlikely.

The second option (that the objector is an opponent of James's position) is the natural conclusion, given the style of a diatribe or even a homily. The difficulty is that this objector does not object, but simply restates the position offered by James. One suggestion is that the phrase ought to be taken as a question: "Do you have faith?" to which James responds that he has deeds.[6] This solution is fraught with difficulties and has won few supporters. A variant possibility is the suggestion that the case made by the objector has been lost, so that all that remains is the response of James.[7] This too is a solution with limited merit.

The third option is perhaps the weakest. While this solution seems to avoid the problems associated with the second option, it is unlikely, given the extremely awkward construction. If this were the situation the more natural construction would probably have been *allos . . . allos* ("one has faith, another one has deeds").[8]

Martin offers the fourth option, and while it may not negotiate the rather difficult grammatical woods with the skill some would wish, it does preserve the basic intent of the verse.[9] In Martin's interpretation, James begins his response to his opponent with the words "Show me" in verse 18. But this requires James to have altered the words of his opponents, so that the "you" in "you have faith" is the opponent of James, and the "I" of "I have deeds" is James himself. While this solves the grammatical problems, it is a rather laborious solution. It does possess, however, the happy benefit of a straightforward reading of the second half of verse 18. According to this view James challenges his opponent to demonstrate faith apart from works—which, of course, is impossible. James then claims to demonstrate faith through deeds. This is consistent with the thought of the letter: Only faith that issues forth in deeds is true faith.

---

6. F. J. A. Hort, *The Epistle of St. James: The Greek Text With Introduction, Commentary As Far As Chapter IV Verse 7, and With Additional Notes* (London: Macmillan, 1909), 60–61.

7. This is the position of H. Windisch, *Die Katholischen Briefe*, ed. H. Preisker (HNT; Tübingen, Mohr, 1951), 16–17.

8. Ropes, *The Epistle of St. James*, 211, opts for this reading, although he is well aware of its shortcomings. The trenchant response of C. F. D. Moule to this interpretation is compelling: "To tell the truth, I cannot think of a *less* likely way to express what J. H. Ropes wants the James passage to mean than what stands there written." This quote is taken from a personal note cited in James B. Adamson, *The Epistle of James*, 137.

9. Ralph P. Martin, *James*, 87.

In the final option James allows his opponent to separate faith from deeds, arguing that each is a component of genuine religion. The great difficulty here is that verse 19 is more naturally read as supporting the position of James. However, it is not inconceivable that verse 19 can be construed as an attempt to support the position of the opponents of James. In either case, the view expressed at the end of verse 18—that there is a legitimate faith without deeds, and another faith with deeds—is consistently denied in James.

"You believe that there is one God. Good! Even the demons believe that—and shudder." If this is still the voice of the opponent of James, then his argument is simply that a type of faith exists as faith without and distinct from deeds. This opponent then refers to the *Shema*,[10] the ancient confession used by Jews and then by Christians ("Hear, O Israel, there is only one God, and no other," cf. Deut. 6:4). He notes that even demons believe this, and this, therefore, is a faith without deeds. To our eyes this seems a tortured reading of verse 19, but it is a possibility. Such a reading would allow for the response of James in the verses that follow, that such a "faith" is so useless as to be no faith at all.

But it is also possible to read this verse in light of the fourth option—that is, that 2:19 continues the response of James to his opponents.[11] If so, he then remarks that to believe in the one God is an excellent starting point, but such an intellectual conclusion is not true faith, for even the demons know this much. Religion that is worth something involves action that grows from the heart. This view has the advantage of nicely picturing those members of the Christian community who refuse to offer concrete assistance to the poor. Instead, they show favoritism by offering only pious verbal nothings. Their sense of spiritual security is false, and their faith is no more salvific than the knowledge that even the demons possess, that there is only one God.

Laws wisely points out, however, that to suppose the belief of the demons in God is merely intellectual is greatly to undervalue the point.[12] The belief of the demons is no mere intellectual assent of passive consequence, for the demons believe "and shudder." The demons believe something about God that occasions a response. Laws argues that James is here referring to the rite of exorcism. By this interpretation there are, then, three types of faith held up for consideration: faith separate from deeds; a faith which is marked by evil deeds (the "faith" of demons); and the faith that James champions, one that results in good deeds.

---

10. Sophie Laws, *The Epistle of James*, 125–26, is not convinced that this constitutes a direct reference to the *Shema*, but is willing to allow the possibility.

11. See Martin, *James*, 87–89.

12. Laws, *The Epistle of James*, 126–28.

Whether or not Laws is right, we may summarize the argument as follows. The speaker of 2:18 holds a position in opposition to that of James (option 2, above). His argument is: (1) Faith and deeds are separate entities; for (2) if faith is validated by deeds, then it can be said to have some existence prior to this validation; thus, (3) faith is both prior to and superior to deeds; and (4) the demons believe without deeds, so therefore a nonsaving faith does indeed exist. While both James and his opponents believe that a faith with deeds exists and is a saving faith, James cannot agree with his opponents that there is a saving "faith" that exists without deeds.

In response James argues that (1) faith and deeds cannot be sundered; (2) the only faith that is worthy of the name is faith that expresses itself in deeds; and (3) faith without deeds is false, since it "does not work"; it fails to accomplish its purpose. This last is a potent point and is able to survive the interpretation of Laws. Faith has a purpose, and that purpose is for the word to grow within us (1:18) until we are mature and complete (1:4). Any "faith" that does not move toward the goal of salvation is therefore not "true" faith.[13] The idea is similar to that of Isaiah 55:11, where God declares that his word always accomplishes the purpose for which he sends it. Anything less is evidence that what is in view is not the word of God.

In understanding verse 20 we are on firmer grammatical and exegetical ground, for this verse clearly contains the words of James. The *de* grants to James's words the force of incredulity: "Don't you understand? Do you need to be convinced?" The pejorative nature of his response is captured in his use of "foolish" (*kene*) as the term can mean both foolishness and deficient moral standing. The point, obviously, is that "faith" without works is "faith" in name only. It cannot be saving faith, because it lacks the strength either to attain the proper end of faith (salvation) or the ability to understand that biblical faith is always tied to character and therefore to action, as the great prophets of the Old Testament demonstrate. James even makes his point with a bit of wry humor in the form of a wordplay: Faith without works (*ergon*) does not work (*arge= a + ergos*).

The Example of Abraham (2:21–24)

JAMES NOW EMPLOYS the example of Abraham to demonstrate the linkage between faith and deeds. This link is not new, he claims, but is in fact the desire of God from the beginning. "Was not our ancestor Abraham considered righteous for what he did when he offered his son Isaac on the altar?" It is possible that the opponent(s) of James had cited Genesis 15:6, which

---

13. There are New Testament parallels to this, especially in the Gospel of John, as the Bridging Contexts section will show.

stated that God reckoned righteousness to Abraham because he believed. James, understanding the revered status of Abraham, wishes to point out that the faith of Abraham was not a sterile intellectual assent; rather, it was a faith that manifested itself in trusting actions that were often great risks, such as the near-sacrifice of Isaac.

James here presents a thoroughly Jewish notion of righteousness, that is, righteousness as covenant fidelity—and fidelity is nothing if it is not about conduct (Isa. 43:9; Matt. 12:37; Rom. 2:6–11; 6:1–12). Righteousness that is true will always compel the righteous to acts of mercy and kindness (see Rom. 2:7). James refers to the example of Abraham, whose trust in God was such that he would risk even his own son. While Paul is chary of such an argument, the author of Hebrews also moves from Genesis 15:6 to the near-sacrifice of Isaac in Genesis 22 (Heb. 11:17–19). It is also possible that in mentioning Abraham, James wishes to imply the hospitality Abraham showed the three travelers in Genesis 18.[14] He performed deeds of mercy because of his faith in God.

The use of "our ancestor" to refer to Abraham is often taken to mean that both the author and audience are Jewish. Certainly it is most natural to see it as referring to Jews. However, the Gospel tradition and Paul make clear that Jewish descent is no guarantee of status as "children of Abraham" (Luke 3:8–9; Rom. 4:1, 16). Note how Clement calls Abraham "our father" while addressing an audience composed of predominantly non-Jewish Christians (*1 Clement* 31:2). In any event, such a statement is natural if even a significant minority within the church were Jewish Christians.

In verse 22 James continues to stress the unity of faith and deeds. "You see" is James's appeal to his opponent to perceive the right logic of the position he is about to articulate yet again, that the faith of Abraham was made complete through his deeds. The term for "made complete" is *eteleiothe*, derived from the same root as "mature and complete" in 1:4. James wants to hold both faith and deeds. The two must mix together for either to be worthwhile. We can never be "made complete" without both.

Verse 23 begins with the connective "and" (*kai*), which James uses to show that Genesis 15:6 is proof of the veracity of the position he has advocated. By showing that the faith of Abraham was faith because his trust was active, he has undercut the possibility of seeing Genesis 15:6 as supporting an exclusive *sola fides* position. Abraham's "faith-work," James argues, is the type of faith that God considers righteous. The attribution "God's friend" is not found in

---

14. While it is true that James cites the near sacrifice of Isaac, within Judaism this event was paired with the mercy displayed by Abraham in Gen. 18 as emblematic of the "reckoned righteousness" of Gen. 15:6. See *A Rabbinic Anthology*, ed. G. G. Montefiore and H. Loewe (New York: Schocken, 1974), no. 1172.

the Old Testament as such, but the Hebrew of Isaiah 41:8 has God referring to Abraham as "my friend," and in 2 Chronicles 20:7 Jehoshaphat refers to Abraham "your friend."

In James's concluding statement concerning Abraham (v. 24), he is as close to contradicting Paul as at any other juncture in the letter. Yet it is important to see that James is actually defending a Pauline position. James does not wish to set "faith" and "deeds" at odds, nor does he wish to deny the importance of faith in justification. His point is that each needs the other in order to be efficacious. Faith alone is insufficient, says James. This is the natural equivalent to Paul's formula of "faith expressing itself through love" (Gal. 5:6 NIV).

The Example of Rahab (2:25–26)

JAMES USES THE example of Rahab to further buttress his claim concerning the unity of faith and deeds. Although a woman of dubious reputation, her actions were evidence of faith. In Jewish tradition Rahab married Joshua and became the ancestor of Jeremiah and Ezekiel (*b. Meg.* 14b, 15a), and in Christian tradition she is included as among the ancestors of Jesus (Matt. 1:5). She showed hospitality to the spies (just as Abraham did to the three strangers). This example is chosen because the church has refused to show hospitality to those whose outward appearance indicated that they had no ability to benefit the church. Yet both Abraham and Rahab showed hospitality to those whose outward appearance mirrored the poor in the church.[15]

"As the body without the spirit is dead, so faith without deeds is dead" (v. 26). With this statement James offers his conclusion. Greek thought created a division between "the body" and "the spirit." In biblical thought, however, this idea has no place. "Flesh" in Hebrew is *baśar*, whether living or dead; *nepeš* ("soul") is what makes a body living. A Greek might say, "I have a soul," but in strict biblical thought we should say "I am a soul." So James here is a good biblical theologian, for he argues that just as *nepeš* describes a living body, so "faith" is properly used to describe a trust in God that by definition is marked by fidelity of behavior.

A "body" by itself is nothing, and a "soul" cannot be a soul apart from a body. In this way James compares faith and deeds. Just as *baśar* indicates flesh, but dead flesh, so "faith" that does not impel the believer to good deeds is no living faith at all. The examples of Abraham and Rahab have been provided to make the case unassailable. When the Spirit and wisdom of God are ours, our hearts are changed, and so then, are our desires and our actions.

---

15. It is also worth noting that both Abraham and Rahab must be seen as proselytes. Joshua 2:11 has Rahab declare that the God of the spies is God in heaven and on earth, and 6:25 says that Rahab lived in Israel.

TWO MAIN ISSUES lodged in this text require careful attention before the lessons James has for us can be applied to the modern world: the relationship between faith and deeds in the New Testament, and the meaning of the term "belief/faith" in the New Testament. Both of these have to do with fidelity to the call of Jesus. Both are also about integrity, that is becoming an integrated person, one in whom beliefs and actions are linked.

Faith and Deeds

THIS IS THE one place where, more than any other, James has achieved notoriety. By all appearances he contradicts the Pauline doctrine of justification by faith, which constitutes an apparent theological problem of no mean stature. It is for this reason that Martin Luther issued his famous condemnation of James.[16] G. E. Ladd says that "the admission of verbal contradiction is unavoidable."[17] It is this "contradiction" that renders this passage perhaps the most discussed in the entire letter.

Summarily put, here is the problem. In Romans 3:28 Paul says "For we maintain that a man is justified by faith apart from observing the law." But in James 2:24 we read, "You see that a person is justified by what he does and not by faith alone." It used to be popular for scholars to posit that James knew Romans and Galatians and was here making a deliberate attempt to refute them.[18] But this is unlikely. Once we move beyond the superficial, the evidence will show that Paul and James are in essential agreement. Because of the historical interest in this issue, as well as its theological importance, a generous amount of space is here allotted to its explication.

The relationship between the free gift of grace and Christian responsibility is less difficult than the limited ability of human language to express it with facility. The problem is threefold: confusion over the meaning of terms, con-

---

16. In the introduction to his first German edition of the New Testament (1522), Luther wrote:

> In fine, Saint John's Gospel and his first epistle, Saint Paul's epistles, especially those to the Romans, Galatians, Ephesians, and Saint Peter's first epistle—these are the books which show thee Christ, and teach thee everything that is needful and blessed for thee to know even though thou never see or hear any other book or doctrine. Therefore is Saint James's epistle a right strawy epistle in comparison with them, for it has no gospel character to it.

Although, as we have seen, Luther has much good to say about various verses in this letter.

17. G. E. Ladd, *A Theology of the New Testament* (Grand Rapids: Eerdmans, 1974), 592.

18. Ibid., 592.

fusion of the use of Genesis 15:6, and the confusion that results from the failure to understand which of the three tenses of salvation are in view.

(1) The first problem, that of verbal similarity, is perhaps the most vexing. It can be resolved once we recognize that words can carry various meanings and that Paul and James intend different meanings in their use of the same terms. For Paul as well as for James, "saving faith" means acceptance of the gospel and includes a personal commitment to Jesus Christ and his mission. Ladd, following Jeremias,[19] understands faith for James as the mere assertion of monotheism.[20] While this is certainly a component of the definition of faith that James embraces, it is insufficient. James argues that the monotheistic "belief" of the demons, while it is a form of faith, is insufficient because it is not salvific. Faith is this monotheistic belief, plus a determination to nurture the word planted within, resulting in acts of Christian love.

When our attention shifts to "deeds," however, the landscape becomes more problematic. Within the Protestant tradition "deeds" are looked on askance, for reliance on deeds is misguided and dangerous. "Faith," however, is good, for we are saved by grace through faith. There is a decidedly anti-Jewish timbre to this received interpretation. Careful scrutiny of the evidence, however, will not support this received tradition. For Paul "deeds" most often, but not always, meant acts of obedience to the Jewish law, which, he argued, were done in order to demonstrate one's election and status in the family of God. Since he came to view this belief as erroneous, it, like the "faith" of the demons in James, was not salvific; it was unable to accomplish the purpose of faith. This is Paul's point in Romans 8:1–4.

For James "deeds" are not the "deeds of the law," but are those deeds of Christian love that fulfill the royal law. A word of encouragement when more is plainly needed is not Christian love. Action is the key, such as visiting widows and orphans (1:27) or standing against any show of favoritism. For James, "deeds" are the acts of charity that flow from a life lived in concert with God, for God is a God preeminently of mercy. Recalling 2:13, James says that any other "faith" will result in not mercy but judgment. That this is the correct interpretation is sealed by the statement of Paul in Galatians 5:6, "For in Christ Jesus neither circumcision nor uncircumcision has any value. The only thing that counts is faith expressing itself through love."

---

19. Joachim Jeremias, "Paul and James," *ExpTim* 66 (1954–1955): 368–71. Jeremias sees in James 2:19 ("the demons believe") a reflection of the rabbinic conception of *'amuna*, which means the assertion of monotheism (370). He does grant that here James refers to a popular conception of faith and that James knows another, the assurance that God hears our prayers. Nevertheless, Jeremias does say that *pistis* "with James means—to admit the existence of God" (370). This limited definition is unsatisfactory.

20. Ladd, *A Theology of the New Testament*, 592.

(2) The second problem involves how both Paul and James use Genesis 15:6.[21] Paul believes that the justification granted to Abraham was the result of the promises of God given to him and sealed by circumcision, the sign of the covenant. Justification was something God *did* in the past, absent any worthiness on the part of Abraham. James, by contrast, passes over the circumcision of Abraham and instead seizes on the near-sacrifice of Isaac. This event he sees as an example of Abraham's faith, a *present* demonstration of what God *had done* in Abraham.

It is striking that the question is almost always posed in terms of James's disagreeing with Paul, as if James might somehow be deficient. In any supposed conflict between Paul and James, we easily and automatically cast James in the role of defendant. Of course, among Protestants there are historical reasons for this, traceable to Luther. But the real question is whether or not the Pauline view is consistent with Jesus' view. It was Jesus who said, "Each tree is recognized by its own fruit" (Luke 6:44), and who also said that many will say, "'Lord, when did we see you hungry or thirsty or a stranger or needing clothes or sick or in prison, and did not help you?' He will reply, 'I tell you the truth, whatever you did not do for one of the least of these, you did not do for me.' Then they will go away to eternal punishment, but the righteous to eternal life" (Matt. 25:44–46). The standard here is the equivalent of James's "deeds."

(3) The final complicating factor involves the temporal location of the "salvation" and therefore the "deeds" in question. In the New Testament generally, and in Paul in particular, salvation is a threefold experience:

It is an accomplished fact: We have been saved (see Eph. 2:8).
It is a present experience: We are being saved (see 1 Cor. 1:18; Phil. 2:12).
It is a future hope: We will be saved (see Rom. 13:11; Phil. 3:20).

Part of the difficulty in rectifying the Paul/James question over deeds is that Paul in Romans 3:28 is speaking of salvation as past event; nothing human beings can do can earn God's forgiveness. But James, when speaking of deeds, has in mind present activity. When he speaks of salvation as past event, he employs the language not of human merit, but of divine providence: "He chose to give us birth through the word of truth" (James 1:18). The thrust of Paul's writings is in total agreement with James here.

To be a Christian, in Paul's mind, is to be alive, to be full of rich, abundant, and pulsating life.[22] It is to enter the service of the living God, "the

---

21. Laws, *The Epistle of James*, 128–30.
22. See G. B. Caird and L. D. Hurst, *New Testament Theology* (Oxford: Clarendon, 1994), 179, 185–90.

God who gives life to the dead and calls things that are not as though they were" (Rom. 4:17). In this newness of life Christians are made competent by God to be "ministers of a new covenant—not of the letter but of the Spirit; for the letter kills, but the Spirit gives life" (2 Cor. 3:6). This Spirit, Paul says, "lives in you" (Rom. 8:11). Here Paul clearly has in mind a life marked by the kind of heart and therefore behavior that marked the life of Jesus. It is to walk a new path, to live "a new life" (6:4).

Paul's insistence on salvation by faith through grace alone stemmed from his own previous experience in Judaism, in which he claims to have misunderstood the Law as the talisman of nationalistic pride. It also came in the context of his long battle with the Judaizers. Once Paul understood that Jew and Gentile are on equal footing before God relative to election and that election could not be based on merit, either personal or national, he was committed to the proposition that grace was a free gift (Rom. 11:5–6). Paul and the Judaizers agreed that the Cross was God's act of salvation, but Paul went beyond this to argue that grace must govern every feature of the Christian life:

> Now this is our boast: Our conscience testifies that we have conducted ourselves in the world, and especially in our relations with you, in the holiness and sincerity that are from God. We have done so not according to worldly wisdom but according to God's grace. (2 Cor. 1:12)

For Paul the grace of God is a potent ethical force:

> For what the law was powerless to do in that it was weakened in the sinful nature, God did by sending his own Son ... in order that the righteous requirements of the law might be fully met in us, who do not live according to the sinful nature, but according to the Spirit. (Rom. 8:3–4)

Here Paul paints an image strikingly similar to James, although the vocabulary palate is different. The "righteous requirements" of the law are to be met, just as James argues for "the perfect law that gives freedom" (James 1:25), the "royal law" (2:8), the "law that gives freedom" (2:12). Both Paul and James have an idea of life lived under the direction of God, whether "the Spirit" with Paul or the implanted word with James (1:21).

For Paul a life under grace and in the Spirit is a life of transformation, beginning with the mind ("Do not conform any longer to the pattern of this world, but be transformed by the renewing of your mind," Rom. 12:2), and continuing to the death of the old life and its patterns ("We died to sin, how can we live in it any longer? ... our old self was crucified with him so that the body of sin might be done away with, that we should no longer be slaves to sin," 6:2, 6), in favor of a new life lived in emulation of the life of our Lord ("count yourselves dead to sin but alive to God in Christ Jesus," 6:11; "For those God foreknew he also predestined to be conformed to the likeness of his Son," 8:29).

Again, the imagery is different, but Paul's thrust is thoroughly consonant with the thought of James. When Paul pleads with the Roman Christians to put aside their conformity with the pattern of this world, he is making the general case of which the plea of James to avoid favoritism is the particular expression. Even the Pauline language of election and conformity to the image of Jesus Christ rings true to James, where in 1:18 he says, "He chose to give us birth through the word of truth, that we might be a kind of first-fruits of all he created." So between James and Paul there is no disagreement of substance, but only one of vocabulary and emphasis. Paul was trying to argue against a false doctrine that deeds of the law apart from faith lead to salvation. James does not see faith by itself as deficient; rather, he argues that true faith always results in good deeds.[23]

But amid this flurry of theology it must be remembered that James, like Jesus, calls us to obedience—a radical obedience. To paraphrase Bonhoeffer, when Christ calls you, he calls you to come and die.[24]

"Belief" and Its Range of Meaning

THIS MULTIFORM RANGE of meanings for the same theological concept is operative not only in drawing comparisons between two different authors or books in the Bible, but it is sometimes present in a single book. In James we encounter various uses of the term "faith." The demons have a "faith," as do the opponents of James. But James would hardly consider either of these a saving faith. Now this variety in meaning might appear troublesome and awkward.

But there is a parallel in the Gospel of John that may shed light on James. In that Gospel the word group *pisteuo/pistis* ("believe/belief") has this character. In John 2:11, after the miracle at Cana, the disciples "put their faith in" Jesus. This belief, we assume, is a saving faith. This assumption appears to be confirmed in 3:16, "For God so loved the world that he gave his one and only Son, that whoever believes in him shall not perish but have eternal life." But in 6:66 many of the disciples who had believed in him "turned back" because of a hard saying and "no longer followed him." So the "belief" of some of the

---

23. Martin, *James*, 81.

24. Dietrich Bonhoeffer, *The Cost of Discipleship*, tr. R. H. Fuller (New York: Macmillan 1960), 99.

disciples was not salvific. In John 11 is recounted the story of the raising of Lazarus. Jesus waits to travel to Bethany until Lazarus has died, and he provides this explanation to his disciples: "For your sake I am glad that I was not there, so that you may believe" (11:14). Jesus apparently holds that the faith the disciples possess is growing toward, but is not yet, saving faith. In 12:42–43 we learn that "many even among the leaders believed in him. But because of the Pharisees they would not confess their faith . . . for they loved praise from men more than praise from God."

In other words, John, like James, can use the word "faith" to plot locations along a continuum. For John there are those who recognize that in Jesus God is at work but refuse to believe. There are those who believe at first, but turn away. There are those who believe but whose desire for worldly praise overpowers their belief. There are those who are growing toward saving faith. Finally, there is saving faith that is manifested in obeying the commands of Jesus (John 15:9–10). For James at least two kinds of "faith" are not true "faith," for they cannot save: the "faith" of the demons and the "faith" of the antinomian party that says there is a "faith" without deeds (James 2:18–19). James holds to only one kind of "faith" that deserves the name, that is true, that has the power to save, and that manifests itself in deeds. This "active faith" flows from a life lived in concert with Jesus, just as in John Jesus asks us to "remain in [his] love" (John 15:9).

THE TEACHING OF James in this passage is a call to integrity, a call to live out the gospel. This "living out" is seen not only in the persuasive power one life can have over others in terms of evangelism, but also in the potency of the gospel of Christ to confront structures of evil that, like the stratification of Roman social culture, infect our world. It is with matters such as these that the following discussion is concerned.

One of the crucial aspects of the teaching of James here is the importance of living lives of Christian integrity. Stephen Carter, the William Nelson Cromwell Professor of Law at Yale University and the author of the influential book *The Culture of Disbelief: How American Law and Politics Trivialize Religious Devotion*, has written a new book titled *Integrity*.[25] Carter says that the definition of integrity in the philosophical literature, which is "living life according to a consistent set of principles," is inadequate. The leaders of the Nazi regime, after all, were consistent in following their warped convictions. Instead, Carter says, integrity means living life according to a "deeply discerned set

---

25. Stephen L. Carter, *Integrity* (New York: Basic Books, 1994).

of principles."[26] Carter is aware that this definition does not guarantee "morality," but he is writing in and for contemporary pluralistic American culture, and one can no longer assume a common religious or Christian moral framework. However, he does point out that the current popular definition of tolerance as the suspension of moral judgment is erroneous, foolhardy, and dangerous. Tolerance in a democracy, he says, means to be open to dialog with those of different opinions, and in contemporary America it ought to mean an openness to dialog with those who embrace an ethic based on religious principle.

James calls us to live consistently according to *Christian* principles. We need to do this for at least three broad reasons. (1) It brings glory to God. Augustine said of God, "You have formed us for yourself, and our hearts are restless till they find rest in you."[27] Our living consistent with his teachings brings God pleasure.

(2) Such a pattern of life is our rightful heritage. James says growing up in faith is what makes us mature and complete (James 1:4). It is ultimately to our benefit that we grow into what God intends for us.

(3) There is something that others find attractive about lives that are lived with consistency. A reporter for the CBS news program *Coast to Coast* staged an experiment.[28] He "lost" his wallet in the back seat of a cab several times in order to see how people would react. In the wallet he placed a business card with his cellular phone number, $23.00, and a shopping list, including a notation to get a "present for dad." Nearly everyone who noticed the wallet in the back seat of the cab called him within minutes and returned it to him with every item intact. Even though some of these "good Samaritans" were working at minimum wage jobs, each refused his offer of the $23.00 as a reward. And so we found Mohammed, Sonia, and the rest attractive because of their honesty and integrity.

Recently I spoke at a conference for people involved in ministries of prayer and evangelism. During one of the breaks I had a conversation with a pastor friend of mine who had been to an evangelism training seminar. After a session one day he had returned to his hotel "pumped up," in his words, to put some of what he had learned into practice. "So that night I prayed that God would put an opportunity before me," he said.

God answered his prayer. The following morning found him in the hotel hot tub. Soon he was joined by three men, all of whom knew each other.

---

26. See Michael Cromartie, "How We Muddle Our Morals," *Books and Culture: A Christian Review* (May/June 1996), 14.

27. Augustine, *Confessions*, 1.1.1.

28. January 29, 1997.

Immediately he sensed that God was answering his prayer. But then these companions began to drink Jack Daniels and to snort cocaine. Suddenly, the scenario did not seem so promising. But my friend entered into conversation with them, which eventually turned to the matter of the professional life of each. Not knowing what to expect, my friend told the men his line of work and that he was in town for a training session in evangelism. One of the men then responded, "That is really interesting. I have a question for you. Can you tell me what 'born again' means? I really do not know. Until recently I laughed at people who said they were 'born again,' but some people I have known for years talk that way now, and the thing is, I have watched them and I know that their lives have been transformed. So, what is 'born again'? I really need to know." The consistent model of Christian living has the power to draw others to the kingdom.

Dietrich Bonhoeffer offers an interesting view on the issue. In his book *The Cost of Discipleship*, this modern martyr[29] draws a distinction between "cheap grace" and "costly grace." "Cheap grace" is a type of faith that does not necessarily lead to actions, because it does not demand a changed heart. "Cheap grace," he says, means

> grace as a doctrine, a principle, a system. It means forgiveness of sins proclaimed as a general truth, the love of God taught as the Christian conception of God. An intellectual assent to that idea is held to be of itself sufficient to secure remission of sins. . . . Cheap grace is the preaching of forgiveness without requiring repentance, baptism without church discipline. . . . Cheap grace is grace without discipleship, grace without the cross, grace without Jesus Christ, living and incarnate.[30]

In contrast to cheap grace, Bonhoeffer defines "costly grace" as "the kingly rule of Christ, for whose sake a man will pluck out the eye which causes him to stumble. . . . Such grace is *costly* because it calls us to follow, and it is *grace* because it calls us to follow *Jesus Christ*."[31] Bonhoeffer makes the point that

---

29. As a young man Bonhoeffer was aware that National Socialism was an attempt to make history without God, and in 1933 he denounced the system that made the Führer its god and idol. He was a leader of the underground confessional church in Germany during World War II. Eventually he became involved in a failed plot to assassinate Hitler and was executed at the concentration camp at Flossenburg on April 9, 1945. For a fuller account, see Thomas Powers, "The Conspiracy That Failed," *The New York Review of Books* (Jan. 9, 1997), 49–54. The article is a review of several books on the so-called "German Resistance" and mentions Bonhoeffer.

30. Dietrich Bonhoeffer, *The Cost of Discipleship*, 45, 47.

31. Ibid., 47.

"cheap grace" convinces the sinner that only those who believe can obey, and thus the sinner is able to engage in the self-delusion of absolution. Since they do not believe, they cannot obey. This, Bonhoeffer claims, is one of the sadly twisted results of cheap grace. Christians must remember and live by both sides of the proposition, "Only he who believes is obedient, and only he who is obedient believes."[32] When Jesus called his disciples, it meant that faith "can no longer mean sitting still and waiting—they must rise and follow him. The call frees them from all earthly ties, and binds them to Jesus Christ alone. They must burn their boats and plunge into absolute insecurity in order to learn the demand and the gift of Christ."[33] Obedience both precedes faith and is the consequence of faith.

Bonhoeffer worked out his salvation in the midst of the Nazi regime in World War II. Americans face a difficult crucible, although we are not always aware of it. It is a crucible with elements to which we have perhaps become jaded, because we distance ourselves from them and claim they bear no relation to our lives. But they are a part of the American landscape. James said we have no business saying to those in need, "Go, I wish you well; keep warm and well fed. . . ." So perhaps we should open our ears and our eyes. Eazy-E, the now-deceased lead rapper of NWA (Niggers With Attitude), consciously "pushed the envelope" of imagery, brazenly rapping lyrics that feature "gunshots as backdrops to their brutal and ugly X-rated tales of drug-dealing, gangbanging and police confrontations." As Eazy-E tells it, gangster rap is something of the alternative press for the underclass in Los Angeles:

> We're telling the real story of what it's like living in places like Compton. We're giving [the fans] reality. We're like reporters. We give them the truth. People where we come from hear so many lies that the truth stands out like a sore thumb.[34]

Critics of American culture rightly decry the untrammeled violence and sexual malevolence that gangster rap employs like grease on the skids of its antinomian crusade not for justice, but for commercial success.[35] But we should be careful to point out that there are issues that have given rise to this hostility. James provides us with the examples of Abraham and Rahab, both of whom perceived a need and sought to meet it. Their faith was not dead

32. Ibid., 69, 76.
33. Ibid., 68.
34. Robert Hilburn, "Rap," *Los Angeles Times Calendar* (April 2, 1989).
35. One of the distinctive features of Los Angeles gangster rap was its unabashed concern for the accumulation of wealth. The New York-based group Public Enemy, in contrast, positioned themselves as the harbingers of Black interests and Black nationalism.

but living. Perhaps the evangelical community has been too slow to recognize the real needs in our society, a complex of factors that can crush those affected. Who will be Abraham or Rahab today?

Recently I had Pastor Willie Jemison of the Oakdale Covenant Church in Chicago speak to one of my classes. When Pastor Jemison came to this church on the south side of Chicago in the early 1970s, he realized that education was the greatest need in the community. Under his leadership the church began to implement a series of educational programs tailored to meet the particular needs in that community. Currently 99 percent of the young people at Oakdale graduate from high school, while the figure is about 50 percent for the community at large; 85 percent of the young people from Oakdale graduate from college, while the figure is about 20 percent for the community at large. Here is a church that has perceived a need and decided to step in and address it.

South-central Los Angeles was, by the mid-1980s, well on its way to becoming a wasteland, deserted by the rest of the economic and social powers of southern California. The area experienced double-digit unemployment, overcrowded schools, and deteriorating housing. A special report in the *Los Angeles Times* claimed that "the Black ghetto is not a viable community . . . it is slowly dying."[36] The Los Angeles Unified School District, then the second largest in the nation, served 600,000 students in classrooms more crowded than those in Mississippi, and with a drop-out rate of between 30 and 50 percent. As California suffered from a regional recession in the 1980s, its per capita student expenditure plunged to thirty-third place among the states, with a per student amount one-third that of the state of New York. A 1989 UCLA study found that poverty was increasing more rapidly among Los Angeles Latinos, especially the youth, than any other urban group in the United States.[37]

There were other inequalities. Southern California experienced a service industry job boom in the 1980s, but the boom was in the suburbs. Young suburban women and men could find work readily available at fast-food establishments and at malls. But for young people in the ghetto, the jobs were as unattainable as if they were on the moon. As Mike Davis points out, there was another product ready to attract the developing business acumen of ghetto youth.[38] A social historian who writes in biting and elegant prose, he

---

36. Mike Davis, *City of Quartz: Excavating the Future in Los Angeles* (New York: Vintage, 1992), 302.
37. Paul Ong, *The Widening Divide: Income Inequality and Poverty in Los Angeles* (UCLA; June 1989), quoted in Mike Davis, *City of Quartz*, 315.
38. Mike Davis, *City of Quartz*, 309.

says, "Through 'crack' they have discovered a vocation for the ghetto in L.A.'s new 'world city' economy." The same story is chronicled by Bruce Springsteen in his song "Sinaloa Cowboys," which he wrote after reading an article in the *Los Angeles Times* about two Mexican brothers who worked in a drug lab in central California. In their eyes this option was more attractive than the conditions experienced by migrant workers. When he introduced the song during a concert in Fresno, one of the major cities in California's agriculture-rich Central Valley, he said, "Sixty years after John Steinbeck wrote *The Grapes of Wrath*, people are working under conditions in the Central Valley that as Americans we really shouldn't tolerate."[39]

The ghetto knows violence that is raw, inhumane, despicable. But in Los Angeles the rhetoric of safety has served to stratify, not unify. In 1965 the legendary Chief Parker of the LAPD told a television audience, "It is estimated that by 1970 45% of the metropolitan area of Los Angeles will be Negro; if you want any protection for your home and family . . . you're going to have to get in and support a strong police department. If you don't do that, come 1970, God help you."[40] Davis relates how in the spring of 1989 the "bad parent" provision of the Street Terrorism Enforcement and Prevention Act of 1988 (STEP) was tested in the arrest of a thirty-seven-year-old South-central woman, whose fifteen-year-old son had been arraigned for gang rape. The triumvirate of press, city attorneys, and police portrayed her as a "welfare queen," who was contributing to the rise of a generation of baby street terrorists. But some reporters dug deeper and found that the official version was faulty. The police had arrested and publicly humiliated a hard-working single-parent mother of three.[41] Davis offers this comment:

> As a result of the war on drugs every non-Anglo teenager in Southern California is now a prisoner of gang paranoia and associated demonology. Vast stretches of the region's sumptuous playgrounds, beaches and entertainment centers have become virtual no-go areas for young Blacks or Chicanos. . . .
>
> Don Jackson, an off-duty policeman from Hawthorne, precisely in order to make a point about de facto apartheid, led some ghetto kids into the Village. They carefully observed the law, yet, predictably, they were stopped, forced to kiss concrete, and searched. Jackson, despite police identification, was arrested for "disturbing the peace." Afterwards at a press conference, Chief Gates excoriated him for "provocations" and a "cheap publicity stunt," descriptions more aptly applied to

---

39. Nicholas Dawidoff, "The Pop Populist," *The New York Times Magazine* (Jan. 26, 1997), 71.
40. Mike Davis, *City of Quartz*, 320, n. 65.
41. Ibid., 283.

the LAPD. Similarly, a few weeks later, a busload of well-dressed Black members of Youth for Christ were humiliatingly surrounded by security guards and frisked for "drugs and weapons" at the popular Magic Mountain amusement park. Park managers adamantly defended their right to search "suspicious" (i.e., Black) youth as a matter of policy.[42]

As Christians we bear a responsibility to those caught in the grip of systemic evil and neglect. We also must recognize that at times we also are caught in the same net. Our desire for status and wealth is but one example. We are called to be Abraham and Rahab to our world.

Of course, the mere presence of systemic evil does not condone the acts of the sinner caught in the system. In his book *Not the Way It's Supposed to Be: A Breviary of Sin*, Cornelius Plantinga quotes Jack Beatty:

> Even poor youths, even poor, ill-educated youths, even poor, ill-educated youths who live in a society suffused by racism, must be responsible for their acts. To believe otherwise is to espouse an environmental determinism nearly as offensive to reason and morality as racism itself. Crime, arson, running amok in the streets, have social contexts, not social causes. The [media blare about] the contexts is an insidious distraction that rests on the presumption that society is responsible for the crimes against it. That is legal and moral nonsense.[43]

Plantinga then asks if society does not at least share in responsibility. I believe he is right. Individuals must be held accountable for their actions. If not, then the grace of God is a sham. But a society in which schools are unequally funded, when public instruction is marked by a legal mandate to avoid attempts to clarify morals, when the judicial system protects rap groups that glamorize the murder of police and inhuman violent behavior toward women, then, Plantinga says, perhaps society does bear some responsibility.

Augustine said that evil is, in effect, the absence of good.[44] Systemic evil may provide a context in which sin is more likely to thrive. But it does not "cause" the decision of a young man to murder a convenience store clerk. One of my childhood friends was shot by the police a decade ago. He had robbed a convenience store using a realistic looking squirt gun. When cornered by the police and ordered to stop, he turned and raised his pseudo-weapon. It was his last mistake. He had turned to robbery to pay for his drug habit. The social conditions in which he lived did not "cause" his death. He made

---

42. Ibid., 284, 286.
43. Cornelius Plantinga Jr., *Not the Way It's Supposed to Be: A Breviary of Sin* (Grand Rapids: Eerdmans, 1995), 64.
44. Augustine, *Confessions*, 7.11.17–12.18.

the decisions that led to it. But social conditions made those decision more likely.

Christopher Lasch, the influential, iconoclastic historian and critic of American culture, once offered his take on the matter relative to religion. According to Lasch,

> [Religion] is a challenge to self-pity and despair, temptations common to all of us, but especially to those born into the wrong social class. . . . Submission to God makes people less submissive in everyday life. It makes them less fearful but also less bitter and resentful, less inclined to make excuses for themselves. Modern social movements, on the other hand, tend to rely on resentment. . . . They distrust any understanding that would seem to "blame the victim." In this way they discourage the assumption of personal responsibility.[45]

It is the expression of sentiments like this that earn Lasch the ire of liberals. His condemnation of corporate capitalism has earned him the ire of conservatives. The Bible affirms that systemic evil is a reality. Paul refers to this evil as the principalities and powers (Rom. 8:38), and James refers to the power of hell (James 3:6). But the Bible also affirms that human beings bear personal responsibility for their actions. Further, James issues a call to Christians that is simple, yet awesome in its scope. What good is faith if you turn your back or close your eyes to others in need. Where are the Abrahams and the Rahabs, whose faith is proved in action?

Perhaps one of the most eloquent and powerful examples of faith in action is that of John Perkins. John Perkins was born in rural Mississippi in 1930. His family was not religious, but in fact, he says, was known for its tough disposition. Growing up in Mississippi he experienced racism and hatred firsthand. As a teenager he watched his older brother die after having been severely beaten by a white deputy sheriff. Shortly thereafter he moved to California and felt he had escaped the crushing conditions of racial hatred and economic oppression of the South.

In 1957 Perkins became a Christian. Shortly thereafter he became involved with a group of Christian businessmen. Two of them asked John to go with them to visit California youth prison camps. These camps were for young men, ages thirteen to seventeen. Most of them, says Perkins, were black.

> A black witness was needed. And that black witness was me. . . . These boys in prison camp often had backgrounds just like mine. Their voices and their accents sounded like guys I grew up with. . . . Like me, they

---

45. Quoted in Mary Ann Glendon, "The Man Who Loved Women and Democracy," *First Things* (February 1977), 43.

came without many skills, without much education. Like me, they didn't have a strong religious background.[46]

But, Perkins realized, he had escaped by God's grace. "So if God had done all this for me, and if He loved these others no less than He did me, what did all this mean? What did it say to *my* plans for *my* 'good' Christian life?"[47]A conviction began to grow in him.

> Real soon the conviction became a command. I remember the night it happened—the night God spoke to me through His Word about going back to Mississippi and starting a ministry for Him there. I was giving my testimony that night to an all-white church in Arcadia, California.
>
> Standing before the crowd of people gathered there, I used as my text Romans 10:1,2, where Paul says, "Brethren, my heart's desire and prayer to God for Israel is, that they might be saved. For I bear them record that they have a zeal for God, but not according to knowledge."
>
> God took the power of Paul's love for His people and shot it through me, saying, "John, my desire for you is that you go back to Mississippi, because I bear your people witness that they have a zeal for God, but it is not enlightened."[48]

Armed with the "full gospel," a message of new life in Christ, and the biblical call to justice, John Perkins, his wife, Vera Mae, and their children, started Voice of Calvary Ministries, beginning in the town of Mendenhall, Mississippi. They started Bible classes for young and old; developed programs to send young people to college; inaugurated a child care center, voter education and registration programs, and leadership development programs; established a housing cooperative, a farmer's cooperative, and a retail cooperative, as well as a health center and a legal aid center—all of this because John Perkins understood that social and economic problems will never be solved until hearts are changed, and that changed hearts do not rest until justice and hope come to full flower. He saw the truth of the gospel, that God in interested in the whole person.

In tones that are characteristically gentle yet probing, John Perkins writes that maybe "evangelical Christians, black and white, were confusing theology with the status quo."[49] In this he stands as a prophet both to the white church, which he accurately says too often ignores its responsibility to all

---

46. John Perkins, *Let Justice Roll Down* (Ventura, Calif.: Regal 1976), 78–79.
47. Ibid., 79.
48. Ibid., 79–80.
49. Ibid., 109.

those created in the image of God, and to the black church, which in his judgment had too often failed to speak out. He describes it this way: "If Voice of Calvary is a model, it is because it is one of the few times that evangelism, social action and community development have been put together in the black and poor community of the United States." Although he was nearly beaten to death in 1970 while in the custody of law enforcement officials following a civil rights demonstration, John Perkins has never lost sight of his vision, his hope, his courage, and his compassion. In the crucible of self-reflection following this torture, the truth of these principles was reified for him.

> I began to see with horror that hate could destroy me. . . . This whole business of hating and hating back. It's what keeps the vicious cycle of racism going. . . . Jesus looked at the mob that lynched him . . . [and] he forgave them. It's a profound, mysterious truth, Jesus' concept of love overpowering hate. I may not see its victory in my lifetime. But I know it's true . . . because it happened to me. On that bed, full of bruises and stitches—God made it true for me. He washed my hatred away and replaced it with a love for the white man in rural Mississippi.[50]

John Perkins has replicated this effective model of community development in Jackson, Mississippi, and Pasadena, California. He is the cofounder and chairman of the Christian Community Development Association, and the publisher of *Urban Family* magazine. He has sought tangible ways to address the social, economic, and spiritual needs of people who, through a combination of personal choice and systemic indifference, are at the margins of our society. These are people who, in his words, God loved "no less than He did me."

John Perkins has taken the call of James seriously and worked to create a place where casual or systemic favoritism finds no home. James warns his readers against empty words, against the pious chant, "Be well, be warm, be fed." Perkins has taken up the struggle to meet these needs and to empower people to meet them for themselves. In the foreword to Dr. Perkins' book *Let Justice Roll Down*, Senator Mark Hatfield wrote:

> This is the story of a black man who was nearly a martyr, and is surely a modern saint. Most of us have never known any of the ruthless poverty, the raw violence and hardened injustice that were inflicted upon John Perkins as a black person in Mississippi. And there are few whom I have ever known whose lives have responded to such overwhelming indignities with such a witness of miraculous compassion, vision and hope.

---

50. Ibid., 204–6.

The story of John Perkins reveals the transforming and revolutionary power of Jesus Christ. . . . [It is a story] about the costs of discipleship . . . [and] the relentless hope and the limitless love which can be born in the hearts of those who follow Jesus.[51]

In the hallowed halls of universities and colleges, in the sanctified confines of churches, issues such as community development, social action, and justice are studied. John Perkins and his family have lived them out in the concrete, with their blood, their sweat, their tears, and their joy. They offer to us a living monument to the potent caliber of hope for what can be—careful study that results in action, a passion for the good of others, and compassion that flows from the very heart of God. These virtues James would have lodge in our hearts and minds, verities whose pursuit is worth the commitment of a lifetime.

---

51. Ibid., 7.

James 3:1–12

NOT MANY OF you should presume to be teachers, my brothers, because you know that we who teach will be judged more strictly. [2]We all stumble in many ways. If anyone is never at fault in what he says, he is a perfect man, able to keep his whole body in check.

[3]When we put bits into the mouths of horses to make them obey us, we can turn the whole animal. [4]Or take ships as an example. Although they are so large and are driven by strong winds, they are steered by a very small rudder wherever the pilot wants to go. [5]Likewise the tongue is a small part of the body, but it makes great boasts. Consider what a great forest is set on fire by a small spark. [6]The tongue also is a fire, a world of evil among the parts of the body. It corrupts the whole person, sets the whole course of his life on fire, and is itself set on fire by hell.

[7]All kinds of animals, birds, reptiles and creatures of the sea are being tamed and have been tamed by man, [8]but no man can tame the tongue. It is a restless evil, full of deadly poison.

[9]With the tongue we praise our Lord and Father, and with it we curse men, who have been made in God's likeness. [10]Out of the same mouth come praise and cursing. My brothers, this should not be. [11]Can both fresh water and salt water flow from the same spring? [12]My brothers, can a fig tree bear olives, or a grapevine bear figs? Neither can a salt spring produce fresh water.

IN THIS SECTION James makes three basic points. (1) Small items, such as the tongue, a rudder, or even one teacher, can and often do control a larger whole, such as the body, a ship, or an entire congregation. (2) One source of evil is hell, the stronghold of Satan. (3) When the tongue is influenced by the forces of hell, the result is severe double-mindedness. This irrationality is seen in that the same tongue may praise God but curse people, who have been made in God's likeness.

The connection between this section and those that have gone before is not immediately obvious,[1] yet it is there. While it is true that James introduces a new notion by discussing teachers, the heart of this section, like that found in 1:19–21, has to do with proper speech. James launches this discussion because verbal attack, in the same manner as the favoritism he has just discussed, has a particularly corrosive and lethal effect on the life of a community, especially a community of faith. Indeed, either of the two discloses that for the false teachers, the targets of James's ire, the community is no distinct community at all, but merely another avenue to personal power. The presence of both verbal attack and favoritism James regards as nothing short of critical—dangerous in the extreme.

Another sinew that binds this section to what has gone before is the frequent use of the word "body" (*soma*). It first appears in reference to the tongue as a part of the human body, but James quickly uses it to refer to the Christian community. Earlier we noted that the opening of the letter is concerned with personal morality, but that with chapter 2 James turns to corporate morality; that continues to be the case here.

A fascinating feature of this passage is that the discussion proceeds on two levels. At first blush the text can be read (and rightly so) in a straightforward fashion—it is about the danger of the tongue, a small part of the body that can do great damage. But we soon realize that we are in the presence of a writer of great facility, for James deftly points to a second level of meaning via his double use of the word "body," referring to both individuals and the Christian church. On this level we see that teachers (and leaders), although a small percentage of the entire body of a Christian community, are able to guide the whole church, just as a rudder guides a ship; with the tongue, leaders can poison the whole community. In 3:4 James notes that the crucial issue with the rudder is the nature of the pilot and his will. The question, then, is whether the teachers are shaped and controlled by the will of God, or by Gehenna.

It should not be overlooked that with chapter 3 James inaugurates a lengthy discussion composed of three blocks of material dealing with pure speech. The first (3:1–12) has to do with his claim that pure speech does not arise from anger or duplicity; in the second (3:13–18) the case is made that pure speech has its origin in wisdom; and in the final section (4:1–10) James argues that pure prayer does not arise from anger, but rather has its home in trust.[2] Here we see many of the themes James has already brought into play writ large.

James's thought in the present section has three layers. The first (3:1–2) is a proverb concerning teachers, which serves to introduce the heart of the

---

1. Sophie Laws, *The Epistle of James*, 140, sees no clear link.
2. See Peter H. Davids, *The Epistle of James*, 135, 149, 155.

section. The second layer (3:3–5) builds on this proverb by discussing the practical difficulty of controlling speech by focusing on the tongue, as if it had a mind of its own. The final layer (3:6–12) also furthers the thought in 3:1–2 by outlining the power of the tongue and its propensity for impropriety. In all of these our author draws on a wealth of images, from animal husbandry to navigation to fire to horticulture, in order to illustrate the power of the tongue for evil or for good.

Teachers and Pure Speech (3:1–2)

VERSE 1 BEGINS with the negative "not" (*me*), in order to emphasize the danger associated with the office of teacher. The responsibilities of teaching in the context of the church are serious, so serious that great deliberation ought to accompany the aspiration. It is also possible, given what James is about to say, that some who exercised that function in the early church should lay it aside. James takes pains to show that he is aware of these demands, for he is a teacher, as the second clause ("we who teach") demonstrates. The use of the first person plural here indicates that the context James has in view is teaching within the Christian community. It should be noted that the New Testament church had a dire need for teachers, but little recourse when it came to examining the qualifications and testing the orthodoxy of these teachers.

The reason for James's warning here is that teachers will receive a more strict judgment if they fail. It is not unlikely that the writer has in mind the teaching of Jesus: "But if anyone causes one of these little ones who believe in me to sin, it would be better for him to have a large millstone hung around his neck and to be drowned in the depths of the sea" (Matt. 18:6; cf. Mark 9:42; Luke 17:2). James does not specifically identify this judgment, but given the teaching just cited, it is logical to assume that James has in mind the eschatological judgment. The fact that James has this judgment in view at other points also leads to this conclusion.

By nature of their position teachers have an inordinately great opportunity to influence others within the congregation. It seems unavoidable that James is blaming certain teachers in the community for teaching false practice, such as favoritism and an erroneously antinomian attitude. Having dealt with each error, he now focuses on the source of those errors, the false teachers themselves. James probably has in mind another of Jesus' teachings: "But I tell you that men will have to give account on the day of judgment for every careless word they have spoken" (Matt. 12:36). The false teachers' words are idle not simply because they are spoken in a thoughtless moment, but because unlike the word of God, they are not able to accomplish their purpose. The doctrine and practice advocated by these teachers do not contribute to the edification of the community, but instead are detrimental.[3]

Within the early church the position of teacher was one of high status. As noted earlier, the human desire for status was endemic to the Roman world, and while many sought to meet this need by joining the *collegia*, some sought illegitimately to meet the need by joining the church. The respect granted to teachers within Judaism ought not to be ignored either.[4] There was evidently a serious problem in this regard in the early church. Without any clear standards, anyone could be put forward as an authority, and even Paul was challenged on this matter on occasion. James, like Paul, issues a plea to accept his authority as paramount over his opponents. But he does so in a fashion not reminiscent of Paul.

In verse 2 James admits a very human truth—none of us is perfect, we all stumble frequently. The word "many" here might refer to either the number or the variety of sins, but most likely refers to both. But there is at least one sin that is common to everyone, the sin of the tongue. At this point James has in mind not only teachers, but all Christians, although, of course, the effects of stumbling in the case of teachers can have far wider effects. But if, James imagines, there were someone who never sinned in speech, then that person would be perfect, for it is much easier to control the body than to control the tongue. The notion of a perfect man (*teleos aner*) must be that of completeness and maturity, just as in 1:4. This is completeness in Christian virtue, not perfect sinlessness.

To "keep [the] whole body in check" implies control of the passions. This, in turn, serves as a link to the *yeṣer* idea discussed earlier and forms another link to 3:6. Speech, and especially the tongue as emblematic of speech, is often the tool of the *yeṣer ha-ra*.[5]

The wisdom tradition had much to say concerning the untamed tongue.[6] But more is at work here, for James has in mind teachings that lead people astray, that teach theological untruth as if it were truth. James insists that someone who is faultless in what he says is able to bridle (*chalinago*; the same

---

3. See G. B. Caird and L. D. Hurst, *New Testament Theology* (Oxford: Clarendon, 1994), 328.

4. Joachim Jeremias, *Jerusalem in the Time of Jesus* (Philadelphia: Fortress, 1969), 243–45, provides a number of examples. The Talmud (*b. Yom.* 71b) relates that one year on the eve of the Day of Atonement a crowd was escorting the high priest to his home. Having spied two scribes, the crowd left the high priest in favor of them.

5. Davids, *The Epistle of James*, 138.

6. Proverbs 16:27–28 says, "A scoundrel plots evil, and his speech is like a scorching fire. A perverse man stirs up dissension, and a gossip separates close friends" (see also 10:8, 11, 19; 18:7–8).

word is used in 1:26) his body. His point, made a number of times in this section, is that a small item (a bit, a rudder, a tongue) can guide and control the larger whole. It should not be lost on us that teachers (and other leaders) in the church fit this image nicely. The same small member can either guide the larger whole to safety or condemn it to the ravages of rancor and falsehood.[7] When the tongue is out of control, it can destroy much good that has already been done; a leader whose teaching is errant can in short order devastate years of careful and healthy growth in the life of a congregation. Such sullied theology was threatening the community to which James wrote, resulting in imperfect practice. He had to put a stop to it and steer the community in the right direction.

The Tongue Can Control Us (3:3–5)

IN VERSES 3–4 James begins a series of illustrations from everyday life meant, in part, to bring home to his readers with especially keen vividness the power of the tongue either to corrode or to nurture. The first two analogies are not quite precise (the tongue does not control the body in the fashion that a bit controls a horse or a rudder a ship), but the meaning is plain enough. The church is controlled by those in leadership roles. Thus, just as the rider directs the horse[8] and the pilot the rudder, so the Christian teacher must be under the direction of the proper authority.[9]

Dibelius argued[10] that 3:3–5 is derived from Hellenistic literature, and this shifting accounts for some of the grammatical difficulty present. While the vocabulary is certainly odd (many of the terms are found only here in Scripture), the vast number of parallels suggest that these images were common in the Hellenistic world. Therefore, no specific parallel is in view. James simply appropriated what he knew to be stock phrases and crafted them to his own ends.

---

7. Early in World War II a shell from the German battleship *Bismarck* sunk the heavy cruiser *Hood*, the pride of the British navy. A great chase commenced, and the *Bismarck* was finally doomed when a torpedo destroyed its rudder, causing it to sail haplessly in circles until a barrage of British naval artillery sent her to the bottom of the Atlantic. See Winston Churchill, *The Grand Alliance* (Boston: Houghton and Mifflin, 1950), 315–19.

8. This was an image known to ancient writers; see Plutarch, *Moralia*, 33.

9. Peter H. Davids, *The Epistle of James*, 139, refers unfavorably to Reicke's explanation that James wishes to link Paul's image of the church as a body to the image of the church as a boat. This begs the dating question, for there is no biblical reference to the church as a ship. The reference to the ark in 1 Peter 3:20 may provide the basis for this picture, but there is no evidence for it.

10. M. Dibelius, *James: A Commentary on the Epistle of James*, rev. H. Greeven, tr. M. A. Williams (Hermeneia; Philadelphia: Fortress, 1976), 185–90.

In verse 5 James displays some of his literary skill, particularly alliteration: The tongue is a small (*mikron*) member (*melos*) but boasts of great things (*megala*). James signals his intention by claiming that the tongue makes boasts, and boasting in the New Testament is generally considered a sin, as it indicates a desire to place oneself in the role of God. Davids[11] points out how James here executes a shift in tone: Both the bit and the rudder were discussed in positive terms, but here the tongue is discussed in terms that are essentially negative. This is because the potential of the tongue is so much greater than that of the bit or the rudder; it is capable of sublime heights, but also of sinking to the most pernicious depths of evil. James's point is that we should not underestimate the powerful potential of leadership positions nor undervalue the damage that can be done through careless or mean-spirited speech.

James then turns to a new image, that of a fire set by a small spark. Here the image is clearly negative. Although there are parallels in Greek literature,[12] the background for this saying is found in Jewish literature. The wisdom tradition especially has much to say about the destructive power of the tongue, at times associating the tongue with images of fire.[13] Few disasters in the ancient world were more feared than fire, as the ancients possessed precious few resources to battle them, [14] even in urban centers.[15] The point of the image is to emphasize the great destructive power of the tongue.

The Power of the Tongue (3:6–12)

IN BLUNT FASHION, having pressed into service some of the strongest terms he has at his command, James makes clear in verse 6 the effects and source of an errant tongue. At this point both levels of meaning are in play: The uncontrolled tongue can cause great harm, and Christian teachers whose teaching in the church is errant cause great harm.

---

11. Davids, *The Epistle of James*, 140.

12. See Ralph P. Martin, *James*, 113.

13. Note Prov. 26:21: "As charcoal to embers and as wood to fire, so is a quarrelsome man for kindling strife" (see also 16:27; Ps. 39:1–3; 120:2–4).

14. In one of his letters to Trajan Pliny makes mention of an urban fire: "While I was inspecting another area of the province, a fire in Nicomedia consumed many private homes and two public buildings, the club for elders and the temple of Isis, even though a road runs between them. It was encouraged at first by a breeze, but it would not have been so violent were it not for the uncaring attitude of the citizens. It seems people stood and watched the disaster, immobile, doing nothing to stop it. Nor is there even one fire engine in town, nor a bucket, nor any other instrument for fighting a fire" (Pliny, *Epistulae*, 10.33).

15. Traditionally the "fires" mentioned here are pictured as forest fires, a tradition the NIV continues. While this is not incorrect, the Greek term used here, *hylen*, is derived from *hyle*, which means a conflagration, whether of timber or cut wood. For this reason the horror of fire in an urban center is not out of the question here.

But beneath the apparently obvious meaning is great complexity. Many of the phrases are enigmatic at best. Furthermore, the first portion of verse 6 contains five terms in the nominative case but only one verb in the indicative (*kathistatai*), here rendered as "(*present*) *among* the parts of the body." The difficulty is to know how best to assign the verb. In addition, the text is marked by a number of variant readings, which has led some commentators to surmise that the text as we have it is corrupt.[16] There is no gainsaying the fact that this passage is difficult to interpret, but we must follow it. To pursue "reconstructed" versions, as some have suggested, is to engage in fancy and to abandon the integrity of the exegetical task.

As we saw above, the statement that the tongue is a fire clearly echoes Old Testament imagery concerning the tongue and inopportune speech. But in choosing to use *kosmos* ("world") James has left us, perhaps intentionally, with a term rich in various meanings. The linkage of this word with "evil" suggests that of the many nuances assigned to *kosmos* in the New Testament, here it must mean the world and its forces opposed to God. A variety of characters inhabit this world, and James clearly believes that the false teachers are citizens of that world, or are at least under the influence of that world, even if they lack this self-awareness.

The point James is making is that the great "world of evil" is seen in smaller, specific examples. On one level the uncontrolled tongue is an example of this world-evil that is opposed to God. On another level, the teachers opposed to James are an example of this same world. Neither the tongue nor the teachers are guided by the Spirit of God, but just as a rudder is controlled by the pilot, the uncontrolled tongue and the false teachers are guided by the forces of Gehenna.

There are other grammatical difficulties with this verse. The NIV has chosen to understand "a world of evil" as grammatically connected to the opening phrase "the tongue is a fire." Most commentators disagree, claiming that the verb "to be" should be understood in the opening phrase, which then becomes a complete sentence. This has the advantage of allowing both occurrences of *glossa* ("tongue") to register in translation: "And the tongue is a fire. The tongue is a wicked world present among our members." But, as Martin points out,[17] there is really little difference between the two translations. The point is that the tongue is often guilty of realizing its potential for evil, and in so doing infects the rest of the body.

This, in fact, is what James says at the end of verse 6, that the tongue can corrupt or stain the entire person (*soma*, lit., "body"). Here is another way of

---

16. See James H. Ropes, *The Epistle of St. James*, 234; James B. Adamson, *The Epistle of James*, 158.

17. Martin, *James*, 115.

making the point that he has already registered: Although small, the tongue controls the larger whole (3:2, 3, 4). James continues his series of negative comments about the tongue in stating that it "sets the whole course of his life on fire." That is, the tongue can corrupt all of life, whether that of an individual or that of a community. Given the double narrative of the passage, James most likely intends this ambiguity.

In his phrase "is itself set on fire by hell," James traces the root of evil, the mouthpiece of which are the teachers and the expressions of which are (particularly) favoritism and antinomianism. The Greek word translated as "hell" is *geenna* (usually transliterated as "Gehenna"), which referred to Ge Hinnom, the valley south of Jerusalem that had become a symbol of the locus of evil and the stronghold of Satan (see Bridging Contexts section). It seems clear that James is arguing that Satan is the ultimate source of the corrosive false teachings offered by the leaders in the church.[18] He had previously identified the *yeṣer ha-ra* (the evil impulse) as a source for evil within a person. Here he identifies a source contributing to the *yeṣer ha-ra*, which is Satan.[19]

In short, James 3:6 captures and intensifies the thrust of 3:3–5, that the tongue is capable of great harm. James achieves this effect through a pastiche of images of great evocative force that, as both Martin and Davids point out,[20] are marked more for their strong impression than for their great grammatical clarity.

In juxtaposition to the inability of human beings to control the tongue, James offers the idea that human beings can train, and have trained, members of the animal kingdom (v. 7). The ancients generally viewed the animal kingdom as symbolic of disorder, but also prided themselves on their ability to tame nature. Perhaps it would be better to say that the ancients believed that reason governed both nature and human convention, and that when human beings were able to harness nature, it was evidence of the potency of the rational spirit in the universe.[21]

But James also clearly has in mind the biblical account of creation, especially God's granting to humankind the right to rule over "the fish of the sea and the birds of the air, over the livestock, over all the earth, and over all the creatures that move along the ground" (Gen. 1:26). James even employs the typical biblical division of the animal world in four classes (cf. also Gen. 9:2).

---

18. This interpretation is strengthened by the appearance of similar themes in 3:15 ("Such 'wisdom' does not come down from heaven, but is earthly, unspiritual, of the devil") and in 4:7 ("Resist the devil").

19. *Gehenna* (here rendered "hell") could function as a circumlocution for Satan, just as "heaven" is frequently a circumlocution for God (see Luke 15:21).

20. Martin, *James*, 116; Davids, *The Epistle of James*, 143–44.

21. Cicero, *De natura deorum*, 2.34.

This oblique reference to creation calls to mind the recurrent *Leitmotiv* of "mature and complete,"[22] which carries the nuance of "proper end." God created human beings for a purpose, and this purpose will not be met by following the false teachers.

James continues his thought: "But no man can tame the tongue. It is a restless evil, full of deadly poison." The inability of the human race to tame the tongue is evidence of the irrational nature of its orientation and effort. The emphasis seems to have shifted from the tongue as a cipher for the church leader to the individual reference. The tongue is described as "restless" or "disorderly" (*akatastaton*),[23] which only serves to heighten the contrast with order and reason, which, by implication, are connected to the teaching of James in contrast to his opponents.

The image James uses here is of a barely and inadequately caged beast, which breaks forth with irrational destructive power. This restless irrationality is akin to the double-mindedness of the tongue, a theme with which we are by now familiar. This destructive power is further colored by the description of the tongue as replete with deadly poison; its arsenal is enhanced by a stock of deadly vitriol.[24]

Having made the claim that the tongue is untrustworthy and duplicitous, James goes on in verse 9 to provide an example. He eschews the use of metaphor to make this point, preferring instead an image drawn from a liturgical setting. This signals the reader that once again the tongue as a cipher for church leaders is at least one of the referents in view. The tongue as the emblem of double-mindedness was known in Judaism,[25] as we have already seen.[26]

According to James, we use the tongue for expressions that are mutually incompatible. The reference to "blessing" is of pointed significance, for it refers to and calls to mind God himself, as well as the relationship between humans and God. As the awareness of the holiness of God developed within Judaism, the Jews devised elliptical ways of speaking of God, one of which was "the Holy One, blessed be He."[27] James hopes to provide with this particularly arresting and poignant example, a stern warning concerning the importance of careful supervision over the tongue.

---

22. See the discussion on this expression in 1:4.

23. Found in the New Testament only here and in James 1:8.

24. The image was not unknown to the Hebrews. Psalm 140:3 says: "They make their tongues as sharp as a serpent's; the poison of vipers is on their lips."

25. Psalm 62:4 says, "With their mouths they bless, but in their hearts they curse."

26. See the discussion on James 1:26, pp. 96–97.

27. Midrash *Bereshith* 1. 1. Cf. also Mark 14:61, which includes the question of the high priest, "Are you the Christ, the Son of the Blessed One?"

To this example James adds another one, which immediately captures attention because of its keen gravity—"with it we curse [our fellow human beings], who have been made in God's likeness." The fact that the verb "curse" (*kataraomai*) occurs in the present tense cements the interpretation that James has in mind a concrete and not hypothetical situation in the church. The question of cursing is a minor but interesting one in the New Testament. Jesus cursed the fig tree (Matt. 21:19), and Paul seems to have been less than immune to cursing when the situation demanded strong talk.[28] But these are the exceptions, as the New Testament generally is against cursing. The idea, obviously, was to limit displays of irrational anger. This fits nicely with the general thrust of James's teaching.

It is also clear that the failure to perceive in one another God's image is a part of the complex. By showing favoritism and by displaying an antinomian spirit that apparently treated the commandment to love one's neighbor as a trifle, certain church leaders were actually encouraging a deviant teaching and practice. Failure to recognize that each of us is created in God's image will eventually allow us to oppress and enslave one another. This is, in fact, a cardinal reason why the worship of foreign gods was outlawed by God, for worship of other gods meant not only the rejection of God, but also the repudiation of his social and ethical standards.

The liturgical setting further exacerbates the importance of the issue. How can worshipers consciously mistreat their fellows and then expect to worship God in purity? So this verse neatly combines the two deviant practices of the church to which James writes.

"Out of the same mouth come praise and cursing. My brothers, this should not be" (v. 10). Drawing perhaps on Psalm 62:4, James alters the image to be a falsehood issued by the mouth—a change that perhaps takes place in order to remind his readers of the words of Jesus in Matthew 15:11: "What goes into a man's mouth does not make him 'unclean,' but what comes out of his mouth, that is what makes him 'unclean.'" Jesus understood actions to be revelatory of character, as the saying "A good tree cannot bear bad fruit" (7:18) attests. He also believed our speech to be revelatory of character, which is the essential point being made here. Our speech comes from the heart.

In verse 11 James includes a phrase of stock Mediterranean wisdom, rendered in Latin as *a fonte puro pura defluit aqua* ("from a pure spring flows pure water"). He also returns to the world of metaphor. A spring from which

---

28. In 1 Cor. 5:5 Paul offers his opinion that the man guilty of incest ought to be handed over to Satan in order to destroy the sinful nature, so that his spirit might be saved; in at least one text (Rom. 3:8) Paul judged that the condemnation of some was well deserved.

issued forth both fresh and salt water was unnatural; in this way James continues to make the point that abusive speech is irrational. The triple image of the illogicality of expecting trees and vines to produce fruit not their own and of a salt spring to produce fresh water are all intended to round out the point he has made again and again. James's use of the phrase "my brothers" (vv. 10–11) suggests an admission on his part that he has said some harsh words to his readers, and he is thus reiterating his affection for them, to recall to their minds the fact that he is one of them, that he has their best interests at heart.

JAMES HAS SKETCHED for us a passage of extraordinary vividness, replete with memorable images ("the tongue is a fire, a world of evil") and spiritual observations ("With the tongue we praise our Lord and Father, and with it we curse men, who have been made in God's likeness"). James was writing to a church deeply divided because of variant teachings propounded by different teachers, though we do not know more than this bare outline. But there are two issues on which he touches that will help us to avoid misstep as we strive to bring this passage to life in our own world. The first concerns the word *geenna* ("hell") in 3:6; the second involves the chief focus of the passage, the susceptibility of the tongue (whether as speech or as emblematic of leaders within the Christian community) to the influence of Satan.

In a passage marked by such rich imagery, these two themes may seem mundane. But they undergird and will in large part control how the issues in the text are applied to contemporary life. The central concern of this passage is power—of Satan, and of the tongue to twist and to corrupt. A proper understanding of the biblical view of power is therefore essential if we are successfully to bridge the gap between the message of James for the first century and for our own. It is for these reasons that these two terms have been selected.

Gehenna. In 3:1–12 James informs us that the evil inclination within us, which is variously in league with and a ready receptor for Satan, is the source of the desire to employ the tongue in hurtful ways. On one level James warns us against ignorance, that "slips" of the tongue may not in fact be innocent or harmless but may very well represent the initial stages of that biological growth of evil to which chapter 1 bears witness. On another level James is warning against leaders who foster not a spirit of cooperation and compassion, but rather envy and strife. These themes will be prominent features of the remainder of the letter.

The NIV uses the term "hell" in 3:6, but behind this English word is the Greek word *geenna*. It is imperative that we understand both the literal and figurative nuances of this term in order to apply its meaning to our own age. Without this understanding, the behavior of leaders and the impure speech of individuals might well be dismissed, in the same manner as a physician might err in dismissing the first signs of cancer in a patient. Such dismissal is not harmless, for the source of the trouble is not innocent, it is Gehenna.

In the Old Testament the Valley of Hinnom (Heb. *gay' hinnon*) formed part of the boundary between the tribes of Judah and Benjamin (Josh. 15:8).[29] It was also the site of the worship of Canaanite gods such as Baal and Molech. In association with these rites child sacrifices were offered there (2 Kings 23:10). Jeremiah said that this valley would be a place of judgment, calling it the "Valley of Slaughter," because of the many Jews who were killed and thrown into the valley by the Babylonians (Jer. 7:29–34). During the second temple period this valley became linked with the idea of fiery judgment and with eschatological judgment (*1 Enoch* 26–27). This caused Gehenna to be associated with the fires of hell, and therefore with hell itself.

There are twelve references to Gehenna in the New Testament. With the exception of this one in James, all are found on the lips of Jesus in the Synoptic Gospels. Here, then, is another link between James and the Jesus tradition. Following the final judgment, Gehenna is a place of punishment and the destruction of the wicked (Matt. 5:22), body and soul are judged in Gehenna (Matt. 10:28; Mark 9:43–47), and this punishment is eternal (Matt. 25:41, 46). Jesus warns against several sins that might cause one to be condemned to Gehenna, including calling a brother a fool (5:22) and giving in to sinful inclinations (5:29–30). These two themes are prominent in James— further evidence of the link between James and Jesus.

In this passage, then, Gehenna is symbolic of the force of Satan. In James 3:15 the false "wisdom" of this world, characterized by envy and bitterness, is attributed to the "demonic" (which the NIV renders "the devil"), and in 4:7 James tells us to "resist the devil." A "whole world of evil" is waiting to ensnare us, and its source is Satan. These are among the most serious terms that James has at his command. He is warning the church: Ignore such speech and the actions of such leaders at your own grave peril!

Power from a biblical perspective. According to James, "The tongue also is a fire. ... It corrupts the whole person ... and is itself set on fire by hell" (3:6). The tongue bears influence far out of proportion to its size. It is also susceptible to the forces of evil. The tongue can be twisted to go about the work of hell. This is stark, uncompromising language, which introduces us again to Satan's power. When our speech demonstrates the capacity to devastate others

---

29. On this issue see H. Bietenhard, "γέεννα," *NIDNTT*, 2:208–9; Duane F. Watson, "Gehenna," *ABD*, 2:926–28.

and even ourselves, our tongues have been bent by the forces of evil. When those in positions of leadership within the church abuse that trust, they are under the influence of the forces of evil. James does not want us to be ignorant of this, for ignorance renders us even more vulnerable to the corrosive ravages of hell. Both the tongue and positions of leadership exercise power, and both easily are compromised. It is critical, therefore, that we understand the biblical view of power.

Lord Acton said, "Power tends to corrupt, and absolute power corrupts absolutely."[30] Acton here has given a secular echo to a theological truth. Daniel told Belshazzar that God was the one who had given to Nebuchadnezzar, his father, "sovereignty and greatness and glory and splendor. . . . But when his heart became arrogant and hardened with pride, he was deposed from his royal throne and stripped of his glory" (Dan. 5:18, 20). According to Scripture, power has the capacity and the tendency to become twisted and perverted. This is significant because in James 3:6, the author links positions of authority (the tongue) and abuse of power (the false teachers, with whom he is at odds) with the font of this calumny, hell. In making this argument James is tapping into a rich biblical tradition that sought to explain the presence and power of evil. It is an understanding shared by James, Paul, and John among the writers of the New Testament.

The first step to understanding how the tongue or people in leadership positions can be "set on fire by hell" and therefore abuse their power is to recognize that the Old Testament affirms that God entrusted humankind with delegated authority. In Genesis 1:26 we read, "Then God said, 'Let us make man in our image, in our likeness, and let them rule over the fish of the sea and the birds of the air, over the livestock, over all the earth, and over all the creatures that move along the ground.'" Humankind, made in the image of God, has been entrusted with delegated authority over all the earth. The Psalms affirm that "the earth is the LORD's" (Ps. 24:1) and that the "highest heavens belong to the LORD, but the earth he has given to man" (115:16). James makes a conscious link to this idea of delegated authority when in James 3:7–8 he refers to the fourfold order of creation.

This combination of delegated authority with creation in God's image is celebrated in Psalm 8, a commentary of sorts on Genesis 1:26–27, which speaks of humankind before the Fall:

> When I consider your heavens,
>   the work of your fingers,

---

30. Lord Acton, "Letter to Bishop Creighton," September 5, 1887. Henry Adams said, "A friend in power is a friend lost" (*The Education of Henry Adams*, ch. 7).

the moon and the stars,
  which you have set in place,
what is man that you are mindful of him,
  the son of man that you care for him?
You made him a little lower than the heavenly beings
  and crowned him with glory and honor.
You made him ruler over the works of your hands;
  you put everything under his feet:
all flocks and herds,
  and the beasts of the field,
the birds of the air,
  and the fish of the sea,
  all that swim the paths of the seas.
O LORD, our Lord,
  how majestic is your name in all the earth! (8:3–9)

Here is affirmed the glory and dominion granted to humankind

The second step to understanding James's idea of the abuse of power is to see that there is something inherent in power that inclines to evil. This is a subplot that finds expression in the apocalyptic sections of Daniel. In Daniel 7 the prophet receives a vision and then relates it:

Daniel said: "In my vision at night I looked, and there before me were the four winds of heaven churning up the great sea. Four great beasts, each different from the others, came up out of the sea.

"The first was like a lion, and it had the wings of an eagle. I watched until its wings were torn off and it was lifted from the ground so that it stood on two feet like a man, and the heart of a man was given to it.

"And there before me was a second beast, which looked like a bear. It was raised up on one of its sides, and it had three ribs in its mouth between its teeth. It was told, 'Get up and eat your fill of flesh!'

"After that, I looked, and there before me was another beast, one that looked like a leopard. And on its back it had four wings like those of a bird. This beast had four heads, and it was given authority to rule.

"After that, in my vision at night I looked, and there before me was a fourth beast—terrifying and frightening and very powerful. It had large iron teeth; it crushed and devoured its victims and trampled underfoot whatever was left. It was different from all the former beasts, and it had ten horns." (Dan. 7:2–7)

The vision opens with a churning sea. The sea represents chaos, the locus of forces opposed to God.[31] The sea is churning at night, both features meant to heighten the sense of danger and evil. Out of the sea come four beasts, representing political powers. They possess dominion, "authority to rule," because God has entrusted humankind with this task. But like Nebuchadnezzar in Daniel 5, the beasts abuse that power. They are told to "eat your fill of flesh" and to "trample underfoot whatever is left."

Daniel, like James, gives voice to the truth that people in positions of power often abuse power, just as the tongue often causes hurt. But Daniel also speaks of the judgment of political power by God—how political powers are stripped of their power, and how "authority, glory and sovereign power" are given to "one like a son of man" (7:13–14). The point of this image is that human institutions possess "authority" because God has delegated that authority to us. However, in our stewardship that authority has been corrupted by evil, it cannot be trusted, and one day God will strip human institutions of the authority we now use inappropriately. Instead, he will give it to the "son of man," God's agent, who will establish God's kingdom. Political power is morally neutral, but it is easily co-opted by the forces of evil.

The third step to perceiving James's idea of power as influenced by hell is to understand these forces of evil. What are they? In the Septuagint rendering of Deuteronomy 32:8–9 we read that when "the Most High gave the nations their inheritance, when he divided all mankind, he set up boundaries for the peoples according to the number of the angels of God. For the Lord's portion is his people, Jacob his allotted inheritance." That is, God appointed heavenly beings to watch over the nations. In 4:19 Israel is warned not to worship these angels, for although they are heavenly beings, they are not God: "And when you look up to the sky and see the sun, the moon and the stars—all the heavenly array—do not be enticed into bowing down to them and worshiping things the LORD your God has apportioned to all the nations under heaven." However, human beings in their ignorance do worship these angels as if they were God, and some of them accept this worship. This accounts for the anger of God with angels.

This is the theme of many psalms. Psalm 82:1–2, for example, says that God sits in judgment of "the gods" (a word referring to angelic spirits): "How long will you defend the unjust and show partiality to the wicked?" His complaint is that these angels have supported the perversion of his standards on earth. Psalm 89:6–7 says that none of the gods can compare with God; 96:4 claims that God is to be feared above the gods; and 97:7 says that the gods should worship God.

---

31. It is for this reason that in Rev. 21:1, when the new heaven and the new earth are described, the first item mentioned is that "there was no longer any sea."

Isaiah likewise echoes this idea and adds the theme of judgment. Isaiah 24:21—22 says:

In that day the LORD will punish
    the powers in the heavens above
    and the kings on the earth below.
They will be herded together
    like prisoners bound in a dungeon;
they will be shut up in prison
    and be punished after many days.

Similarly, Isaiah 34:2—4 says:

The LORD is angry with all nations;
    his wrath is upon all their armies.
He will totally destroy them,
    he will give them over to slaughter.
Their slain will be thrown out,
    their dead bodies will send up a stench;
    the mountains will be soaked with their blood.
All the stars of the heavens will be dissolved
    and the sky rolled up like a scroll;
all the starry host will fall
    like withered leaves from the vine,
    like shriveled figs from the fig tree.

Note here the close association of the angels with the human political forces they represent. Standing behind many human institutions are the supernatural forces of evil. This is particularly true of the political order, whether manifested in governments, in the bureaucratic culture of corporations, or in university politics.

This is essentially the view of John and of Paul. In John's Gospel it is the Romans who execute false judgment against Jesus, having had their hand forced by the Jewish authorities (John 19:12—16). But behind both stands Satan. The Jewish authorities do not realize it, but they are, says Jesus, the children of Satan (John 8:44). Speaking of his death at the hands of the Romans Jesus says, "I will not speak with you much longer, for the prince of this world is coming" (14:30). Satan stands behind the political forces that, ignorant of his presence, are bent to his will.

Paul presents us with a slightly more enlarged canvas. He claims that these angels are the rulers of this age and that they are in league with Satan, "the god of this age" (2 Cor. 4:4), "the ruler of the kingdom of the air" (Eph. 2:2). Paul claims that these rulers stand behind the forces of political power, specifically the political forces that executed Jesus: "None of the rulers of this age understood it, for if they had, they would not have crucified the Lord of glory" (1 Cor. 2:8). In Colossians 2:15 the apostle writes that these rulers, along with their earthly minions, have been defeated in the Cross: "And having disarmed the powers and authorities, he made a public spectacle of them, triumphing over them by the cross." Christ's victory is so complete that, like the victims of Roman might, the principalities and powers are made to parade in shame before the conqueror. Yet, Paul affirms, the defeated powers are still dangerous: "For our struggle is not against flesh and blood, but against the rulers, against the authorities, against the powers of this dark world and against the spiritual forces of evil in the heavenly realms" (Eph. 6:12).

The Bible, therefore, argues that the political order is morally neutral but inherently weak and easily corrupted by Satan. Examples are not hard to come by. Serbian soldiers defend their complicity in acts of murder and torture with the claim that they were merely following orders. Supervisors pass over deserving employees to grant a promotion to a relative. Governments conduct nuclear tests in order to determine the effects of radiation by exposing soldiers to nuclear fallout, but do not inform them of the danger.

Political power is dangerous, precisely because it is power. Without political power, Adolf Hitler would have remained nothing more than a petty, malevolent malcontent carrying on a lecherous, incestuous affair with his niece.[32] But because he came to control a modern nation-state, he could wreck untold carnage. Stalin might have spent his life as nothing more than a moody family tyrant, privately gnawing on his ambitions and reading his favorite novel, a Russian translation of Edgar Rice Burroughs' *Tarzan of the Apes*.[33] Yet because of the power of the state, he has excelled all others who reside in the long corridor of human depravity in the grisly business of murder.

Parents can cripple the spirit of their children through withering critical speech. The tongue has the power to devastate a small child. Power even in the church is open to abuse. To the explication of this theme we now turn.

THE CENTRAL THRUST of this passage has to do with power, and specifically with its wrong application. Persons in position of leadership fall prey to its allure, even leadership within the church. Each of us has the power to inflict pain on others through our speech. Finally,

---

32. William Manchester, *The Last Lion: Winston Spencer Churchill; Visions of Glory; 1874–1932* (Boston: Little, Brown, 1983), 867, 870.

33. Ibid., 876.

the world in which we live is awash in the abuse of power, which makes it all the more difficult and necessary to remain unattracted to the abuse of power.

The text offers us three significant issues for application. Towering over the others is the question of teachers and the power that is theirs by virtue of position. Because James offers us warnings concerning teachers and leadership, the discussion will focus on some of the perils teachers face. The second major issue has to do with the power of the tongue to inflict damage and pain. But the idea that allows these other two to achieve clarity is expressed in James's phrase "a world of evil." He wishes to remind his readers that Satan is capable of great evil, and he employs this phrase to create a terrible vision of warning. Without diligence, the church can become too much like this world of evil, even though those within the church are blissfully ignorant of the slide toward depravity. Certainly this was the case in the congregation to which James has directed his letter.

The world of evil. The tongue can inaugurate a "world of evil" (3:6), just as a tiny spark can cause a huge fire. Human experience confirms this. Augustine said that all of us, as a result of the Fall, have a bent toward perversity.[34] The tongue is a restless evil, whose source is hell; we allow Satan to twist and pervert us. Because of this creeping malevolence, we fail to recognize the image of God in others (see 3:9). There is no shortage of evidence in our culture for this irrational, malignant character of evil.

A high school yearbook editor in Indiana takes vengeance on her rivals by defacing their yearbook photographs. The books appear with teeth blacked out and underarm hair penciled in.

The mother of an aspiring thirteen-year-old cheerleader in Texas contracts with a hit man to murder the mother of her daughter's rival. Her hope is that the grieving girl will not try out for the cheerleading squad.

In 1993 the town of Lakewood, California made the national news as a result of a scandal involving teenagers, peer pressure, and irrational evil. A number of the members of a high school football team had formed a club called the "Spur Posse," in which the members competed with each other to see how many times they could have sexual relations with different women. They impudently kept score, and some had scores in the fifties and sixties. It was shocking enough that many members of this gang were proud of their behavior, but more shocking that the parents of some defended their sons. "Nothing my boy did was anything any red-blooded American boy wouldn't do at his age," said one father. Others blamed the girls, referring to them as "trash."[35]

---

34. Augustine, *De correptione et gratia,* 9.
35. Cornelius Plantinga Jr., *Not The Way It's Supposed to Be: A Breviary of Sin* (Grand Rapids: Eerdmans, 1995), 163—64, 180—81.

The movie "Trainspotting," which became a minor classic in the mid-1990s, also illustrates this "world of evil."[36] The movie opens as Mark Renton, the unofficial ringleader of a group of heroin addicts in Edinburgh, is shooting up in the flat of his supplier. As we watch this scene, we hear Renton's voice offering commentary: "Who needs reasons when you've got heroin?" In their irrational relentless pursuit of the drug, the young men will steal from their families and each other. Even the death of an infant as a result of neglect does not deter them—Renton and the mother of the dead baby promptly cook up another batch of poison. At the conclusion of the film Renton, having stolen from his friends and leaving them in the lurch, says, "So why did I do it? I could give a million reasons, all false. The truth is, I'm a bad person."

Renton, like Augustine, understood that sin is more than being misled, or a casual error, or "worst of all, a 'life-style choice.' It is a full-speed plunge into the hissing cauldron of lust followed by a soothing pickling in the juices of self-love."[37] Humans want to know the experience of sin, the self-indulgence. But Augustine knows what Renton does not know: Sin is its own penalty—it becomes tiresome, and it eventually kills.

In her award winning novel *A Map of the World*, Jane Hamilton introduces us to Alice, a woman whose innocent negligence led to the tragic drowning death of the daughter of her best friend and neighbor. Reflecting on this event and its aftermath, Alice says:

> I used to think that if you fell from grace it was more likely than not the result of one stupendous error, or else some unfortunate accident. I hadn't learned that it can happen so gradually that you don't lose your stomach or hurt yourself in the landing. You don't necessarily lose the motion, I've found it takes at least two and generally three things to alter the course of a life: You slip around once, and then again, and one more time, and there you are, feeling, for a moment, that it was sudden, your arrival at the bottom of the heap.[38]

As James said, when desire is conceived, it gives birth to sin; and sin, when it is full-grown, gives birth to death (1:15). The process is not always obvious, but its effect is sudden, and with shock we realize that we are at the bottom of the heap.

Sin, according to Plantinga, is like cancer—it kills because it reproduces.[39] Sin echoes down the generations. Family systems marked by incest and abuse

---

36. J. A. Hanson, "It's Heavy, Man" (a review of the movie "Trainspotting"), *Regeneration Quarterly*, 2 (Fall 1996): 41.
37. Ibid.
38. Jane Hamilton, *A Map of the World* (New York: Anchor Books/Doubleday, 1994), 3.
39. Plantinga, *Not The Way It's Supposed to Be*, 55.

perpetuate themselves. Violence between ethnic groups or between families continues long after the original reasons have been lost in the haze of time. In Shakespeare's *Romeo and Juliet*, the Montagues and the Capulets continued to kill each other because ... that was what Montagues and Capulets were supposed to do. One lie leads to another. The tongue is emblematic of this evil. It is a "world of evil" (3:6), a restless, irrational wickedness full of poison (3:9), a malicious spark that causes conflagration (3:6).

The temptations of leadership. The creeping malevolence of sin manifests itself in the allure and pitfall of political power. "The body," said Soranus, "is sick with desire."[40] One of the most potent of these desires is that of political power. Daniel made this point concerning Nebuchadnezzar. James deals with it here in the guise of teachers who abused their position by teaching and practicing false doctrine. In recent years it has surfaced in national politics with the ascendancy of the politics of Dick Morris, which may be called the politics of style over substance. Morris, President Clinton's now disgraced political advisor, helped to usher in the era of constant testing of public opinion. The result has been the disquieting sensation that the President of the United States does not stand for anything except the currently popular.[41]

In his recent book, *Behind the Oval Office: Winning the Presidency in the Nineties*,[42] Dick Morris happily claims that he was one of the first to engage in negative advertising. Gary Wills says that Morris, and others like him, are "willing to do whatever it takes, and they subordinate other considerations to the electoral appeal of their client."[43] Morris explains his motivation in stark terms: "I needed the [power] fix too badly."[44] He claims that the success of the Clinton campaign was its ability to know the current mood of the country and to shape the President's message to fit that mood. In order to do this, Wills points out, constant polling was required, which costs a great deal of money. The "real scandal," in Wills' view, was not Morris's long-running affair with a prostitute, but that the Clinton White House was in such dire need of funds to support this election apparatus that it engaged in measures of

---

40. Soranus, *Gynaecology*, 1.30. Soranus was born in Ephesus late in the first century A.D. He studied medicine in Alexandria and practiced in Rome under Trajan (A.D. 98–117) and Hadrian (117–138).

41. Churchill had little use for opinion polls. He said, "It is not a good thing always to be feeling your pulse and taking your temperature. Although one has to do it sometimes, you do not want to make a habit of it. I have heard it said that a Government should keep its ear to the ground, but they should also remember that this is not a very dignified attitude" (Manchester, *The Last Lion*, 106–7).

42. Dick Morris, *Behind the Oval Office: Winning the Presidency in the Nineties* (New York: Random House, 1997).

43. Garry Wills, "The Real Scandal," *The New York Review of Books* (Feb. 20, 1997), 4.

44. Ibid.

questionable ethics. "The money raised from foreign sources was a measure of the desperate search for all possible sources of income."[45] This all-consuming need for reelection to political power left the President badly out of focus. Reflecting on conversations with the President, Morris says,

> Clinton complained bitterly at having to raise this much money. . . . "I can't think. I can't act. I can't do anything except go to fund raisers and shake hands. You want me to issue executive orders; I can't focus on a thing but the next fundraiser. Hillary can't, Al can't—we're all getting sick and crazy because of it."[46]

The same disease readily can infect teachers and leaders within the Christian church. The teachers in James's congregation were advocating practices that mirrored the standards of the Roman empire. In our day, some Christians advocate a domination of the political process by Christian and even evangelical values. In a democracy each citizen has a right to have his or her views aired, as Stephen Carter has been wise to point out.[47] However, Christians should not forget that the state is not to be trusted; it is no substitute for the church.

Some evangelical churches dangerously confuse "American" values with those of the New Testament. One church recently emerged from a long battle concerning the placement of the flag of the United States on the platform. Many in the congregation felt the suggestion that the flag be removed was an attack on patriotism. They pointed out that their fathers and brothers had died for freedom, including religious freedom, while fighting under the flag of the United States. Whether they realized it or not, such placement sends a powerful, if at times subtle, message: The United States is God's agent, and therefore whatever the United States chooses to do is somehow sanctioned by God.

There is no gainsaying that this country has often stood against oppression and the forces of evil, and in such cases the United States should be lauded. But our history is a spotted history, and to confuse the state with the church of Jesus Christ is a danger every bit as deadly as that which confronted

---

45. Ibid., 6.

46. Quoted in ibid.

47. Stephen L. Carter, *The Culture of Disbelief: How American Law and Politics Trivialize Religious Devotion* (New York: Basic Books, 1993). On pages 4–5 Carter cites this example: "When Hillary Rodham Clinton was seen wearing a cross around her neck at some of the public events surrounding her husband's inauguration as President of the United States, many observers were aghast, and one television commentator asked whether it was appropriate for the First Lady to display so openly a religious symbol. But if the First Lady can't do it, then certainly the President can't do it, which would bar from ever holding the office an Orthodox Jew under a religious compulsion to wear a yarmulke."

James in his church. The annals of history demonstrate that governments tend toward power at the expense of the interests of the many. Solomon traded away entire villages, inhabitants and all, to pay debts. The British government reneged on promises to France and Czechoslovakia in an attempt to buy peace with Hitler. The United States government has broken innumerable promises to Native Americans. The state simply is not overly interested in the cause of Christ, and we confuse the two at our great peril.

Some evangelical churches choose to avoid the problem by remaining silent on the issues of the day. This naive refusal to address critical issues is neither biblical nor safe. The "Christian response" to welfare reform, abortion, gay rights, intervention in Bosnia, homelessness in America, and other issues are not easily discerned, for they are enormously complicated. But their complexity is no excuse to forego honest biblical dialogue in search of a response informed by faith and the Spirit of God. To do otherwise is to baptize secular ideology of whatever stripe and call it Christian.

The lives and decisions of Dietrich Bonhoeffer and Alexandr Menn provide marvelous examples. Both men lived under regimes hostile to the faith, and both refused to follow the lead of church leaders who accommodated to these regimes. Bonhoeffer was a Lutheran pastor in Nazi Germany and reached the amazing conclusion that morality demanded of him participation in a plot to kill Hitler. Such decisions are not reached lightly, but come only after careful prayer, study, and reflection.

Alexandr Menn was murdered on September 9, 1990. Menn was an orthodox priest, the spiritual advisor to Alexandr Solzhenitsyn and Andrei Sakharov. He was an outspoken critic of the Soviet system. Two months before he was struck from behind with an ax, he was interviewed on radio, and the broadcast was heard across Russia. He was asked the question, "Does one need to be a Christian, and if one does, then why?" Menn began by saying:

Man always seeks God. The normal state of man is, to some extent, to be connected with a higher power, even when the higher power in the human mind is distorted, and turned into something secular. Eras of Stalinism ... and all other isms seek some false god even if God is taken away. This turns to idol worship, but still the inner instinct of seeking God is there. ... I believe that everything that is of value in Christianity is valuable only because it belongs to Christ. If it doesn't belong to Christ, it belongs to the same degree to Islam or Buddhism. So every religion is an attempt to reach God. But Jesus Christ is the answer.[48]

48. Larry Woiwode, "A Martyr Who Lives," *Books and Culture: A Christian Review* (March/April 1996), 23–25.

It was precisely this type of boldness in the face of government opposition that signaled his death warrant. The night before he was murdered, Menn said these words in a lecture in Moscow: "No living creature, except for man, is able to take a risk, and even the risk of death, for the sake of truth." Menn was able to identify the politically acceptable Christianity of some of his Orthodox superiors and to live instead for the truth. The political order has its own agenda, and that agenda is often injurious to the cause of Christ.

This desire for power among Christians manifests itself in other ways too, as people often use the local congregation as an opportunity for wielding power. This is sometimes true of pastors who arrogate to themselves the power to make every decision in the life of the church. A close friend of mine in Chicago is about to leave his church. He is happy with the congregation and is confident of the preaching of the pastor. But the inability of that pastor to allow anyone else, even the boards, to make decisions has left my friend feeling weary beyond description. The pastor's nearly pathological need to control leaves him open to the blindness and arrogance of self-delusion. This self-delusion has already given rise to destructive behavior, as some who have been critical of his need for power have found themselves the target of verbal slander. Desire for power and the evil of the tongue often walk hand in hand.

Sometimes it is laypersons who are guilty. My pastor recalls a man during his intern days who was upsetting many in the congregation. This man claimed that God had called him to exercise the spiritual gift of rebuke. The fact that this particular spiritual gift is not mentioned in the New Testament did not faze him. Apparently believing that he was acting as God's agent, this man had begun to terrorize the congregation with his frequent and insensitive accusations of imperfection. I am not a psychologist, but it seems to me that here was a case of a person wrapping himself in the mantle of spirituality in order to exercise a human and petty need to improve his self-image by decimating the self-image of others.

Another classic case involves a trustee board at a church where a friend of mine is pastor. Apparently one member would spend a half hour arguing against the purchase of a $45 coffee maker in favor of one costing $35. A number of people in the church refused to serve on the board while this man was serving. A few years later, however, this gentleman became involved in a program dedicated to working with new Christians in the church. "This," he said later, "revolutionized my life." He began to see that his earlier efforts at serving God were actually functions of his own need to be in control. The tongue does indeed have the power to inflict deep wounds. He apologized to the congregation, recognizing the times he had said hurtful things, all in the pursuit of petty goals.

Finally, the desire for power can make itself felt in doctrinal issues. James wrote against teachers who had altered the gospel. In our day there are similar teachings and practices within the Christian community. Some expressions of the faith, or perversions of it, advocate an overly rigorous doctrine. One example is the growing Church of Christ (Boston). As a graduate student and university pastor I became acquainted with this group. The students I knew who were involved with this church told me that it teaches a harsh, selectively literalistic biblical ethic, and tells its members that they are the only "true" Christians. Recently a former student and good friend encountered this church here in Chicago. After attending one service, he was invited to a lunch with the pastor. At this meeting the pastor informed my friend that his spiritual life was seriously inadequate and that the teaching he had received in his home church was so lacking as to be substandard. My friend went home, found a web site devoted to persons who are "recovering" from this group, and discovered a long letter written by a woman whose experience paralleled his.[49] This type of exclusivism has been a hallmark of heresy since Paul battled the "super-apostles."

But we need venture no further than the broad mix of evangelicalism to discern vestiges of this overly strong attitude. Philip Yancey has worked as a Christian journalist for twenty-five years. During President Bill Clinton's first term in office, Yancey and other journalists were invited to a breakfast with the President at the White House. Clinton told them, "Sometimes I feel like a spiritual orphan," because he had seen the bumper stickers that proclaimed, "A vote for Bill Clinton is a sin against God." In the article he wrote following that breakfast, Yancey noted that Clinton's faith "was not a posturing for political expediency, but an integral part of who he was."[50] In the aftermath of that article Yancey received a barrage of letters, most attacking him for portraying the President in a somewhat favorable light. "In my 25 years of journalism, I have received my share of mixed reviews. Even so, as I read through stacks of vituperative letters, I got a strong sense for why the world at large does not automatically associate the word 'grace' with evangelical Christians."[51] In our desire to be "right," we may well alienate the very people Christ came to save.

---

49. As of this writing the email address for this web site is (http://www.anacapa.net/~lesid/icc/icc.htm). A more general website sponsored by ex-members may be found at (http://www/reveal.org/).

50. Philip Yancey, "A State of Ungrace. In Fighting the Culture Wars: Has the Church Forgotten Its Central Message?" *Christianity Today* (Feb. 3, 1997), 32.

51. Ibid.

But the church can also be too soft. The spectacle of John Spong, the Episcopal bishop for the Diocese of New Jersey, is a case in point. He has argued for the permissibility of sexual relations outside of marriage for both heterosexuals and homosexuals, claiming that "sex outside of marriage can be holy and life-giving in some circumstances."[52] He denies the virgin birth and the bodily resurrection of Jesus. In these and other ways his teachings are far removed from scriptural warrant. Another example involves the Interfaith Alliance, which has recently begun to surface in the American public consciousness. This self-described "moderate" group, started with funds from the Democratic Congressional Campaign Committee, aims to counter the "extremism" of the right-wing Christian Coalition. Its executive director is Jill Hannauer, who as a student at the University of Colorado tried to stop Bill McCartney from leading his players in a moment of silence before football games. This seems a curious pedigree.[53]

Christian teachers and leaders can also stray when there is an overemphasis on one truth or on one doctrine. The "Signs and Wonders" movement made startling claims about God's desire to heal all Christians in the 1980s. Wimber claimed that sickness was caused by Satan and that the performance of "signs and wonders" by Christians was God's plan for world evangelization. Recently John Wimber's own experience of cancer has led to a more balanced biblical view.[54] Two generations ago the dispensational movement was marked by a denial of the contemporary application of spiritual gifts. Today this hard edge is being dulled on the whetstone of biblical teaching and experience.

Among the many temptations that involve teaching and leadership positions within the church is that we are not careful enough in the evaluative process. Count Axel Gustafsson Oxenstierna, the Chancellor of Sweden in the seventeenth century, once said, "Behold, my son, with what little wisdom the world is ruled."[55] That this is true takes little perspicacity to see. But part of the blame lies with ourselves, for we routinely take far too little time in evaluating those we choose for leadership, and we too easily allow ourselves to be duped. Thucydides said, "So little trouble do men take in the search for truth, they readily accept whatever comes first hand."[56] The ancient Athenians, having expelled the tyrant Pisistratos, allowed him back in the city under the guise of an ama-

---

52. C. Stephen Evans, "Why I Feel Sorry for Bishop Spong," *Books and Culture: A Christian Review* (January/February 1997), 5.

53. Richard John Neuhaus, "The Public Square," *First Things* 71 (March 1997): 69.

54. See John Wimber, "Signs, Wonders and Cancer," *Christianity Today* (Oct. 7, 1996), 49–51.

55. The saying has been attributed to many others throughout history.

56. Thucydides, *History of the Peloponessian War*, 1.20.

---

teurish ruse. Pisistratos found a striking peasant girl, dressed her as Athena, and placed her standing before him in a chariot. He then sent heralds into the city of Athens, proclaiming that Athena herself was reinstating Pisistratos as tyrant. The Athenians, legendary for their wisdom, nonetheless acquiesced.[57]

This same tendency to be too trusting can be seen in this century. In the chaos of Germany between the wars, the church in large measure failed to discern in Adolf Hitler a man and a mission that deserved not trust but careful scrutiny, even condemnation. In this context a number of issues came to confluence, not the least of which was the paucity of any tradition of opposition to the state within the German church. As is often true of American Christians, many German believers saw the interests of the state as commensurate with the interests of their faith. Some adopted the motto, "The Swastika on our breasts, the Cross in our hearts." Their pastors donned Nazi uniforms as they sang Nazi hymns. Philip Yancey comments, "Too late did they learn that once again the church had been seduced by the power of the state."[58]

But it was not only the German Protestants who failed to see the imminent danger. In September of 1938 there was a well-organized plot to oust Hitler, composed of high-ranking elements of the German military. It may have succeeded if British Prime Minister Neville Chamberlain had not caved in to Hitler on the question of Czechoslovakia. The German conspirators believed that all the British had to do to bully Hitler into submission was to send "an energetic military man who, if necessary, can shout and hit the table with a riding crop."[59] Instead Chamberlain went to Munich and capitulated. It was a monumental failure to read the signs.

We as Christians often fail to read the signs as well. At times churches choose pastors who, although godly, are poor fits for the congregation that calls them. More significantly and at times tragically, we are often too trusting in an era of sexual abuse perpetrated by clergy. Our pastors deserve and need our support, our forgiveness, and our mercy, but they also need our honest care. James says that we all stumble in many ways. Clergy stumble too. Some are driven by a desire for power or money, as the not-too-distant cases of Jim Bakker and Oral Roberts illustrate. Jim Bakker and his organizations bilked trusting souls out of millions of dollars, and he spent time in prison as a result of this debacle. Great damage has been suffered by the cause of Christ in the wake of this scandal. Other clergy simply crave authority. These are very human faults. But congregations owe it to themselves and to their leaders to provide adequate systems of support and care for those in positions

---

57. Herodotus, *History*, 1.60.
58. Yancey, "A State of Ungrace," 36.
59. Quoted in Thomas Powers, "The Conspiracy That Failed," *The New York Review of Books* (Jan. 9, 1997), 50.

of authority, to ensure that the teaching and practice remains biblical. This provides insurance against theological error on one side, and the devastation of the pastor, teacher, or leader by the congregation on the other.

The power of the tongue. According to James, the tongue has great potential, but it is unstable. With it we both praise God and vilify our neighbor (3:9–10). This is irrational, he says—and rightly so. It is also an accurate depiction of our lives as Christians. It is this irrational power of the tongue to cause evil that led Henri Frederick Amiel to write, "In order to see Christianity, one must forget almost all the Christians."[60]

Human beings have the propensity to utter words that are ill-considered, and these sometimes do damage to others or to ourselves. Early in World War I Winston Churchill served the British nation as First Lord of the Admiralty. He had coaxed into service a retired British naval hero, John "Jacky" Fisher, to serve as First Sea Lord, the equivalent of the Chief of Naval Operations in the United States. They worked well together for some time, but as the plans for the Dardanelles strategy progressed, it became obvious to many people that the elderly Fisher was becoming unstable. In fact, the blame for the failed Dardenelles strategy and the disaster of Gallipolli lies not with Churchill, but was principally due to the procrastination of both Prime Minister Asquith and secretary of state for war Kitchener, and secondarily with Fisher, who seemed unable to give consistent advice. Fisher also maneuvered to have Churchill removed from his duties as First Lord of the Admiralty, a plan in which he was successful, but which involved his own removal from office.

No longer a member of the cabinet, but still a member of the House of Commons, Churchill chose to serve in the infantry and was involved in trench warfare in Flanders. Several months later, he returned to the House of Commons, and on March 7, 1916, delivered what William Manchester has called "one of the most unfortunate speeches of his life." After offering an insightful critique of certain features of the government's prosecution of the war, he then uttered a fateful sentence, one that sent him again into political exile: "I urge the First Lord of the Admiralty without delay to fortify himself, to vitalise and animate his Board of Admiralty by recalling Lord Fisher to his post as First Sea Lord."[61]

The House of Commons, says Manchester, was stunned. Former Prime Minster Balfour, at this point a political enemy of Churchill, saw his opportunity. Balfour pointed out that in Churchill's farewell speech the previous autumn he "told us that the First Sea Lord, Lord Fisher, did not give him, when he was serving in the same Admiralty with him, either the clear guidance

---

60. Henri Frederick Amiel, *Journal* (Aug. 30, 1887).
61. Manchester, *The Last Lion*, 596.

before the event or the firm support after it which he was entitled to expect. . . ." Further, said Balfour, Churchill now claims that Fisher is "nevertheless the man who ought to be given as a supporter and a guide to anybody who happens to hold at this moment the responsible position of First Lord of the Admiralty. It is a paradox of the wildest and most extravagant kind." Balfour concluded with a remark calculated to condemn Churchill to oblivion: "I should regard myself as contemptible beyond the power of expression if I were to yield an inch to a demand of such a kind, made in such a way."[62]

Such cases are not limited to the arena of politics. Before joining the academic world full-time, I spent ten years in parish ministry, where I encountered legions of examples that verify James's statement. Some were unintentional, such as the time during a low-key social gathering that a pastor, in an off-hand remark, offered his opinion concerning a social issue of the day. His innocent remark, reported to others, led to division within the church and the departure of several families with children whose lives had been touched by this particular social issue. But the families did not approach the pastor to ask for his version of the remark. They denied the pastor the chance to provide theological context for his remarks. Neither did the pastor pursue the families; instead, he began to talk about what he supposed was their motivation in leaving. The result was a healthy store of mutual bad feelings, all created by ill-considered speech run rampant.

The misuse of tongue by leaders within the church contributes to a wide swath of discontent concerning the church. Dennis Ngien tells a story that is emblematic of this discontent, but also of its transformation.

> My neighbor, an arrogant and wealthy businessman, scorned the church for many years. Whenever church members phoned him, he would criticize them: "You church people are only interested in my money. You don't care for me; you only care about my pocketbook." But then he became ill and was paralyzed. When I went to visit him, to my utter surprise his entire room looked like a flower shop, and cards were posted everywhere on the wall. The flowers and cards came from church members whom he so disdained for many years. Posted on the wall, facing his bed, was a big sheet of paper with these words on it: "I was wrong. The church does care." Later he became a Christian, all because of the church's willingness to risk loving vulnerability.[63]

In this case, the same "tongue," the voice of the church, which first had been experienced without the grace and compassion of Jesus, had made its true

---

62. Ibid., 597.
63. Dennis Ngien, "The God Who Suffers," *Christianity Today* (Feb. 3, 1997), 41.

nature known. With the tongue we can unwittingly drive people away or draw them near. The difference is the wisdom of God and sensitivity to his Spirit.

There are also times in which we use speech with the deliberate intent to hurt. The world of the academy is something of a mystery to most of us, but even here common human foibles and failings are evident. I once heard a disturbing story that bears this out—a story that involves tenure. Within the politics of the university this is among the most sacrosanct of issues. Normally the case of a professor eligible for tenure is debated first at the departmental level, with the recommendation of the department then forwarded to a variety of committees. For obvious reasons, the comments made during such discussions must be held in strictest confidence. In this case a senior professor abused this privilege. For reasons known only to him, he told a junior professor that a second senior professor had spoken against the junior professor during his tenure review. This left the junior professor bitter and angry, and for more than a decade he nursed a grudge. Unfortunately, it was all a lie. For more than a decade what had been a burgeoning friendship lay abused and dormant, strangled by a malicious lie.

Sometimes the greatest hurt is meted out by family members. Winston Churchill was ignored by both his parents. His father, Lord Randolph Churchill, detested Winston; his mother merely paid him no attention. That Winston was a disappointment as a student (he scored 53 percent in English composition on his entrance exam to Sandhurst, the British military academy) seemed to confirm their parental opinion and, in their minds, justified parental neglect. Upon graduation from Sandhurst young Winston imagined that his father would be proud. Instead Randolf was furious that he had not scored high enough to make it into the 60th rifles, a "crack regiment." Randolf wrote a letter to his son containing these venomous words:

> Do not think I am going to take the trouble of writing to you long letters after every failure you commit and undergo. . . . I no longer attach the slightest weight to anything you may say about your own acquirements & exploits. . . . If you cannot prevent yourself from leading the idle useless unprofitable life you have had during your schooldays & later months, you will become a mere social wastrel one of the hundreds of the public school failures, and you will degenerate into a shabby unhappy & futile existence. If that is so you have to bear all the blame for such misfortunes yourself.[64]

Randolf ended the letter brutally: "Your mother sends her love."

---

64. Manchester, *The Last Lion*, 182–83.

Even in church such intentional barbs are let loose. Recently I was on the phone with an old friend who lives thousands of miles away. When I inquired about church life, he became quiet and sad. There had been some rough times in their church, and several prominent members of the church had let loose with some poison-tipped barbs directed at my friend and his wife. Following this the two of them felt that others within the church had become purposeful in avoiding them. My friend continues to attend the church regularly, but his wife has experienced deep hurt and attends only rarely. How petty we are, and how hurtful!

Sometimes we tell lies to hide culpability. In the early months of 1997 the American public became increasingly interested in the campaign fundraising efforts of the Clinton administration and the Democratic National Committee, in particular the propriety of appearing to "sell" access to the President. The *New York Times* reported that in 1995 President Clinton "personally approved a plan under which the Democratic Party rewarded some top donors with meals, coffees, golf outings and morning jogs with him and with overnight stays in the Lincoln bedroom. . . ."[65] Amid the growing furor, President Clinton, on February 25, 1997, said, "The Lincoln Bedroom was never sold."[66]

Yet, according to the *Times* report, some "Democratic fund-raisers explicitly sold invitations to White House coffees with President Clinton and offered to arrange invitations for a price, usually $50,000 but as much as $100,000." The *Times* also published a copy of a memo in the President's handwriting dated to 1995: "Yes, pursue all three and promptly. And get other names at 100,000 and 50,000 or more. . . . Ready to start overnights right away. Give me the top 10 list back, along w/ the 100, 50,000."[67] The *Times* also reported that while officials of the Clinton administration claimed that invitations to White House events were never sold, "several contributors and fund-raisers . . . said that was not true. 'I don't understand why they continue to deny the obvious,' said a fund-raiser. . . ."[68]

The church is not immune from this phenomenon either. I have a friend who is a clinical psychologist. Some years ago a young woman, the daughter of a prominent pastor, came under her care. It soon became evident that her father was guilty of physically abusing his daughter. This was not a case of creative memory, for there was incontrovertible proof in the form of witnesses and hospital records. Her father denied the charges. The members of the church board, trusting their friend and pastor, defended him energetically. Over the course of several months the matter was played out in a highly

---

65. *New York Times* (Feb. 26, 1997): 1.
66. Ibid.
67. Ibid.
68. Ibid., 13.

public fashion. Finally, the pastor admitted culpability. He had lied, he said, to save the church from scandal and to save himself. The result was catastrophic for the church. The elders who had trusted the pastor were duped by him and fell into disgrace in the eyes of both church and community. In this case the tongue perpetuated an evil and spread the venom of the original evil, infecting all who came into contact with it. How many lies were told to cover the original lie, which covered the sin of abuse? How much faithfulness and integrity were besmirched because of that first lie? Our words, when sinful, grow in malevolent effect far more quickly than we imagine. This is a case in which the tongue of a pastor, in telling a selfish lie, infected and destroyed an entire congregation.

In the chapter entitled "Queen Alice" of his *Through the Looking Glass*, Lewis Carroll has the Red Queen say, "When once you've said a thing, that fixes it, and you must take the consequences." Our tongues may be small, but like a tiny spark that sets a blaze, our tongues can do untold damage to others.

Several years ago I was backpacking with some friends in northern California. On the morning of the last day, during a thunderstorm, we realized that a forest fire was not far away. As the day wore on, the air became increasingly thick with smoke. All day long we could hear and sometimes see the planes as they prepared to drop fire-arresting chemicals on the blaze. When we reached our car and turned on the radio, we learned that the fire had burned to the area where we had camped just the night before. After burning several hundred acres, the fire was arrested by a combination of the storm and the efforts of fire fighters. It had started as the result of one careless match. There is great potential stored up in the tongue, just as there is great potential in the position of teacher. Both must be exercised with the wisdom of God.

James 3:13–18

WHO IS WISE and understanding among you? Let him show it by his good life, by deeds done in the humility that comes from wisdom. [14]But if you harbor bitter envy and selfish ambition in your hearts, do not boast about it or deny the truth. [15]Such "wisdom" does not come down from heaven but is earthly, unspiritual, of the devil. [16]For where you have envy and selfish ambition, there you find disorder and every evil practice.

[17]But the wisdom that comes from heaven is first of all pure; then peace-loving, considerate, submissive, full of mercy and good fruit, impartial and sincere. [18]Peacemakers who sow in peace raise a harvest of righteousness.

Original Meaning

JAMES HERE OFFERS us a series of clear contrasts between two kinds of wisdom. This passage is also a fine example of the essential unity of the letter, despite the opinion of many that the letter is an ill-fitting collection of moral teachings.[1] The early portion of chapter 3 dealt with the problem of false teachers and their dangerous teaching by employing the image of the tongue. This "fire" (3:5–12) is almost certainly the cause of the bitter envy, ambition, and divisions discussed in the present section.

James holds up for approbation the wise teacher and the wisdom that comes from God and contrasts it with the false wisdom offered by his opponents. James also continues here his discussion of the source of the evil within us. In chapter 1 James touched on the presence of the *yeṣer ha-ra* within us, and in 3:6 he referred to Gehenna, a circumlocution for Satan. In 3:15 James offers a more direct observation: Some within the church are exhibiting behaviors that are "of the devil." This telescopic series of statements concerning the source of evil therefore anchors this passage firmly within the letter as a whole. Clearly we have here the product of careful thought, for it is marked by clarity of thematic structure and dexterity of presentation.

---

1. Based largely on grammatical evidence, Dibelius argued that this section was originally an independent unit, as there appeared to be "no connection of thought" to the preceding argument in James (M. Dibelius, *A Commentary on the Epistle of James*, rev. H. Greeven, tr. M. A. Williams [Hermeneia; Philadelphia: Fortress, 1976], 207). However one weighs the grammatical evidence, there are, in fact, numerous connections.

Five pieces of evidence demonstrate this care on the part of our author. (1) The entire section is marked by the idea of wisdom, which serves to bracket the passage and appears in verses 13 and 17. (2) These verses employ two catalogues: a list of vices with their corresponding evil origins, and a list of virtues with their corresponding wholesome origins. Note particularly the descending order found in verse 15: "earthly, unspiritual, [and finally] of the devil." (3) The list of virtues in verse 17 is marked by assonance (see below). (4) The use of wisdom (*sophia*) suggests a contrast with the "wisdom" of the teachers James has called into question.[2] Furthermore, the themes of discordant community life, envy, and ambition are present not only here but in the preceding sections. In fact, this section serves as a kind of summary statement for what has gone before, positing that teachers and others should not misuse the tongue, but rather develop authentic Christian virtues. (5) Finally, the passage contains an earlier and prominent theme: Faith without works is dead (2:14–26). The theme appears here in terms of heavenly wisdom and the sort of deeds that are its evidence and confirmation.

James here offers a contrast of two wisdoms. *False* wisdom is marked by "envy" and "selfish ambition," two traits that are the tangible result of false teaching within the lives of those who follow it. James notes these and points out that such traits cannot be of God; therefore, the teaching that spawns them is false. The result of these traits in action is disorder and even "evil practice" within the Christian community. James has already told us that he believes faith results in good deeds (2:14–26). He now reveals that aberrant faith also reveals itself by its deeds. Once again we are reminded of the teaching of Jesus: "Likewise every good tree bears good fruit, but a bad tree bears bad fruit" (Matt. 7:17).

True wisdom reveals itself by several markers as well. These include "deeds done in the humility that comes from wisdom" (James 3:13). Such deads reveal a person connected to the "truth" (v. 14)—a term James reserves for the proper understanding of the Christian life, one that combines a healthy cultivation of the word and shows itself in action. Those who follow true wisdom are described by seven attributes, which function as the mirror images of the blunt description of the false teachers present in verses 14–16. The practical result of this wise teaching is peace within the community. This is not a false peace at any cost, for James is insistent on placing his convictions

---

2. As Paul argued in 1 Corinthians 1, the "wisdom" of this world (the pursuit of which is dominated by self-interest, the desire for wealth, and the desire for status) is diametrically opposed to the wisdom of God. James has made a case similar to that of Paul in 1 Cor. 2 and 3.

beyond equivocation. It is, rather, the peace that comes from making correct but difficult decisions.

As far as James's structure here is concerned, the opening verse establishes the topic to be discussed. It is followed by a double list of virtues and vices. Worldly wisdom (3:14–16) as offered by the teachers with whom James is at odds is characterized by ambition and a desire to seek status through wealth or the securing of a position of power. True wisdom (3:13, 17) implies a vision of heaven, is marked by humility, and results in good deeds. The passage concludes with an apt proverb: "Peacemakers who sow in peace raise a harvest of righteousness."

Pure Speech Comes From Wisdom

JAMES BEGINS BY offering an alternative vision of wisdom to that of his opponents, that true wisdom is marked not by ambition and a desire for status, but rather by humility. The chief interpretive problem of verse 13 is the identification of the "who" that opens the passage. Clearly the teachers whom James has opposed are in view. They have arrogated to themselves a position of authority as those qualified to instruct the Christian community, and in so doing have offered themselves as "wise," just as the false teachers of 1 Corinthians 1:19 laid claim to the mantle of wisdom. In James's eyes, however, it is a wisdom of the world and therefore false. But it is also likely that many others within the church are within the field of the author's gaze. Certainly there were some, perhaps more than a few, who were captivated by the message of these teachers, a message that spoke to their human desires to attain privilege and status.

The fact that James connects someone who is wise (*sophos*) and understanding (*epistemon*) is significant. In the LXX these two terms are frequently linked. In Deuteronomy 1:13, 15 the terms refer to leaders, but in 4:6 they appear in tandem and refer to the people at large.[3] To follow God's decrees is the hallmark of wisdom. Other nations, the Hebrews are promised, will call them wise if their deeds match the decrees of God. Just as in James, the leaders of Deuteronomy 1:13, 15 must have deeds to match their words.

James next offers a rapier-thrust definition of wisdom intended to devastate the position of his opponents. True wisdom, he claims, results in humility and good deeds shown in a "good life." The noun the NIV translates as "life" is *anastrophe*, which is better rendered "way of life" or "mode of life"—a term

---

3. See also Dan. 5:12, in which Daniel is described as a man with a "keen mind and knowledge and understanding." In Job 28:28 God, apparently addressing the entire human community through Job, says, "The fear of the Lord—that is wisdom, and to shun evil is understanding."

used favorably by 1 Peter (1:15; 2:12; 3:1—2, 16). The force of the term indicates that these deeds of humility relate to the core of the Christian. True believers radiate such principles and actions.

The contrast is not between a practical wisdom that results in action and an earthly wisdom that affects only the life of the mind, as Martin seems to suggest.[4] The "worldly wisdom" of the false teachers has not been so irenic or ineffectual. It has had its corrosive effects. This acid force has manifested itself in concrete actions—acts of favoritism within the Christian community and a legitimizing of actions that are at odds with the "law of love." Rather, the contrast is between the different origins of these two "wisdoms" and between the different actions that follow in train.

The phrase *en prauteti sophias* ("the humility that comes from wisdom") is somewhat unwieldy, suggesting that its origin is Hebrew and not Greek. There are parallels in both the Old Testament and the New. Neither Moses (see Num. 12:1—3) nor Jesus (see Matt. 11:29) were interested in personal popularity or power, nor did they defend themselves, but in humility pointed others to God.[5] In similar fashion the Christian in humility is to do good deeds to the glory of God. This is the spirit of true wisdom.

Verse 14 presents a contrasting picture: a bitter and selfish person. Here, instead of the indirect address of verse 13 ("Who ... among you"), James becomes more direct: "If you. ..." Although James writes a conditional clause, the rhetorical force is such that it is a statement of fact and accusation. The term the NIV translates as "bitter envy" is *zelon pikron. Zelon* is derived from *zelos,* which is often translated into English as "zeal." It can bear a negative nuance,[6] often depicting some overblown and therefore inappropriate sense of devotion to God. Paul describes his own past as marked by a zeal for God in persecuting the church.[7] The term can also be used in the positive sense,[8] but of course any zeal has the potential for great destruction if turned. In this case zeal for self-interest has resulted in attitudes of envy and desire, which engulf whatever better judgment may have been present.

The term the NIV translates as "selfish ambition" is *eritheia*. Some argue that this word is derived from *eris*, which can mean "discord."[9] However, others point out that the word is rare outside the New Testament; its only appear-

---

4. Ralph P. Martin, *James,* 129.

5. Peter H. Davids, *The Epistle of James,* 150.

6. See Rom. 13:13; 2 Cor. 12:20; Gal. 5:20.

7. Phil. 3:6. See also Rom. 10:2, where Paul describes the Israelites—"they are zealous for God, but their zeal is not based on knowledge."

8. See 1 Kings 19:10, 14; John 2:17; 2 Cor. 7:7; esp. 11:2, where Paul speaks of "godly jealousy."

9. Paul uses it this way; see 2 Cor. 12:20; Gal. 5:20, two texts cited above.

ance prior to the New Testament is in Aristotle, who uses it to mean the self-seeking pursuit of political power by unjust means.[10] This more precise rendering makes sense here. Paul's use of *eris* appears in lists of vices and, together with *zelos*, describes leaders who cause discord by claiming superior wisdom and by gathering to themselves followers while they charge others in the church with a lack of spirituality. Discord has come to the Christian community as a result of their status-seeking, and they have usurped the spiritual offices of the church in order to teach and propagate this worldly philosophy.

To understand James's urging these teachers and their followers to refrain from "boast[ing] about it" (v. 14), we must first understand to what the "it" refers. Most likely this refers to the wisdom they claim. So we might translate: "Do not boast about your worldly wisdom, because to do so is only to deny the truth even more clearly." This causal sense is endorsed by Ropes.[11] What the teachers falsely call "wisdom" is in fact the virulent work of the *yeser ha-ra* in human hearts. There is a heavenly truth—a truth they deny, a truth that is the polar opposite of the "truth" they disseminate.

Significantly, in verse 15 James does not call what his opponents espouse wisdom, preferring to refer to it in veiled fashion. Their "wisdom" is not from God, which can be had simply by asking (1:5). In saying this James makes a clear argument that the wisdom of these teachers is not neutral or trivial. He does this by arranging the sources of this "wisdom" in an escalating crescendo of perniciousness. The first is *epigeios*, or "earthbound." Here the image of the world, as elsewhere in James, plays a negative role. "Earthly" by definition is less pure and inferior, and in this instance refers to the forces arrayed against God. James also intends to remind his readers that the world is at odds with God. He is saying, "Do not fool yourself into thinking that this attitude is in concert with God, for such is a lie."

Next, this wisdom is *psychikos*, or "unspiritual." This is a fairly unusual word, found in only four other locations in the New Testament.[12] Paul uses the term to describe the "natural man,"[13] as it is drawn from Genesis 2:7, where God breathes life into Adam and he becomes a living *psyche*. In this regard it can denote the unrealized potential to respond positively to God. *Psychikos* was sometimes used by heterodox groups to describe their opponents.[14] The term therefore denoted beings possessing merely life, bereft of

---

10. Aristotle, *Politics*, 5.3.

11. James H. Ropes, *The Epistle of St. James*, 246.

12. 1 Cor. 2:14; 15:44, 46; Jude 19.

13. See G. B. Caird and L. D. Hurst, *New Testament Theology* (Oxford: Clarendon 1994), 99-100.

14. Tertullian (*Against Praxeas*, 1.6) relates that the Montanists branded the orthodox with this term.

the touch of the Spirit of God. Such persons were responsive only to natural stimuli. The false teachers had accused James of this and of a lack of wisdom. Deftly James causes this accusation to turn in their hands. He points out that the activity of the false teachers, this self-righteous name-calling, is in fact a facade that is the result of the very natural, base, and unspiritual desire for personal status and prestige.

Such "wisdom" is, worst of all, demonic in origin. This term, *daimoniodes*, is rare; it appears nowhere else in Scripture and is not to be found in Greek literature before James. There are two options as to its meaning: (1) This teaching and its derivative behavior is instigated by demons and the unwholesome spiritual world; or (2) the behavior depicted here is similar to that of the demons. There is no good reason to suppose that James did not have the first in mind.

In verse 16 James argues from the perspective of the practical. The wisdom of his opponents, rooted in "envy and selfish ambition," has done nothing to strengthen the body, but rather has served only to bring "disorder and every evil practice." True wisdom does not confuse issues of primary allegiance with those of secondary or tertiary character.[15] It does not brook the discord that results from selfish personal interest. The source of such tumult and mean-spirited talk is Satan. The word the NIV renders as "disorder" is *akatastasia*, the same word used in 1:8 for the unstable, double-minded person. Here, as in 3:8, the scenario is writ large as the subject is not an individual, but the Christian community. This teaching has not added to the church, but instead has caused the church seriously to question its direction, and even its heart and soul. Combined with this is all manner of evil practice.

James goes on, then, to outline what he considers to be among the most important results of heavenly wisdom. He does so in a list of virtues similar to those given by Paul in his list of "the fruit of the Spirit." James has offered seven for consideration. First, this wisdom is marked by purity. The Greek term, *hagne*, is unusual.[16] It connotes the absence of the spiritual, ethical, and behavioral imperfections that are necessarily a part of the double-minded person. The idea is found in the Old Testament, usually in connection with the character of God. God's words are pure (Ps. 12:6); and the ways of the righteous are pure, not bent (Prov. 21:8), because their lives mirror God's character. Here, then, is another reference to the rightful "end" or "purpose" of humankind.[17] A person marked by purity partakes of the character of God,

---

15. While the speech of Jesus is often hyperbolic—"If anyone comes to me and does not hate his father and mother . . . he cannot be my disciple" (Luke 14:26)—the point is clear: Jesus demands our primary allegiance.

16. See also Phil. 4:8; 1 John 3:3.

17. See the discussion concerning the meaning of "mature" and "complete" in 1:4 and 3:7.

following after God with "unmixed motives."[18] Purity is listed first because in many ways it is the most important, paving the way for the others.

James has arranged the remaining seven virtues to employ assonance, first with *e*, then with *a*: peace-loving (*eirenike*), considerate (*epieikes*), submissive (*eupeithes*), full of mercy (*meste eleous*), good fruit (*karpon agathon*), impartial (*adiakritos*), and sincere (*anupokritos*). Such wisdom also creates a peace-making spirit. This is of particular importance here, given the problem of discord in the church.

"Considerate" is usually associated with justice, especially with the administration of justice, and suggests someone who does not abuse a position of power, but remains calm and sober and true to the highest ideals of such a position.[19]

"Submissive" can mean "trusting" and "easily persuaded." It does not indicate a person without convictions or one easily swayed. Rather, it conjures the image of a sober, thinking, and intuitive person who recognizes the truth when heard and willingly receives such instruction. Together the pair denote someone who is both gentle and reasonable, whether in a position of authority or of subservience.

James next mentions "full of mercy" and "good fruits" (*karpon agathon*). Earlier, he has told us that true religion is evidenced by acts of kindness (1:27) and that faith is seen in deeds of love (2:15–18).

Finally, James offers for consideration "impartial and sincere." The first is a word of great rarity, found only here in the New Testament. It is the opposite of "double-minded," a word James has used frequently. Wisdom, then, is without double-mindedness; it possesses a singularity of purpose in its trust in God. "Sincere" is a fine capstone to the list, as it also means "without hypocrisy."

Taken as a whole these words counteract the divisive and party spirit and prompt an openness to God's leading, so that even the teachers James opposes might "see the light."

In his final comment, James not surprisingly focuses on peace, given the discord in the church. Righteousness and peace are regularly linked in the Old Testament (see Ps. 85:10; Isa. 32:17). Isaiah 32–33 is of particular importance, as in these chapters the image of cultivation is linked with righteousness and peace.

The phrase "harvest of righteousness" is somewhat difficult in that the genitive can be read as either "the harvest that belongs to righteousness" or "the harvest that consists of righteousness." In the first righteousness has a fruit

---

18. Davids, *The Epistle of James*, 154.
19. In 1 Tim. 3:3 Paul uses it to describe the ideal behavior of church leaders.

that will be produced in the context of peace; in the second "peace" is the condition that gives rise to righteousness. Laws[20] insightfully argues that the "harvest of righteousness" is in fact wisdom. If she is correct, then the argument of James is as follows: (1) Where there is divisiveness, there is no wisdom; (2) wisdom is peaceable; (3) therefore, the peacemakers are the ones who possess wisdom; and (4) the ones who create tumult and discord do not possess wisdom, however much they protest to the opposite. The opponents of James have claimed, either explicitly or implicitly, to possess a superior wisdom. By defining wisdom in biblical terms, James has shown his opponents to be purveyors of a highly corrosive brew of worldly wisdom and deficient teaching. In short, he has shown them to be *psychikoi*, the very charge they leveled at James.

Bridging Contexts

THE PASSAGE BEFORE us is comprised of a discussion of true and false wisdom. Such teaching is not simply an arid intellectual exercise. Rather, in the experience of James teaching about God is always potent, extending to all areas of human endeavor. Pure teaching and sullied teaching both have effects. He is at pains in this section to make those effects clear. James sums up this section by encouraging his readers to be peacemakers.

The most significant single issue for investigation in this section is the biblical notion of peace. There are several reasons for this. (1) Peace is the point of the concluding proverb, and this is a clear sign that the idea of peace is significant for our author. (2) Wisdom, the gift from God (1:5), is needed to help us achieve maturity, and maturity is connected to righteousness. Righteousness is, as James tells us, the harvest realized by peacemakers. (3) Thus, peace is the idea that gathers together a number of disparate ideas that are at work in this passage, as the wisdom of God leads to the peace and wholeness God desires of and for us. Unless this is discerned, we will be unable to understand the richness of James's thought, and we will be tempted to seek contemporary applications that settle for inferior, abiblical notions of peace. It is for these reasons that "peace" is the subject of this Bridging Contexts section.

The richly textured Old Testament notion of "peace" (*šalom*) is one of those ideas that can legitimately be linked to a single word. *Šalom* means "to be whole, to be healthy, to be complete." In this regard it is distinct from most words for peace. For example, the Greek word *homonoia* ("harmony") originally conveyed only a negative meaning, denoting the absence of political

---

20. Sophie Laws, *The Epistle of James*, 165–66.

turmoil within a city. Only later did this word come to possess a positive nuance. But *šalom* bore from the outset a primarily positive meaning. In the LXX *eirene* ("peace") is regularly used to translate *šalom*, and it occurs over 250 times.[21] While other terms can be used, depending on the nuance of *šalom* in a given context, in the LXX *eirene* appears when the wholeness and well-being that is of God is in view.

Šalom was employed in the Old Testament in a dizzying variety of ways. The daily greeting in Israel was *šalom 'alekem* ("peace be upon you"), a blessing and greeting meaning "may you be well."[22] The Old Testament also contrasts peace with warfare, but the emphasis is on peace as close and harmonious relations among peoples.[23] *Šalom* is used of prosperity (Ps. 73:3), physical health (38:3), and salvation (Isa. 43:7). It can also be used in connection with death. The promise to Abraham is, "You, however, will go to your fathers in peace and be buried at a good old age" (Gen. 15:15). *Šalom* is likewise connected to the covenant. In Numbers 25:12 the Lord says to Moses, "I am making my covenant of peace. . . ."

True wholeness, true peace, is intimately linked with the character of God. This idea is present in Psalm 34:14, where the psalmist says, "Turn from evil and do good; seek peace and pursue it." Here we see the notion of peace linked to the twin ideas of justice and righteousness, which together are integral components of the character of God. We should not forget that the definition James has offered for "true religion" is the embodiment of the notion of justice and righteousness: to visit widows and orphans (James 1:27). In Psalm 34 peace is substantial, it is linked to the very core of God's character, and it must be pursued. The idea of "truth" ('*emet*) is added to this complex when in Zechariah 8:16–17, 19 God addresses the inhabitants of Jerusalem and Judah:

> "Speak the truth to each other, and render true and sound judgment in your courts; do not plot evil against your neighbor, and do not love to swear falsely. I hate all this," declares the LORD. . . . "Therefore love truth and peace."

Of course, the reality of life dictates that peace such as this is rarely known. For this reason peace has a future orientation as well. The "Prince of Peace" is the agent of God who brings God's justice, truth, and peace.

---

21. H. Beck, C. Brown, "Peace," *NIDNTT*, 2:777.

22. Joseph P. Healey, "Peace," *ABD*, 5:206.

23. In 1 Kings 5:4 Solomon says, "The LORD my God has given me rest on every side, and there is no adversary or disaster." In Judg. 4:17 we read, "Sisera, however, fled on foot to the tent of Jael, the wife of Heber the Kenite, because there were friendly relations between Jabin king of Hazor and the clan of Heber the Kenite."

In the New Testament the idea of peace is prominent in the teachings of Jesus. It is significant that in the Beatitudes the term "peacemaker" is one of virility; all the other characteristics mentioned by Jesus "designate a state or an attitude, while this one describes a concrete act."[24] Peace, then, is the creation and maintenance of a state of truth, honesty, righteousness, and justice. This notion of wholeness in terms of social relations has obvious merit, given the context in the church of James. But the question of truth and justice should not be overlooked.

When James encourages his readers to be "peacemakers who sow in peace [and who] raise a harvest of righteousness," it is this complex idea of *šalom* to which he refers. Justice, righteousness, and peace are central to the character of God. To develop such character in ourselves and within the Christian community has been a frequent theme throughout the course of this letter. What remains is to consider how its use as revealed here can be applied today.

 EVANGELICALS WOULD DO well to recapture the biblical idea of peace. In practice we often confuse the biblical idea of peace with its impoverished modern counterpart, the absence of obvious tension. We do this in part because we find it expedient in the short run to avoid disagreement and the tension it brings.

In a passage in Thucydides, a Corinthian delegation attempted to persuade the Athenians to join their cause with the words, "The true path of expediency is the path of right."[25] The Corinthians spoke the truth, but in the long annals of human history there is little evidence to support the popularity of their view. Our more typical course of action is to succumb to the temptation of the path that in prospect seems to afford the least resistance and the smallest chance of personal harm. Having registered our choice, we honor it with pious rationalizations.

The evangelical church is not immune from this pervasive malady. In fact, it is surprising how frequently the contemporary evangelical church has blindly chosen nonbiblical ideas of "peace" instead of the more profound biblical idea. Routinely we pursue peace as "absence or denial of tension within the body" over peace as "wholeness within the body." Most evangelical churches I know of are petrified of tension; thus, discussion of issues that might cause conflict is suppressed. In the last four months I have heard a number of such stories—some fresh, some the memories of events long past.

---

24. William Klassen, "Peace," *ABD*, 5:209.
25. Thucydides, *The History of the Peloponnesian War*, 1.42.

- To the surprise of many within a congregation, one of their associate pastors was dismissed. A few in the congregation knew that there were problems afoot, and others felt the pastor in question was not effective. Many others, however, disagreed, having found the pastor quite helpful. The announcement of dismissal, therefore, was a shock. Still more surprising to many was the service on the last Sunday of the pastor's tenure. A litany was prepared, in which both the pastor and the congregation read appeals of forgiveness asked of one another. To many in the congregation this seemed excessively odd. There has been no further discussion.
- The entire executive board of a church resigned, claiming that the pastor was "running the church" through his friends instead of through the elected board structure. Tension between the pastor and the board had been growing for nearly a year. The congregation at large had been deliberately and effectively shielded from this growing tension by both parties. Both had begun to elicit support for their positions from selected members of the congregation. To most, however, knowledge of this development came only with the mass resignation. This brinkmanship soured the spirit of the church, and attendance dropped 45 percent.
- A volunteer counselor with the youth group was found in a mildly compromising position with a female student. The volunteer was dismissed from the high school counseling staff, and the pastoral staff at the church decided to cover up the incident. Nonetheless, reports of the incident began to circulate in the small community, many of them wildly exaggerated. The church continued to stonewall the truth. Respect for the church in the community, which had been high, began a rapid free-fall.
- After two years of prayer and deliberation, a congregation decided to move forward with plans to build a new and larger sanctuary, a plan with which the pastor was in full accord. During the week following the vote, however, several members of the congregation met secretly with the pastor and convinced him to change his mind. The following Sunday the pastor dutifully announced that he now viewed the plans to build a new sanctuary "sinful." The pastor soon left the church, realizing that he had been manipulated. The leaders of the "coup" and the elected leaders of the church have refused in the ensuing decade to speak with each other or about that chapter in the history of the church, citing the need to "keep peace" within the congregation.
- A new senior pastor announces to the congregation that he desires the entire staff to stay in place, but in private makes it clear to one staff

member that his resignation is required. The resignation comes as a surprise to many, and when asked if he is being "forced out," the staff person lies with the words, "in the interests of peace and the welfare of the church."

- A church member and frequent soloist is upset because the pastor has not agreed with her wish to be the featured Sunday morning soloist at least twice a month. She and her family leave the church, and no one besides the two principals knows why. When asked, neither will speak of the matter.
- A church that has remained at two hundred members for fifteen years has called a new pastor. He quickly realizes that there is a difficult family in the church. This couple insists on having their own way, even to the point of offering threats during business meetings of the church. Many church members commiserate with the new pastor and inform him that this couple has dominated the church for years, but no one wishes to go through the unpleasantness of crossing them. The pastor learns that the husband has been brought up on charges of child abuse in the past, and in a private session informs him that he can no longer work with the youth of the church. Realizing that the pastor cannot speak of this publicly, the man attempts to malign the pastor for excluding him from ministry. The pastor is days away from accepting a call to another church before the leadership finally stands up to this controlling couple.

None of these cases is simple. There are, as always, mitigating circumstances that must be considered. One of these is the protection of the privacy of individuals, whether pastors or members of the congregation. A second is often cited, the Pauline demand to protect the unity of the church in order to keep "peace" in the church. It is important to recognize that this command appears in a particular context in Philippians, a context in which Paul argues for the unity of the church, not so much as an end in itself but so the church may be firmly fastened upon its primary task, which he says is the spread of the gospel (Phil. 1:27; 4:2–3). If the church is consumed with divisions over tertiary issues to the extent that primary concerns are left unattended, then a not insignificant evil has been committed. In some of these situations listed above, either mitigating factor could legitimately be invoked. Nonetheless, there is something about contemporary evangelicalism that comes up short when compared to the biblical idea of peace.

Recently I asked a colleague to lead one of my classes through a discussion of "Christian community." She began by inquiring of the students their impressions of relationships within the church. The initial responses were slow and halting, but within two minutes they came fast and furious. I dutifully recorded as many of their answers as I could. Here is the list:

- People put up a facade.
- Relationships are basically superficial.
- Most of the time people are not sincere.
- But there are plenty of people who are caring.
- It often feels artificial.
- People are really "nice," as in the appearance of peace.
- People are usually considerate.
- When people are friendly, it is usually with other Christians; it is not usually extended to those outside the church.
- People are too busy.
- The church is not egalitarian, but highly structured.
- The church is hierarchical, with clear, unspoken rules of power: pastor, deacons, long-time members, and wealthy members have the power.
- People want to avoid conflict.

My colleague then asked them why they think this is so, given the biblical model of Christian community. Once again I recorded as many of their answers as I could:

- We have other priorities—money, appearance, recognition.
- We are dishonest with ourselves about these, our true priorities.
- We fear persecution by the world.
- We are afraid of the consequences of the truth. We often avoid telling someone else the truth, and we tell ourselves this is because we wish to protect their feelings. But we know the real reason is that we don't want to have to deal with the potential unpleasantness of the situation.
- We are afraid of facing the fact that we cannot live up to biblical standards.
- We realize we cannot make a difference in the world or even in our church, so why try?

Finally, she asked them to describe the values our culture seems to extol or which mark our culture:

- Materialism—we want things.
- We want attention, even fame.
- We desire greed, power, status.
- We are careless about other people, especially people we do not know.
- Our culture loves temptation.

- Self-protection
- Fear
- Aggression
- Envy
- Pride, not humility
- Assumption. We do not bother to find out; we simply make assumptions about people and judge them on superficial grounds, without really knowing them.

In our desire to preserve what is an unbiblical "peace," have we produced a situation of such unbiblical proportions? I was struck by several issues as I heard my students speak. I was impressed that they identified themselves with the deeper issues in the second group of responses. I was also struck by their fear of not measuring up to God's standards. This is wholly commensurate with James. His letter teaches adherence to an exacting standard. But it also teaches the forgiveness of God and the truth that as the word is planted within and is nurtured, the Christian can grow into "perfection" (1:4, 18).

The final point that struck me about these three lists was the degree of correspondence between them and the list of vices outlined by James. His catalogue of evil in chapter 3 is frighteningly similar to the model of the biological growth of evil pictured in 1:15. These vices have their origin in desires that are "earthly, unspiritual, of the devil" (3:15), which lead to "envy and selfish ambition," which in turn cause "disorder" (3:16) within the Christian community. James steadfastly refuses to allow us to view such developments as trivial. Their origin is unwholesome, and however innocent or irenic the garb in which initially they are clothed, ultimately they are a cancer in the body.

It is for this reason that James used unreservedly strong language in 3:1–12 in his discussion of false teachers, false teaching, and the devastating effect these have on the community. Do not be fooled or cowed, James intones. Such teaching, and the failure to recognize and resist it, is dangerous in the extreme. The poison begins innocently, in the fertile receptacle of our minds and hearts. It grows to dominate our actions. Finally, through our actions it spreads to infect the community around us. The most effective course to avoid this evil, James reminds us, is to walk firmly and with resolve in the path of heavenly wisdom and its fruits.

The impressions of my students do not, of course, convey the entire picture of American evangelicalism. There is more that can be said, much of it positive. But they are nonetheless accurate in pointing to features that, if not the entirety of the landscape, are nonetheless present. These impressions must be set in contrast with the catalogue James has left for us concerning a life in accord with "wisdom that comes from heaven," which results in peace.

In 3:13 James speaks of heavenly wisdom placing its stamp upon an entire "mode of life" (*anastrophes*). The seven traits he outlines make for such a "consistent life" shaped by heavenly wisdom: It is "pure, then peace-loving, considerate, submissive, full of mercy and good fruit, impartial and sincere." Together these are the characteristics of the peacemaker in 3:18.

"Purity" reflects God's character. A pure person follows God's decrees with motives unmixed. For such an individual the cleansing of 4:7–8 is unnecessary. The motives of the soloist mentioned above were not unmixed. She may well have imagined only pure motives, but I am confident most observers would detect a self-centered *prima donna* attitude at work here, not the humble and unselfish attitude extolled by James.

There are also cases in which mitigating circumstances might apply. Several years ago a friend of mine became friends with the members of a Christian heavy-metal band. Proudly she told me how the band would throw Bibles into the audience during their performances. While I hold reservations about the wisdom of this style of ministry and evangelism, it may be effective for some. She also showed me pictures of herself with the band members. I could not help but notice their pants. They were leather and skin-tight, so tight that nothing was left to the imagination—precisely the sort of pants that members of heavy-metal bands in the secular music industry wore. Perhaps I am something of a prude, but this seemed a mixed message to me.

As we have seen, "considerate" is usually associated with justice, particularly the avoidance of the abuse of power. Power has been an issue much in my mind of late. Some time ago I was asked to speak to a group of pastors about church governance, specifically about the role of the pastor, the boards, and the congregation in terms of the New Testament. With but a little probing I realized that the real issue was power. At least the most vocal members of the steering committee wished to see justification for greater power in the hands of the pastor. I am chary of power, as I believe James to be. But he places before us a key characteristic for those in power: consideration.

The first pastor I served under continues to have my utmost respect as a man of integrity, character, and consideration. Although superficially he can appear brusque, and although many view him as dictatorial (during those early years he once told me, "If you don't know which way the vote in your board is going to go, then you have not done your homework"), I know better, for I have the privilege of knowing him well. Several times during the three years we worked together I saw him absorb misplaced and misdirected vituperation because he had the integrity not to reveal confidential information or information that might be damaging to someone else. In the years since, I have known many leaders, and nearly everyone has failed this very test. This pastor is a man who is unswerving in his dedication to see the work of Christ go forward and is diligent in attempting to discern the voice of God. He will not countenance wavering when the integrity of the gospel or the work of Christ is at issue. But he remains tolerant and even untroubled by misinformed forces that often work to his great personal detriment.

James includes in this list of virtues "submissive," meaning one who recognizes the truth of God when it is heard and willingly submits to it. After spending more than a decade in pastoral ministry, I cast my lot with the academy, becoming a full-time professor in 1992. People often ask me which I prefer, and I can honestly say that both have appeal for me and that in my present capacity I am able to move in both worlds. But there is one aspect of pastoral ministry that I miss with passionate longing—the joy of working with a leadership team. During my last five years in ministry I had the privilege of working with a group of leaders, each of us solidly committed to God, to each other, and to the goals we had prayerfully established. Often we disagreed on precisely how to reach a certain goal; but once a decision was made, each of us willingly made ourselves submissive to that plan, that strategy, that program.

Such teamwork is not cheaply bought. We were a diverse group: black, Asian, white, even some from foreign countries; some were from wealth, others grew up in poverty. It took honesty, risk, and hours together—hours of play as well as work. I particularly remember one long drive with one of our minority leaders. There had been tension between us born of misunderstanding. After five hours of small talk and with only twenty minutes to our destination, I finally fortified my anemic courage and said, "I am concerned about our friendship." The reply surprised me, "What friendship?" We spent the next two hours in deep and honest discussion, sometimes painful, but always in the knowledge that we shared a love of Christ and a love for each other. These virtues of honesty, submissiveness, and compassion suffused our leadership team, and working with them was one of the most extraordinary experiences of my life.

"Mercy" and "good fruit" go together, for mercy has a practical orientation that by definition manifests itself in "good fruit." Mercy is not pity, for pity can be simply the emotion of concern that passes as quickly as the shadow of a cloud. Mercy is compassion that drives one to action. Jesus once addressed the Pharisees: "Therefore I tell you that the kingdom of God will be taken away from you and given to people who will produce its fruit" (Matt. 21:43). Fruit, as we have repeatedly seen, comes from the heart, from character, and character can be shaped.

The film *Rain Man* is in some ways a parable of redemption. Tom Cruise plays Charlie Babbitt, a smooth-talking, sleazy salesman who returns home when he learns that his estranged father has died. When the will is read,

Charlie receives only the Buick convertible from his youth. The remaining millions of his father's estate is left to his institutionalized, autistic older brother Raymond, a brother Charlie did not even know he had. Much of the movie is made up of Charlie trying to hustle the money from Raymond or trying to parlay Raymond's amazing mathematical talents into a fortune in Las Vegas. But a change begins to take place within Charlie. He begins to care for Raymond, even against his own will. His heart changes, and as this change gains in depth and confidence, Charlie begins to do for Raymond more than for himself.

This is a "good fruit" from the heart. There may have been a core of right-eousness in the hearts and minds of that small cadre of people who torpedoed the building plans of the congregation, but in the mix was a desire to control, a hatred of losing, and a selfish urge to have the church remain "just the way we like it." Honest reflection may very well have revealed the true origin of their desires.

The final pair of virtues, "impartial" and "sincere" also go together. For James these describe a person who is not double-minded. It is the person who knows the heart of God and therefore the priorities of God. As we have seen earlier, one of the stickiest problems is knowing how to balance "peacemaking" with sticking to principle. One of the keys is understanding the priorities of God. For James these are, in short form, (1) devotion to the spiritual life, so that the word may be planted in you and grow strong; (2) care of the poor and marginalized, not only of their dignity, but also of their material circumstances; (3) a willingness frequently to take stock of oneself, to ensure that the virtues, and not the vices, are growing strong; and (4) the willingness to know the truth of the gospel and stand up for it when it is threatened. But we must remember that even the false teachers were "dear brothers" to James. For "sincerity" conveys the idea of treating all people equally, of holding to both truth and love.

Inherent to the biblical idea of peace is a standard, a caste of heart and mind and consequent behavior congruent with God, and which is, therefore, nonnegotiable. Peace at any price is not peace, as human history readily demonstrates. The horrors of World War I left the peoples of the former allied powers longing for peace and nearly pathologically incapable of believing that another war would ever begin. When the League of Nations conducted a poll on the issue of international disarmament, 10.4 million Britons were in favor, only 870,000 opposed.[26] As the inhumanity of the new Nazi regime became more obvious, the British government, and indeed world

---

26. William Manchester, *The Last Lion: Winston Spencer Churchill; Alone; 1932–1940* (Boston: Little, Brown, and Co., 1988), 95.

opinion, seemed blind to the obvious. After an interview with *der Führer*, a British journalist wrote that Hitler had "large, brown eyes—so large and so brown that one might actually grow lyrical about them if one were a woman."[27] In fact, the eyes of the dictator of Germany were blue. The Jewish American journalist Walter Lippmann wrote an article in which he extolled Hitler as "civilized," and spoke of Nazi persecution of the Jews as a way to "satisfy" the German desire to "conquer somebody."[28]

British diplomats, who should have known better, believed that Hitler was basically a man of peace, who wanted only to recover for Germany a modicum of prestige and security. Speaking for the government of Prime Minister Ramsay MacDonald in the House of Commons on March 23, 1933, Anthony Eden said that it is necessary to "appease" Hitler, because if appeased his anger would cool and Germany would become sensible and stable. "Appeasement" at first meant allowing Germany to break the conditions of the Versailles Treaty and forge a military arsenal equal to that of France. Later it came to mean allowing Germany to overrun countries such as Czechoslovakia, countries that Great Britain had sworn to defend. In this way was the honor and integrity of Great Britain compromised. Finally, of course, it meant descent into the cataclysm of another world war. In the early 1930s these British diplomats did not understand the untrammeled voraciousness of evil. Soon enough they would. The *yeṣer ha-ra*, Gehenna, Satan—these are voracious and uncompromising. They are not to be trifled with.

The members of the congregation who allowed one couple to dominate church life sought peace through appeasement. They allowed themselves to impugn the integrity of the biblical call to community by holding to the promise of "peace" in the congregation. By placing their feet on this path, they condemned the church to more than a decade of envy, bitterness, and strife. Peace that leads to righteousness is peace that steadfastly refuses to let go of its standard: justice, righteousness, and the wisdom of God. Peace bought at their sacrifice is not biblical peace.

---

27. Ibid., 82.
28. *New York Herald Tribune* (May 12, 1933).

James 4:1–10

WHAT CAUSES FIGHTS and quarrels among you? Don't they come from your desires that battle within you? ²You want something but don't get it. You kill and covet, but you cannot have what you want. You quarrel and fight. You do not have, because you do not ask God. ³When you ask, you do not receive, because you ask with wrong motives, that you may spend what you get on your pleasures.

⁴You adulterous people, don't you know that friendship with the world is hatred toward God? Anyone who chooses to be a friend of the world becomes an enemy of God. ⁵Or do you think Scripture says without reason that the spirit he caused to live in us envies intensely? ⁶But he gives us more grace. That is why Scripture says:

"God opposes the proud
    but gives grace to the humble."

⁷Submit yourselves, then, to God. Resist the devil, and he will flee from you. ⁸Come near to God and he will come near to you. Wash your hands, you sinners, and purify your hearts, you double-minded. ⁹Grieve, mourn and wail. Change your laughter to mourning and your joy to gloom. ¹⁰Humble yourselves before the Lord, and he will lift you up.

<table>
<tr><td>Original
Meaning</td><td>THERE ARE SEVERAL ties between this passage and those which preceded, in spite of a variety of commentators who tell us otherwise.[1] The section just completed (3:13–18) was concerned</td></tr>
</table>

with true wisdom that issues forth in peace and false wisdom that results in disorder and strife. Here James again discusses disorder (4:2) that results from this same false wisdom, the ultimate source of which is the devil (4:7).

This section also continues enumerating the escalating steps in evil. In 1:14 James introduced the evil desire. In 3:6 he opined that Gehenna was the cause of the tongue's fire. In 3:15 the origin of the "wisdom" of the world was

---

1. Sophie Laws, *The Epistle of James*, 167, sees no structural connection, but does observe that the transition is "understandable."

identified as lodged in the demonic. Here in 4:7 Christians are now told to resist the devil. The pride fostered and nurtured by false wisdom must be humbled, which is the point of the somber grieving of 4:9. The pride of 4:6 is linked to the boasting of 3:14; the selfish ambition of 3:14 is linked to the human heart that needs cleansing (4:8). Finally, the statement that "friendship with the world is hatred toward God" (4:4) refers to the passionate desire of some in the community to seek status and prestige as their surrounding culture defined it. In this pursuit they showed favoritism and displayed an unwillingness to understand the law of love, thereby showing themselves opposed to God.

In these verses James once again points out the two choices arrayed before the church. This is a theme that we have seen before,[2] but here it takes on special significance. The author has just finished laying before us a full dress presentation of the source, origin, and results of the ways of earth and the ways of heaven. He has provided a concrete example of the biological model of the growth of sin offered in chapter 1. So here the two ways are set with particular clarity and urgency before his readers: earthly wisdom or heavenly wisdom, self-interest or the law of love, self-exaltation or exaltation at the hand of God. His language is powerful and graphic: Resist the devil/come near to God; wash your hands/purify your hearts; grieve and mourn/turn joy to gloom; humble yourselves/God will lift you up. The seriousness of the matter is confirmed in the harsh vocabulary James marshals: They "kill" (4:2); they are an "adulterous people" (4:4), whose actions make them "an enemy of God" (4:4); they are "sinners" (4:8).

James 4:1–10 is composed of three sections, of which the first two offer diagnoses of the problems rampant in the church, while the third offers a solution. In verses 1–3 James chastises his readers for their prayers, for these are marked by anger and selfish desire, not by an attitude of trust in God. In verses 4–6 James points out that there are substantial and significant differences between the values of the Roman empire and life lived according to God's desires. A choice must be made; no one can satisfy the demands of both. Then, in verses 7–10, James offers his solution to the various problems besetting the church as he issues a call to repentance.

Prayers Offered in Anger and Desire (4:1–3)

AT THE END of chapter 3 James laid before his readers a positive summation: A harvest of righteousness is promised those who are peacemakers. The rich agricultural image of the verse is particularly striking, given the heavy reliance

---

2. See the discussion of the two ways in the Original Meaning section of 1:16–18 (pp. 75–78).

on horticultural language James has chosen to employ. Here he turns his probing eye once again to the debilitating effects of the philosophy of false wisdom: "What causes fights and quarrels among you?" James knows full well the answer, so this and the other question in verse 1 are rhetorical in nature.

James returns to the problem of the tongue and compares the effects of the tongue under the influence of false wisdom with rather serious parallels: "fights" (*polemoi*) and "quarrels" (*machai*).[3] Along with his earlier description James paints a picture of a Christian community deeply divided, composed of a variety of groups, some of them marked by different combinations of unwholesome practices. The church is beset by jealousy, selfish ambition, slander, anger, a willingness to depart from received teaching, and a host of other ills that follow the pattern of their culture.

The fact that James refers to no specific dispute might signal to us a situation so rife with tensions that the church was at a standstill. In any event, the conflict is clearly within the Christian community,[4] as this is certainly the meaning of *en hymin* ("among you"). In other words, certain teachers had won a following by offering a philosophy that encouraged the pursuit of status as taught by society and unbridled by any authentic Christian witness. This in turn allowed a false belief to germinate and flourish that all of one's old prejudices could exist and thrive within the church. For this reason some were showing favoritism, while others were exploiting the poor. Arrayed against these were believers loyal to the gospel, who correctly understood the threat. The members of this group reacted variously to those following the teachers of false wisdom—some wanting peace at any price, others advocating a fight for the soul of the church.

In the second part of verse 1, James wisely points to a two-layered interpretation, just like the one sustained throughout 3:1–12. Just as there are mixed within each of us as individuals motives and emotions wholesome and unwholesome, so within the Christian community there is a wide variety of impulses. James says their disputes come from the desires (*hedone*) within them. The rabbis believed that the impulses, the *yeṣarim*, had their seats in various organs or "members" of the human body; therefore, the members of the body were "at war" with one another—pulled one way by conscience, then another way by the evil desire.[5]

---

3. The term *machai* is related to *machaira*, the Greek word Homer uses to indicate a short sword or a long knife. *Machai* is often reserved for battles without weapons; these battles can be physical or verbal.

4. Recall the decision to define "twelve tribes," "brothers," and "the rich" as each referring to Christians.

5. Although later than the New Testament, these rabbinic sayings are evidence of this "war" among the members of the body. "R. Simeon b. Levi said: The evil *yetzer* of a man waxes

This image is not unknown elsewhere in the New Testament. First Peter 2:11 speaks of "sinful desires," which "war against your soul." In Romans 7:22–23 Paul speaks of the two "laws" within him: "For in my inner being I delight in God's law; but I see another law at work in the members of my body, waging war ... and making me a prisoner of the law of sin at work within my members" (cf. also Gal. 5:17). In speaking of these "desires" we might have expected James to use the term *epithymia*, as he did in James 1:14–15. But *hedone*, like *epithymia*, while semantically neutral, can (as here) carry a negative meaning, such as "sinful passion."[6] The term is used in 4 Maccabees 1:25–26: "And there is in pleasure a malicious disposition." If this passage is the background for the use of *hedone* here, then James's point is that such a person strives against God. However, in Titus 3:3 *hedone* and *epithymia* appear as synonyms, so the use of *hedone* here may be due to stylistic reasons.

It is the passions, or more properly the decision to cultivate rather than control the passions, that have contributed to the problems within the church. These passions (untrammeled desire for power and authority, a desire for popularity within the eyes of the powerful, etc.) constitute a state of double-mindedness. The members of the congregation are pushed this way and that, first by their conscience, then by the evil impulse.

In verse 2a James punctuates his message by noting that unrestrained desire can never be fulfilled. His words "You kill and covet, but you cannot have what you want" refers to present difficulties. Several commentators have attempted to see "murder" (*phoneuete*) as metaphorical.[7] Martin desires to treat it literally, but his reconstruction is not convincing.[8] Yet we must agree that the term can and perhaps should be understood literally, even if we do not know the particulars. It is possible, as Martin suggests, that various positions on Roman rule existed within the church, just as it is beyond doubt that various positions on Roman culture were present. Certainly the poor saw those who collaborated with the Romans as traitors. It is significant that James adds the reason for this killing as covetousness. If "killing" is the tool that still does not bring the desired result, then James is explaining that vio-

---

strong against him day by day, and seeks to kill him, and if God did not help him, man could not prevail against it" (*Kiddushin* 30b). "The Rabbis say: so hard is the evil *yetzer* that even its Creator calls it evil, as it is said, 'For the *yetzer* of man's heart is evil from his youth' (Genesis 8:21)" (*Kiddushin* 30b). In the Talmud, *b. Nedarim* 32a–32b, the numerical value of *ha-satan* (Satan) is 364, which, claims the Talmud, means that Satan has power over human beings for 364 days a year, but not on the day of Atonement. The Talmud goes on to say that humans are composed of 248 body parts, and the "Good Urge" and the "Evil Urge" struggle over the body as a whole, each lodging in various body parts.

6. See James H. Ropes, *The Epistle of St. James*, 253–54.

7. See comments of Ralph P. Martin, *James*, 146.

8. Martin argues that some of the Christians to whom James writes were former Zealots.

lence is never a solution worthy of pursuit. To choose the path of violence is to place oneself within a vicious cycle of retribution. Only the peace offered by God can stop such a tragic web of circumstances.

But there are other difficulties with verse 2. The standard edition of the Greek text sees three propositions here: "You desire and you do not have; you murder and you are jealous and you cannot get what you want; you quarrel and you fight." This rendering is followed by the NIV and places "murder/kill" in the role of a preliminary condition that results in unrequited desire. Many commentators prefer a different punctuation, one that sees this verse composed of two parallel statements of cause and effect: "You desire and you do not have, so you murder; you are jealous and you cannot get what you want, so you quarrel and fight." Murder, then, becomes a consequence of desire that is not realized, rather than a constituent part of that desire. This mitigates the force of the argument for seeing murder as literal.

That last part of verse 2 contains a theme we have already seen (1:5). Here James must be expecting his readers to think in ultimate terms. What they want is not status, but rather what they hope status will bring to them: a sense of wholeness, joy, and peace. James asserts that believers do not have what they are seeking because they have been searching for it in alleys that are blind and in fields that are infertile. They should ask God, who gives wisdom (1:5), and this is a wisdom that results in wholeness and peace.

In Matthew 7:7 Jesus gave an unconditional promise that prayer would be answered. James in verse 3 makes explicit what Jesus left implicit: You do not receive because you ask God not for wisdom, but for selfish pleasures that by definition are not in the interests of the Christian community. Much has been made of the curious use of the middle and active voices in 4:2–3.[9] But the significant point is that the readers of James ask with the wrong motives, and therefore for the wrong things.

According to the Old Testament, God answered the prayers of the just, because they were offered in righteousness. Note Psalm 34:14–17:

> Turn from evil and do good;
>> seek peace and pursue it.
> The eyes of the LORD are on the righteous
>> and his ears are attentive to their cry;

---

9. Some see the middle voice as marker of the prayer of the heart and the active voice denoting the prayer of the lips. F. J. A. Hort, *The Epistle of St. James: The Greek Text with Introduction, Commentary As Far As Chapter IV Verse 7, and Additional Notes* (London: Macmillan, 1909), 89, saw the middle voice as the designation of asking for something and the active voice designating the asking of a person.

the face of the LORD is against those who do evil. . . .
The righteous cry out, and the LORD hears them. . . ."

James points out that the "prayers" his readers have offered are marked by their desire for "pleasures." The Greek word for "spend" here is *dapanao*, which here has a negative connotation, just as it did in the parable of the prodigal son (Luke 15:13–14). The prayer was not answered positively because, in part, the prayer assumed a certain arrogance, the presumption that the one praying knew what was best. God's wisdom is often at odds with our own, and this was the case here. What is needed, of course, is patience and a willingness to be molded by God. These were evidently absent from James's readers.

The Bane of Compromise (4:4–6)

IN VERSE 4 James adopts the mantle of elder and offers a rebuke as to errant children. By designating them "adulterous people," he recalls a frequent Old Testament rebuke,[10] offers an echo of the teaching of Jesus in Matthew 12:39, and artfully holds out to his readers inclusion even as he wields the whip of chastisement. James is trying to shame them by reminding them of their commitment to the faith.

James's reference to friendship with the world closely parallels a phrase employed by Paul in 2 Timothy 3:4 ("lovers of pleasure rather than lovers of God") and by John in 1 John 2:15 ("Do not love the world or anything in the world. If anyone loves the world, the love of the Father is not in him."). We are, then, in touch with a broad tradition. "The world" here assumes its semantic function as the forces and elements opposed to God, or, more precisely, the whole complex of human institutions, values, and traditions that knowingly or unwittingly are arrayed against God.[11]

Martin notes that the choice to be apart from God is deliberate.[12] While the grammar may support this, the thrust of James's argument does not. True, some choose friendship with the world in the full knowledge that this constitutes enmity with God, and some of these continue to maintain the facade of a relationship with the Christian community. Perhaps James suspects this of the teachers he opposes. But many choose friendship with the world with-

---

10. The premise of the book of Hosea is that the people of Israel have been adulterous (see also Jer. 3:7–10).

11. As we have seen, in Dan. 7 this is pictured as four beasts (human governments and institutions) that stamp on the earth and devour flesh, but whose dominion is taken away by the Son of Man in order to institute God's kingdom.

12. Martin, *James*, 148. He points out that the verb "chooses" (*boulomai*) implies a conscious choice. Of course people often make conscious choices in ignorance of the ramifications, especially if duplicity is involved.

out realizing that it means enmity with God. This is probably his chief point, for the phrase "adulterous generation" is always used in Scripture of those who assume they are in a covenant relationship with God. Why else would James seek to win them back by argument and then rebuke?

Like the prophets of old James wants his audience to wake up, rub the sleep from their eyes, look in the mirror (1:23), and see themselves as they really are. What has appeared to them as sound teaching and practice is actually apostasy. It amounts to the worship of a false god. There is no middle ground where one can stand and remain unsullied (1:27). To continue to follow this false teaching is no mere trifle; it is to join hands with evil. They have not sensed the dire straits in which they stand, and James sounds for them the warning klaxon.

Verse 5 presents at least two problems of interpretation. (1) What Scripture does James have in mind, for there is no Old Testament text to correspond to the quote. In the next verse James cites Proverbs 3:34, but this verse hardly suffices here. It is possible that we have here a loose paraphrase of Exodus 34:14: "Do not worship any other god, for the LORD, whose name is Jealous, is a jealous God." It is also possible that James here summarizes the many Old Testament passages that speak of the jealousy of God when the worship and ultimate allegiance on the part of human beings is in view. James's point is that God earnestly desires his spirit to reside in us.[13]

(2) This leads us to another problem: What is the subject and what is the object of the verb "longs for" (*epipothei*)? The NIV has chosen to muddy the waters by conflating two consecutive Greek terms, *phthonon* ("envy, jealousy") and *epipothei*. It is best to treat *phthonon* as an adverb ("with envy, with jealousy") and to see "God" as the subject and "the spirit" as the object of the verb. This leaves us with the following translation: "Out of jealousy he longs for the spirit that he made to live in us." This is the interpretation chosen by the NRSV (cf. NIV text note). Other renderings are, of course, possible and grammatically defensible. The subject could be the Holy Spirit, in which case the translation would be, "The Holy Spirit that he sent to live in us desires us for himself alone." This, however, leaves us not distantly removed from where we find ourselves if God is the subject.[14] In any case, the point is, plainly, that God

---

13. In John 14:17 Jesus refers to the Spirit in him who will be in them once his crucifixion and resurrection are accomplished: "You know him, for he lives with you and will be in you." In 14:23 Jesus speaks even more deeply of this love-relationship between God the Father, Son, and Spirit and with human beings: "My Father will love him, and we will come to him and make our home with him."

14. Note text note on this verse in NIV. The subject could also be the human spirit: "The spirit that he caused to live in us is one of jealousy and envy." This translation leaves us with the human spirit bent toward friendship with the world. This is not off the mark, but it does

desires with all of his heart for us to come home and to live with and in him, for us to ask for his wisdom. Instead, we follow the wisdom of the world, whether knowingly or unwittingly, and by following that errant path we can never achieve what we truly seek.

In verse 6 James holds out a lifeline to those who have apparently been ignorant of the gravity of their situation. God's grace, he says, is still available and abundant for them. God's demands can be harsh, but he always provides the means to follow him. This holds true even in the case of those active in cultivating a friendship with the world. James probably has in view a panoply of gifts, such as wisdom, the Holy Spirit, forgiveness, salvation, Jesus Christ himself, and many others.

The Scripture James quotes here is Proverbs 3:34: "He mocks proud mockers but gives grace to the humble." He uses this verse as the headwaters for a cascade of ten commands. Its thrust is that God opposes the proud because they seem to have little interest in anyone but themselves, often exploiting the poor; and that God grants grace to the poor and needy because they trust in him, having no other recourse (1:6, 12; 2:5; 5:8). In this case the proud and arrogant have already shown their stripes: They have demonstrated favoritism based on wealth and status as the Roman world demanded, and they have therefore unveiled themselves as the friends of that world and at enmity with God. Further, they have arrogated themselves the right to proclaim as faith a functional denial of the very teaching of Jesus, specifically the law of love.

Repentance and Forgiveness (4:7–10)

VERSE 7 OPENS a series of ten imperatives, or commands, built on the foundation laid in verse 6. These commands comprise James's recipe for humility before God. To "submit" (*hypotasso*) is normally used in reference to human authority, but the point is plain and the alternatives stark: "You may think you have been serving God, but you have not. Change, then, by submitting to God." The idea of submission carries with it the full range intended by the term *repentance*, which is not only a change of direction, but also a humble and contrite spirit. If this path is chosen, the response of God is forgiveness, as James has just reminded us in verse 6 ("he gives us more grace"). James then expands these points.

The first component of submission to God is to "resist the devil." The word "resist" (*anthistemi*) is the same one used by the LXX in Proverbs 3:34: "God opposes the proud." James flatly claims that Satan is the ultimate source of

---

seem to make less sense of the current trajectory of James's argument. Furthermore, the subject of the verb *katokisen* (to dwell) is God, and it makes the most sense for James to have the same subject for both verbs.

evil.[15] Perhaps he has employed this elaborate escalating technique (the *yeṣer ha-ra* in 1:14; Gehenna in 3:6; the demonic in 3:15; the devil here) in order to mirror the craftiness of Satan himself. The idea that the devil can be resisted is known in both Jewish and Christian thought.[16] Within the theology of the New Testament the power of Satan was severely curtailed at the Crucifixion/Resurrection, and it is possible that James has this in mind. The promise here is that with resistance, the devil will flee. Certainly the resistance of Jesus in the desert put Satan to flight, at least for a time (Luke 4:13).

The correlate to "resist the devil" is "come near to God" (4:8). As Martin wisely points out,[17] this coming to God is an act of contrition, not one of conversion. It involves the renunciation of all the practices and teachings that he has catalogued up to this point in the letter.

James has carefully laid the groundwork in the realm of general teaching concerning purity and evil. In chapters 2 and 3 he became specific. Now, having established this portrait of evil (unwholesome practice, teaching, origin, and goal), he commands renunciation while holding out the promise of gracious forgiveness. This he states in typically Jewish terms of washing and purity. The call of James is to a reorientation to God and his purposes in our world, purposes that touch on the social, cultural, and economic juggernauts with which human beings must reckon. The linkage of "hand" and "heart" is typically Jewish. The Psalms, for instance, frequently speak of the connection between inner disposition and outward acts (Ps. 24:4; 73:13).

"Sinners" is an interesting choice, as it was precisely these people with whom Jesus associated, much to the consternation of the religious authorities (Matt. 9:10–13). The word "double-minded" James has used earlier to describe the unstable who doubt God (1:8). Here it refers to those who try to live in two natures, one of the world and one of God. This sort of double allegiance is not possible.

To the admonition to cleanse themselves James adds obvious and perhaps even public acts of contrition (v. 9). The verb that opens this sentence, "grieve" (*talaiporeo*), is a common one in the Prophets (e.g., Jer. 4:8; Joel 2:12–13), used to convey the news that the time is one of great and imminent danger. The matters James has put on the table are not trifles. Similarly, the idea of changing laughter to mourning was used in Amos 8:10 to spark a sudden awareness of guilt and repentance. By such signs the prophets warned

---

15. See the discussion "Satan, evil, and trials" on James 1:2–11 (pp. 56–58), and the discussion of 1:13–15 (pp. 72–75).

16. The discussion of the armor of God in Eph. 6 includes the idea that against the powers and the spiritual forces of evil Christians can "stand their ground" when properly prepared. First Peter 5:9 also commands Christians to "resist" the devil.

17. Martin, *James*, 153.

of sudden catastrophe that the people had brought on themselves by their studied indifference to the poor and therefore to God as well.

In urging grief and a shift from laughter to mourning and joy to gloom, James reminds his readers that the false paths they thought would lead to true laughter and joy are dead ends and need to be abandoned. This abandonment must carry with it a recognition that the pursuit of these old false paths has not only grieved God, but endangered the Christian community and harmed many of their sisters and brothers. The recognition of such hurt carries with it an awareness of guilt and responsibility that are not appropriately mixed with laughter and joy.

The verb that begins verse 10, "humble yourselves" (*tapeinoo*), speaks not only of contrition and repentance, but also points to the penitent being in the presence of the Lord. By employing this word group both here and in verse 6, James has offered a clear stylistic clue to the unity of the passage. Humility is opposed to the attitude of reckless, arrogant indifference to God, which has characterized the instruction and practice of the false teachers. The promise of forgiveness is that God will then "lift you up" (*hypsoo*). This verb normally carries a metaphorical sense.[18] Those who followed the false teachers desired wholeness and joy. James points out here that in their true form these can only be found through humility before God.

James is no mere moralist. His thought, moral though it may be, is grounded in and supported by theology. In this section he reveals that his community was threatened by practices based on passions, by a capitulation to the standards and practices of "the world," and by pride. In response he has pointed out that following the passions only results in involvement in a ruthless and ultimately fruitless circle. The passions cannot lead us to our true goal, because they are essentially self-interested. He has also pointed out that one must choose between the world and God; there is no middle ground, and there must be no equivocation. Finally, he has made a case that pride is a feature of the standards of the world, and its antidote is humility.

THE CENTRAL THRUST of this passage is aptly expressed in verse 7, "Submit yourselves, then, to God." In order to make this point James employs two devices that require some explication. The first is associated with the idiomatic expression "Come near"; the second is

---

18. It is a part of the enduring attraction and interest of the "spiritual gospel" that in John this verb bears a literal sense (see John 12:32, "But I, when I am lifted up from the earth, will draw all men to myself").

---

the meaning of the imagery of temple and sacrifice, which James calls upon in order to make his appeal.

Come near. With this phrase James taps into the language of eschatology, in which the phrase "come near" means "has arrived." When in Mark 1:15 Jesus says, "The kingdom of God is near," he means that with his activity the kingdom of God has begun to arrive. He does not mean that it is on its way. The point is made in Lamentations 4:18:

> Men stalked us at every step
>> so we could not walk in our streets.
> Our end was near, our days were numbered,
>> for our end had come.

The phrase is also used relative to sacrifice. To "come near to present the offerings" (Lev. 21:21) means being so close to the altar that a sacrifice can be offered on it. To "come near to God," then, is more than simply to resolve to improve one's spiritual life. It is fully to enter the presence of God, to reside there, to be comfortable there, to be at home. James uses this imagery because he wishes to remind his readers of God's longing to know them. The challenge is no less daunting, nor is the importance any less grave, as we consider the significance of this language and its meaning for the modern period. To "abide" in the presence of God, and for God to "abide" in us, as John's Gospel puts it, is the task before us.

Temple and sacrifice. When James says, "Come near to God and he will come near to you. Wash your hands, you sinners, and purify your hearts, you double-minded. . . . Humble yourselves before the Lord, and he will lift you up" (4:8–10), he is employing the image of the temple and the language of sacrifice. The Hebrews pictured repugnance to the pollution of sin in the moral realm in terms of aversion to dirtiness in the physical realm. The Old Testament temple ritual contained a double distinction that was rooted in this imagery of physical pollution: "You must distinguish between the holy and the common, between the unclean and the clean" (Lev. 10:10). In the Old Testament the unclean was "that which disqualified a person from participation in worship, so that in effect he was debarred from the presence of God."[19]

Sacrifice was the process by which this barrier was eliminated. Items that were unclean were unfit for use by Jews.[20] Clean items were acceptable, and

---

19. G. B. Caird, *The Language and Imagery of the Bible* (Philadelphia: Westminster, 1980), 17.

20. This seems to be the issue in John 4:9, where Jesus asks the Samaritan woman for a drink. The text adds the comment, "Jews have no dealings with Samaritans." Whatever the verb (*synchraomai*) means, it cannot signify complete noninteraction, for the disciples have gone into Sychar to secure food. Many years ago David Daube argued that *synchraomai*

such items were divided into "the holy" (acceptable for and dedicated to God) and "the common" (acceptable for everyday use). Persons rendered unclean were not allowed access to the sanctuary and were therefore symbolically denied access to God. Sin relegated the offender barred from God's presence. In a passage replete with temple imagery, Isaiah expresses horror, for he has seen God and instinctively senses his own unworthiness and imagines impending catastrophe:

> "Woe to me!" I cried. "I am ruined! For I am a man of unclean lips, and I live among a people of unclean lips, and my eyes have seen the King, the LORD Almighty."
> Then one of the seraphs flew to me with a live coal in his hand, which he had taken with tongs from the altar. With it he touched my mouth and said, "See, this has touched your lips; your guilt is taken away and your sin atoned for." (Isa. 6:5–7)

The stain of sin extended beyond the individual because the Hebrews recognized the communal nature of human existence. Sin, therefore, had the capacity to defile the very land of Israel.

> Do not pollute the land where you are. Bloodshed pollutes the land, and atonement cannot be made for the land on which blood has been shed, except by the blood of the one who shed it. Do not defile the land where you live and where I dwell, for I, the LORD, dwell among the Israelites. (Num. 35:33–34)

It is God's desire to live among his people, and together God and people form community. Defilement makes this difficult, if not impossible. The theological richness of the vista we have encountered here is such that associated with sacrifice are four ideas that express different but interpenetrating aspects of the role of sacrifice within Israel.[21] Each of them has bearing on this section of James: *community, offering, power,* and *commemoration.* In employing the images of washing, purity, and drawing near to God, James is building upon these ideas. His community was no community at all, but was fraught with divisions that needed to be mended. Sacrifice was needed to cleanse the community and effect this healing, and so James asks his readers to sacrifice their self-interest by submitting to God. James knows that the

---

means "to use together with" and therefore concerns issues of purity in the preparation of food (David Daube, *The New Testament and Rabbinic Judaism* [Univ. of London: Altone Press, 1956], 375–79; cf. his earlier article, "Jesus and the Samaritan Woman," *JBL* 69 [1950]: 137–47; see also John Marsh, *The Gospel of Saint John* [Middlesex: Penguin, 1971], 210).

21. This entire section is indebted to G. B. Caird and L. D. Hurst, *New Testament Theology* (Oxford: Clarendon, 1994), 150–52.

---

power to heal his community resides in God alone. He used the language of sacrifice to remind his community of this power.

(1) One of the more curious features of the Old Testament image of sacrifice was its connection to *community*. Sacrifice was an integral part of any ceremony celebrating the covenant between God and his people, for they were, collectively, *his* people.

> Moses took half of the blood and put it in bowls, and the other half he sprinkled on the altar. Then he opened the Book of the Covenant and read it to the people. They responded, "We will do everything the LORD has said; we will obey."
> Moses then took the blood, sprinkled it on the people and said, "This is the blood of the covenant that the LORD has made with you in accordance with these words." (Ex. 24:6–8)

Sacrifice, then, was a necessary precursor that pointed toward the essential unity of the people involved. The covenant was with God, but it was a covenant *of the people* as a whole, not only of the people as a collection of individuals. At this point it is easy to see why James chose the language of sacrifice. His community, ostensibly a "covenanted" community, evinced few of the hallmarks of such a community. They were a fractious, judgmental, and self-interested group of individuals. This sacrifice imagery was intended to remind them of the vision for community that resided in both the idea and the living reality of the covenant. They were invited not only to remember, but also in the present to experience the presence of God in and among them. In so doing they would gain God's wisdom, and in due time his peace and righteousness.

But sacrifice imagery also casts its influence into the modern period, for we are culturally far more enamored of individualism than were even the targets of James's rebuke. The challenge is to apply the message and meaning of sacrifice to our own day. Enamored as we are of individualism, evangelicals often find it easier to argue for structural change than to submit themselves to the hard work of learning to live together in community.

(2) *Sacrifice* was also a symbol of loyalty and gratitude to God, offered by his people out of gratitude for his forgiveness. The sacrifice was neither bribe nor payment, for the Hebrews were well aware that neither would be efficacious. The sacrifice was to be without blemish, a symbol of the desire of the penitent to be similarly pure. But even here there was a corporate dimension: "If the anointed priest sins, bringing guilt on the people, he must bring to the LORD a young bull without defect as a sin offering for the sin he has committed" (Lev. 4:3). Here we see not only the forgiving nature of God, but also the influence of a leader. If the priest sinned, the stain of his sin could spread to the entire people. This was the darker side of community.

Just as in James's day there were leaders whose actions sullied the larger community, so today there are such leaders. To these leaders and to their followers God offers his forgiveness, trusting that in gratitude we will embrace it.

(3) The rite of sacrifice in the Old Testament was connected to the release and explosion of *power*, for blood stood for life. A passage in Leviticus demonstrates that certain offerings have the ability to render holy whatever comes into physical contact with them: "The sin offering is to be slaughtered before the LORD in the place the burnt offering is slaughtered; it is most holy. . . . Whatever touches any of the flesh will become holy" (Lev. 6:25, 27). In John 6:53–56 Jesus elaborated on this theme:

> Jesus said to them, "I tell you the truth, unless you eat the flesh of the Son of Man and drink his blood, you have no life in you. Whoever eats my flesh and drinks my blood has eternal life, and I will raise him up at the last day. For my flesh is real food and my blood is real drink. Whoever eats my flesh and drinks my blood remains in me, and I in him."

Here Jesus speaks of the power of his sacrificial blood to render holy.

In connection with this theme James weaves together a number of others. He points out that we do not receive from God when we ask, for we are asking for the wrong things (James 4:3). Last term a student approached me, aware only that I am a professor, and asked me for assistance on a mathematics problem. For as long as I can remember, mathematics has made as much sense to me as voodoo. Of me she was asking the wrong question. Her question proved that she did not know me. Similarly, our determination to ask God for the wrong things only underscores how little we know of God.

This realization, then, allows James to take us to the next step—a call for humility (4:6). The attitude of humility allows us clearer vision, to see our own need for God and to perceive his answer. Thus adorned, we are ready to enter his presence (4:8). It is important to note that purity is not required as a precondition. Purity systems often suffer from a dangerous misconstrual. In practice they tend toward the expectation of purity as a precondition for instead of the purpose of the sacrificial rite. "Unclean" becomes misidentified with "common."

It is for this reason that Jesus said, "It is not the healthy who need a doctor, but the sick. But go and learn what this means: 'I desire mercy, not sacrifice.' For I have not come to call the righteous, but sinners" (Matt. 9:12–13). Jesus here quotes Hosea 6:6, and in doing so emphasizes that sacrifice involves cleansing. There is no point in reserving sacrifice only for those already clean. Furthermore, sacrifice is not an end, it is a means to allow for the development of godly character (here mercy as emblematic of the character of God) within his people. For our purposes the point is that forgiveness of God is available, no matter how sullied we find ourselves to be.

(4) In the annual Passover celebration, and particularly in the sacrifice associated with it, Israel *commemorated* her liberation from slavery in Egypt. It does not seem unjustified to see James urging his congregation to break free from the shackles of bondage to false wisdom that they have willingly but perhaps unwittingly taken on.

This idea of purity saw further developments within certain quarters of Judaism. The New Testament speaks of the "tradition of the elders" (Matt. 15:1–2), a purity system observed by the Pharisees that existed in oral form at the time of Jesus and was reduced to writing between A.D. 160–200 in a written document known as the Mishnah.[22] The Mishnah and therefore its precursor, the oral law, had as their object the "preservation, cultivation and application to life of 'the Law' (Torah). . . ."[23] There is a strenuous debate concerning the degree to which the Mishnah reflects the actual teachings and practices of Pharisees in first-century Palestine, and in fact what we can actually know about these Pharisees.[24] What we can say is that first-century Pharisees were interested in preserving holiness in part by preserving purity.

The oral tradition served as a first warning device, a barrier around Torah. Torah declares that no work is to be done on Sabbath. Mishnah asks the question, "What, precisely, constitutes work?" and answers it. To follow Mishnah means that the sanctity of Torah will remain intact. Of course, Jesus had little use for this tradition ("Why do you break the command of God for the sake of your tradition? . . . You nullify the word of God for the sake of your tradition"; Matt. 15:3, 6); he even had the temerity to break the Torah injunction concerning rest on the Sabbath. Jesus complained that in its desire to preserve the holiness of God, Judaism had excluded most of its adherents from drawing near to God for cleansing. Some traditions within the Judaism of his day failed to see that compassion, not purity as separation, is at the heart of God's character. The point for Jesus and for James is that drawing near to God need not be done only in a state of purity. Drawing near to God is done because of a desire and even a resolve to become and continue to live clean and pure before God. The heavy use of temple imagery in James 4 is designed to recall this practice of atonement.

---

22. Eugene J. Lipman, *The Mishnah: Oral Traditions of Judaism* (New York: Schocken 1974), 18.

23. Herbert Danby, *The Mishnah: Translated From the Hebrew With Introduction and Brief Explanatory Notes* (Oxford: Oxford Univ. Press, 1933), xiii.

24. A good summary of the debate can be found in Jacob Neusner, "Mr. Sanders' Pharisees and Mine: A Response to E. P. Sanders, *Jewish Law from Jesus to the Mishnah*," *SJT* 44 (1991): 73–95. Sanders and Neusner are the most prominent of the partners in this debate.

BY PRESSING INTO service the image of sacrifice and the language of drawing near to God, James has deftly pointed our attention toward forgiveness, community, and submission to God. It is in relation to this last that he counsels us to resist the devil. Many other themes in this passage have been discussed already (the pride and effects of false wisdom, the corrupting power of sin, leadership and the abuse of power), so that drawing near to God, forgiveness, and community will occupy our discussion here. But there is another reason. James has devoted a great deal of space to error within the church, and in this passage he discusses the forgiveness available to us. Therefore, coming near to God is the central thrust of the passage.

This passage implores us to draw near to God in order to be forgiven. The appeal is general, but especially it is directed to leaders within the church who are misusing their position and status. The "fights and quarrels" mentioned in verse 1 are the result of following internal desires, desires often in conflict with the purposes of God. As an antidote James advocates forgiveness. Forgiveness is a complicated business. Some of us find it difficult to forgive others, and some of us cannot, it seems, forgive ourselves. All of us need to be reminded of the love of our Father in heaven, who has forgiven us. Forgiveness also allows for the development of true community, which is James's hope here. Finally, James speaks of resisting the devil.

God is forgiving; he washes us clean. In his powerful and alluring novel *Atticus*, Ron Hansen offers a masterful retelling of Jesus' parable of the love and forgiveness that God lavishly bestows on us. Atticus, a sixty-seven-year-old Colorado cattleman, has two sons. The older son, Frank, is married and a state senator. The younger one, Scott, is brilliant but impetuous. Some years before, Scott had lost control of the family car on a winter day, and in the resulting crash his mother was killed. After spending some time in mental hospitals, Scott drifted to Mexico, where he led a scarred, profligate life. At Christmas he returns home, and in the midst of his father's inquiry about his life and activity, Scott says:

> I just *am* Dad. You've got one son who's a huge success any Father'd be proud of, and you've got one son who's a slacker and using up your hard-earned cash on just getting by from week to week. Hell, I'm forty years old. You oughta be used to me being a failure by now.[25]

---

25. Ron Hansen, *Atticus* (New York: HarperCollins, 1996), 7.

Shortly after this interchange Scott goes for a walk and comes upon the vehicle in which his mother died. Atticus, growing concerned, looks for his son and finds him sitting in the car. Tenderly but painfully Hansen allows us to understand the depth of Scott's self-loathing, and part of the reason he believes he is beyond forgiveness.

The milkwhite Thunderbird [was] just as it was sixteen years ago when Scott took Serena to the store. The high speed of the accident had destroyed one headlight and crumpled up the right fender and hood like writing paper meant to be thrown away. The right wheel titled on its axle as though it had not been fully bolted on, and the rubber tire shredded from it like black clothing scraps.

Atticus walked around to the driver's side and opened the door. The iron complained at his pull but Scott did not look up, he stayed as he was, in his father's red plaid hunting coat, just sitting there, one wrist atop the big steering wheel, his right hand gingerly touching the windshield glass where it was crushed and spiderwebbed on the passenger's side. A milky light was filtering through the half-inch screen of snow. Atticus asked, "You okay?"

Scott pressed his cold-reddened fingertips into a crack and said, "Wondered if her hair was still there. Crows must be nesting with it."[26]

Soon Scott returns to Mexico, and in an effort to escape his problems but with an astonishing lack of sensitivity to his family, he fakes his own suicide. He then watches from a distance as Atticus searches for clues in the Mexican village where Scott has lived.

You've put him through hell, I thought, *again and again.* . . .
I felt humiliatingly unequal to his faithfulness, his loyalty, his love, as if I were heir to some foreign genes that my father had no part in.[27]

Finally, however, the truth comes out, and Scott reveals to his father that he is, indeed, alive.

I asked, "Will you forgive me?" And I felt forgiven even as I said it. . . .
His shifty second son was there, found and alive, and if there was hurt in his face and he seemed to have visited every room in hell, it hardly mattered now; Atticus was flooded with joy. He's had his mind set on just one thing and got surprised by the far better.[28]

---

26. Ibid., 19–20.
27. Ibid., 227, 238.
28. Ibid., 240, 243.

To the great disappointment of Atticus, Scott seemed to express no inter-est in coming home to Colorado. Nearly a year passed, and then one day, the son returns.

> Looking for the flush of a second bloom from his wife's perenni-als, Atticus got his sheep shears and knelt in the garden in June, cut-ting back the penstemon, rockcress, stork's-bills, and daisies. A soft rain began to fall as he heaped the green clippings on gunnysack and hauled it out back to the compost pile, and then he heard a far-car on the highway. Why he didn't know, but Atticus walked to the front yard, taking off his gloves, and he saw a yellow taxi heading toward the house. And while his son was still a long way off, his father rushed out to greet him.[29]

In humility, James says, come near to God, and he will come near to you. As Atticus forgave Scott and wished only to lift him up, so God will forgive you, and he will lift you up.

Forgiving others. It is often difficult to forgive others, especially if some-one has been the author of great personal tragedy. The relatives of murder victims tell television interviewers that they want the death penalty meted out. There is within us a bent to revenge and a desire for "justice" that is sometimes at odds with the gospel. Some months ago I was speaking with an old friend, and our discussion turned to his conversation with a mutual friend who had suffered a great personal tragedy at the hands of a criminal. My friend said, "I asked him how he felt about the perpetrator, and he said, 'I have forgiven him.' That is not natural," my friend added; "it is not normal." He is right.

In his book *Improving Your Serve*, Charles R. Swindoll tells the story of Aaron, a seminary student who took a job as a bus driver in order to pay his tuition. A small gang of "tough kids" got on his bus and refused to pay the fare. After several days of this behavior, Aaron spotted a policeman, pulled over, and reported the situation to the officer. The officer made them pay and got off the bus. A few minutes later Aaron was attacked by the gang. When he awoke, the bus was empty, blood was all over his shirt, two teeth were missing, his eyes were swollen, and his money was gone. Aaron decided to press charges. Swindoll continues:

> In walked Aaron and his attorney plus the angry gang members who glared across the room in his direction. Suddenly he was seized with a whole new series of thoughts. Not bitter ones, but compassionate

---

29. Ibid., 247.

ones!... After there had been a plea of guilty, Aaron (to the surprise of his attorney and everybody else in the courtroom) stood to his feet and requested permission to speak. "Your honor, I would like you to total up all the days of punishment against these men—all the time sentenced against them—and I request that you allow me to go to jail in their place." The judge didn't know whether to spit or wind his watch. Both attorneys were stunned. As Aaron looked over at the gang members (whose mouths and eyes looked like saucers), he smiled and said quietly, "It's because I forgive you."

The dumbfounded judge, when he reached a level of composure, said rather firmly, "Young man, you're out of order. This sort of thing has never happened before!" To which the young man replied with genius insight: "Oh, yes, it has, your honor.... Yes, it has. It happened over nineteen centuries ago when a man from Galilee paid the penalty that all mankind deserved."[30]

Swindoll concludes that through personal pain and assault, Aaron learned the beauty of forgiveness, as God has forgiven us.

Forgiving ourselves. In the early to middle 1980s I worked with youth in the San Francisco Bay area. During one eighteen-month span I came to know several teenage women who had been the victims of sexual abuse as children. One young woman was Sarah. After I had known her for about a month, it became clear to me that she wanted to tell me something. She began to say that she had done something bad, so bad that God could never forgive her. I assured her that God always forgives. Over the course of a few weeks she told me of certain things she had done, none of which were startling. Finally, she revealed that as a child she had been sexually abused. The event was long past. The police had been informed, and the perpetrator, a relative, was in jail. But in her eyes she felt she was somehow responsible. "I must have done something to encourage him," she said. She also felt guilty for causing the imprisonment of a relative. She was absolutely certain, she said, that God could never forgive her for such evil.

Several years ago a young lady became dear to my wife and me. We first met Ruth when she was sixteen. Her parents had divorced when she was an infant, and she had just come to live with her father. It soon became clear to us that there was a deep shadow cast over Ruth's life, and before long she confided in us. Ruth had been sexually abused by a series of men in her mother's life following the divorce. The pain of these experiences had seared her. Like many victims of this most aggressive and twisted of evils, Ruth somehow felt

---

30. Charles R. Swindoll, *Improving Your Serve: The Art of Unselfish Living* (Waco, Tex.: Word, 1981), 54–57.

responsible. What must she have done to deserve this? Had she somehow enticed these men? Was it all just a fantasy, and if so, what kind of person was she?

Ruth was a victim of what has been labeled Self-Inflicted Violence Syndrome (SIV) or Self-Mutilation Syndrome.[31] She would slash her wrists, purposely burn herself, or lacerate her legs. These were not attempts at suicide, nor, she said, were they cries for attention. In fact, she usually tried to hide her handiwork. Ruth suffered a form of self-induced mental torture; she simply could not get the emotional pain out of her mind. When this pain became too intense, she would mutilate herself, for this intense physical pain afforded a buffer, an alternative that crowded out her emotional pain. Over the space of seven years Ruth would begin and then withdraw from therapy, because therapy forced her to confront the memories and emotional pain. In the midst of this multiyear struggle, Ruth questioned the forgiveness of God. Ruth had committed her life to the Lord, but she harbored doubts that anyone, especially a God of holiness, could forgive her.

In my first year teaching at North Park I encountered a wonderful, bright young student. Mary was twenty-one, unmarried, and the mother of a four-year-old son. After seven weeks of class had transpired, she came to see me in my office. She wanted, she said, to "talk about God." I asked her what experience she had with the Christian faith. She told me that as a child she had attended a Christian after-school program, but that the pastor of the sponsoring church told her that the pants she sometimes wore proved that "she was evil," and Mary did not go back. As she told this story, she began to cry. If God considered her wardrobe "evil," what must he think of an unwed seventeen-year-old mother? She told me that she had been searching for God, praying to God that she might find someone with whom she could talk about God; but, she said, "I am so evil God does not listen to my prayers."

"Mary," I said, "what are we doing right now?" During the next hour I was able to assure her that God was a God of forgiveness and that he wants us to come near him so we can be washed clean.

In all three of the above situations, the women in one way or another expressed the difficulty of experiencing God's forgiveness. Yet it seems obvious to me that an equally difficult struggle was the ability of each to forgive herself of real or imagined guilt.

---

31. Bessel A. van der Kolk, J. Christopher Perry, and Judith Lewis Herman, "Childhood Origins of Self-Destructive Behavior," *American Journal of Psychiatry* 148 (December 1991): 1665–71; Beth S. Brodsdky, Marylene Cloitre, and Rebecca A. Dulit, "Relationship of Dissociation to Self-Mutilation and Childhood Abuse in Borderline Personality Disorder," *American Journal of Psychiatry*, 152 (December 1995): 1788–92.

Leadership and forgiveness. James lodges a stern warning in reminding us that friendship with the world is enmity toward God. This warning is addressed to those in leadership positions in addition to those who follow. In this fashion he links an overly healthy desire to accommodate with the world with the error of misdirected leadership. In his church, leaders had advocated that the sin of favoritism was not, in fact, sin, but that certain cultural norms were fully commensurate with the gospel. This position James attacked, even while offering to those preaching it, and to those seduced by it, the promise of God's forgiveness.

It is a sad commentary that the modern church is not bereft of parallels. Tom F. Driver, a one-time student of Paul Tillich, remembers his mentor: "I felt that his apologia was not addressed to unbelievers nearly so much as to persons like me who had been Christian all our lives and had now come to a time when we did not really know what Christianity was about, for it seemed at odds with our culture."[32] This, of course, is quite the point. The bane and blindness of liberal Christianity includes the assumption that there should be a warm joining of hands between culture and Christianity. But the Bible often compels us to stand for values radically at odds with those of our culture. To suppose otherwise is to misunderstand Scripture at the most basic level. As James says, "friendship with the world is hatred toward God" (4:4).

The bane and blindness of conservative Christianity is to assume that the only dangers are on the left. The shoals on the evangelical right can be those of zeal, of excoriation, or of numbness. In our zeal for truth, evangelicals often offer the spectacle of religious cannibalism, as we devour one another. The divisive battle current in the Southern Baptist denomination is a case in point.[33] Evangelicals are also guilty of a blanket excoriation of the world. "Friendship with the world" refers to embracing the standards of the world. But there are not infrequent points of correspondence. Christians should affirm what is true and worthwhile in our culture instead of offering churlish blanket condemnations.

Evangelicals are also prone to inaction. The atrophied silence of evangelical churches during the civil rights movement stands as a mute witness of shame. The biblical principles that evangelicals claim to hold so dear—the principles of righteousness and justice to which James gave voice when

---

32. Richard John Neuhaus, "The Public Square," *First Things* 70 (February 1997): 69.

33. Timothy C. Morgan, "SBC Targets Clinton, Disney, Jews," *Christianity Today* (July 1996), 66. Morgan quotes outgoing Southern Baptist Convention President James Henry Jr. as pleading for greater understanding and unity: "We as Southern Baptists are a diverse people. We must appreciate and appropriate this diversity for the common good." The comments of new President Tom Ellit were less conciliatory. See also Keith Hinson, "University Independence Sparks Renewed Tensions," *Christianity Today* (Feb. 3, 1997), 81.

he said, "Religion that God our Father accepts as pure and faultless is this: to look after orphans and widows in their distress and to keep oneself from being polluted by the world" (1:27)—were in large measure ignored. Instead we opted for the safe course of measured inaction, sanctioned by the winds of American political conservatism. We became "numb," to use Walter Bruegemann's phrase. [34]

We easily become "numb." In the prologue to his book *Whereon to Stand*, Daniel Berrigan writes:

> How bloodstained is our lifetime ... [the] throwaway lives, the anonymous poor, the multitudes commonly considered of no worth ... As for those who teach or preach or remain silent and so consent ... we must speak of a crime, a sin. [35]

The journal *First Things* reports that a group of Episcopalian priests in Brooklyn are alleged to have imported young men from Brazil to engage in acts of a grotesque sexual nature. The story broke, predictably, in *Penthouse* magazine. [36] *Penthouse* quoted Long Island Bishop Orris G. "Jay" Walker, "If they were consenting adults, my position is that they were certainly free to take that action." *Penthouse* offered this bitterly ironic observation: These men became "playthings for priests whose commitment to the Scriptures had long ago been replaced by a pursuit of pleasure that would have fit nicely in Sodom and Gomorrah." [37] When *Penthouse* offers such a critique of Christian leaders, the situation is dark indeed.

A number of Episcopalian bishops have responded by issuing a statement called, "Where It Is Corrupt, Purify It." The statement alludes to the Richter trial, which concluded that the Episcopal Church has no "core doctrine" in the area of human sexuality; therefore, the ordination of active homosexuals violates neither the doctrine nor the discipline of the church. The ruling has sparked strong protest, particularly as the idea of "core doctrine" seems to have been created for this response. [38] The statement by the bishops also cites the long-term position of the Presiding Bishop of the Episcopal Church, the Most Reverend Edmond L. Browning: "In this Church there shall be no

---

34. Walter Brueggemann, *The Prophetic Imagination* (Philadelphia: Fortress, 1978), 46.

35. Daniel Berrigan, *Whereon to Stand: The Acts of the Apostles and Ourselves* (Baltimore: Fortkamp, 1991), xxiii.

36. A number of documents related to this issue, including the statement "Where It Is Corrupt, Purify It," are available at (http://www.episcopalian.org/EU/Press_Releases/index.htm).

37. *Penthouse* (December 1996), 42, quoted in the United Voice editorial "Penthouse Rebukes the Church," available at the website listed in note 36.

38. See the document "A Response to the Opinion of the Court for the Trial of a Bishop," available at the website listed in note 36.

outcasts." As the protesting bishops imply, this is a naive statement. The Bible certainly teaches compassion for all, but the Bible also teaches the corrosive power of sin.

The statement by the bishops offers this trenchant observation: "In a Church in which nearly half of the active bishops have declared their support—in principle—of the ordination of non-celibate homosexual persons, we must not be surprised when some of their clergy take them at their word."[39] The statement by the bishops further issues a call for the Episcopal Church to "provide clear and binding standards regarding the sexual behavior of clergy." The bishops acknowledge that grave error has occurred and suggest an attitude of humility and a process pointing to forgiveness.[40]

In each of these cases, whether the sin involved is one of commission or omission, what is required, as James pointed out long ago, is humility—humility before God's will revealed in Scripture, humility before the Lord, and humility before others. The sacrifice of Jesus can wash us clean, if we will draw near.

Community. James 4:1–10 offers a strong call to community, and especially community created by a spirit of humility and forgiveness.[41] The Bridging Contexts section has demonstrated the critical significance of the need to create strong community, and especially of repentance and forgiveness as a means to establish such a community. Certainly the congregation to which James wrote needed such direction.

Our world is awash in facsimiles of true community. An avenue often attempted by evangelicals in America is that of reforming the state. In his warmly positive review of Guenter Lewy's *Why America Needs Religion: Secular Modernity and Its Discontents*, J. Budziszewski emphasizes a point that Lewy himself notes when he quotes from the document "Evangelicals and Catholics Together": "To propose that securing civil virtue is the purpose of religion is blasphemous. To deny that securing civil virtue is a benefit of religion is blindness."[42] It seems odd that Lewy not only sees the need for religious underpinnings to effect a moral society, he even understands that it takes an active belief in God to animate these moral principles. When he began writing the book, Lewy writes, he was a "secular humanist" bent on demonstrating the

---

39. Richard John Neuhaus, "The Public Square," 71.

40. The question of homosexuality from a clinical perspective is insightfully treated by Elizabeth Moberly, "Homosexuality and Truth," *First Things* 71 (March 1997): 30–33. She points out that many recent studies on the biological origin of homosexual behavior are inconclusive. She advocates "respect for truth and respect for people" (33).

41. See the Contemporary Significance sections to 3:1–12; 3:13–18, pp. 188–202, 212–20.

42. J. Budziszewski, "Second Thoughts of a Secularist," *First Things* 72 (April 1997): 43.

superfluous nature of religious values. But in his research, he came to see the importance of these values and to eschew the label "secular humanist" for "nontheist."

Even so, Lewy points us in the right direction. Far too often evangelical Christians decry the paucity of moral values in this country and seek structural change. This may take the form of legislative action to bar certain kinds of medical procedures, or it may simply be idle talk about the need for prayer in the public schools. While these are not wrong-headed, they are incomplete answers. Ron Sider points out that evangelicals are "all over the waterfront"[43] on these issues. Evangelicals are zealous conservatives when attacking programs they do not like, arguing for limited government. "Then, when the issues change to abortion, euthanasia, and pornography, the same people loudly demand vigorous government action."[44]

Sider claims that evangelicals need to work out carefully the specific policy implications of biblical faith. We need, he says, an evangelical political philosophy. At this point I become nervous, for as we have seen, institutions, and particularly political institutions, while morally neutral, are easily co-opted by Satan and for this reason cannot blindly be trusted. Sider actually provides an example. The Reagan administration skillfully manipulated the American people over the question of school prayer during the 1984 campaign. In an effort to secure the vote of the religious right, the campaign

> decided to stage a fake drive to pass a constitutional amendment on school prayer. But first they asked a conservative senator to do a head count. When he reported insufficient votes to pass the bill, the Reagan staffer replied, "Good, we just wanted to make sure that it could not pass before we began the battle." The whole House then rallied the leaders of the Religious Right and promised to twist arms to pass the bill on the prayer amendment. But it was all a farce. Evangelicals did not understand either the politics or the substance of the issue.

Sider argues that evangelicals need to "articulate a view of government, human rights, the relation of church and state, democracy, private ownership and market economies, civil society (especially the family), and the like."[45] He is correct, as long as we adopt a biblical view of government. Government is not the body of Christ, nor can we expect it to be. When evangelicals confuse Christian faith with certain political interests, they are choosing

---

43. Ronald J. Sider, "Can We Agree to Agree?" *Books and Culture: A Christian Review* (January/February 1997), 27.
44. Ibid.
45. Ibid.

friendship with the world over friendship with God. They are mistaking the possibility of an external framework for the deeper values that only the church of Jesus Christ can inspire.

Lewy's solution is one of externals—embracing the "morals" of religious faith without necessitating the living faith itself. Many centuries ago in ancient Israel such a code was developed; it may be found in the book of Proverbs, which offers sterling wisdom for the pragmatic and even boring realities of life. For example, "Lazy hands make a man poor, but diligent hands bring wealth" (Prov. 10:4). This is good advice, and it should be followed. But life at times confronts us with painful realities for which the book of Proverbs offers little salve.

A powerful example is the story of Job. As the story begins, Satan claims that Job fears God only because God has rewarded him for being so industrious. "You have blessed the work of his hands. . . . But stretch out your hand and strike everything he has, and he will surely curse you to your face" (Job 1:10–11). The challenge of Satan to God is whether or not there is any authentic faith in Job. There is no necessary impulse in the system enshrined in Proverbs to drive human beings into a living relationship with God. Such a system could, with profit, remain simply external.

Job's friends certainly seem to believe in this external cause and effect worldview of Proverbs: "Consider now: Who, being innocent, has ever perished?" Eliphaz asks Job (Job 4:7). This view God found wanting. If tragedy strikes, the only cause Job's friends can conceive of is sin. Their world is simple: The good are blessed, the wicked are not. But life is not always so simple. Cicero once observed, "Laws bereft of moral quality are worthless."[46] Unless there is some set of deeply held beliefs that animate the moral character of law, the law and the moral system that law seeks to create remain external. The book of Job serves to remind us that religious mores are good, but without the living faith within, they are hollow if elegant shells.

Evangelicals must do more than work for structural change, for structures are weak and easily co-opted by Satan. The heart must change, for without these deeper values, the law is external. James implores us to draw near to God, not merely to adopt moral guidelines of which God would approve.

Resist the devil. When James says, "Resist the devil, and he will flee from you," he is aligning himself with solid biblical teaching. Satan can be resisted, primarily because he is weaker than God. I recall my Old Testament professor in seminary remarking that the entrance of the serpent in Genesis 3 is unspectacular when compared to the resplendence of God's activity in Genesis 1 and 2, because the Bible wishes to stress the overwhelming majesty of

---

46. *Leges sine moribus vanae.*

God. In the New Testament, as we have seen,[47] Satan's power has been vastly curtailed after the resurrection of Jesus. The rabbis also thought of the power of Satan as strong, but a power from which the study of Torah offered protection: "Raba said, Though God created the *Yetzer ha-Ra*, He created the Law, as an antidote [lit. spice] against it."[48] The question is, of course, whether the devil "flees" today.

As a young graduate student in the San Francisco area in 1981, I took a class on prayer from Robert Munger, the pastor emeritus of First Presbyterian Church, Berkeley, and of University Presbyterian Church, Seattle. An essential element of the course was a time of prayer in small groups of three, in which we shared concerns and prayed for one another. After perhaps six weeks one of the members of my group of three missed a class. This left me alone with a woman in her mid-thirties. As we went off to pray, she told me a story that seemed to me fantastic. The night before, she said, she was awakened at 1:00 A.M. to hear her young son screaming in his bedroom. She rushed to his room, only to encounter what she described as a malevolent presence inhabiting the room and choking the life out of her son. She struggled against this presence, picked up her son, ran from the house, and she had not been back.

She then paused for several long seconds before adding, "I used to be a witch." She admitted she had been active with wiccans in the San Francisco area for many years before she became a Christian. In fact, over her fireplace mantle was hanging a macramé weaving of the zodiac symbol, the very one she had used as a part of her previous religious activity as a witch. She felt certain that this symbol was somehow involved. She then asked me, "What do you think I should do?" Realizing I was in over my head, I said, "I think you should tell this to Dr. Munger." In the weeks that followed, this woman told me that Dr. Munger had spoken with her, that they had prayed together, and that she knew that the devil had fled before the onslaught of prayer and her growing confidence in the presence and power of Christ.

In the opening pages of his book *Christian Missions and the Judgment of God*, David M. Paton many decades ago offered this sage commentary:

> But let our confidence be sober, and rooted in a Faith that knows all about Evil. Our world is one world—in God's design. ... [My] father ... said once that passing through Shanghai in 1935 had finally convinced him of the existence of the Devil, for in the appalling nexus of evil in Shanghai there seemed to him to be something at work

---

47. See the Bridging Contexts section to James 3:1–12, pp. 187–88.
48. *Baba Batra*, 16a.

beyond what could be accounted for by the follies and wickedness of mankind.

The Devil, then, must also be given his due. Mr. C. S. Lewis suggested in the preface to the *Screwtape Letters* that it is equally dangerous to our race to display either too much or too little interest in the Devil. Interested too deeply, we assign to the operations of the Devil events which can be adequately explained by common or garden sin, abnormal psychology and the like, and indulge in those orgies of witch-hunting which stain the history of the Church. Scornfully enlightened, and ignoring the well-authenticated phenomena of demon-possession (whether in the Gospel accounts of Palestine or in modern Africa or China), we allow the Devil a wider field for his operations by the very fact that we are off our guard. Both these attitudes are common; and not to be imitated. We may usefully preserve … that proper agnosticism without which there can be no true faith; only, if we allow for the operations of the Devil, let us be very clear that God is sovereign.[49]

Satan at times operates boldly and personally, at other times more slyly and through structures of power and authority. At still other times, such as in a cutting word unerringly directed, the fringe of his evil is felt; but this periphery points to the full weight of his malevolence. It must not be taken too lightly or too seriously, as Lewis has said. And it must be remembered that God is sovereign and that the devil will flee if resisted.

---

49. David M. Paton, *Christian Missions and the Judgment of God* (London: SCM, 1953), 15.

James 4:11–17

BROTHERS, DO NOT slander one another. Anyone who speaks against his brother or judges him speaks against the law and judges it. When you judge the law, you are not keeping it, but sitting in judgment on it. ¹²There is only one Lawgiver and Judge, the one who is able to save and destroy. But you—who are you to judge your neighbor?

¹³Now listen, you who say, "Today or tomorrow we will go to this or that city, spend a year there, carry on business and make money." ¹⁴Why, you do not even know what will happen tomorrow. What is your life? You are a mist that appears for a little while and then vanishes. ¹⁵Instead, you ought to say, "If it is the Lord's will, we will live and do this or that." ¹⁶As it is, you boast and brag. All such boasting is evil. ¹⁷Anyone, then, who knows the good he ought to do and doesn't do it, sins.

Original Meaning

HAVING ISSUED A call to repentance and forgiveness, James begins a short section in which he discusses a variety of problems within the community. The first problem is unwholesome speech in the form of name-calling and the spreading of lies. James counters this by showing how such behavior abrogates the law of loving the neighbor. The second problem has to do with an unhealthy fascination with making money, which James counters with a reminder that money is only temporary. What binds this passage together and to earlier ones is the power of the tongue, here understood primarily in the individual sense. The tongue can be used to slander others (vv. 11–12) and to boast of such empty things as wealth and status (vv. 13–17).

This passage divides neatly into two sections. In the first, the author argues in favor of a pure speech that does not condemn. He then turns his attention to the wealthy and offers teaching that extends through 5:6.

Pure Speech Does Not Condemn (4:11–12)

IN VERSE 11, James uses the term "brothers," binding himself to the church to which he writes. The verb the NIV renders as "slander" is *katalaleo*, which means "to speak ill of," though it can also carry the more narrowly focused meaning of speaking falsely. Whether this speech is false or true, James has in mind harsh criticism and condemnation. Such verbal attacks were among the "quarrels and fights" referred to in 4:1–2.

There is no shortage of similar material in the Old and New Testaments. In the Old Testament parallels can be found in the Pentateuch,[1] the Psalms,[2] and the wisdom tradition.[3] In the New Testament the term appears in several of the lists of vices (Rom. 1:30; 2 Cor. 12:20). But the clear foil is Leviticus 19:18, with its command to "love your neighbor as yourself." This command is "the law" referred to in this passage. James points out that anyone who speaks disdainfully of a sister or brother is, in fact, breaking this "royal law" (cf. 2:8). Continuing in such behavior is no trifling matter. It does more than break the law, it treats the law as if it did not matter, as if it were not in force. In short, it judges the law and finds it not worthy of adherence.

What is so keenly disturbing for James is the central place this command occupied in the ethical teaching of Jesus.[4] To ignore this command is, in effect, to repudiate Christ and to render the self-description "Christian" a falsehood.[5] This "speaking ill" of sisters and brothers is closely allied to the ill treatment of them in 2:1–7, and the flagrant refusal to follow the royal law recalls James's teaching in 2:8–13. The New Testament contains various injunctions against judging (Matt. 7:1–5; Rom. 2:1; 1 Cor. 4:5), but the reason given here, that judging breaks the law, pertains to James alone among the authors of the New Testament.

As in 2:10–11 James is not content to allow his case to rest on the meager foundation of the law itself. Rather, he discusses the law in terms of the personal authority of God, who stands behind the law (4:12). Here James is again in touch with a widely held tradition, that Christians should not judge others. Certainly this is a part of the Jesus tradition, for Jesus says in Matthew 7:1: "Do not judge, or you too will be judged" (cf. also Rom. 2:1; 1 Cor. 4:5). Only God has the right to judge, as he is the lawgiver. In the LXX Psalm 9:20 uses the term *nomothetes* ("lawgiver") to refer to the action of God. God alone, as Davids points out,[6] has authority over life and death (Gen. 18:25; Deut. 32:39), and only he has the ultimate power to save or to destroy (1 Sam. 2:6; Matt. 10:28).

According to James, when we judge others, we not only arrogate to ourselves what belongs to God alone, we also invite and pronounce judgment on ourselves. This is not meant to exclude honest and healthy discussion

---

1. See Lev. 19:16, "Do not go about spreading slander among your people."
2. See Ps. 101:5, "Whoever slanders his neighbor in secret, him will I put to silence."
3. See Prov. 10:18, "He who conceals his hatred has lying lips, and whoever spreads slander is a fool."
4. See L. D. Hurst, "The Ethics of Jesus," *DJG*, 210–22.
5. See the discussion relative to "true membership" and the rich in James 1:2–11.
6. Peter H. Davids, *The Epistle of James*, 170.

among believers, but it is to make clear a strong warning that the line demarking proper from sinful discourse is easily and often unknowingly crossed. James also points out that none of us is without stain, and we are deserving of the same judgment we so righteously place at the feet of others. It is possible that a part of the sting here is to avoid giving the church an unsavory reputation within the community at large.

Do Not Boast, For Tomorrow Is Uncertain (4:13–17)

IN VERSE 13 we have an example of the educated Greek style of James, as it begins with the construction *age nun*, translated by the NIV as "now listen." The construction is rare in the New Testament (found only here and in 5:1). It is common, however, in the world of Hellenistic literature.[7] The term is meant to convey tones of insistent and even brusque address.[8] While there is some debate as to the identity of the group intended by the phrase "you who say," there is no reason to suppose that James does not have in mind members of the Christian community.

Many argue that the absence of the term "brothers" indicates that James is now referring to some outside the church, but this is not as strong a position as is often supposed, for several reasons. (1) It makes little sense to argue that any outside the church would be interested in what James has to say on these matters. (2) James has already referred to members of the church in harsh terms without the designation "brothers." In 4:1–10 Christians were referred to by a variety of terms that are less than favorable ("adulterous people" in 4:4; in need of washing and purifying because they are "sinners" in 4:8). (3) James 4:15 contains the phrase "if it is the Lord's will," which is surely a marker that Christians are in view. In any event, we have here a group of merchants with some close tie to the church.

Verse 13 also contains a quotation; presumably James has heard that such statements have been on the lips of the merchants in the city. There is a potent Old Testament tradition of distrust of merchants and traders (Prov. 20:23; Mic. 6:11), but this does not seem to be the appropriate background here. Rather, the idea seems to be that the desire to make a profit has become such a towering priority that it has overshadowed everything else. This amounts to a smug certainty with no room for God. If this is correct, it recalls the merchants who, in the words of Amos, trample the needy as they anxiously await the end of the Sabbath so they can make more money (Amos 8:4–5). The parable of the rich fool, who relies on his stored wealth, also comes to mind (Luke 12:16–21).

7. See Epictetus, *Discourses*, 1.2.20.
8. See James H. Ropes, *The Epistle of St. James*, 276.

James is not arguing against the making of money, or even against the desire to make money; rather, he is against the attitude of self-contained certainty, the same smug attitude that marked the teaching of the false teachers. Such certainty is revelatory of an attitude that does not take God seriously enough, a mind-set for which the making of money outstrips devotion to God in importance. The desire betrays friendship with the world and is, therefore, enmity with God. Beyond this, of course, is another sin, for many in the church have not seen the poor as their sisters and brothers. They have not shared with them, but have showed favoritism.[9] There is no discernible difference in their lives for having come to know Jesus.

At this point it is proper to ask about these traders and merchants. Davids[10] seems to think that they were in business at the local marketplace and had not yet become wealthy.[11] Rather, their plans were to build a fortune. But Laws[12] insightfully argues that these must be traders on an international scale, as the verb used by James (*emporeuomai*) indicates a distinction between the wholesale traveling traders (*emporoi*) and the local merchants (*kapeloi*). More significant is the allusion to traveling to other cities. As Gerd Theissen has pointed out,[13] travel was expensive, one of the markers of wealth of such magnitude as to warrant the attention of government officials.[14] Yet we know of several New Testament Christians with that kind of wealth. Chloe, for example, a female leader in the church in Corinth, had enough money to send some of her "people" with a message to Paul (1 Cor. 1:11). So the reference to travel and the considerable resources that such travel indicates do not necessarily preclude these traders from membership in the church.

---

9. The eminent sociologist Rodney Stark has recently published a book, *The Rise of Christianity*, in which he says that Christianity grew because of its theology—a remarkable assertion given the usual attitude of sociologists toward religion. Stark says that "Christians introduced into a world of hatred and cruelty a totally new concept about humanity—that you had a responsibility to be compassionate and caring to everyone" (see review in *Chicago Tribune*, March 27, 1997).

10. Davids, *The Epistle of James*, 170–71.

11. "Wealthy," of course, is a hopelessly inaccurate term, as what might appear to be a staggering fortune to a Galilean fisherman would be insignificant to an equestrian. Wealth was relative to location, status, and background.

12. Sophie Laws, *The Epistle of James*, 190.

13. Gerd Theissen, *The Social Setting of Pauline Christianity: Essays on Corinth*, ed. and tr. by John H. Schütz (Philadelphia: Fortress 1982), 91–96.

14. Of course travel does not necessarily indicate the wealth of the traveler. But someone with wealth paid the bill. As is the case with so much else in the ancient world, the gaps in our knowledge about travel and its implications are disturbing. For example, why would Pliny feel the need illegally to secure an imperial travel permit so his wife could return to Rome on the occasion of the death of her grandfather? See Pliny, *Epistulae*, 10.45–46.

Verse 14 begins with *hoitines*, which means "you who are those who," and refers to the "you who say" of verse 13. In spite of all their careful planning (all the verbs in the quotation in v. 13 are in the future tense: "will go," "[will] spend a year there," "[will] carry on business," "[will] make money"), the future is uncertain. There is a clear connection to the rich in 1:10–11, who, in spite of their feelings of security, will be brought low. There James said that the rich and their riches will fade like a flower. Here the life of human beings can be compared to a mist that vanishes even as it is apprehended, with an ease and swiftness that takes the breath away.

The idea of the uncertainty of riches is universal, but Old Testament parallels are instructive. Proverbs 27:1 says, "Do not boast about tomorrow, for you do not know what a day may bring forth." Hosea 13:3, in speaking of the people who have turned from God, says, "Therefore they will be like the morning mist, like the early dew that disappears, like chaff swirling from a threshing floor, like smoke escaping through a window." These are the same images as in James: Making plans without considering God is evidence of idiocy, because life is transitory. The parable of Jesus concerning the house built on sand comes quickly to mind (see Matt. 7:24–27; cf. Luke 12:16–21; also Job 7:7, 9; Ps. 39:5).

For James the real question is how to approach life when the outcome is uncertain. His answer is to trust in God's graciousness, not in human plans. This is, in fact, one of the central messages of the Old Testament prophets. To trust in one's own devices is foolish in light of the fact that one can trust in God.

It is a great oddity that there is no clear biblical referent for the formula James records in 4:15, although the idea of the Lord's will pervades Scripture (e.g., Prov. 19:21). While the many close parallels in Greek and Latin literature[15] may betray a reference to the multiracial church, this is only supposition. This verse makes it clear that James is not against planning. Rather, James wants such planning to be given its proper priority, and none higher. God must be in control of such planning.

In verse 16, James sets limits on speech. He has already mentioned boasting: The poor may boast (1:9), and mercy boasts in the face of judgment (2:13), but the tongue should not boast (3:5). The merchants are not excoriated for the wealth they possess, or even for the pursuit of more. Rather, the rub is that they do so without reference to God, and they boast about it. As Laws observes,[16] the issue here is spiritual, not material or even (primar-

---

15. See Plato, *Alcibiades*, 135D. In this passage Socrates says, "if it be God's will" (*hoti ean theos ethele*).

16. Laws, *The Epistle of James*, 193.

ily) social. Boasting in our own accomplishments and/or in our own plans, on our own terms, is the issue. As long as God is not in control of such endeavors, boasting is evil.

Two points need to be made here. (1) The saying of Jesus regarding alms-giving ("So when you give to the needy, do not announce it with trumpets, as the hypocrites do in the synagogues and on the streets, to be honored by men. I tell you the truth, they have received their reward in full," Matt. 6:2) illuminates this passage. The attitude God desires is one that seeks his favor, not the praise of the world. (2) "Evil" is a strong word. Other less harsh words were at the command of James, yet he chose this one. Boasting is not for James a trivial matter.

This boasting is the sin mentioned in 4:13: The merchants plan and carry on as if God were unimportant or did not even exist. Instead, they should have made their plans in prayer and in the anticipation that God may in fact change these plans. They ought to be alert to the "new thing" that God may do. The merchants may be superficially pious in church, but their attitude if not their actions are boastful of their independence from God.

In verse 17, James shifts to the third person singular from the second person plural, indicating that he is quoting a proverb (as in 2:13; 3:18). Laws wonders how this verse connects with the others in this passage, but then she believes that the merchants are not members of the church. If, however, the merchants are members of the church, the connection is obvious, and James is saying, "Now that you know what is right, do it!"

James is possibly commenting here on Proverbs 3:27–28:

> Do not withhold good from those who deserve it,
>   when it is in your power to act.
> Do not say to your neighbor,
>   "Come back later; I'll give it tomorrow"—
>   when you now have it with you.

However, there are similar sayings in a variety of sources from the ancient world. Ultimately, the precise identification of the source is not important. James here argues that sins of both commission and omission are grievous, especially when done knowingly. The making of plans as though the future is certain is itself a sin, because functionally it is a denial of God, either his importance or even his very existence. Then to boast about it is a further sin. James may perhaps be building on the saying of Jesus in Luke 12:47: "That servant who knows his master's will and does not get ready or does not do what his master wants will be beaten with many blows." Knowledge of right places us under a moral obligation to do right.

Bridging Contexts

THE TWO CHIEF issues in this passage are judging and boasting in wealth. Each requires clarification before application can begin.

Judging. In 4:11–12 are several variations of the idea of "judge," all of them forms of the Greek verb *krino* ("judge").[17] In the LXX *krino* is used to render three different Hebrew words: *šapat, dyn,* and *ryb.* This conflation lent to *krino* a wide range of meanings. The first word, *šapat,* can mean both "to judge" and "to rule." The second one, *dyn,* can mean "to judge," "to punish," and "to obtain justice for someone." The third one, *ryb,* can mean "to quarrel" and "to carry out a lawsuit."

In ancient Israel justice was about more than adherence to some abstract moral standard; it also included fidelity to a sense of peace and health within the community. Sometimes this meant that the wealthy were expected to sacrifice in the interests of the poor. Also in ancient Israel, all justice was attributed to God; he is the Lord and judge (see Deut. 1:17). God judges the nations, and on the "day of the LORD" he will destroy all ungodliness (see Isa. 2:12, 17–18).

In the New Testament *krino* and the idea of judging can mean "to approve," "to distinguish," and "to consider." But the term can also possess a forensic meaning, such as "to judge," "to condemn," and "to punish." The question of humans acting as judges is not without controversy in the New Testament. On the one hand, Paul says that the apostles and the church have a responsibility to judge. When confronted with serious sin within the congregation, he wrote: "What business is it of mine to judge outside the church? Are you not to judge those inside? God will judge those outside. 'Expel the wicked man from among you'" (1 Cor. 5:12–13). Elsewhere Christians are commanded to exercise judgment in spiritual matters: "Dear friends, do not believe every spirit, but test the spirits to see whether they are from God, because many false prophets have gone out into the world" (1 John 4:1).

On the other hand, there are frequent commands to avoid judging others. Jesus said, for example, "Do not judge, or you too will be judged. For in the same way you judge others, you will be judged, and with the measure you use, it will be measured to you" (Matt. 7:1–2). Paul likewise records this sentiment when in Romans 2:1 he writes: "You, therefore, have no excuse, you who pass judgment on someone else, for at whatever point you judge the other, you are condemning yourself, because you who pass judgment do the same things."

---

17. See W. Schneider, "Judgment," *NIDNTT* 2:362–67.

Clearly we are dealing with two different issues. There is an injunction to avoid judging, but there is also the command to display judgment within the church. In fact, even James's warnings about judging are a form of the very judgment he seems to condemn. What is the path out of this problem?

In both Testaments all judgment is assigned to God. Judgment on the part of human beings, therefore, is lodged within the wider context of God's judgment. God assigns to Jesus the task of judging. Jesus is God's representative, though the authority to judge rests with God.[18] When Jesus says, "Do not judge, or you too will be judged," he is reflecting the awesome and fearful nature of the task. To the church God has delegated the task of judging in matters that affect its members. For this reason James and Paul can and do judge. However, they remind us that in judging we are acting in God's stead, and therefore exceptional care and restraint must be observed. God does not take it lightly when his name and honor are invoked inappropriately. To render judgment in the flippant, arrogant, and harsh fashion that some in his church have been doing, James finds reprehensible and foolhardy. God will defend the cause of those maligned.

In summary, three points are prominent. (1) God alone has the right to judge. He is the lawgiver, the author of justice and righteousness. (2) God at times delegates that responsibility. He delegated it to Jesus, and in certain functions he delegates it to us. When exercising this role, however, we serve not as our own agents, but as the representatives of God. In some areas we are commanded to judge, such as in the case of spiritual discernment. But in all such areas we are to judge not in accordance to our own foibles and proclivities, or even according to personal convictions, but only in concert with the standards of God. This is the only true template. (3) We often judge inappropriately. When we use slander, misinform for ulterior motive, or seek what appears to our eyes to be "the good," we are doing more than sinning against our neighbor. We are breaking trust with God; and in so doing, we are, in fact, judging ourselves. We demonstrate our lack of understanding of God our Father, and we place ourselves in jeopardy.

Merchants and traders. An unfortunate reality of the study of ancient Mediterranean history is that so little can be known about traders (*negotiatores*). What little we do know comes from disparate sources, principally occasional references in literature and citations in tax codes. The various codes all leave

---

18. The Gospel of John clearly adheres to this pattern. God is the judge (cf. 8:50, where Jesus says, "I am not seeking glory for myself, but there is one who seeks it, and he is the judge"). John also argues that Jesus has been delegated the authority to judge by God, for in 5:22 Jesus says, "The Father judges no one, but has entrusted all judgment to the Son." That Jesus judges in fidelity to God's appointment is affirmed in 5:30, when Jesus says, "I judge only as I hear, and my judgment is just."

this group ill-defined, but generally they include all who made their living buying and selling, such as merchants, shopkeepers, moneylenders, and prostitutes.[19]

For many years a tax existed on traders, the *collatio lustralis*. Both pagan and Christian sources speak of it as a terrible burden.[20] When outlawed, its place was taken by rents on imperial estates. We can only deduce that the imperial *coloni*[21] far outnumbered the traders. We do know that the demand for most goods was low. After all, the vast bulk of the population often had trouble securing sufficient food. Most of the goods needed were manufactured locally, with the peasant population making virtually everything that was needed in their own homes. There were exceptions, such as the fabric industry, for which, as one might expect, the production facilities were located near the wool and cotton growing lands. Most local elites had their need for cloaks, shoes, and other items filled by traveling salespersons. Such traders rarely became rich, except by the standards of the poor. A trader in the Spanish market, for example, left an inheritance to his family of seventy pounds of gold.[22] This was a great sum by local standards. But a senator of even modest means might expect income of one thousand to fifteen hundred pounds of gold annually.

Such traders were not trusted and were commonly considered to be inveterate liars. Proverbs 20:23 says, "The LORD detests differing weights, and dishonest scales do not please him." Micah says, "Shall I acquit a man with dishonest scales, with a bag of false weights?" (Mic. 6:11). For these reasons traders were usually barred from the decurionate (the local city government). Callistratus tells us that it would be disgraceful for traders to be elected to the decurionate because it is likely that they will be flogged.[23] In summary, there were few traders, but they did exist, often traveling for long periods. The wealth they could amass was little compared to the decurions. But in the eyes of the poor they were both rich and august.

The Roman economy was essentially agricultural, with trade comprising a fraction of the total gross production. The fact that the tax on traders could be replaced by rents on the imperial estates demonstrates not only the limited number of traders, but the relative unimportance of trade in the Roman economy. In this world traders held a position of low status, except in relation to the poor. It is possible, therefore, that some of these traders may have

---

19. See A. H. M. Jones, "The Economic Life of the Towns of the Roman Empire," *The Roman Economy*, ed. P. A. Brunt (Oxford: Blackwell, 1974), 35–60.

20. Libanius, *Orationes*, 46.22.

21. The term *coloni* signifies free peasants who were legally tied to the land.

22. Palladius, *Lausiac History*, 15.

23. Callistratus, *Digest*, 50.2.12.

joined the Christian movement in part because it afforded the opportunity for status and display of wealth denied them in Roman culture at large. Certainly the complaint of James indicates that the interest of these traders was self-directed instead of directed toward the church.

Our world is quite different. In Chicago, where I live, thousands make their livings trading products that do not even exist yet. At the Chicago Board of Trade millions of dollars are made and lost speculating on the future price of orange juice or pork bellies. To trade in the price of imagined products would have been inconceivable to James. In spite of this difference, however, there are similarities. Like those early traders, we can and do boast in and rely on our standing in terms of public opinion, our reputation, our wealth, the security of our jobs, and countless other false foundations.

 THE CHURCH TO which James wrote had adopted as their own a philosophy that was errant and misguided. In this passage James points out two manifestations of this aberrant philosophy: Christians were given to judging one another without considering that God delegated that authority to them, and they boasted in their own strength and resources.

Impious judging. Five days after I graduated from college, I joined the staff of a large church on the San Francisco Peninsula, just north of the Silicon Valley. Friends, relatives, and even strangers, when they learned of my place of employ, offered some variation of, "It must be great to work at a place where everybody gets along, where everybody trusts each other, where there is no political maneuvering." It took little time for that fantasy to evaporate in the hard light of experience. It is unfortunate, but true, that the contemporary church is no less immune to the virus of slander, ill-talk, and harsh criticism than the church to which James wrote so long ago. We find ourselves, as Luther said, *simil iustus et peccator*, "at once justified and sinful."[24]

During the next fifteen years as I served in local churches, I witnessed astounding acts of Christian devotion and selfless service done with integrity and sacrifice. But I also witnessed evidence of another kind. Early on I watched as a plot hatched by some volunteers was set in motion. Their plan included ill-talk, half-truths, and misinformation concerning a pastor, which eventuated in his removal. They executed their strategy with precision and granted to it a veneer of spirituality, claiming to be acting "for the good of

---

24. Martin Luther, *Lectures on Romans*, ed. Hilton C. Oswald (Concordia: St. Louis, 1972), 258–60 (v. 25 of *Luther's Works*).

the church." These volunteers were privy to various planning meetings and virtually all the decisions made by the pastor in question, never disagreeing with him openly. But as soon as the meetings were over, they spread their vitriol to others. Questions were raised in secret about the wisdom of the decisions made, and subtle hints were left concerning the misuse of funds. These "charges" were without foundation, but the effect was the same.

There are even more egregious examples. I know of a case in my own denomination in which men and women in local church leadership falsified official minutes of the church and lied to the annual meeting of the congregation about others in the church. Their rationale? That although the church had voted for a certain position, the decision was a poor one, and this, they felt, justified their arrogating to themselves the right to work against the position taken by the church. To do so they were compelled to act in ways that maligned others. When finally confronted, they protested pure motives, if not righteous actions. No one wants to believe that this can happen in the church, but it does.

Such deviousness is not limited to the local church. My own denomination is a case in point. The Evangelical Covenant Church in America was founded by Swedish pietist immigrants. To this country they brought a robust belief in the authority of Scripture and a commitment to the essential nature of the experience of new life in Christ. But in the early 1900s growing tensions within the denomination became clear. Over the years harsh, unkind, and untrue words were spoken and written. Each side was certain that it stood with the angels, and each was certain that the very soul of the denomination was at stake. Feelings were hurt, careers damaged, and untold misery experienced by family and friends. One of the principal players in the controversy wrote that at the time the convictions and actions of both sides seemed noble and pure, but in retrospect "some of us ... displayed a regrettable party spirit. I confess that I carry my full share of guilt for the unwarranted apotheosis of something which, in the words of Nietzsche, was 'human, all too human.'"[25] We have the capacity to speak ill-considered and even slanderous words about each other within the church, even though we know that James says such behavior only brings condemnation on our own heads.

There are, I think, several steps we can take to avoid this pitfall. (1) *We must remember that the end does not necessarily justify the means.* Near the end of his life Cicero witnessed the destruction of what he considered the best of Roman civilization, and he bitterly said, "When you are no longer what you

---

25. Karl A. Olson, "The Covenant Constitution and Its History," *Narthex*, 3/1 (February 1983), 11.

were, then there is no reason left for living."[26] It is possible "to win," as had Cicero's enemies, but at the terrible price of character and integrity. There are times when our desire to see a goal come to fruition so overwhelms us that the process of its achievement nullifies its effect.

Few questions are as important to the church of Jesus Christ as that of leadership. One of the truly discouraging features of my coming to maturity was the realization that in church politics the end often seems to justify the means. Mike was a young intern serving as a youth director at a church. He was recently married and set to attend seminary in the fall. He planned on resigning in May so that he and his new wife could move across the state and spend the summer settling into marriage and familiarizing themselves with the town that would be their home for the next three years. Mike's supervisor knew of his plans, but did not want to interrupt his own vacation schedule in order to conduct a search for a replacement. So he convinced Mike to stay until a week before classes began. His motive was selfish, although he told Mike it would be "better for the kids." His lie was convenient for him, but not for Mike. He abused his position, and although the stakes were not high, this abuse revealed something of a double-minded heart.

Recently a good friend of mine, a regional official for his denomination, told me a sad story concerning the administrator to whom he once reported. This administrator is gifted in many ways, and my friend has tremendous respect for her. But she had made some enemies among those who viewed her as an interloper. From my friend's perspective this woman had done a great job, but the reaction against her had taken the form of a well-organized cabal. Several prominent persons within the district had decided to have her removed from office. They made charges that they believed were true, but many of which were without foundation. They misled some of her support staff and misused the information gained thereby. In their eyes it was essential for "the good of the district" that she lose her position. But the process they chose, one of duplicity, subterfuge, and misrepresentation, was not worthy of the cause of Christ. The goal before their eyes must have seemed to them so pure and rarefied, but the path they chose to reach it sullied and polluted not only the goal, but themselves.

(2) *Stretch for biblical open-mindedness.* Hindsight, the saying goes, is always 20/20. James has implored his readers to repent. To him the need for repentance was obvious. To his readers it was not so. There is something about faith that tends toward certainty. But certainty can be dangerous when it makes us blind. Jesus, like James, tried strenuously to open the eyes of his contemporaries to see their need for repentance. He implored them, "Stop judging

---

26. Cicero, *Ad Familiares*, 7.

by mere appearances, and make a right judgment" (John 7:24). In no uncertain terms he warned them, "Woe to you, blind guides!" (Matt. 23:16). In frustration he said to them, "If you were blind, you would not be guilty of sin; but now that you claim you can see, your guilt remains" (John 9:41).

History teaches that we are foolish if we imagine we are immune from the same tendency. What ensures the honesty and integrity of our faith and practice is, in part, a healthy biblical self-critique. Paul says that, in a flash, he came to realize that his trust in the law was actually a form of idolatry that had prevented him from seeing the light (Rom. 10:1–4; 2 Cor. 3:7–4:6). Peter persisted to maintain a practice of separation from Gentiles until the vision recorded in Acts 10. Both were open to self-critique against the standards of Scripture and the Spirit. Such critique involves the courage and integrity to attempt to discern the wisdom of other positions. Above all, it means to test our own convictions, as well as those of others, on the anvil of the biblical witness.

Several years ago a good friend of mine, who as a young man became a millionaire in the clothing business, reported to his friends that his life had been transformed by reading John F. Alexander's *Your Money or Your Life*.[27] It convicted him concerning his use of money and God's call on his life. God sometimes speaks to us, as he did to Paul, through the careful consideration of a position we do not hold. We must remain open to his leading. We owe it to ourselves to read and to study positions taken by other Christians, remembering to evaluate them on the basis of the biblical record and in light of the Spirit.

(3) *Commit to personal integrity and biblical fidelity.* Debates concerning women in ministry, the ordination of practicing homosexuals, leadership styles, and the merits of leaders are often politically charged and highly emotional. Frequently there is little reason attendant to the debates and often a lack of civility. James begs us to commit to personal integrity and biblical fidelity.

Let us not "win" at the sacrifice of our principles. Integrity means that we are willing to say in public what we say in private. "I am going to tell you something that he said, only I need you to keep it confidential" is a seedbed for Satan to do his work. Remember, when we judge, we do so as God's designated agents. God will not brook falsehood, misleading, or duplicity. We may "win," and in so doing wreck carnage on our victim, and yet be certain that the cause is just. But such a victory is pyrrhic and tainted, and it will be the cause of our own condemnation.

---

27. John F. Alexander, *Your Money or Your Life: A New Look at Jesus' View of Wealth and Power* (San Francisco: Harper and Row, 1986).

The idiocy of boasting in the uncertain. When James counsels us that tomorrow is never certain, he is right. The ancients knew this and spoke of capricious fortune that governed the lives of women and men. Perhaps the most ready examples of the unpredictable winds of life are those involving finance. Americans are fascinated with money, and particularly with financial abundance. There is something more than a desire for financial security at work here. We are intent on affluence. Our culture is captivated with wealth, with its acquisition and display. In this regard we are not too far removed from the traders whom James knew.

Infomercials crowd the television channels on the weekends, featuring testimonials from former wage earners who, after a short correspondence course, became millionaires buying real estate with no money down and working only ten hours a week. The complimentary airline magazines are replete with video courses offered by financial and success "gurus" who promise easy money. Millions flock to Atlantic City and Las Vegas every year, hoping for a big score. The advertising industry fuels this malady, as everything from luxury cars to recreation and vacation options, clothing, homes, cigarettes, kitchen cabinets, and top-of-the-line toilet tissue is hawked, with the emphasis on wealth and luxury. In case some little-used corner of our conscience is disturbed by this self-interest, the advertisers assure us that we deserve and need such opulence.

This is a twisting of the American dream. In the movie *The Jerk* we are exposed to a comedic dark vision of the American dream. Steve Martin plays a penniless simpleton who travels to the city, accidentally invents a hot-selling product, and thereby becomes a millionaire. But the product proves to have adverse physical effects, and soon the character played by Martin loses everything. This rags to riches to rags story parodies the American dream that any of us can become rich. But it also points out the transitory nature of financial wealth.

In the first place wealth is not easy to acquire. It is true that the American social and cultural landscape is studded with success stories that like of the billionaire H. Ross Perot. It may even be possible to become a millionaire buying real estate with no money down, but as James reminds us, this is not the point. Financial affluence is like the mist; it can disappear even as we grasp it. The wise person does not make his or her finances the bedrock of personal security. Only God deserves that status. But this requires honest evaluation of our own lives and priorities. God does not desire to be a mere ornament clinging desperately to the surface of our lives.

Of course, for most Americans financial affluence is beyond the realm of possibility. During 1996 pay and benefits for US workers rose by an average of only 2.9 percent, according to the Labor Department. The AFL-CIO notes that in 1965 the average CEO made forty-four times the average salary package of the average worker. In 1996 the difference was two hundred times.[28]

Not only is wealth difficult to accumulate, but it is equally difficult to maintain. I once knew a real estate mogul. He was a Christian and served on the deaconate of his church. When video tape technology was set to become widely available to the American public, he made two crucial decisions that together were the equivalent of risking his financial health. Both turned out to be mistakes. The first was to risk a good portion of his wealth buying stock in a "sure thing" electronics firm, which turned out to be the opposite. The second involved a major deal to develop a large tract of land. Everyone said his plan was brilliant. The land in question was ideally located, and the timing seemed perfect. A year after he purchased the land, the value had doubled. But soon a horrific series of events began to transpire. Legal problems concerning title arose, serious environmental questions were posed, and several of his partners backed out. The deal collapsed around him. In both he suffered huge losses. The enhanced financial security for which he hoped, which everyone said was a foregone conclusion, easily within his grasp, dissipated like the morning mist, disturbed by even the lightest of breezes.

Investors in foreign markets take no fewer chances. In his review of the book *Kremlin Capitalism*,[29] Robert Cottrell points out that years of communist rule have left managers and workers woefully unprepared for the essential savvy needed in a market economy. Instead of selling the majority of shares in an industrial enterprise to an "investor who would bring the entire amount of capital necessary to modernize and restructure the firm" in order to make it healthy, most Russian managers and workers prefer to maintain ownership of an increasingly outdated plant. Such behavior the authors label as "suicidal."[30] There are other dangers to investing in Russia. "In 1995 alone the Russian Business Roundtable, an organization of leading executives, lost nine of its top thirty officials to assassins."[31]

Sadly, many in Christian ministry betray the same smug certainty in wealth and position. Jim and Tammy Faye Bakker and their PTL (Praise the Lord) ministry are a case study in the virulent spread of the desire for and false assurance in financial security. Most of the Bakker's close associates were caught in a web of expanding lies, all set in the context of a ministry that once was viable. The desire for money perverted Bakker and his closest associates

28. *Chicago Tribune* (May 11, 1997).

29. Joseph R. Blasi, Maya Kroumova, and Douglas Kruse, *Kremlin Capitalism: The Privatization of the Russian Economy* (Ithaca, N.Y.: Cornell Univ. Press, 1996).

30. Robert Cottrell, "Russia: The New Oligarchy," *New York Review of Books* (March 27, 1977), 28.

31. Ibid., 30.

in a fashion that was not only thorough, but also subtle enough that they did not recognize their own infection until it was too late and thousands of innocent, trusting people had suffered, as had the reputation of the church of Jesus Christ. Neither Bakker nor his associates ever dreamed that their world of affluence could dissipate so quickly and completely.

In his surprisingly sympathetic review of the newest books by Jim Bakker and Tammy Faye Messner,[32] Martin Gardner catalogues the sad story of a Christian minister seduced by the limelight and money, and the rapid spread of this infection. Richard Dortch, Bakker's co-pastor, who paid Jessica Hahn $363,700 in hush money, was sentenced to eight years in prison and fined $200,000. Another of Bakker's top assistants, David Taggart, and his brother James, PTL's interior decorator, were convicted in 1989 of tax evasion to the tune of $500,000. Each was sentenced to seventeen years in prison. Jim Toms, Bakker's friend and attorney, pled guilty to embezzling $1.4 million from his clients. Roe Messner, Bakker's friend, contractor for the defunct Heritage USA Christian theme park, and current husband of Bakker's ex-wife, was indicted by a Wichita, Kansas court for hiding $400,000 from the government when he declared bankruptcy in the aftermath of the PTL scandal. The desire for wealth cloaked itself in the guise of authentic ministry and proved a deadly foe.

Gardner writes that while Jim Bakker was in prison, he came to understand that his "health and wealth" gospel was wrong. Gardner quotes Bakker as saying, "To my surprise, after months of studying Jesus, I concluded that He did not have one good thing to say about money. . . . I had to face the awful truth that I had been preaching false doctrine for years and hadn't even known it!"[33] Gardner continues that Bakker no longer believes the frequent justification Tammy offered for their material luxury: "We were worth it."

Of course, the other factor is what people everywhere think wealth will get them: happiness. A recent survey asking this question of Americans, "What will make you happier," yielded 32 percent who answered, "If I were smarter," and 48 percent who said, "If I were rich." This is one of the great false beliefs of our time. University of Illinois psychologist Ed Diener and his colleagues surveyed forty-nine of the wealthiest Americans (according to the listing in *Forbes* magazine). They reported only slightly higher levels of happiness than is the average among all Americans. Of these forty-nine Americans, each with a net worth over $100 million, 80 percent agreed with the statement that "money can increase *or* decrease happiness, depending on how it is used." Many of those surveyed said that they were basically

---

32. Martin Gardner, "How He Lost It," *The New York Review of Books* (May 29, 1997), 29–32.
33. Ibid., 30.

unhappy, and one of these enormously wealthy persons reported that he could never remember being happy.

In 1957 the per capita income in the US, expressed in 1990 dollars, was $7,500; in 1990 it had doubled to $15,000. Yet in both 1957 and 1990 only 33 percent of those surveyed by the University of Chicago National Opinion Center said that they were "very happy." We are twice as wealthy, but no happier. In fact, between 1956 and 1988 the percentage of Americans who reported that they were "pretty well satisfied" with their financial situation actually dropped from 42 percent to 30 percent. Wealth does not bring happiness.

Erno Rubik, the inventor of the Rubik's cube, was transformed by the success of his product from a $150-a-month professor to the richest person in Hungary. Yet when he was showing an interviewer through his new mansion, replete with pool, three-car garage, and a sauna, the interviewer noticed that there was no dining room. "Do you plan to have many people over for dinner?" Rubik was asked. "I hope not," was his reply.[34]

The unexpected can bring sudden wealth, as it did for Erno Rubik. But more often, it seems, the unexpected brings not good news, but bad. During the early stages of the Peloponnesian War, when the Athenians had suffered an unforeseen blow, Pericles spoke to them, saying, "When the unexpected happens, suddenly and against all calculations and well laid plans, it takes the heart out of you. . . ."[35] When the unexpected happens, we too are shaken. We rely on wealth, yet the stock market crash of 1987 wiped out a man I knew who was only six months from retirement. We rely on the security of our jobs, yet the "peace dividend" occasioned by the collapse of the Soviet Union led to Lockheed laying off more than 20,000 of its 30,000 plus employees at its Sunnyvale, California plant. We rely on a myriad of resources that are, in the words of the Bible, only mist. Life is unpredictable, James says, and we are foolish if we rely on anything other than God.

For Christians to rely on anything other than God is to lack integrity; it is to be double-minded. Integrity is what James is aiming at. Our world seems bereft of integrity. Tobacco companies maintained for decades that they had no knowledge that nicotine was addictive, but in March of 1997 one company admitted what the rest of us suspected for years: The companies knew the addictive properties of nicotine and lied to the rest of us. The pursuit of wealth, apparently, was more highly valued than truth.

Countries fare no better. While claiming to stand for human rights and publicly declaring abhorrence at the massacre in Tiananmen Square, the gov-

---

34. For these examples see David G. Myers, *The Pursuit of Happiness: Who Is Happy and Why* (New York: William Morrow, 1992), 40–42.

35. Thucydides, *History of the Peloponnesian War*, 2.61.

ernment of the United States continues to extend Most Favored Nation Trading Status to the People's Republic of China.[36] But this gulf is really an extension of the gulf within the human soul. We are torn, one way by the *yeṣer ha-ra*, another by the *yeṣer ha-tov*. And yet James implores us to be *integrated* people, consistent, marked by integrity, and mature. How is this accomplished?

In his slender volume *Shaping Character*,[37] Arthur F. Holmes outlines a course of action with the intended result of creating ordered minds and hearts within us, alert to the leading of the Spirit and to the teaching of Scripture. Holmes points out that ethics has been marginalized in our culture, and that most Americans display a functionally relativistic attitude: "It is right for me, but it may not be right for you."[38] In response Holmes outlines eleven steps in the development of this integrated Christian moral identity.

- *Consciousness raising*: becoming aware of the wider world outside ourselves, the pain and suffering of others, the systemic abuses that are the manifestations of Satan's continued perverse influence over our world.
- *Consciousness sensitizing*: feeling compassion for those caught in the web of this evil.
- *Values analysis*: understanding the values that nations, companies, and other people have and which in practice shape their behaviors.
- *Values clarification*: becoming aware of the values that we as individuals and organizations functionally embrace.
- *Values criticism*: asking ourselves hard questions concerning these values: Are they the ones that ought to be operative in our individual and corporate lives?
- *Moral imagination*: thinking in universal terms in order to construct a moral framework based on biblical principles.

---

36. President Clinton promised while campaigning for the presidency to do his best to address human rights violations in China, but on May 28, 1993, he abandoned that promise, claiming that economic engagement with China would improve the positions of all. This has proven to be a hollow position. At least the Reagan administration's position vis-à-vis South Africa did assist in the end of apartheid. No parallel development is in the offing in China.

37. Arthur F. Holmes, *Shaping Character: Moral Education in the Christian College* (Grand Rapids: Eerdmans, 1991).

38. The work of sociologist James Davison Hunter seems to bear this out. His research has led him to two conclusions. (1) Most Americans believe in God and the existence of absolutes. (2) Most Americans do not feel it is appropriate to impose a universal set of moral principles on others. This split Hunter attributes to the success of the media in convincing Americans of the "rightness" of moral relativism. The irony of this is, of course, bitterly amusing. See Richard John Neuhaus, "Tongue-Tied in Public," *First Things* 70 (February 1997), 58–59.

- *Ethical analysis*: exploring the elements of morally complex situations. For example, the Bible is against lying, but was it right to lie to the Gestapo in order to preserve the lives of Jews hiding within the home?
- *Moral decision-making*: having the courage to act on the results of the analytical task just completed.
- *Acting as responsible agents*: making such moral decisions on a consistent basis; the practice of moral action helps to seal such principles in our hearts.
- *Virtue development*: developing godly character, not simply right behaviors. For this reason spiritual development and moral development walk with joined hands. As Jesus said, a good tree bears good fruit.
- *Moral identity*: becoming a unified person, what James 1:4 calls mature and complete.

Holmes argues that life affords us with myriad ethical decisions, and we often base these decisions on a set of rules that we find near at hand. These rules are based, in turn, on principles, which ultimately have some foundational base. Jesus operated in this fashion. When confronted with the problem of divorce, he went behind the Mosaic Law to the foundational basis of Judaism, the doctrine of creation, and derived from this a principle that men and women are to learn to love and forgive one another. Wolfhart Pannenberg has recently argued in precisely this fashion relative to contemporary ethical problems facing the church.[39] Such a process points us to dependence on God instead of on our possessions or ourselves.

Jesus made decisions on the basis of principles rooted in Scripture and a sensitivity to the will of God. James would have us lead lives of similar fidelity—lives that integrate actions, mind, and heart. This is the life of Christian character. Otherwise, we too easily know the good but fail to do it. Now that you know not to judge, and now that you know to trust only in God—do it!

---

39. Wolfhart Pannenberg, "Revelation and the Homosexual Experience," *Christianity Today* (Nov. 11, 1996), 35, 37.

James 5:1–6

NOW LISTEN, YOU rich people, weep and wail because
of the misery that is coming upon you. ²Your wealth
has rotted, and moths have eaten your clothes. ³Your
gold and silver are corroded. Their corrosion will testify
against you and eat your flesh like fire. You have hoarded
wealth in the last days. ⁴Look! The wages you failed to pay
the workmen who mowed your fields are crying out against
you. The cries of the harvesters have reached the ears of the
Lord Almighty. ⁵You have lived on earth in luxury and self-
indulgence. You have fattened yourselves in the day of slaughter. ⁶You have condemned and murdered innocent men, who
were not opposing you.

JAMES SHIFTS HIS attention from the merchant
class, which has just received the benefit of his
honest negative assessment, to the landowning
class, which will receive the same. The two sec-
tions are linked by the common thread of the desire for wealth. James assumes
the mantle not of teacher or preacher but of prophet, for his warnings are the
warnings of coming destruction and wrath.

Martin holds that the parallel to the Old Testament prophets indicates that
the rich landowners must be unbelievers.[1] This is indicative of one of the most
common fallacies of New Testament scholarship.[2] James could reasonably

---

1. Ralph P. Martin, *James*, 172; Sophie Laws, *The Epistle of James*, 195; and Peter H. Davids,
The Epistle of James, 174, also see the rich landowners as outside the Christian church.

2. G. B. Caird, "The Development of the Doctrine of Christ in the New Testament,"
Christ For Us Today, ed. N. Pittenger (London: SCM, 1968), 69–70, pointed out that as
helpful as the original meaning of a term may be, the only issue of prime importance is to
understand what the author intended by that term.

Parallels to the New Testament in other literatures and religions are in themselves
no evidence of dependence; and, even where dependence can be proved, the fact
remains that to trace a word, an idea, or a practice to its origin helps us very little to
explain what it means in its new setting. A probe into the pre-Mosaic origins of the
Jewish Passover tells us nothing about the Christian Eucharist. Bultmann has told us
the Prologue to the Fourth Gospel had a previous existence as a Gnostic hymn, and
for all I know he may be right. But even if this could be proved beyond reasonable

expect errant Christian brothers and sisters to recognize themselves in the negative descriptions borrowed from the prophets. Further, as Martin himself notes, the harsh tones James has employed in previous sections (1:9–11; 2:2–4, 5–12, 15–16; 4:13–17) were directed at some within the Christian community, especially at those who gloried in their own status and position as opposed to the more humble within the church.

This section serves many purposes. It warns the rich of their coming destruction; and although there is no clear call to repentance here, it is not unreasonable to surmise that such is the implication. James also makes clear the fate of those who persist in claiming true Christian identity without the concomitant life of practice he has outlined. Finally, the passage offers hope to the righteous who suffer, since the fate of those who cause this suffering is the opposite of their own fate.

The preeminent fault described here is the desire for possession. Wealth (fine clothing, gold, and silver) is hoarded, and yet it is of no avail. Produce has decayed in the storehouse, clothing has been decimated by moths, gold and silver that once was bright has become dull with age and disuse. But possession is also manifested in the willingness to be niggardly in paying wages. This life of self-interested and irresponsible luxury is nothing short of murder, for the rich have seen the poverty of the poor around them and have failed to take action.

The tone evident in this passage is more strident than in 4:11–17. Here the rich landowners are threatened with judgment *prior* to a description of their sins (5:3). The merchants were not criticized for their wealth as such, but here that seems to be the case.

As to structure, the passage is a neat unit, containing a condemnation of the indifferent landed gentry that recalls the vocabulary and tone of the great prophets. There are discernible transitions, however. Verse 1 stands as a sharp introductory warning. Verses 2–3 compose a brief catalogue of riches that have been stored against difficult times, but which are useless nonetheless, because they represent trust in human planning. Verses 4–6, which offer a laconic inventory of particular sins perpetrated against the poor and the common people by this landed class, form the basis for the wrath and judgment about to befall them.

---

doubt, it would be a fact of singularly little importance to the commentator on the Gospel. What the hymn meant to its suppostitious Gnostic author may provide an interesting exercise for the antiquarian. But for the exegesis of the Gospel all that matters is what it meant to the Evangelist; and this we can discover only by reading the Gospel.

Condemning Introduction (5:1)

JAMES BEGINS BY condemning the unfeeling and selfish attitude of the wealthy landowners. As in 4:13, he uses the rare phrase *age nun* ("Now listen"). In spite of this similarity, however, this group is not the same as the "you who say" of 4:13 (i.e., the merchants). On the other hand, though members of these two groups would themselves be keenly aware of the differences between them, to the common people they are essentially alike, for both have the same malady: an irrational desire for and trust in wealth.

Laws[3] observes that "the rich" is unqualified. James apparently makes no allowance for the possibility of a rich landowner who does not oppress the poor. He calls for a sudden opening of the eyes for the rich, to see that they are, in fact, oppressing the poor.

These wealthy people must "weep and wail." "Weep" (*klaio*) means to respond to disaster in a rightful manner—to weep from the depths of one's being in grief and remorse. "Wail" (*ololuzo*) means to howl, especially as a result of sudden and unexpected evil and regret (see Isa. 15:2–3, 5; Jer. 13:7; Lam. 1:1–2 as Old Testament parallels). This remorse is justified because the lot of these rich is "misery" (*talaiporia*, a word used only here and in Rom. 3:16 in the New Testament). James may indeed have Jeremiah 12:3 within view: "Set them apart for the day of slaughter." The reason is not their wealth per se, but the fact that they have not sought to use their wealth to alleviate the sufferings of the poor. In fact, their desire for wealth is the cause of much of this suffering in a direct fashion, for the poor work for the landowners.

A Catalogue of Futility (5:2–3)

HAVING CONDEMNED THE wealthy landowners for their indifference, James next points out that riches are worthless when it comes to eternal salvation. The terms used here ("wealth," "clothes," "gold and silver") comprise a standard catalogue of riches in the ancient world, especially if "wealth" refers to land and its produce. The produce of the land has "rotted," and the clothing has been eaten by moths (cf. Job 13:28: "So man wastes away like something rotten, like a garment eaten by moths"). The gold and silver have corroded or rusted. Technically these metals do not rust, but James is painting with the eye of a prophet.

It is both a measure of his skill as a stylist and his indebtedness to the prophetic tradition that James uses these three verbs in the perfect tense. The decay has not yet taken place, but the eye of a prophet sees the result as clear as the daybreak is to the watchers on the wall. The wealthy still

---

3. Sophie Laws, *The Epistle of James*, 197.

enjoy the benefit of their wealth and station; but unless they repent, their destiny is set, and James can see it.

The corrosion of the precious metals is called into the dock as a witness against the wealthy. In Matthew 6:20 Jesus said, "But store up for yourself treasures in heaven, where moth and rust do not destroy." This corrosion acts not only on the metals, but with far more serious import on the flesh of the wealthy, just as a fire ravages all before it. The idea, of course, is that their wealth will accuse these landowners, especially since in spite of the signs, they have continued to hoard "wealth" even though these are "the last days" (v. 3).

This is not to say that James is imagining an imminent Parousia. Rather, just as it would be criminally ridiculous to hoard wealth when the Parousia is imminent, so Christians who have heard Jesus' message and yet shortchange needy workers and hoard wealth are morally liable. The treasure awaiting them is not fine clothing or gold, but "misery." Like the citizens of Carthage who reveled in the circus while their city was under siege and then was stormed by Genseric in A.D. 439,[4] the wealthy landowners have been about a task that seemed important to them at the time, but which on further reflection can only be judged idiotic. Alternatively, the idea can be taken figuratively, that this behavior stores up a "treasure" of punishment soon to be delivered.

James provides four reasons for the wealthy landowners to weep: Their wealth is temporal and subject to the ravages of time; they are guilty of a crime against their sisters and brothers; they will be judged and condemned for this selfish use of temporal goods; and they have been adding to their material treasure as if the world will go on forever.

An Inventory of Selfishness (5:4–6)

JAMES NOW LISTS specific behaviors that have contributed to the hoarding of wealth. For one thing, they have not paid their hired laborers their due, thereby robbing their own neighbors of earned pay.[5] The wages due to the workers but still in the treasury of the owner were crying out the iniquity, just

---

4. Salvian, *On the Governance of God*, 6.12.

5. Most of the time these landlords were absentee landlords. Tacitus (*Annals*, 12.23) tells us of Roman senators who owned vast estates in far provinces. Pliny considered purchasing a certain estate near many others that he owned but had never visited. He worried that it might be a poor purchase, because he liked to have estates in far-flung areas since it "amused" him to travel about (Pliny, *Epistulae*, 3.19); half of the Roman province of Africa was owned by six landlords (idem, *Natural History*, 18.35). During the reign of Trajan only 7 percent of the population owned 40 percent of various regions in Italy (Geza Alföldy, *The Social History of Rome*, tr. D. Braud and F. Pollock [Baltimore: Johns Hopkins Univ. Press, Baltimore, 1988], 107). Likewise, Luke 12:16–21 and 14:18–19 speak of wealth in crops and land; while Matt. 25:14–30 speaks of money-lending as an avenue to wealth.

as the blood of Abel cried out from the ground concerning the sin of Cain (Gen. 4:10). Here is an image of great power. The murder of Abel by Cain is perhaps the archetypal sin, and his blood cried out to God. To compare the present sin to the murder of Abel is to emphasize its grievous nature—it is far more serious than the landowners have imagined. Moreover, the Bible makes it clear that God is the defender of the poor and oppressed.

The combination of these two themes grants to this passage special power and poignancy. Because God has already heard the cry, the voice of judgment against the wealthy has already begun to sound. James says that the double cry (of the workers and of the wages) has reached the ears of "the Lord Almighty." Here the NIV has done a disservice, for James uses the expression *kurios sabaoth*, "the Lord of hosts" (a phrase appearing only here and in Rom. 9:29 in the New Testament). This phrase conjures up the image of God going to war against the wealthy to defend his oppressed poor.[6]

In verse 5 James turns his attention from the hardship imposed on others to the ease and sloth of the wealthy. He levies two allegations: (1) They have lived lives of "luxury" and gross "indulgence." The strength of the terms suggests that there is more here than simply a life of pleasure. Rather, the terms imply such superabundance that this life of luxury is pursued at the expense of others and with an attitude of unfeeling dismissal toward them. The phrase "on earth" (lit., "on the land") rightly identifies land ownership and agriculture as the basis of real and inherited wealth in antiquity.[7] The opening phrase, "you have lived," also points with accuracy to the fact that wealth tended to be hereditary.[8]

The point of verse 5 recalls the parable of the rich man and Lazarus in Luke 16:19–31. In both the rich have received in this life all the comfort they will have. They can expect nothing but torment in the next life.

Martin wisely points out that unlike the merchants in 4:13–17, who do wrong, these landowners fail to do anything, even in the face of great misery![9] This is supported by the term "self-indulgence" (*spataleo*; cf. also 1 Tim.

---

6. In the LXX Isa. 5:9 has the phrase *kyriou sabaoth*, who declares the vacancy of the fine houses of the landowning class.

7. Pliny (*Epistulae*, 3.19) writes there are three ways to make money: inheritance, loaning at interest, and marrying into money. By inheritance he meant land, which was the only sure basis for wealth. Cato recommended the cultivation of a cash crop, such as olive oil (Cato, *De Agri Cultura*, 2.7).

8. The American notion of "climbing the ladder" of economic success would have made no sense to the ancients. As M. Woloch ("Four Leading Families in Roman Athens," *Historia* 18 [1969]) has pointed out, to an astonishingly high degree wealth and status remained the province of rigidly secure groups of families in any given locale.

9. Ralph P. Martin, *James*, 180.

5:6), which James sees as a great sin, a denial of God and of our common humanity. This point he makes with astonishing clarity in the final sentence of verse 5: "You have fattened yourselves in the day of slaughter." Few behaviors are more despicable than profiting from the deaths of others. The NIV does not do justice to the force of the Greek text. A better translation would be, "You have gorged your hearts in the day of slaughter." This conveys the sense of complete self-interest and indulging all lusts without thought of shame.

"In the days of slaughter" is a somewhat problematic phrase. The verse clearly betrays an eschatological dimension, yet the preposition *en* is used, not *eis*, which one would expect if a future orientation were in view. Perhaps the best way to resolve the problem is to understand that for James, the day of reckoning has already begun—the day of judgment as well as the day of the slaughter of the enemies of God (Jer. 46:10). This harmonizes nicely with the Gospel accounts of the sayings of Jesus; as we have seen, James is able to write in such a way.

(2) The final accusation aimed at the landed class is their plotting of the wrongful treatment and even murder of the innocent (v. 6). This verse presents difficulty if taken literally; but apart from the abhorrence such a reading creates, there are little grounds, grammatical or otherwise, from seeing it in any way other than literal. The death referred to here may be the result of starvation caused by the withholding of wages. Or perhaps, like the powerful landed gentry everywhere in the empire, these men saw themselves as the kings of their own land.[10] Justice in the empire was due the citizen, not the noncitizen. Their victims did not oppose them, probably because they could not.[11] They suffered and died, and the landed class was not even aware of their plight. This is perhaps an even more grievous offense than if the wealthy were watching this suffering with sickening glee.

There is an ancient tradition that suggests that the "innocent" (lit., "righteous") one is Jesus himself (James uses the singular here; cf. Acts 3:14; 7:52; 1 Peter 3:18; 1 John 2:1). Apart from understanding the church as the cor-

---

10. Amos 5:11–12 speaks of this: "You trample on the poor and force him to give you grain. Therefore, though you have built stone mansions, you will not live in them; though you have planted lush vineyards, you will not drink their wine. . . . You oppress the righteous and take bribes and you deprive the poor of justice in the courts."

11. Plutarch tells us that Cato considered himself the law on his estates, presiding over even capital trials (Plutarch, *Marcus Cato*, 21.3–7). Other practices endorsed by Cato, such as the chain-gang for slaves (Cato, *De Agri Cultura*, 56) and his advice that the owner or the representative of the owner arrogate to themselves the role of judge and jury (see Plutarch, *Marcus Cato*, 145), demonstrate with crystal clarity that Roman justice was for Roman citizens, and even then especially in urban settings.

porate Christ, there is little merit for this view. On the other hand, we should not assume that the idea of the corporate Christ is a mere unimportant curiosity. The wealthy should understand that God takes it personally when we treat others like garbage, as if they do not deserve even our attention as they die. In Matthew 25:31–46 Jesus says that he considers our treatment of the poor, the imprisoned, and the thirsty to be our treatment of him.

THIS SECTION IS a warning of judgment to wealthy landowners, whom James charges with insensitivity and even murder because of their lives of luxurious excess. Today's farmer uses complex and expensive machinery. But in the ancient world there were no such options. Instead, wealthy landowners who fancied themselves "farmers" employed slaves and poor free persons on their land. Such persons were among the wealthiest in the empire. Today the superrich rarely make their money in agricultural production. For this reason we must investigate both ancient patterns of wealth and land ownership as well as contemporary parallels in order to understand the contemporary significance of the passage.

James threatens the wealthy with judgment *prior* to his describing their sins. To the traders in 4:13–18 James had pronounced judgment only *after* their sins were recounted. What accounts for this curious change? The answer to this question is that in the ancient world, rural land holdings and their produce were the source of real wealth.

A wealthy landowner was, by definition, an exploiter of the poor. The parables of Jesus indicate that wealth was associated with the production of olive oil, grain, ownership of land, and lending money at interest (Matt. 20:1–16; 25:14–30; Luke 7:41–43; 12:16–21). Cato had definite advice on running a successful farm: Sell surplus grain and wine, sell olive oil (but only if the price is right), and sell old and worn-out oxen and slaves.[12] Plutarch relates that he made money not only in cash crops, but also in land speculation, being careful to buy from distressed sellers and to pick property which "could not be ruined by Jupiter."[13] Cicero knew that

> the professions which require either a higher degree of intelligence or which no small benefit to society is given, for instance medicine and architecture and teaching, these are acceptable for those whose social position makes them appropriate. Trade, if on a small scale, is vulgar; but if wholesale and on a large scale ... it even seems to deserve the

---

12. Cato, *De Agri Cultura*, 2.7.
13. Plutarch, *Cato*, 21.5–6.

highest respect. ... But of all the occupations by which gain is secured, none is more profitable or more delightful than agriculture.[14]

Of course, Cicero had in mind not farmers as we understand the term, but only those wealthy enough to own estates. Pliny agreed, offering his advice that a fortune was waiting to be made in the production of wine![15] Modern scholarship has proven Pliny right.[16]

Varro tells us that agriculture was carried out by three types of means: articulate (people), inarticulate (cattle), and mute (farm implements).[17] "All agriculture," he wrote, "is carried on by human beings—either slaves, freemen, or both." The only freemen who farmed were either the very poor or those hired to work off debt. Slaves were the usual source of labor, but he preferred free peasant *coloni*. His discussion presupposes large estates owned by absentee landlords and overseen by foremen, either slave or *liberti*, and worked by slaves, *liberti*, and free poor. Every aspect of the lives of these human machines (Varro called such workers "equipment"[18]) was dictated by the landlord through the agency of the foreman: whom they married, how they were paid, how they were punished. Although agriculture and especially the cultivation of cash crops were regarded as the surest route to wealth, none of the elite wanted to do the work themselves.[19]

According to James, the wealthy landowners were not paying their laborers their due. We have already seen how the wealthy made their money by cultivation of cash crops. Philostratus, in his *Life of Apollonius*, relates an unnerving account of the selfishness and indifference of the wealthy:

> Bread riots are no such easy matter ... but Apollonius was able ... to cope with people in this temper. ... [In Aspendus] the price of even vetch was high, the people were living on siege rations, because the ruling class had put the entire supply of grain under lock and key so that they could export it at an ever greater profit![20]

James has accused the wealthy landowners with murder. This passage from Philostratus confirms that James could very well be speaking literally. Such was the indifference of the wealthy and the strength of their addiction to money.

---

14. Cicero, *De Officiis*, 42.

15. Pliny, *Natural History*, 14.5.47–57.

16. N. Purcell, "Wine and Wealth in Ancient Italy," *Journal of Roman Studies*, 75 (1985): 1–19.

17. Varro, *Rerum Rusticarum*, 1.17.1–7.

18. Ibid., 1.17.7.

19. Cf. also Philostratus (*Vit. Soph.*, 547–48), who tells us that the fabulously wealthy Athenian of the early empire, Herodes Atticus, became wealthy through his landed estates worked by poor tenant farmers.

20. Philostratus, *Vit. Apollonius*, 1.15.

The Roman historian Sallust decried this crass desire for money, which, in his view, had infected and destroyed his beloved Rome. Speaking of generations of Romans only recently dead he writes:

> But when our nation had become great because of toil and justice … the lust for money, and then for power overcame them, these were, I think, the root of all evils. For avarice destroyed honor, and integrity … and taught instead insolence and cruelty.[21]

Ganymede, one of the guests at Trimalchio's dinner party in *The Satyricon* of Petronius, complained that prices were so high even he could not afford bread. "And so," he said, "the little people suffer."[22] Juvenal said that *Pecunia* ("money") was a goddess that was worshiped:

> Let money carry the day, let the sacred office be given to one who came but yesterday with white feet into our city. For no god is held in such reverence among us as wealth, even though you, evil money, have no temple of your own, as yet we have raised no altars to money in the fashion that we worship Peace and Honor, Victory and Virtue, or Concord.[23]

Peasants bore the brunt of severe circumstances,[24] including taxation. Peasants in Judea carried the burden of the temple tax, Roman tribute,[25] special taxes,[26] and the tax for the building programs of Herod, which, said Josephus, "bled the country dry."[27] Estimates of a 40 percent tax rate on these peasants are not unreasonable.[28] The devastating famine of A.D. 46–48 only exacerbated these conditions.

---

21. Sallust, *The War With Cataline*, 10.

22. Petronius, *Satyricon*, 44.

23. Juvenal, *Satires*, 1.110–16.

24. See Gerd Theissen, *The Shadow of the Galilean*, tr. John Bowden (Philadelphia: Fortress, 1987), 75–82; S. Applebaum, "Judaea As a Roman Province: The Countryside As a Political and Economic Factor," *ANRW*, 2nd series, ed. H. Temprorini and W. Haase (Berlin: Walter de Gruyter, 1977), 8:355–99.

25. Josephus (*Antiquities*, 14.202–3) writes, "Gauis Caesar, Imperator for the second time, commanded that they shall pay a tax for the city of Jerusalem … every year except the seventh … in addition, they shall also pay tithes to Hyrcannus and his sons, just as they paid to their forebears."

26. Josephus (*Jewish War*, 1.219–22) relates how the populations of several towns were sold into slavery when they were late paying their taxes.

27. Josephus, *Antiquities*, 17.304–8.

28. See Richard Horsley and John Hanson, *Bandits, Prophets, and Messiahs, Popular Movements in the Time of Jesus* (San Francisco: Harper and Row, 1985), 55–56.

James has offered us a warning concerning wealth, its power, and its peril. The ancients knew the acidic power of money. Seneca said, "Unfortunately, we esteem a man for his wealth, and not his soul."[29] James calls us to a sudden opening of our eyes, to see that as evangelicals in the wealthiest nation in human history, we bear a responsibility to understand the power and peril of our wealth and to use it responsibly. Like the Romans, we esteem people for their wealth, and not so often for their souls. Popular magazines glamorize the glitterati and their money, whether the source of this wealth is business (Donald Trump or Bill Gates), Hollywood (Liz Taylor or Arnold Schwarzenegger), or music (Michael Jackson or Madonna).

In spite of the fact that wealth does *not* bring happiness,[30] American newsstands are glutted with periodicals devoted to wealth and its acquisition. They bear titles such as *Forbes, The Wall Street Journal, Business Week, Fortune, Entrepreneur,* and astonishingly, *Money.*[31] Like Roman society, we as individuals and as a culture are fascinated with money. Seeker-sensitive churches often make it a creed to refrain from speaking of money, lest the congregation be "offended." In the American evangelical subculture we regularly bow to the goddess *Pecunia,* whether in the money we spend on church buildings, or in the selection of church officers based on wealth and status.

Recently I spoke at a gathering of church leaders in the Detroit area, where I shared lunch with a denominational administrator. As we enjoyed our meal in the cafeteria of a lovely church, he paused, cast his gaze around the room, and spoke in low tones, "Sometimes I worry about the money we spend on ourselves. How many starving children could be fed for a year with the money spent making this facility beautiful, as opposed to merely functional?" James calls us to open our eyes. The first step to integrity in this issue is, as my friend has done, to wonder and to ask the question.

Ronald J. Sider, in his book *Rich Christians in an Age of Hunger: A Biblical Study,* quotes from a sermon by Paul E. Toms, former President of the National Association of Evangelicals: "I read sometime ago that Upton Sinclair, the author, read this passage (James 5:1–7) to a group of ministers. Then he attributed the passage to Emma Goldman, who at the time was an anarchist agitator. The ministers were indignant, and their response was, 'This woman ought to be deported at once!'" Sider responds trenchantly:

---

29. Seneca, *Epistulae,* 41.7.

30. See David G. Myers, *The Pursuit of Happiness: Who Is Happy and Why* (New York: William Morrow and Company, 1992), 40–42.

31. The cover story for the June 1997 issue of *Money* was "How to Build Wealth On Even a Modest Income."

Most Christians in the Northern Hemisphere simply do not believe Jesus' teaching about the deadly danger of possessions. We all know that Jesus warned that possessions are highly dangerous—so dangerous in fact that it is extremely difficult for a rich person to be a Christian at all. "It is easier for a camel to go through the eye of a needle than for a rich man to enter the kingdom of God" [Luke 18:24–25]. . . . But we do not believe Jesus. Christians in the United States live in the richest society in the history of the world surrounded by a billion hungry neighbors. Yet . . . we insist on more and more. If Jesus was so un-American that he considered riches dangerous, then we must ignore or reinterpret his message.[32]

Sider points out too that this message concerning wealth goes beyond Jesus and James. Paul writes, for example in 1 Timothy 6:9–10:

People who want to get rich fall into temptation and a trap and into many foolish and harmful desires that plunge men into ruin and destruction. For the love of money is a root of all kinds of evil. Some people, eager for money, have wandered from the faith and pierced themselves with many griefs.

The love of money is the root of all kinds of evil. The Latin phrase is *radix omnium malorum avaritia*, and during the Reformation the acrostic ROMA was popular as a symbol of the perceived abuses of the Roman church.[33] Here began a sin of pride that marks the Protestant tradition. Protestantism has long been characterized by a barely concealed pride that it is free from the stain of the sin of avarice, but today it is a pride without warrant. There is ample evidence that Protestants are as guilty of this sin as the Catholic hierarchy of the sixteenth century. From the New Testament to Sallust the message is the same: Money has an attractive power that is lethal in its effects.

I used to think, when I was a child, that Christ might have been exaggerating when he warned about the dangers of wealth. Today I know better. I know how hard it is to be rich and still keep the milk of human kindness. Money has a dangerous way of putting scales on one's eyes, a dangerous way of freezing people's hands, eyes, lips and hearts.[34]

---

32. Ronald J. Sider, *Rich Christians in an Age of Hunger: A Biblical Study* (New York: Paulist, 1977), 131.

33. See Lewis W. Spitz, *The Renaissance and Reformation Movements*, v. 2, *The Reformation* (St. Louis: Concordia, 1971), 313.

34. Dom Heldert Camara, *Revolution Through Peace* (New York: Harper, 1971), 142–43, quoted in Ronald J. Sider, *Rich Christians in an Age of Hunger*, 122.

MONEY POSES A grave danger that the church ignores at its peril. As James warns us, the love of money will garner judgment from God. Money has the potential to cause us to ignore God and to become callous to the needs of our brothers and sisters, and it will result in judgment if we have used wealth selfishly. The love of money has this power because we are so easily blinded to the strength of its allure, and we ignore it to our peril.

The power and peril of wealth: We ignore God. James asks of us an important question: Has our wealth blinded us to God? Has our desire for security and even excess so significantly dulled our ears that we barely hear God's voice? Is Ron Sider correct when he says that we are so influenced by our culture that we must either ignore the call of Jesus, or else radically reinterpret it?

Every two years I teach a class called "Christian Studies," which encourages students to think seriously about the call of Christ on our lives in this increasingly complicated world. The course combines a study of biblical passages; the reading of diverse books on matters of theology, ethics, and contemporary issues; and a variety of presentations by persons whose lives and ministries are marked by a passionate love for God and concern for others. One of my speakers is Erika Carney, a young graduate of North Park College whose vision is to care for, love, and support young people in the community immediately surrounding the school. Ours is an urban campus, and our neighborhood is marked by the usual urban "problems."

A few years ago Erika felt led to begin an after-school program for the young people in the area. What started out as a one-afternoon-per-week opportunity to play pool in the North Park recreation lounge has expanded to include a full-range of options for junior high and senior high school students, including academic assistance and a youth ministry program. Erika calls it "After Hours," and the program has been recognized by Senator Paul Simon and President Clinton. In 1996 Erika was invited to fly to Washington to meet with President Clinton, where the "After Hours" program was recognized as one of the best volunteer programs in America. One student who heard Erika address the class was Anji Ecker. This is her account:

> I know that I have a desire to find a passion as Erika has found. She has helped me to have a desire to seek out my "passion" so that I can get to the stage where I can *live it*. Erika pointed out a passage in *Compassion*[35]

---

35. Donald P. McNeill, Douglas A. Morrison, Henri J. M. Nouwen, *Compassion: A Reflection on the Christian Life* (Garden City, N.Y.: Doubleday, 1982).

that she felt summarized the challenge she is confronted with. It relates to the command given to us by Jesus: "Be compassionate as your Father is compassionate." This command does not restate the obvious, something we already wanted but had forgotten, an idea in line with our natural aspirations. On the contrary, it is a call that goes right against that grain; that turns us completely around and requires a total conversion of heart and mind. It is indeed a radical call, a call that goes to the roots of our lives.

From what I know about Erika, she could have done anything. She shared how some people back home questioned her judgment because of her choice of occupation and told her she would "grow out of it." I think she has lived firsthand what this passage is talking about. She has gone against the grain, against that "upward pull" towards fame, riches, and higher positions. I can see what a "radical call" it really is, and as graduation day approaches, it seems all the more radical. My tendencies are to look toward jobs that will make the most money so that I can fill my life with "things." Erika's example has challenged me to find something more meaningful, something that "requires a total conversion of heart and mind."

Society encourages us to go in an upward direction. By "upward direction" I mean striving for things like better salaries and more prestigious positions. The "downward pull" that *Compassion* refers to is what Jesus' life reflected. "Instead of striving for a higher position, more power, and more influence, Jesus moves from the heights to the depths, from victory to defeat, from riches to poverty, from triumphs to suffering, from life to death," says Karl Barth.

Anji has correctly grasped the message of James. It does not sound sweet to our ears, because, as Anji says, our society encourages the upward direction. But James is not interested in molding the gospel into a shape demanded by society. Instead, he calls us to a sober and steady gaze at our lives as individuals and as the church, urging a sudden "opening of the eyes" concerning wealth.

Money has made us blind, just as Sallust said of his own sisters and brothers. Archbishop Oscar Romero[36] commented on the same point when he said:

How many there are that would better not call themselves Christians, because they have no faith. They have more faith in their money and

---

36. Archbishop Oscar Romero of San Salvador, El Salvador, was assassinated on March 24, 1980. He had been Archbishop of San Salvador for three years. During this time he had weekly spoken out against the combination of wealthy elites and the government for their systematic campaign of torture and murder. This earned him their ire, and eventually his martyrdom. Pope John Paul II said Oscar Romero surrendered his life "for the church and

possessions than in the God who fashioned their possessions and their money.[37]

The power and the peril of wealth: We ignore our sisters and brothers. What would James think of the way American evangelical churches and parishioners spend money? We spend millions on new sanctuaries, sound systems, and Christian conferences for the family. We are generally upper middle class, owning luxury cars, swimming pools, and the latest clothes. Are these wrong, or do they merely indicate that a mid-point can be found and that greater balance is needed?

In 1997 Michael Horowitz of the Hudson Institute began developing concern for persecuted Christians around the world. In a similar fashion A. M. (Abe) Rosenthal has been using his column in the *New York Times* to highlight the plight of those persecuted simply because they are Christians, especially in China. Both of these men are Jews, and both are intent on shaming Americans, and (perhaps especially) American Christians, into feeling concern for fellow believers. What does it say of American evangelicalism when we are so obviously myopically self-interested?

Paul Marshall and Lela Gilbert, in their joint book, *Their Blood Cries Out: The Growing Worldwide Persecution of Christians*,[38] think they know. They point out that more Christians regularly attend worship in China than in all of Western Europe, and that some 75 percent of Christians today are persons of color living in the Third World. American Christians, the authors allege, are either so marked by some vague post-colonial guilt that they refuse to take a moral stand against any other country, especially when the issue is persecution of Christians (after all, Christianity is the epitome of dead white European male hegemony); or else they are so captivated by personal spirituality and anesthetized by the climate-controlled upholstered environment of their worship services that they ignore God and the needs of others.

Surely Marshall and Gilbert are not wholly wrong! The human rights abuses in China constitute a case in point. The conservative Christian magazine *World* quoted Clinton's National Security Advisor Samuel Berger as saying, "We cannot say that human rights conditions in China are better today than they were a year ago."[39] Even *The Nation*, proud of its arch-liberal

---

the people of his beloved country" (see Oscar Romero, *The Violence of Love: The Pastoral Wisdom of Archbishop Oscar Romero*, compiled and trans. James R. Brockman [San Francisco: Harper and Row, 1988], xii).

37. Ibid., 162.

38. Paul Marshall and Lela Gilbert, *Their Blood Cries Out: The Growing Worldwide Persecution of Christians* (Dallas: Word, 1997).

39. *World* (May 31/June 7, 1997), 10.

reputation, finds little redeeming about the Clinton Administration's attempt to defend its China policy.[40]

Before Donorgate weakened his hand, President Clinton was planning to push for permanent M.F.N. (Most Favored Nation) trading status and early and easy accession of China into the World Trade Organization. The Administration argues that free markets and growth will generate a middle class and an evolution to democracy—that entangling China in global treaties and laws, from missile nonproliferation to the W.T.O., will foster the rule of law within the country.

The argument lacks only evidence. Chinese repression is worse since the Clinton Administration backed off linking trade and human rights. The Chinese leaders do not share the assumption that capitalism requires democracy. More than 150 million people are officially described as migrant unemployed in China. Inequality is stark; corruption rife. Multinationals want order enforced, property protected, and labor disciplined. They find the authoritarian Chinese regime attractive, not repellent.

Here is a case of astonishing consensus across ideological lines, and yet there is little concern expressed in the American evangelical community. In the interests of money, personal ease, and personal spiritual renewal, we turn a blank stare on sisters and brothers in Christ in China. We are, perhaps, so inoculated and deadened by our culture that we simply do not care, or we believe there is nothing we can do. Our government, as a government, cannot be trusted to be about the work of the church of Jesus Christ. But does not this task involve concern for non-Christians as well as Christians?

James has consistently taught that our relationship with God shapes character, and character influences and even determines our actions, perhaps especially how we treat others.[41] The mutually implicatory character of these

---

40. Robert L. Borosage, "China Syndrome," *The Nation* (June 9, 1997), 6–7.

41. Luther captured this idea perfectly. The great Luther scholar and Stanford professor, Lewis W. Spitz, put it this way (*The Protestant Reformation: 1517–1559* [New York: Harper and Row, 1985], 86):

The Christian lives by faith alone, a faith which is trust in Christ (*fiducia*) not merely belief (*credulitas*). It must be the individual's personal faith (*fides explicita*), not a general agreement with the facts of the biblical account (*fides historica*) or acquiescence in the stand of the church (*fides implicita*). Faith is the life of the heart (*via cordis*) which unsettles poise and insists upon man's transformation, growth in holiness of life. Luther hoped to be known as the doctor of good works (*doctor operum bonorum*). The man of faith produces good works; it is not the works that make man good, as Aristotle argues in the *Nicomachaean Ethics*. Man is at the same time righteous and a sinner (*simul justus et peccator*); he is righteous in God's eyes when forgiven for Christ's sake, yet while on the earth he remains partially a sinner in his own eyes and in those of his neighbor. He is justified in hope, sinner in reality (*justus in spe, peccator in re*). Nevertheless, man

two dynamics is aptly captured by Oscar Romero in a passage in which he speaks of the liberating power of the gospel:

> The church's social teaching tells everyone that the Christian religion does not have a merely horizontal meaning, or a merely spiritualistic meaning that overlooks the wretchedness that surrounds it. It is a looking at God, and from God at one's neighbor as a brother or sister, and an awareness that "whatever you did to one of these, you did to me." ... It would be worthless to have economic liberation in which all the poor had their own house, their own money, but were all sinners, their hearts estranged from God. What good would it be? There are nations at present that are economically and socially quite advanced, for example those of northern Europe, and yet how much vice and excess![42]

James argues for faith as a "life of the heart," which unsettles poise and insists on our transformation. Do we use our wealth and influence for peace and justice? Do we care about our brothers and sisters in Christ throughout the world? Do we allow the Holy Spirit and Scripture to "unsettle" us and pursue the truth wherever it leads? If our eyes were "suddenly to open," what would we see? James has compared the sin of the landowners to the sin of Cain. It is a sin far more grievous than they had imagined. They were to weep and wail for the misery that was about to befall them.

The power and peril of wealth: judgment. James pronounces a stern warning to the wealthy. He does not condemn wealth as such. Rather, he condemns an attitude toward wealth that deadens the wealthy towards others and causes them to live in excess even as their brothers and sisters are in need. Jesus offered a similar warning of judgment when he spoke of the sheep and the goats in Matthew 25:31–46. Ezekiel spoke of the judgment and destruction of Sodom:

> Now this was the sin of your sister Sodom: She and her daughters were arrogant, overfed and unconcerned; they did not help the poor and needy. They were haughty and did detestable things before me. Therefore I did away with them as you have seen. (Ezek. 16:49–50)

James warns us that our bent to ignore God and others while enjoying material goods and that our desire for money render us open to misery and

---

can and should grow in holiness of life or sanctification. The most prominent emphases in Luther's ethics were responsibility, gratitude, and stewardship, as expressions of love of God and fellow man, the neighbor in need of love.

42. Oscar Romero, *The Violence of Love*, 3, 10.

judgment. The idea of judgment in the New Testament is enormously complex; it includes both chastening judgment, which has as its aim restoration (1 Cor. 11:32), and separation from God and eternal destruction (John 3:19; Heb. 10:27). It is unclear which James has in mind, but neither is to be coveted. At the very least the "misery" he imagines is the realization that the wealth and the material goods in which we have trusted have turned; they have proved untrustworthy, having rotted before our eyes.

But we should not forget that Jesus taught a lesson as hard and difficult as flint. Some who call him "Lord, Lord" he will not recognize on the Day of Judgment, because they did not offer the cup of cool water to another person in need (Matt. 25:31–46). To those whom he does not recognize the King will say, "Depart from me, you who are cursed, into the eternal fire prepared for the devil and his angels" (v. 41).

James does not condemn riches per se, but rather the fact that the wealthy have not sought to use their wealth to alleviate the sufferings of the poor. American evangelicals are wealthy, satiated, and at ease. So the appeal of James resounds across the centuries to our ears. We must open our eyes to the Scriptures and our ears to God, and we must prayerfully consider how best to use our money. Our failure to act, says James, is a sin more grievous than we have imagined.

James 5:7-11

🌿

BE PATIENT, THEN, brothers, until the Lord's coming. See how the farmer waits for the land to yield its valuable crop and how patient he is for the autumn and spring rains. ⁸You too, be patient and stand firm, because the Lord's coming is near. ⁹Don't grumble against each other, brothers, or you will be judged. The Judge is standing at the door!

¹⁰Brothers, as an example of patience in the face of suffering, take the prophets who spoke in the name of the Lord. ¹¹As you know, we consider blessed those who have persevered. You have heard of Job's perseverance and have seen what the Lord finally brought about. The Lord is full of compassion and mercy.

FROM THIS POINT to the end of the letter is the last major section of James. It has much in common with the section immediately preceding it, including, not insignificantly, an eschatological orientation. The present section is concerned with a call to patience. The next section (5:12–18) has to do with general issues regarding the health of the church (oaths, prayer, sickness). The final section (5:19–20) is a call to the church members to do just what James has done in this letter: call back to faith those who have wandered.

James 5:7–11 is a call to patient living under adverse circumstances. The root word for patience, *makrothymeo*, occurs four times in these five verses. Another term, *hypomone*, which the NIV renders as "perseverance," occurs twice. These two words are close parallels, and in Colossians 1:11 are virtual synonyms. The root *makrothymeo* carries the idea of waiting with calm and expectancy, and the words associated with *hypomone* convey the sense of patient endurance and fortitude.

This passage consists of one tight argument, but with three discernible components. In the first (vv. 7–8) James calls us to patience and provides an example from everyday life. He draws the conclusion that we too should be patient. Next (v. 9) James affirms that patience must be mixed with the harmony that results from controlled speech and behavior; thus he counsels against complaining about one another. In the final section (vv. 10–11) he returns to the issue of patience, citing the biblical examples of the prophets and Job.

The passage also offers an interesting bit of Christology. In verses 10 and 11 James uses the word *kyrios* in reference to the Old Testament examples of Job and the prophets. This word here must refer to God. But in 5:7 James has used the phrase *parousias tou kyriou* ("the Lord's coming"), and it is difficult to see how this phrase can be applied to anyone other than Jesus Christ. Jesus Christ, in other words, is Lord!

The Call to Patience (5:7–8)

As FRANCIS HAS convincingly argued, these verses begin the closing section of the letter.[1] Yet there is much that binds it with previous ones, especially the return of the term "brothers," which James here as elsewhere uses to remind his readers that although he has offered them strong rebuke, he is their brother and they are all one in Christ. While in 5:1–6 the emphasis is on the wealthy, here the lion's share of James's thought is directed to the poor.

Christians are enjoined to be patient until the Lord comes (*parousia tou kuriou;* lit., "coming of the Lord"). The use of *parousia* here signals the expected return of Jesus, and so "Lord," a term often and most recently used in James (5:4) to refer to God, here refers to Jesus. While we are on ground too infirm to build a grand Christological edifice, the implication should not be missed. Many argue that James is wholly without Christology. While it is an accurate assessment that Christological concerns and language are largely absent from James, here a statement of high Christology is present. This *parousia* will include Jesus Christ's setting the oppressed free (cf. Luke 4:16–21). But the waiting is a long process, and in its difficult shoals the temptation to criticize will be overpowering. For this reason James offers for consideration a series of illustrations.

As a practical illustration of such patience, James refers to a farmer who waits patiently for harvest time and for the autumn and spring rains. In the eastern Mediterranean two seasons of rain are normal and necessary for a successful crop.[2] The emphasis here is double, not only on patience, but also on the surety of the farmer that the rains and the harvest will indeed come, each in its due season. This waiting is hard psychologically, for in the presence of the vagaries of weather that determine the success of the crop, the farmer is helpless. But the waiting also involves a good deal of hard work and encounters with the vicissitudes of normal existence.

In a similar manner the Christian and the Christian community must wait patiently for the coming of the Lord, for nothing can be done to speed the

---

1. Fred O. Francis, "The Form and Function of the Opening and Closing Paragraphs of James and 1 John," *ZNW* 61 (1970): 110–16.

2. Cf. Mishnah, *Taanith* 1.1–7, which refers to this.

parousia on its way. The waiting is often hard. Difficulties within the community must be dealt with, and the correct understanding and practice of the faith and works dynamic must be taught and maintained. It is easily misunderstood, as the letter itself demonstrates. Certainly James is calling on Christians to allow God to judge the wicked. To arrogate to ourselves this task is to call down God's judgment on ourselves.

Verse 8 recalls the Markan account of the opening of Jesus' ministry, as both use the same verb, *engizo*. The perfect tense of this verb, *engiken*, is ambiguous, in part because the language of nearness involves ambiguity. When Judas "drew near" to kiss Jesus, he made contact with Jesus. So *engiken* can mean "is coming shortly" (as it does here), or it can mean "has arrived." This ambiguity is intentional in Mark 1:15, where Jesus announces: "The time has come. . . . The kingdom of God is near." Of course *parousia* in James 5:7 is a technical term indicating the coming of Christ. Although the evidence is mounting that the early church did not anticipate the imminent return of Christ,[3] it must be admitted that this conclusion cannot be dismissed out of hand.

Furthermore, in the phrase "until the Lord comes," the word "until" (*eos*) can carry not only the nuance of time, but also of purpose. Whether or not James envisioned an imminent return of Christ, perhaps the point here is that as Christians we are to live in community one with another as if the new day has already dawned. This second reading is not inconsistent with the general sweep of the New Testament.[4] This idea reminds James's readers that every day ought to be lived with the same devotion to Christian principles and morals as if it were the last day. Otherwise, we will be guilty of sloth "in the day of slaughter" (5:5).

Avoid Complaining (5:9)

IF WE ARE correct in seeing that this section has as its primary audience the poor, who suffer the darts and lethal indifference of the merchants (cf. 4:13–17) and the landed gentry (cf. 5:1–6), then in verse 9 James has a warning for them as well: In spite of the abuse you have enured, do not grumble. The key term here, as Davids notes,[5] is *kat' allelon* ("against each other"). James reminds the poor that the wealthy, so often the self-imposed enemies of the poor, are sisters and brothers, fellow believers in Christ. Even understandable

---

3. Marcus Borg, "An Orthodoxy Reconsidered: The 'End of the World Jesus,'" *The Glory of Christ in the New Testament: Essays in Christology in Memory of George Bradford Caird*, eds. L. D. Hurst and N. T. Wright (Oxford: Clarendon, 1987), 207–17.

4. See G. B. Caird and L. D. Hurst, *New Testament Theology* (Oxford: Clarendon 1994), 32–33.

5. Peter H. Davids, *The Epistle of James*, 184–85.

feelings of enmity for what they may have suffered at the hands of the indifferent wealthy lays the poor open to judgment. Only Christ, the Judge, has the right so to criticize. Internal bickering is an evil that can easily beset and occupy the church, thereby preventing it from its primary task.

Life does bring trials, of course, but no one is served by the cultivation of a spirit of complaining. James would have us remember 3:16 and 4:2, that complaining leads not to peace but to disorder, nor does it do anything to alleviate the real problem. James buttresses his point by reminding his readers that judgment is coming and that he has already enjoined them in the name of the Judge from speaking any kind of evil one against another (4:11).

Biblical Examples of Patience (5:10–11)

JAMES CLEARLY EXPECTS his readers to be familiar with biblical examples of patient suffering.[6] The prophets as the messengers of God experienced suffering.[7] But they endured, patiently and hopefully waiting for the judgment and the mercy of God. Laws notes the growing tradition of the prophets as martyrs, but also comments that only Zechariah son of Jehoiada (see 1 Chron. 24:20–22) met a violent death.[8] Of course, one can be a martyr without suffering persecution unto death. The prophets "spoke in the name of the Lord," which indicates that in this world those who assume the name of God as their banner will suffer.

Such a course of action also brings with it the high honor and regard of earning the label "blessed" (v. 11). The grammar of this verse suggests that this "blessedness" is reserved for those who have been found faithful to the end. Of course, it might also be the case that our intoning the judgment of such "blessedness" must wait until the end, while someone like Job enjoyed its experience while still alive. But perhaps primary in James's mind is that those who have gone into the presence of God with such a life of perseverance are truly "blessed." The idea that blessedness is a reward for those who endure is widely represented in the New Testament and is found on the lips of Jesus as well (Matt. 5:10–12; 23:29–36).

From the example of the prophets James turns to the specific example of Job. This choice seems odd to many interpreters, for Job complained bitterly

---

6. This is obvious. It also confirms our earlier decision to see the landowners of 5:1–6 as members of the Christian community and familiar enough with the Old Testament to see in their own behavior a parallel to the wealthy castigated by the prophets.

7. Similar sentiments regarding himself and his people were not infrequently on the lips of Jesus, even as he anticipated his own final persecution and death (see Matt. 23:37; Luke 9:22).

8. Sophie Laws, *The Epistle of James*, 214.

to God.[9] They posit that James may have been thinking of the apocryphal *Testament of Job*, in which Job is patient while his wife does the complaining. There is much that commends this hypothesis.[10] But while attractive, it accepts a too simple reading of Job. In fact, Job remains faithful to the picture of God he possessed, and he questioned only the accuracy of that picture. Like some of the psalmists,[11] Job's complaint to God was a complaint born out of faith. As a result of his sufferings, he gained greater knowledge of God, which may indeed be God's purpose and the hope James has as the result of the sufferings that are the background to this passage.

James employs a phrase that has occasioned no little speculation. The phrase the NIV renders *to telos kuriou eidete* as "you . . . have seen what the Lord finally brought about," is better translated "the end [*to telos*] of the Lord you saw." It is possible that *to telos* here refers either to Jesus' crucifixion[12] or to his *parousia*, so that one can "see" what has yet to happen, just as the prophets could see the coming catastrophe.[13]

However, it is more likely that *to telos* refers to the "purpose" or "plan" of the Lord.[14] The death and resurrection of Jesus as the conclusion of this plan may be said to encapsulate the entire design, but we are on safer ground if we simply point to the plan as a whole. The plan of the Lord in the life of the believer, as James has been at great pains to point out, is to live a life of Christian virtue based on accurate teaching. The successful pursuit of such a course of action will lead to being called "blessed." Suffering is used by God to produce Christians who are mature, who understand the dynamic of faith and deeds, and who pursue peace and not disorder.

Finally, the purpose and plan of God includes his "compassion and mercy." We have seen these themes before (4:6), but James knows that human beings are not only in constant need of the assurance of grace and forgiveness, but also in constant need of the fact of God's grace and forgiveness.

---

9. See the argument in Ralph P. Martin, *James*, 194 (though Martin does not have sympathy with this view).

10. There are four chief reasons. (1) The term *hypomone* ("perseverance") and its cognates, which appear in 5:11, are prominent in James (1:3, 4, 12), yet occur only once in Job in the LXX (14:9), and even then it is not clear that it refers to Job. However, *hypomone* and its cognate forms are frequent in the *Testament of Job*. (2) In the *Testament of Job* the complaints are found on the lips of his wife, but not on those of Job. (3) The testing is portrayed as parallel to the testing of Abraham and is clearly satanic. (4) The charity of Job is stressed.

11. See, for example, Ps. 6 or Ps. 69:1, in which the psalmist declares, "Save me, O God, for the waters have come up to my neck." In these, and other "psalms of lament," the psalmist wonders if God hears his cry and if God will be true to the covenant and answer.

12. Augustine surmised that this referred to the death of Jesus; see Martin, *James*, 195.

13. See the discussion on pp. 269–70.

14. See Caird and Hurst, *New Testament Theology*, 27–30. *Telos* can mean both "end" in the sense of termination and "end" in the sense of goal.

Bridging Contexts

JAMES FOCUSES HERE on patience in the context of adversity and on the need to avoid judging others, specifically the ones causing the adversity. The picture is made both more interesting and more difficult in that he has chosen to employ the language of eschatology to make his point: "Be patient, then, brothers, until the Lord's coming" (5:7). This introduces the question of the role that eschatological language plays in this passage.

The question of the imminent *parousia* ("appearance") or return of Christ is one of the thorniest in the New Testament. On the one hand, a number of passages seem to suggest that Jesus and the early Christians believed in an imminent *parousia*. Some scholars argue that Paul in 1 Thessalonians clearly believes that the *parousia* is about to occur, and that therefore 2 Thessalonians must not be Pauline, since it posits a different eschatological scheme.[15] On the other hand, there is the incontrovertible fact that the *parousia* has yet to take place. What does the New Testament teach on this issue?

The difficulty begins with the meaning of the word "eschatology" itself.[16] The *Oxford English Dictionary* of 1891 and 1933 defines it as "the department of theological science concerned with the four last things, death, judgement, heaven, and hell." This classic definition is essentially concerned with the fate of the individual. In more recent years the word has come to refer to the destiny of the world. The difficulty, then, is that we employ one word to describe two very different forms of understanding the future: the one individual and the other cosmic.

This difficulty is further compounded by two other matters: the uses of eschatological language and the eschatological beliefs of Jesus. Eschatological language is enormously flexible and is often used to describe a variety of other doctrines, much as an overnight envelope can carry a wide variety of types of correspondence. Isaiah, for instance, had a vision of the restoration of Paradise, in which the wolf and the lamb will live together, the leopard will lie down with the goat, the cow will feed the bear and their young will lie down together, the lion will eat straw, and a child will play with a cobra (Isa. 11:1–9). The vision is cast in what we would call eschatological language; but it is not about eschatology, but rather about an ideal earthly kingdom. Eschatological language is here used to describe a future historical hope.

---

15. See, for example, R. H. Fuller, *A Critical Introduction to the New Testament* (London: Duckworth, 1966), 57–58. But R. Jewett, in his *The Thessalonian Correspondence: Pauline Rhetoric and Millenarian Piety* (Philadelphia: Fortress, 1986), 16–18, summarizing the work of many others, has effectively argued for Pauline authorship of both letters.

16. Caird and Hurst, *New Testament Theology*, 243 (for a full discussion of the issue see 243–67).

An even more clear example is found in Isaiah 13, a passage that contains a description of the Day of the Lord and employs eschatological language:

See, the day of the LORD is coming
    —a cruel day, with wrath and fierce anger—
to make the land desolate
    and destroy the sinners within it.
The stars of heaven and their constellations
    will not show their light.
The rising sun will be darkened
    and the moon will not give its light.
I will punish the world for its evil,
    the wicked for their sins.
I will put an end to the arrogance of the haughty
    and will humble the pride of the ruthless. (Isa. 13:9–11)

Although cast in typically eschatological language, the wider context makes clear that Isaiah is speaking of the coming invasion of the Medes. The prophets, then, were able to picture historical crises in the language of eschatology, because each crisis was a dress rehearsal for the ultimate crisis, when the nation faced the questions of life and death.

Jesus also spoke in these terms. In Luke 17:20–24 he said:

The kingdom of God does not come with your careful observation, nor will people say, "Here it is," or "There it is," because the kingdom of God is within you.

. . . The time is coming when you will long to see one of the days of the Son of Man, but you will not see it. Men will tell you, "There he is!" or "Here he is!" Do not go running off after them. For the Son of Man in his day will be like the lightning, which flashes and lights up the sky from one end to the other.

On the one hand, Jesus said that there will be no signs; yet on the other, there will be signs across the heavens. The conundrum is resolved when we realize that Jesus was speaking of two different realities—one historical, the other that of eschatological hope.

Luke 21 makes this even more explicit. In this chapter Jesus predicts wars and rumors of wars, and armies surrounding Jerusalem. The chapter ends with the prediction of the coming of the Son of Man and the saying that "this generation will certainly not pass away until all these things have happened" (21:32). But Jesus also counsels his followers to attempt to "escape all that is about to happen" (21:36). He could not have been so naive as to suggest that his followers could escape the final consummation of the kingdom, for there is no escape from this. The answer, of course, is that like the Old Testament prophets, Jesus is using eschatological language to discuss both historical events and the final denouement of history—that is, the coming destruction of Jerusalem and his *parousia*.

This means that, Schweitzer to the contrary, Jesus did not envision an imminent *parousia*. Schweitzer's misguided picture of an "end-of-the-world" Jesus led him to believe that Jesus preached an impractical ethical system for this brief interim (*Interimsethik*), which could never serve for an extended period.[17] While Schweitzer was wrong about the return of Christ, his recognition that the ethic preached by Christ was to be in force is sound. Those who follow Jesus are to live as if the kingdom were already fully realized.

In the present case the reference to the Lord's return is not so much about the *parousia* as it serves the interests of the spiritual life. James knows that the promise of the return of the Lord gives hope to those who are suffering. The spirituals of African-American slaves betray this same spirit. Songs like "I Am Bound for the Promised Land"[18] and "Steal Away"[19] emphasize the expectation of heaven in order to divert attention from the hell of earthly existence.[20] James wishes the poor to do more than wait expectantly for the Lord's coming. He wants them to take advantage of this time of suffering. For this reason he uses the image of the farmer, who waits patiently during the growing season, knowing that this is the only sure route to harvest.

I spent a part of my childhood on my uncle's grain farm in the Sacramento Valley of California. Each October my uncle planted wheat and oats, and through the long winter he watched as the plants sprouted, and then grew strong and tall. Finally, in the heat of June, he began harvest. The end

---

17. See L. D. Hurst, "The Ethics of Jesus," *DJG*, 210.
18. I am bound for the promised land;
    I am bound for the promised land:
    O, who will come and go with me?
    I am bound for the promised land.
19. Steal away, steal away,
    Steal away to Jesus,
    Steal away, steal away home,
    I ain't got long to stay here.
20. Albert J. Raboteau, *Slave Religion: The "Invisible Institution" in the Antebellum South* (New York: Oxford Univ. Press, 1978), notes that slave owners and even missionaries believed that the otherworldly emphasis of Christianity rendered a force for docility among slaves (290). However, Raboteau goes on to say, Christianity has often been the seedbed of subversion on moral grounds. Raboteau cites the case of the slave Henry Atkinson, who said, "I heard the white minister preach, and I thought within myself, I will seek a better world—here I am in bondage, and if there is a better world above, where I shall not be pulled and hauled about and tormented, as I am in this, I will seek it." But Raboteau also notes that Henry Atkinson made good on an escape attempt (303–4).

result was the harvest, but the harvest was not possible without the growth accomplished during the long hard months of winter. So it is with the spiritual life. Our destiny is to be with Christ, but it is often in the crucible of difficulty that God prepares us for that day. James uses the example of the prophets and of Job, persons whose lives were marked by difficult circumstances they often did not understand, but in which God forged their spiritual character. James, as my wife says, desires us to shift our attention from what is happening to us to what God is forming in us.

But the language of eschatology may serve another correlative function in this passage. James has here discussed judgment. The New Testament generally links ethics with a positive image—for instance, when Paul says that God desires that we be "conformed to the likeness of his Son" (Rom. 8:29). But here James is not reticent to apply the image of the Judge who is about to arrive. He has already given similar warnings of sudden reckoning unlooked for, employing the image of a fragile flower that withers in the heat of the day (James 1:11) or of wealth that has become worthless in the storehouse (5:2–3).

Nor is James alone in this. Jesus uttered a stern warning of eschatological judgment based on acts of compassion (Matt. 25:31–46), and he could offer a more positive inducement: "Be merciful, just as your Father is merciful" (Luke 6:36). James hopes that the believers to whom he writes will remember the generosity of God (James 1:5), in whose name they belong (2:7), and will live lives of humility and compassion, just as did Jesus. But he is not afraid to remind them, when necessary, that God is also the Judge. Given the consequences, this is less a threat than it is the warning shout of a dear friend. Nor should it be forgotten that eschatological judgment is two-sided, comprised of both damnation and the promised reward.

 JAMES CONCENTRATES ON two teachings here. (1) Patience is important because it allows for Christian growth in the midst of difficult times. (2) We should not judge others, even if they are the source of the difficulties we face. Both of these have applications in our lives.

Patience. James argues for patience because he wants us to wait for the Lord's coming, and as was the case with Job and the prophets, our character is forged on the anvil of difficulty. It is not surprising that eschatological teaching should be found in close correspondence with teaching concerning patience during difficulties, because "eschatology arises out of the clash between faith in a benevolent purpose of God and the harsh facts of a ruthless world."[21]

---

21. Caird and Hurst, *New Testament Theology*, 244.

People in times of trouble naturally hope for release, and there is no doubt that many of the early Christians hoped for release from this world in the form of Christ's return. Certainly a variety of events in that first century created a burgeoning of eschatological excitement in each weary breast. Palestine knew "wars and rumors of wars," as Jesus had predicted (Mark 13:7), which had their devastating appearance in the Jewish war of A.D. 66–70. Caligula declared his intention to erect a statue of himself in the temple in Jerusalem, which must have seemed a fulfillment of "the abomination that causes desolation" (cf. 13:14). But James uses the language of eschatology in order to prepare his readers for spiritual growth. Within the history of Christian spirituality, difficult circumstances (a) are considered a normal and necessary part of the process of spiritual growth, (b) require a certain attitude in order to be dealt with most effectively, and (c) bear certain results.

Difficulties are normal and necessary. John of the Cross and Theophan the Recluse are examples of the widespread belief that suffering is a normal and even necessary part of the spiritual lives of Christians. John of the Cross was born in Castille in 1542 and became a Carmelite monk in 1564. Theresa of Avila placed him in charge of the order, and through this position as well as his writings, he became prominent in the Catholic reform movement. He was later arrested and put in confinement by those who opposed him, and during this period he wrote his *The Dark Night of the Soul.* The book describes the fashion in which God works on the human soul, through sorrow and darkness, not only through joy and light. He wrote:

> Into this dark night souls begin to enter when God draws them forth from the state of beginners—which is the state of those that meditate on the spiritual road—and begins to set them in the state of progressives—which is that of those who are already contemplatives ... to the end that we may better understand and explain what night is this through which the soul passes, and for what cause God sets it therein, it will be well here to touch first of all upon certain characteristics of beginners. ... it must be known, then, that the soul, after it has been definitely converted to the service of God, is, as a rule, spiritually nurtured and caressed by God, even as is the tender child by its loving mother, who warms it with the heart of her bosom and nurtures it with sweet milk and soft and pleasant food, and carries it and caresses it in her arms; but, as the child grows bigger, the mother gradually ceases caressing it, and, hiding her tender love, puts bitter aloes upon her sweet breast, sets down the child from her arms and makes it walk upon its feet, so that it may lose the habits of a child and betake itself to more important and substantial occupations. The loving mother is

like the grace of God, for, as soon as the soul is regenerated by its new warmth and fervour for the service of God . . . it will be seen how many blessings the dark night of which we shall afterwards treat brings with it, since it cleanses the soul and purifies it from all these imperfections.[22]

John clearly understood that what we perceive as difficulty and trial God can and does use for his purposes and our spiritual growth, even if we find the experience painful and distressing. This is a theme James introduced in chapter 1.

For Theophan the Recluse, suffering was a necessity and should be expected.

It must be realized that the true sign of spiritual endeavour and the price of success in it is suffering. One who proceeds without suffering will bear no fruit. . . . Every struggle in the soul's training, whether physical or mental, that is not accompanied by suffering, that does not require the utmost effort, will bear no fruit. . . . Many people have worked and continue to work without pain, but because of its absence they are strangers to purity. . . .[23]

The proper attitudes. Among the several attitudes necessary for correctly perceiving adversity as an opportunity for spiritual growth are three represented by Thomas Merton, Henri Nouwen, and Catherine of Genoa.

One of the difficulties we moderns have with the spiritual disciplines is our addiction to ease and to "feeling good." But how we "feel" has little, if anything, to do with the spiritual benefit of a situation. Thomas Merton makes this point well in his *Contemplative Prayer*:

If we bear with hardship in prayer and wait patiently for the time of grace, we may well discover that meditation and prayer are very joyful experiences. We should not, however, judge the value of our meditation by "how we feel." A hard and apparently fruitless meditation may in fact be much more valuable than one that is easy, happy, enlightened, and apparently a big success.[24]

Another deadly force relative to spiritual maturity is the allure of our world. Henri Nouwen argues that great determination is needed in order to overcome this peril. Nouwen was a Catholic priest, and until his death in

---

22. John of the Cross, *The Dark Night of the Soul*, 1.1–3.

23. Theophan the Recluse, quoted in *A Guide to Prayer for Ministers and Other Servants*, eds. Reuben P. Job and Norman Shawchuck (Nashville: The Upper Room, 1983), 113–14.

24. Thomas Merton, *Contemplative Prayer* (Garden City, N.Y.: Doubleday [Image Books], 1971), 34.

1997 was loved by Catholics and evangelicals alike for his writings on and example of the spiritual life. In his book *Making All Things New*, Nouwen argues that God gets our attention and saves us from the allure of the world by encouraging us to deny the priorities of the world and to summon up our stern resolve and determined effort:

> The spiritual life is a gift. It is the gift of the Holy Spirit, who lifts us up into the kingdom of God's love. But to say that being lifted up into the kingdom of love is a divine gift does not mean that we wait patiently until the gift is offered to us.
>
> Jesus tells us to set our hearts on the kingdom. Setting our hearts on something involves not only our serious aspiration but also strong determination. A spiritual life requires human effort. The forces that keep pulling us back into a worry-filled life are far from easy to overcome.
>
> "How hard it is," Jesus exclaims, "to enter the kingdom of God!" (Mark 10:23, JB). And to convince us of the need for hard work, he says, "If anyone wants to be a follower of mine, let him renounce himself and take up his cross and follow me" (Matt. 16:24, JB).[25]

Nouwen, like James, tells us that active patience is needed.

Similarly, Catherine of Genoa encourages us to throw ourselves into the arms of God and not to rely on worldly possessions. Her biography bears out the truth of her words. Catherine was born into a prosperous and important religious family in 1447. In 1463 she married a man committed to wealth and its increase, and this was the source of no little tension. But when her husband lost the bulk of his fortune, the two of them decided to live and work among the poor in Genoa. In this life she found greater joy and fulfillment than when she enjoyed wealth and ease. Her main work is called *Life and Teachings*, and in it she writes:

> I . . . saw others who were fighting against their evil inclinations and forcing themselves to resist them. But I saw that the more they struggled against them, the more they committed them. So I said to them, "You are right in lamenting your sins and imperfections, and I would be lamenting with you if it were not for the fact that God is holding me. You cannot defend yourself and I cannot defend myself. The thing we must do is renounce the care of ourselves unto God, who can defend our true self. Only then can God do for us what we cannot do for ourselves."
>
> As to the renouncing of ourselves, I told them, "Take a piece of bread and eat it. When you have eaten it, its substance goes into you

---

25. Henri J. M. Nouwen, *Making All Things New: An Invitation to the Spiritual Life* (San Francisco: Harper and Row, 1981), 65–66.

to nourish the body and the rest is eliminated because your body no longer needs it. For the body is more important than the bread; it was created as a means, but it is not to remain forever with us. Likewise, we must remove all evil inclinations from our bodies; they cannot live on within us, lest we die."[26]

According to Catherine, the world and material goods cannot compare with joy that comes with spiritual growth. This is a lesson that cuts with keen and sharp agility, piercing to the heart of the materialistic American ethos.

The results of perseverance through adversity. Patience in adversity brings benefits, argues James. Many of the giants of Christian spirituality agree. Thomas à Kempis notes that perseverance in adversity cleanses us, Benedict of Nursia shows that it creates humility, and Malcolm Muggeridge argues that it allows us to minister to others.

Thomas à Kempis became a monk at the age of nineteen in 1399. His great spiritual treatise, *The Imitation of Christ*, is his most significant work (though some believe that it was written by Gerhard Groote and edited by Thomas). In the following passage Thomas discusses the usefulness of difficulties:

> And yet, temptations can be useful to us even though they seem to cause us nothing but pain. They are useful because they can make us humble, they can cleanse us, and they can teach us. All of the saints passed through times of temptation and tribulation, and they used them to make progress in the spiritual life. ... No one is completely free of temptations because the source of temptation is in ourselves. ... We cannot win this battle by running away alone; the key to victory is true humility and patience; in them we overcome the enemy.[27]

Benedict of Nursia was born in A.D. 480, and in 529 he founded a monastery at Monte Cassino. Christianity had been made the favored religion of the empire by Constantine more than a century earlier, and Benedict saw that already the faith had begun to be mixed with the secular. In this context Benedict wrote *The Rule*, a justly famous set of disciplines for the spiritual life. In the following passage Benedict writes on the spiritual fruit of humility. He sees affliction and difficulty as one of the tools God uses to develop this trait in our lives:

> The fourth step of humility is accepting the hardships of the commandments and enduring with patience the injuries and afflictions we face. We are called to endure and not grow weary or give up, but to

---

26. Richard J. Foster and James Bryan Smith (eds.), *Devotional Classic: Selected Readings for Individuals and Groups* (San Francisco: HarperCollins, 1993), 213–14.
27. Thomas à Kempis, *The Imitation of Christ*, 13.2–3.

hold fast. The Scriptures teach us, "They that persevere unto the end shall be saved."

Those who have faith must bear every disagreeable thing for the Lord, keeping in mind the promise, "But in all these things we shall overcome because of Him who loves us." God shall try us by fire just as silver is tried and purified. Our Lord teaches us that when we are struck on one cheek, we must turn the other; when asked for a piece of our clothing, give the whole thing; when asked to go one mile, go two; when we are cursed by others, we must bless them.[28]

How different are we, who wish to see justice rendered unto our enemies, and how weak is our will to forgive.

In a poignantly honest passage Malcolm Muggeridge reflects on the choices he made in life and points out that choosing to remain in conditions that our culture would label crazy allows one to grow in spiritual stature. He writes:

> I ran away and stayed away; Mother Teresa moved in and stayed. That was the difference. She, a nun, rather slightly built, with a few rupees in her pocket; not particularly clever, or particularly gifted in the arts of persuasion. Just with this Christian love shining about her; in her heart and on her lips. Just prepared to follow her Lord, and in accordance with his instructions regard every derelict left to die in the streets as him, to hear in the cry of every abandoned child, even in the tiny squeak of the discarded fetus, the cry of the Bethlehem child; to recognize in every leper's stumps the hands which once touched heads and made them calm, brought back health to sick flesh and twisted limbs. As for my expiations on Bengal's wretched social conditions—I regret to say that I doubt whether, in any divine accounting, they will equal one single quizzical half smile bestowed by Mother Teresa on a street urchin who happened to catch her eye.[29]

Muggeridge points out that one benefit from patient endurance of affliction is that we are granted the opportunity to minister to others who are similarly afflicted. These are hard words, but true. My wife and I have been married for fifteen years and are without children. The physicians say that we will never be able to have children. The manic and unexpected emotions of this painful want are difficult to describe. But my wife and I have been able

---

28. Foster and Smith, *Devotional Classics*, 179.

29. Malcolm Muggeridge, *Something Beautiful for God*, quoted in *A Guide to Prayer for Ministers and Other Servants*, eds. Reuben P. Job and Norman Shawchuck (Nashville: The Upper Room, 1983), 111.

to come alongside others who face similar pain—the pain of a mother whose child died in childbirth, or that of couples who, like ourselves, are without children. I cannot say that we take great comfort in this role, but we have found it to be a role that we can play.

Do not judge. James has already provided teaching on the question of passing judgment (4:11–12), but he does so here again. He warns the poor against taking judgment, even righteous judgment, into their own hands, because the wealthy who have been their oppressors are also their brothers and sisters in Christ. The call of James is to love these brothers and sisters in the concrete, not just in the abstract. This is no light task. Eric Hoffer, the San Francisco longshoreman-philosopher made famous in the 1960s, once observed, "It is easier to love humanity than to love your neighbor."[30]

One of the striking issues in this passage is that the wealthy who have exploited the poor have not even asked for forgiveness, and yet James urges the poor to forgive. This is one of the most difficult issues that faces a human being. In her remarkable novel *The River Beyond the World*, Janet Peery touches on this theme. The novel is the story of Luisa, who as a young girl lives with her mother and with Chavela, her aunt. Chavela is often cruel, especially to Luisa.

> Once, when her mother was grinding corn, Luisa asked why Chavela was so mean. "Hearts are made two ways," her mother said. "Some are full with what they're given, no matter how small, and others can't forget what they can't have."
>
> "She's mean," Luisa insisted. "And that's a sin."
>
> Her mother stopped to cool the mano, then sprinkled kernels onto the metate and blew on them to give them courage. She shook her head. "Forgive her."
>
> "She never asks."
>
> Her mother shook her arms, then resumed rolling. The corn crunched between the stones. "All the more reason."[31]

There is great wisdom in this passage. Yeats once said that a life of such compassion and denial eventually deadens the spirit—"Too long a sacrifice / Can make a stone of the heart"[32]—but Yeats had not considered the heart that is full of service to God. Luisa is justified in her anger and condemnation of Chavela, for she is a cruel and undeserving aunt. It would be unnatural for Luisa to forgive her aunt, yet her mother wisely offers such counsel.

---

30. Eric Hoffer, interview with Eric Severeid of CBS News (Nov. 14, 1967).
31. Janet Peery, *The River Beyond the World* (New York: Picador, 1996), 9.
32. W. B. Yeats, "Easter, 1916," lines 57–58.

A murderer who confesses and seems to display signs of remorse moves us, generally, to the serious consideration of leniency. After all, we all have erred, we all have had irrational impulses, and we all can, perhaps, imagine ourselves in a similar position. But a remorseless criminal earns our hatred and our irrational fear, for we cannot conceive of such a brazen and indifferent attitude. So it is with these wealthy in James 5. They may be vaguely aware that some of their poor employees have died as a result of their demand for luxurious ease (as 5:6 suggests). But they have no notion of the individuals they have harmed. In such cases it is usual for the wronged and maligned to desire some measure of vengeance, but James forbids it. To demand vengeance is to be guilty of the very crime committed against them. "The Judge," James says, "is standing at the door!" (5:9).

James says that God does not wish us to condemn one another. Behind this statement stands another reason, namely, that we can too easily become guilty of the same sins ourselves. We are to be patient and refrain from condemnation, for each is a necessary ingredient for the spiritual journey to which James calls us. To condemn is to sink to the level of those who perpetrate wrong. To endure with patience is to set one's feet on the path to spiritual maturity.

James 5:12–18

⚘

ABOVE ALL, MY brothers, do not swear—not by heaven or by earth or by anything else. Let your "Yes" be yes, and your "No," no, or you will be condemned. [13]Is any one of you in trouble? He should pray. Is anyone happy? Let him sing songs of praise. [14]Is any one of you sick? He should call the elders of the church to pray over him and anoint him with oil in the name of the Lord. [15]And the prayer offered in faith will make the sick person well; the Lord will raise him up. If he has sinned, he will be forgiven. [16]Therefore confess your sins to each other and pray for each other so that you may be healed. The prayer of a righteous man is powerful and effective.

[117]Elijah was a man just like us. He prayed earnestly that it would not rain, and it did not rain on the land for three and a half years. [18]Again he prayed, and the heavens gave rain, and the earth produced its crops.

JAMES IS ABOUT to conclude his letter. As he does so, he focuses on three themes present in the beginning of his letter: speech, prayer, and suffering. Just as the letter began with a double opening, James presents us with something of a double ending. In 5:7–11 he discussed trials, rich versus poor, and pure speech, three themes that have dominated the letter as a whole. Now he places a cap on his discussion by emphasizing pure speech (prayer) and its power in times of adversity.

Verses 12–18 have two natural sections. Verse 12 is an injunction against the making of oaths, while verses 13–18 concern prayer. The passage moves from the situation of one who is suffering, to one who is joyful, back to one who is suffering. What binds the entire passage together is that both sections have to do with our address of God and with the use of the tongue.

The Taking of Oaths (5:12)

"ABOVE ALL" (PRO *panton*) means "most importantly" or "but especially." However, given the care with which James has developed other themes—for example, the great stress he has placed on patience—it would be odd indeed if James were saying that his message concerning oaths he regards as the single most important in the entire letter.[1] Rather, the term ought to be understood as "finally" or "to sum up"; that is, James is alerting his readers that the letter is about to conclude.

Any attempt to defend the present placement of this saying must show how it connects either with what has gone before or with what comes after. As many have noted, this logion appears out of place. However, when seen as an inappropriate use of the tongue in contradistinction to the proper uses pointed out in 5:13–18, it is clear that this verse has a rightful place here. This, of course, connects the verse with what comes after. But what about the preceding section? Martin[2] believes that Reicke is correct when he argues that the swearing of oaths is a sign of the impatience displayed by the poor who live under the cavalier and unchristian treatment of the wealthy in their community. Since James has counseled these poor to be patient and to wait for the deliverance of God, Reicke's insight may well be accurate.

The point at issue in this verse is the taking of an oath, that is, invoking the name of God in order to buttress the truthfulness of what one has said. Here James is fully in line with the teaching of the Old Testament that false swearing and the giving of oaths is forbidden. Leviticus 19:12, for instance, says, "Do not swear falsely by my name and so profane the name of your God. I am the LORD" (cf. also Jer. 5:2; Hos. 4:2; Mal. 3:5).

But the issue is not entirely without wrinkle. In Genesis 22:16 God swears by his own name (cf. Heb. 6:13–18). In the passage from Leviticus just cited, "false swearing" is prohibited, leaving "truthful swearing" an open question. In the Ten Commandments the taking of an oath is not strictly prohibited, but it is limited to those matters that one can accomplish (see Ex. 20:7). Here too the issue is to avoid invoking the name of God in an oath that is false. God, after all, is the one whose words always accomplish his purpose (Isa. 55:11). Human beings, on the other hand, utter words that "will not stand up" (8:10) and that "fall to the ground" (1 Sam. 3:19).

To invoke God's name falsely, then, is to involve God in a falsehood. The problem is, of course, that sometimes human beings utter falsehoods knowingly, but at other times we are unable to accomplish what we intend. The prohibition recognizes this and serves to limit and to exclude these unintentional infelicities. Certainly the Old Testament reveals a developing problem with conscious falsehood (see Jer. 5:2; 7:9–10).

But there are other wrinkles on the matter. In Exodus 22:10–11 an oath "before the LORD" is demanded, the point being that such an oath ensures the truthfulness of testimony. It seems, in other words, that the point of the

---

1. See Peter H. Davids, *The Epistle of James*, 189.
2. Ralph P. Martin, *James*, 203.

Scriptures was to avoid using the name of the Lord in an oath concerning the future, because human beings are incapable of assuring that what they promise will come true. This makes sense in the context in James, as James has recently argued that such "certainty" is a sign of godless *hybris* (James 4:13–17). But in the case of testimony concerning past events, the name of the Lord serves as a guarantor of truthfulness.

Judaism developed the idea that the best policy was to avoid the use of the name of God in any oath.[3] Jesus seemed to agree, adding in a startling coda such forms of oath-taking are of satanic origin (Matt. 5:34–37). He also criticized the Pharisees for what he regarded as semantic circumlocutions in the taking of oaths (23:16–22).

There is, in fact, a close similarity between James's and Jesus' teaching in Matthew 5:34–37. The Matthean text is studded with more detail, including every element mentioned by James.

Matthew 5:34–37	James 5:12
Do not swear at all:	Do not swear—
either by heaven, for it is God's throne;	not by heaven,
or by the earth, for it is his footstool;	or by earth
or by Jerusalem, for it is the city of the Great King.	or by anything else
And do not swear by your head, for you cannot make even one hair white or black.	
Simply let your "Yes" be "Yes" and your "No," "No";	Let your "Yes" be yes and your "No," no,
anything beyond this comes from the evil one.	or you will be condemned.

Some see this as evidence of the primitive nature of James, as the Matthean saying is more complex and therefore, so the logic goes, must be later. However, it is just as likely that James is drawing on a saying of Jesus and has simply shortened it. Furthermore, the idea that "simple" must mean "primitive" or "early," and "complex" must by necessity mean late is a falsehood,[4] in spite of its enduring appeal.

---

3. Sirach 23:9, 11.

4. G. B. Caird, "The Development of the Doctrine of Christ in the New Testament," *Christ For Us Today*, ed. N. Pittenger (London: SCM, 1968), 66–80.

There are a number of parallels to this formula within Judaism. The formula in *Ruth Rabba* 3.18 (ascribed to Rabbi Huna) is, "The yes of the righteous is yes, and the no, no." In the Talmud (*Nedarim* 20a) we read, "Never make a practice of vowing, for ultimately you will trespass in the matter of oaths." Josephus writes in reference to the Essenes, "Every statement of theirs is surer than an oath; and with them swearing is avoided, for they think it worse than perjury. For they say that he who is untrustworthy except when he appeals to God, is already under condemnation."[5]

Why does James offer this counsel? (1) to avoid the situation of Jephthah, who swore an oath that bound him to disastrous consequences (Judg. 11:30–39); (2) to ensure that Christians are not influenced by pagan oath-swearing formulae; (3) to maintain a high standard of truth in all speech; and (4) to avoid involving God in a falsehood if, by chance, what we intend we are unable to accomplish. The consequences for each of these is to fall under the judgment of condemnation, and this James wants us to avoid.

Prayer (5:13–18)

WHILE THE MOST obvious feature of this section may seem to be healing, more specifically, the prayer over and anointing of the sick (v. 15), the true theme of the passage is prayer (v. 16). The entire section is caught up by issues involving prayer, as prayer is mentioned in every verse. James here deals with the prayer of the individual (v. 13), the prayer of the elders (vv. 14–15), the prayers of friends and companions for one another (v. 16), and finally the prayer of the righteous prophet Elijah (vv. 17–18).[6]

The first issue raised is that of suffering (v. 13a). This clearly forms a bridge to 5:7–11. We also see here how James is bringing his letter to a close, as this theme formed the first issue raised in the letter (1:2). James is well aware that life, and perhaps especially the Christian life, is one in which we experience trouble—and in such a way that we may feel tempted to call the goodness of God and of our fellow human beings into question. In such times James advocates neither anger nor stoic resignation, for the former poisons the spirit and the latter dulls the mind. Instead, he advocates prayer. It is a response that allows us to be active and positive and keeps us in communication with God.

Some see this verse as combining a declarative statement with an imperative: "There is among you one who suffers. He should pray!" Yet whether this or the more traditional reading (an interrogative followed by an imperative)

---

5. *Antiquities*, 15.10.
6. This is based on the work of J. A. Motyer, *The Message of James*, 186–208.

is chosen, the force is the same. In times of distress, the best recourse is to prayer.

The Greek word for "trouble" here is *kakopatheo*, which means "to suffer misfortune"; this word is normally not used of illness. Davids offers the opinion that the word indicates not a specific misfortune, but rather the "inner experience of having to endure misfortune."[7] As in chapter 1, James is not advocating a prayer for the removal of the cause of trouble so much as for the strength to endure the present troublesome situation.

Then James discusses the case of those who are happy. The word he uses (*euthymeo*) conveys something far more than the superficial happiness dependent upon circumstance. Rather, it refers to a deeply rooted happiness, a contentment of the heart.[8] James is referring to the believer who, through prayer, can be in good spirits even when transitory conditions are difficult because of a deep-seated trust in the trustworthiness of God. The word translated "sing songs of praise" (*psallo*) originally meant "to play the harp." It is used frequently in the Psalms, as one would expect (e.g., Ps. 33:2; 98:4–5; 149:3).

In this verse of "trouble" and being "happy," it is not unlikely that James has in mind the psalms of lament, which feature an honest questioning of God that seems to border on doubt, but which always conclude with a statement of praise and trust. The psalmist may feel abandoned: "But now you have rejected and humbled us" (44:9); but always this "doubt" is in the context of the covenant relationship—"Rise up and help us; redeem us because of your unfailing love" (44:26). James likewise wants his readers to remember that God desires and deserves our prayers and praise in both difficult and pleasant times.

Having dealt with two occasions for prayer, James now turns to a third, illness. The word for "sick" is *astheneo*, which has a wide range of meanings having to do with weakness of any kind. It is the word Paul used to signify his "thorn in flesh," classifying it as a "weakness" he was glad to bear, for his weakness allowed Christ's power to be evident in him (2 Cor 12:7–10). But as Davids points out,[9] there are reasons for concluding that *astheneo* here is more narrow in meaning, that is, physical illness. The use of the word *sozo* ("to make whole") and the participle *ton kamnonta* ("the sick person") in 5:15, and the use of *kakopatheo* for distress apart from illness, all indicate that James means physical illness in 5:14.

The sick person should call the elders of the congregation to come, to pray over him, and to anoint him with oil. *Proskaleomai* ("to call") suggests that

---

7. Davids, *The Epistle of James*, 191.
8. D. Moo, *The Letter of James*, 175.
9. Davids, *The Epistle of James*, 192.

the situation is dire and requires measures that are somewhat extreme. The word "elders" is used in the Gospels of Jewish leaders in the synagogue, but throughout the remainder of the New Testament it signifies leaders in the Christian church.[10] The entire group of these local leaders is to be called. James knows nothing of a particular person or charisma known as a "faith healer/healing," such as some claimed to have and was recognized by Paul in the Corinthian church (1 Cor. 12:9, 28, 30). That is, we are not dealing with an example of "faith healing" here. Rather, the act of prayer and anointing for healing is undertaken by the recognized leaders of the church. In 5:13 the person in "trouble" was urged to pray for himself or herself; here the sick person is asked to call others to minister.

Two actions are to be undertaken. The sick person is to be "prayed over." To pray for healing was not unknown within Judaism (see Ps. 35:13; 41:4.). Regarding the anointing, the grammar is not clear whether the oil is to be applied before or during the prayer, and it is probably of little importance. It is also unclear if hands are to be laid on the sick person, although this is not unlikely. The absence of any clear direction to "lay hands on" the sick person is surprising, given the practice of Jesus (Mark 6:5) and his followers (Acts 9:17). Of course, the "laying on of hands" might be presupposed in the application of oil.

It is obvious that the basis for this action is the firm belief that God is the source of healing, for the anointing is to be done "in the name of the Lord." There are four possibilities as to the precise implication of the phrase.[11] It could mean (1) by calling on the name of the Lord (cf. Luke 10:17), or (2) by an appeal to the power associated with the name of the Lord (cf. Acts 3:6), or (3) as one who has been commissioned by the Lord (cf. Gal. 1:1, 15), or (4) consciously assembled as a Christian community (cf. 1 Cor. 5:4). Ultimately, it matters little, for the point is that the Lord is at work in the actions of the elders, who are God's representatives. Any healing is due to his power and action, not to any human effort.

Anointing the sick with oil is mentioned twice elsewhere in the New Testament. In Luke 10:34 Jesus, in relating the parable of the Good Samaritan, says that the Samaritan bandaged the wounds of the man left for dead by the robbers, "pouring on oil and wine." The other reference is Mark 6:13, something of a *locus classicus* for modern faith healers. Although Mark 6:5 says Jesus could do no miracles in Nazareth, the same verse relates that he healed a few people, though he apparently did not use oil. In the next pericope

---

10. See Acts 11:30; 1 Tim. 5:17–19; 1 Peter 5:1; see also L. Coenen, "Bishop," *NIDNTT*, 1:192–201.

11. Martin, *James*, 208.

Jesus commissions the Twelve, and Mark tells us (v. 13) that they anointed the sick with oil. It is not insignificant that in this verse the anointing of the sick is clearly separate from exorcism. The implication is that Jesus discerns a difference between sickness caused by natural means and sickness that is of satanic origin.

As in the previous section, "the Lord" must be Jesus. This tells us that although James is nearly without a discernible Christology, what Christology he does possess is high.[12]

Two reasons are generally given for the anointing.[13] (1) Some scholars see it as symbolic of God's unceasing interest in his people during times of duress. It was an essential feature of the developing faith of Israel that what God deemed best for Israel was not always what Israel deemed best. Thus, the great prophets could argue that the military and political defeat of Israel and Judah signaled not the impotence of God, but rather God's power and purpose at work. With this background in view, the anointing mentioned here is not done with a certainty that God will heal, but with the certainty that God cares. To pray with certainty that God will heal seems to contravene one of the prominent themes of the letter, namely, to endure difficulties because God can use them to bring about his purpose in our lives.

(2) Other scholars see this anointing as practical and medicinal. Olive oil was thought to bear medicinal powers of wide application in the ancient world.[14] Its use here was clearly with the expectation that physical healing could occur.[15]

Whatever the precise definition and meaning of the act of anointing, it is "the prayer offered in faith" (or, better, "the fervent request offered in faith"), *not* the anointing, that makes the sick person well (v. 15). This is a point frequently missed in the intricacies of the matter of anointing. The emphasis should fall on the "fervent faith," that is, a prayer that expresses trust in God and that flows from a deep commitment to God (cf. vv. 17–18). The prayer and the faith is, evidently, that of the elders, since only the prayer of the elders is mentioned. The question of precisely what kind of "faith" is in

---

12. See comments on 5:7–11, p. 285.

13. On this matter see Martin, *James*, 208–9.

14. Olive oil was used for a variety of medicinal purposes, including cleansing and soothing wounds (Isa. 1:6; Luke 10:34). Herod tried a hot oil bath to heal a variety of internal and external ailments (Josephus, *Antiquities*, 17:172); and Pliny tells us that oil was used to treat the gums and teeth, to keep the body supple, to neutralize "all poisons," to restore vigor if fatigued, to serve as a laxative, and to improve vision (when mixed with honey) (Pliny, *Natural History*, 23.39–40).

15. J. Wilkerson, "Healing in the Epistle of James," *SJT* 24 (1971): 326–45, argues that the oil was a medical and not a religious procedure. His point is that the church should embrace all forms of healing, and should support them through prayer.

view and therefore efficacious is an important one, but this is a matter better treated in the Bridging Contexts section.

This prayer carries with it two results: (1) The sick person is made well (*sozo*); and (2) the Lord will raise him up (*egeiro*). The verb *sozo* is most often used in the New Testament in reference to eschatology and the salvation of believers, and this may be the intent of language here (which implies the resurrection—cf. "will raise him up"). Because of this, a number of commentators see this issue as about spiritual death, not physical health. The verb "to be healed" (*iaomai*) in 5:16 is normally reserved for physical healing, but can be used for spiritual healing.

The chief issue, then, is whether the future verbs "to save," "to raise up," and "to be forgiven" refer to eschatological and therefore spiritual healing, or to physical healing. While these verbs can be made to bear eschatological nuance, the weight of the grammatical and lexical evidence is on the side of a physical understanding of the passage. After all, the person about whom this is written is still alive! While it is possible that James has both in view, it is difficult to escape the conclusion that at the very least he is speaking of physical healing of an illness. To avoid this conclusion on the basis of a predetermined theology does injustice to the text. On the other hand, James has counseled patience in the face of affliction. The key to resolving this apparent dilemma is found in the discerning prayer of the elders.

The first sentence of verse 16, where James implies that sin can cause sickness, goes with verse 15. This is sound New Testament teaching, fully in harmony with the remainder of the New Testament. But the New Testament does not teach that all sickness is the result of sin (see John 9:1–3), or that all sin causes sickness, or that God always desires to remove maladies from besetting us (cf. Paul's thorn in the flesh in 2 Cor. 12:7–10). But James clearly teaches here that sickness caused by sin can be alleviated through public confession and prayer for healing. The fact that elders are not mentioned in verse 16a does not necessarily indicate that a new case is in view, but rather buttresses the idea that the prayer of faith pertains to elders and to others as well.

In verse 16b James introduces a new line of thought, the example of "a righteous man." The prayer of such a person, says James, is both "powerful and effective." The "righteous man" is the one who is committed to doing God's will and to cultivating a relationship with God that knows God's heart. The participle *energoumene* means "is able to do" (if understood in the middle voice) or "is enabled to do [by the Spirit of God]" (if understood in the passive voice). Either choice is feasible grammatically. In either case the prayer has a powerful effect. Such a prayer can have noticeable consequences on a person whose sickness is the result of sin, as long as (or especially if) the sin has been confessed.

James has already made reference to three Old Testament exemplars (Abraham, Rahab, and Job). To this list he now adds a fourth, the prophet Elijah, to whom he appeals as an example of a person of faith. For Elijah prayer was a function of faith and trust in God, even in the face of a difficult situation.

Elijah was a man "like us" (*homoipathes hemin*), an expression that conveys the sense of the same limitations. Luke uses the same expression in Acts 14:15, when Paul and Barnabas attempt to convince the citizens of Lystra that they are not divine beings, but people just like anyone else. James's point is that such a prayer is possible for the people he is addressing. The phrase "prayed earnestly" (or, more literally, "by prayer he prayed") is a Semitism, conveying the sense of intense prayer. Because Elijah was a man of sincere faith, he discerned God's heart, and his prayer was honored by God.

James refers here to the account given in 1 Kings 17–18. First Kings does not tell us specifically that Elijah prayed for rain to cease and then for rain to start again, but his praying is implied throughout the story (cf. his prayer for the widow's son in 17:20–24 and for fire from heaven in 18:36–37). The reference to "three and a half years" is surprising, because 18:1 mentions simply that the drought ended "in the third year." Likely James, similar to Luke (Luke 4:25), is reflecting apocalyptic symbolism, in which "three and a half" is a number of sinister omen, since it is half of the number seven, the perfect number (cf. Dan. 7:25; Rev. 12:6, 14; 13:5).

James concludes with the thought that just as the prayer of the righteous Elijah resulted in the refreshing of the earth, so the prayer of the righteous believer can result in the refreshing and healing of a Christian afflicted by sickness caused by sin.

THIS PASSAGE IS primarily concerned with prayer, and in fact touches a number of types of prayer. Perhaps the most problematic for us is the question of healing prayer. Several years ago I spoke at a small gathering of Christian leaders where the question of the "charismatic" gifts (healing, tongues, prophecy, etc.) was before us. Although a group of only twenty, we held widely divergent and firmly held beliefs. Some believed that only the gift of healing, and then only on rare occasions, was a true work of the Spirit today, while some others seemed ready to declare those who held the first view to be in need of exorcism! Because of the controversial nature of the issue of sickness, sin, and healing, we will focus on that in this section.

Recently I traveled to another city for a speaking engagement. After checking in to my hotel room I unpacked, washed my face, and turned on the television. I had not been cruising through the stations long before I had found the local Christian station and heard a preacher say, "Sickness is caused by Satan, and God wants you to be well." Later, referring to prayers of healing that are apparently without effect, he said, "You have got to have enough faith; otherwise God will not heal you." Such statements betray a decidedly unbiblical approach to the question of sickness. What can we say about the matter, based on the evidence of the New Testament?

(1) While the New Testament does argue that sickness can be the result of sin, this is not *necessarily* the case. In John 9:1–5 Jesus and the disciples encountered a man born blind. The question of the disciples, "Rabbi, who sinned, this man or his parents, that he was born blind?" betrayed their belief in the necessary link between sin and sickness. Jesus did not share their presumption. He responded that this particular malady was not due to any specific sin at all. In short, while sickness is often related to sin, it is not necessarily so. For this reason we should be slow to ascribe to any sickness a source rooted in sin or the demonic.

(2) God can and does use sickness and affliction for his purposes. In 2 Corinthians 12:7–10 Paul discusses his "thorn in [the] flesh," which he calls a "messenger of Satan." He relates that he prayed to be relieved of this affliction. If ever there was a test case for the theology of the televangelist I was watching, this is it. Satan had afflicted Paul, and Paul was a man of unquestioned faith. Yet Paul says that God allowed this affliction in order to keep him humble. What was apparently a physical affliction (Paul calls it "a thorn in my *flesh*") was used by God for a spiritual purpose. What is more, Paul, as a result of prayer, understood it in this fashion. He was able to bear the affliction because God revealed to him its purpose. This is precisely the point James made in 1:5.[16]

(3) The *ability* of Jesus to perform the miraculous has nothing at all to do with the "faith" of the sick person. Jesus does not "need" the faith of the sick person in order to heal, as if he requires some external boost of energy to be effective. The question, actually, is the *quality* of faith. Jesus often did not perform "miracles" when he discerned that the result would be belief in his ability as a wonder-worker, as opposed to belief in his person and message.

This comes through strongly in John 6:60–66, a passage that follows the feeding of the five thousand and the difficult teaching of Jesus that his disciples must eat the flesh and drink the blood of the Son of Man. John then writes that many of his disciples left him. They had seen his signs and "believed" (cf. John 2:11), yet their belief was anemic. It had no staying power. They wanted a Jesus they could possess only on their own terms.

---

16. Cf. also Heb. 11:32–40.

Jesus desires a faith that penetrates behind the miraculous to the core of his message and of his person, that understands and accepts him on his terms.

(4) Since sickness can be caused by sin and even by demonic possession, Jesus was interested in healing. This is no less true in our day. Sometimes the sin involved is addiction to alcohol or other substances that causes us to ignore our responsibilities to family and community. Sometimes it is a penchant to sinful behaviors, such as physical or sexual abuse. Sometimes it is an emotional sickness caused by bitterness or envy. In all of these areas, and many others, God desires to heal. And he calls us to pray. Many of these themes are further developed in the various types of prayer James describes here. To these we shall now turn.

AT HEART, THIS passage is about prayer, concerning which James discusses a wide variety of types: prayer and joy in adversity, prayer for the sick, the prayer of confession within community, and the prayer of the righteous.

Prayer and joy in adversity. In 5:13 James counsels prayer in adversity, and he links this prayer to joy in the face of adversity. At times our reticence to embrace pain and loss is understandable, for it is often difficult to discern God's grace.[17] Several persons close to me have recently found themselves in such situations: One couple is mourning their murdered child, another couple has learned that one of them has inoperable cancer. In scenarios such as these, we need to be honest and admit that God's ways are often inscrutable to us.

Not all adversity is as difficult to bear as these, but to find joy amid any adverse situation is, frankly, alien to our culture. We inhabit a social and cultural world in which a great premium is placed on the elimination of discomfort. For example, our television sets advertise comfort in everything from leather car upholstery to sofa-recliners to lower house payments to searching for a dentist; such commercials demonstrate that Americans have an appetite for the elimination of stress and pain.

In the face of this potent cultural norm evangelicals need to go against the grain and appropriate a biblical understanding of adversity. James has provided several steps for us to follow. The first is to see that God uses adversity in the interests of spiritual preparation. Hannah More (1745–1833) was born to privilege near Bristol, England. As a young woman she was the friend

---

17. See the book by Gerald Sittser, *A Grace Disguised: How the Soul Grows Through Loss* (Grand Rapids: Zondervan, 1996), which explores through personal tragedy the relationship between suffering loss and experiencing God's grace.

of Sir Joshua Reynolds, Edmund Burke, and the actor David Garrick. She became a famous poet and dramatist, but her deepening friendship with John Newton, the converted former slave trader, deepened her interest in spiritual things. She began to see her powerful desire for personal fame as incompatible with the spiritual life, and increasingly she was uncomfortable with the social scene in London. She finally "retired" to the area near Bristol, where she suffered from asthma and bronchitis. In the 1780s she became active in the campaign to end the slave trade, working with John Newton, William Wilberforce, and the Clapham Sect. She said:

> Affliction is the school in which great virtues are acquired and in which great characters are formed. It is like a spiritual gymnasium in which the disciples of Christ are trained in robust exercise, hardy exertion and severe conflict.
>
> We do not hear of military heroes in peacetime, nor of the most distinguished saints in the quiet and unmolested periods of church history. The courage in the warrior and the devotion in the saint continue to survive, ready to be brought into action when perils beset the country or trials assail the Church, but it must be admitted that in long periods of inaction both are susceptible to decay.[18]

But prayer in adversity also urges us to renounce the materialism and the self-centeredness of the world. This has been a constant theme in James. This is also stock wisdom, although our culture seems to ignore it. "Rule your desires, lest your desires rule you," said Publius Syrus.[19] St. Serafim of Sarow (1749–1833) once said:[20]

> It is better for us to despise what is not ours, i.e., the temporal and passing, and desire our own, i.e. incorruption and immortality. For when we shall be incorruptible and immortal ... we shall be joined in a union with God surpassing the mind, like the heavenly minds. For we shall be like the angels, and sons of God, "being the sons of the resurrection" (Lk. 20:36).

Adversity is also a sign of God's love and care, and through prayer we can begin to recognize it as such. Hannah More wrote:

> If a surgeon were to put into the hand of a wounded patient the probe or the scalpel, how tenderly would he treat himself! How

---

18. Hannah More, *Religion of the Heart*, ed. Hal M. Helms (Orleans, Miss.: Paraclete 1993), 198.

19. Publius Syrus, *Sententiae*, 50.

20. Brenda Meehan, *Holy Women of Russia: The Lives of Five Orthodox Women Offer Spiritual Guidance for Today* (Crestwood, N.Y.: St. Vladimir's Seminary Press, 1997), 4.

skin-deep would be the examination, how slight the incision! The patient would escape the pain, but the wound might prove fatal. The surgeon therefore wisely uses his instruments himself. He goes deep perhaps, but not deeper than the case demands. The pain may be acute, but the life is persevered.

Thus Him whose hand we are, is too good and loves us too well to trust us with our own surgery. He knows that we will not contradict our own inclinations, that we will not impose on ourselves any voluntary pain, however necessary the infliction, however healthful the effect. God graciously does this for us Himself because otherwise He knows it would never be done.[21]

In another passage Hannah More combines the renunciation of the world, spiritual preparation, and the joy that comes in the face of adversity.

It is among the mercies of God that he strengthens servants by hardening them through adverse circumstances, instead of leaving them to languish under the shining but withering sun of unclouded prosperity. When they cannot be attracted to Him by gentler influences, He sends these storms and tempests which purify while they alarm. Our gracious Father knows how long the happiness of eternity will be for His children.[22]

Still another reason that suffering is the lot of Christians is that Christ suffered. In Colossians 1:24 Paul wrote, "Now I rejoice in what was suffered for you, and I fill up in my flesh what was lacking in regard to Christ's afflictions, for the sake of his body, which is the church." Paul reminds us that we are to be fellow sufferers with Christ by participating in "the fellowship of sharing in his sufferings" (Phil. 3:10).

There is a kind of suffering that is redemptive suffering, a difficult concept for us to understand, since we share the culture of recliners and ease. Our whole society is dedicated to avoiding suffering. Richard Foster, in his book *Prayer: Finding the Heart's True Home*, notes that we need to find value in suffering. Jesus was a man of sorrows, Foster reminds us. Christians who speak of "victory" have perhaps missed what Foster calls the "sacrament of suffering." There is a triumph to suffering, but it goes *through* suffering, and not *around* it.[23]

---

21. More, *Religion of the Heart*, 199–200.

22. Ibid., 202.

23. Richard Foster, *Prayer: Finding the Heart's True Home* (San Francisco: Harper, 1992), 219.

Finally, prayer allows us to understand what God is forming in us through this suffering. Sue Monk Kidd writes of an experience she had once while on a spiritual retreat, an experience that exposes our culturally imposed need for frenetic activity that we so glibly confuse with progress:

One day after morning prayers, I walked to the edge of the pond and sat on the grass. I listened to the wind sigh over the water and tried to be still, to simply be there and wait in the moment. But almost instantly my inner chaos rose up. The need to keep moving, to act, to solve everything overpowered me. I got to my feet.

As I returned to the guest quarters, I noticed a monk, ski cap pulled over his ears, sitting perfectly still beneath a tree. There was such reverence in his silhouette, such tranquil sturdiness, that I paused to watch. He was the picture of waiting.

Later I sought him out. "I saw you sitting beneath the tree—just sitting there so still. How is it that you can wait so patiently in the moment? I can't seem to get used to the idea of doing nothing."

He broke into a wonderful grin. "Well, there's the problem right there, young lady. You've bought into the cultural myth that when you're waiting you're doing nothing."

Then he took his hands and placed them on my shoulders, peered straight into my eyes and said, "I hope that you'll hear what I'm about to tell you. I hope you'll hear it all the way down to your toes. When you're waiting, you're *not* doing nothing. You're doing the most important something there is. You're allowing you soul to grow up. If you can't be still and wait, you can't become what God created you to be."[24]

The wisdom of this monk is clear. When we wait before God, as James says, he allows us to see what he is forming in us. Prayer is the necessary discipline.

Prayerful contemplation allows us to slow down, to let our soul "grow up" and catch a glimpse of God's purpose in allowing us to experience affliction. But we are not good at waiting. We are not good at being still before God. Before my wife and I moved to Chicago, we lived in Northern California. For some fifteen years I had led backpacking trips into the Sierra Nevada mountains, much of the time with groups of Christian students. Many of these students had never been in the mountains before, and five days in the mountains, hiking as high as twelve thousand feet, allowed them to distance themselves from the crush and pull of their lives and to gain a new appreciation for those "important things" of which the monk spoke. A typical plan was to find

---

24. Sue Monk Kidd, *When the Heart Waits: Spiritual Direction for Life's Sacred Questions* (San Francisco: Harper, 1990), 21–22.

camp early on the fourth day and to spend the afternoon on "solo." I would send the students around the lake or down the river to be alone for six hours. Some of them had never had an experience like this. I remember quite clearly one sixteen-year-old say, "I can't do it, I'll be bored! I've never been alone for more than fifteen minutes!" To her surprise, she liked the experience.

On one occasion a young man was suffering grievously from a difficult and even dangerous family situation. We had spent many hours speaking of this circumstance over the previous months, and he was bewildered by it. When the solo time was up, he returned to camp, silent but somehow calm. Later that evening he told me that during this quiet time of prayer, God had revealed something that surprised him, but the more he thought about it the more sense it made. God had told him that his own family struggle was training him in patience and in encouragement.

Prayer for the sick. When James instructs his readers to ask the elders to pray and to anoint them with oil when sick, he leads us to the matter of healing prayer. Richard Foster tells the story of his first experience with healing prayer. It involved a man who had led a mission of thirty-three men in World War II. They found themselves pinned down by enemy gunfire. He prayed all night for deliverance, but instead all but six men were killed. This experience left him a confirmed atheist. But since that day he had not been able to sleep. Foster asked if he could pray for the man, who agreed. The prayer was for emotional healing and included, as an afterthought, the ability to sleep through the night. The man returned a week later with this report: "Every night I have slept soundly, and each morning I have awakened with a hymn on my mind. And I am happy . . . happy for the first time in twenty-eight years."[25] This experience convinced Foster that the healing ministry of Jesus is intended for the whole person—physical, emotional, mental, and spiritual.

Many in the evangelical community are skeptical of healing prayer. This is not necessarily a bad thing. Healthy agnosticism prevents us from being deceived by the antichrists, who also can work signs and wonders.[26] But James says we are to be about the task of healing prayer. Richard Foster offers four steps in this regard.[27] (1) We must listen to God and to people, and allow our spirits to discern the Holy Spirit. (2) We must ask—with boldness. When his friend Melanchthon was sick, Luther "besought the Almighty with great vigor . . . quoting from Scripture all the promises I could remem-

25. Foster, *Prayer: Finding the Heart's True Home*, 205.

26. Cf. Mark 13:22–23, where Jesus warns, "For false Christs and false prophets will appear and perform signs and miracles to deceive the elect. . . . So be on your guard."

27. Foster, *Prayer: Finding the Heart's True Home*, 210–16.

ber."[28] (3) We must believe. Foster calls us to exercise the confident assurance in the faithfulness of God. (4) We must give thanks to God for his compassion and his mercy.

From birth until I left home for college, I attended a fine evangelical church near San Francisco. It was a church not hostile to obvious displays of the power of the Holy Spirit, but not one that encouraged them. However, there was a lady in the church who, years before, at about the age of sixty, had undergone surgery, during which the physicians discovered cancer laced through her viscera. They abandoned the surgical plan and informed her that she had at most six months to live. She asked the pastor and elders to anoint her with oil and pray for healing, which they did. Six months later a second surgery was done, and to the surprise of the surgeons, there was no cancer to be found. The woman lived into her nineties, a witness to the power of prayer.

However, not everyone we pray for will be healed. A physician friend of mine who is also a devout Christian confided in me that over the years he had grown tired of and even angry about the pastors who entered the rooms of patients with a too smug false surety and confidence. "Often, not always, but often," he said, "they promise a good deal more than gets delivered." His heart is for the patients, whose faith may waver as a result. These pastors, my friend believes, have yet to understand the "sacrament of suffering."

Richard Foster says that there are any number of reasons why healing does not take place. Heading the list is the possibility that we have misinterpreted the focus of our prayer when the Spirit prompts us to pray. Others include a failure to use the available medical resources because we do not wish to see medical science as an avenue God can use for healing. Perhaps we have not prayed specifically enough. In any event, Foster wisely directs us away from laying the blame on the patient and urges us always to act with compassion, being sensitive to the pain and weakened state of the patient.[29]

Confession and community. James tells us to confess our sins to each other and to pray for one another. Here surfaces his passion for true spiritual community, as is seen also in his use of the term "brothers" throughout the letter.

James asks us to confess to each other publicly for at least two reasons. (1) It is the practice of vulnerability. The church to which James wrote was rife with arrogance, power politics, and dissension. In order to combat these forces James here urges public vulnerability. Proverbs says, "A gentle answer turns away wrath" (Prov. 15:1), and James here offers similar advice. The

---

28. Quoted in ibid., 211.
29. Ibid., 206–7.

practice of vulnerability and confession will cool tempers and help heal the divisions within the church. James is advocating the model of Jesus, to become the servant and to become vulnerable before others. As well, confession of wrongs committed against sisters and brothers is a sure path to interpersonal healing.

(2) Richard Foster points out that both Moses and Daniel, although innocent, identified themselves with the sins of their people.[30] On Mount Sinai Moses asks God to forgive the people for their sin regarding the golden calf, and if God will not, Moses offers his own life (Ex. 32:31–32). Daniel prays, "We have sinned and done wrong . . . we have not listened . . . we have not obeyed the Lord our God" (Dan. 9:5–10). To this list we can add Nehemiah (see Neh. 1:6), and of course, Jesus, who identified with us unto death.

James calls us to put aside vain personal concerns and willingly shoulder a responsibility not technically ours. In this fashion we become the community of the faithful. When the allies liberated the Ravensbrück concentration camp, a scrap of paper was found next to the body of a dead child. On it was written a prayer:

> O Lord, remember not only the men and women of good will, but also those of ill will. But do not only remember the suffering they have inflicted on us; remember the fruits we bought, thanks to this suffering: our comradeship, our loyalty, our humility, the courage, the generosity, the greatness of heart which has grown out of all this. And when they come to judgment, let all the fruits that we have borne be their forgiveness.[31]

The prayer of the righteous. The final type of prayer James mentions is that of the righteous person. Such a prayer is powerful because the righteous person has discerned God's leading already. Such wise saints are found in every congregation and deserve the careful attention of church leadership, even if the church leaders are successful "business" types. But patient supplication is also beneficial in that God rewards the persistence of the widow who prays day and night (Luke 18:1–8). Elijah is singled out because his heart was sensitive to God. The point here is that sin hinders our ability to pray. God certainly hears the prayers of the sinful, but sin dulls our sensitivity to God, and we become less and less in tune with him. This is what James meant in 4:3 when he scolded his brothers and sisters for asking wrongly.

---

30. Foster, *Prayer: Finding the Heart's True Home*, 221–22.
31. From Rob Goldman, "Healing the World by Our Wounds," *The Other Side* 27, no. 6 (November/December 1991): 24.

James also says that the prayer of the righteous person is powerful and effective. As we have seen, the righteous person is in touch with the heart of God. Many people like this speak of a sensation of energy flowing through and from them when they pray for others, especially when they lay their hands on them. Richard Foster knows this sensation and adds, "I cannot make the flow of heavenly life happen, but I can stop it. If I resist or refuse to be an open conduit for God's power to come into a person, it will stop."[32] While many within the evangelical camp are less enthusiastic than Foster concerning the contemporary display of the Spirit's power in this fashion, all of us can agree that we are to be conduits of God's love, but that we can and, sadly, often do serve to block its flow.

32. Foster, *Prayer: Finding the Heart's True Home*, 209.

James 5:19–20

MY BROTHERS, IF one of you should wander from the truth and someone should bring him back, ²⁰remember this: Whoever turns a sinner from the error of his way will save him from death and cover over a multitude of sins.

IN THIS LACONIC conclusion James returns to the themes of sin and forgiveness. In so doing he reveals his pastoral heart. The passage is related to the previous section in that forgiveness follows confession. James's opponents in the church have arrogated to themselves the right to teach, and to teach a doctrine clearly at odds with the Jesus tradition, a tradition James knows.

In its effects this false teaching was savagely corrosive of the true faith. It exalted an impudent antinomian spirit pervasive enough to dismiss even the great commandment, and it claimed that "faith" is separate from any particular ethic.[1] It also extolled the values of Roman provincial society, and in so doing portrayed the Christian church as one among the many *collegia*, and thus an avenue for social climbing and social stratification for the scores who were not (or only marginally) included in the broader political and social life of the civic community. Yet to these purveyors of pernicious doctrine, James holds out the hand of forgiveness and encourages others in the Christian church to win them back to the true faith. Here is a model of the very teaching he has put forward. This is an apt conclusion, for the entire letter is written to turn and prevent people from error.

The passage is short—in fact, a single sentence. But it should not be missed that in this one sentence James marshals no less than three significant theological ideas: (1) Christians have the opportunity and the responsibility to care for one another through the task of loving doctrinal and moral correction. The theme here is not evangelism, but the care and maintenance of the Christian community. (2) The penalty for sin is death; James will not equivocate on this. (3) In this process, the agent of reconciliation "covers" a multitude of sins.

---

1. Paul found himself in a similar situation when he wrote 1 Corinthians. There members of the Christian community had also sought to use the church as an avenue to exalt themselves and had arrogated to themselves the mantle of teacher and prophet in order to validate these theological and cultural positions.

The usual Pauline concluding elements (greetings and personal comments to individuals with whom he is familiar, as well as a benediction) are not in James's arsenal. Instead, he ends with an exhortation to seek out those who in teaching and practice have wandered from the truth. This implies, of course, an exhortation to avoid disobedience.[2]

As he has frequently done, James uses the phrase "my brothers" to remind his readers of his relationship to them, a relationship marked by warm interpersonal regard and by a shared status before God. In urging Christians to seek and save those wandering, James aptly sums up the core thrust of the letter. The many particular errors he has catalogued (misuse of the tongue, jealousy, desire for social status at the expense of brothers and sisters in the faith, disputatiousness, false teaching concerning faith and works) can be summed up as markers of wandering ways. That James is directing this conclusion to the Christian community does not come out strongly enough in the NIV, which renders *tis en humin* with "one of you;" it probably should be translated as "one among you."

The word used for "wander" is *planao*, which can mean "lead astray" as well as "wander." The implication is that this "wandering" is not wholly innocent. The wanderer may understand that the path chosen is a deviant path; or if the wanderer has pursued the path accidentally or unconsciously, those teaching and practicing this error are certainly conscious of it as different from the truth that they know. This term conjures up a rich array of Old Testament references, most having to do with transgression of the law, and more particularly with idolatry (see, e.g., Prov. 14:8; Isa. 9:15–16; Jer. 23:17; Ezek. 33:19). It is possible that this deliberate waywardness James sees as somehow influenced by Satan. He has already made reference to this possibility (James 3:15; 4:7), and such teaching is consonant with the witness of the New Testament generally (cf. Rom. 1:27; Eph. 4:14; 1 Peter 2:25).

The wanderer has wandered from "the truth" (*aletheia*). For James truth is not simply something to be believed, but also and necessarily something to be practiced. It is much closer to our English word "conviction." The Bible reflects this in its penchant to speak of truth as a way to go, a path to be followed, the "way of ... truth" (Matt. 22:16; cf. Ps. 26:3). And the wanderer is not left to his or her own devices; the burden of reclamation is laid on the community. In this James has much in common with Paul in 2 Corinthians 5:18–21. While Paul seems to be referring to the initial conversion and James to a second turning back to God, both are "conversions."

---

2. Ralph P. Martin, *James*, 218, is accurate but not technically correct to claim that James concludes with a call to refrain from disobedience.

James concludes his letter in a surprisingly abrupt fashion (v. 20). The person who "turns" the errant wanderer saves the wanderer from sins. The Greek word James uses for "turn" is *epistrepho*. The idea here probably owes its origin to two passages in Ezekiel. The first is Ezekiel 33:11:

> Say to them, "As surely as I live, declares the Sovereign LORD, I take no pleasure in the death of the wicked, but rather that they turn from their ways and live. Turn! Turn from your evil ways! Why will you die, O house of Israel?"

The other passage is Ezekiel 34, in which calumny is called down on the false shepherds of Israel, and God as Israel's true shepherd is extolled. One of the functions God assigns to himself is that of seeking and saving those who wander. Furthermore, God will appoint for Israel a true shepherd, his servant David, who will carry out the same tasks.[3] Thus, those who seek and save the wandering are truly the people of God, for they are like God. "Death" (*thanatos*) here is, of course, spiritual death. Consonant with the teaching of the Bible generally, this death has eternal consequences (Deut. 30:19; Job 8:13).

When we come to the phrase "cover a multitude of sins," we enter a difficult landscape. Certainly the idea here is to forgive sins. The action of the high priest on the Day of Atonement was to cover (*kaphar/kippur*) the sins of the people by sprinkling blood on the atonement cover, the lid of the ark (Lev. 16:15–16), and James is drawing on that image. What is not so clear is the identity of the one who is saved from death, and of the one whose sins are covered. The NIV has made an exegetical decision on the first matter, clearly indicating that it is the wanderer who is saved from death. This is a sound decision theologically, as it comports with the thrust of James and with the theology of Ezekiel. It is also a good decision grammatically, although the grammar would also support the idea that the one saving the wanderer is also saved by that action.

The second matter suffers from the same grammatical ambiguity, and in this case there is less of a theological trajectory to serve as a reference. It is likely that James intends the "covering" of the sins of both the wanderer and the one who saves the errant party. We also should not forget that James lays responsibility for the wanderer on the Christian community generally. In fact, this is just one example of the sort of mutual care and responsibility that he expects of all within the Christian community.

James ends his letter abruptly by reminding his readers that the wise person walks with God in wisdom. Sin is a problem both corporate and personal.

---

3. Here again is a striking similarity to Jesus (see esp. Matt. 18:12–14; Luke 15:3–7; 19:10).

It is subtle, tenacious, and dangerous; it should not be underestimated. Christians have a responsibility to their world and to one another.

A CLEAR PRIORITY for James has been to establish the idea of the church as community. For this reason he has used the term "brothers," he has spoken of shared concerns, and he has asked the church to confess their sins publicly. Now James adds to the list: He instructs the church as a whole to seek and save the lost and the wandering.

This idea of Christian community does not come naturally to us. A good friend of mine is a pastor on staff of a church of nearly four thousand members. Their list of pastoral staff positions is astounding: Senior Pastor, Executive Pastor, three Senior Associate Pastors, Pastor for Education Ministries, Pastor for Outreach, Pastor for Small-Group Ministries, Minister of Visitation, Singles Pastor, Director of Student Ministries, College Pastor, High School Pastor, Junior High Pastor, and Director of Children's Ministries. A church of this size may very well need this many pastors, with these tightly focused job descriptions. But there is a not too savory side-effect to this creeping specialization, for it often creates a sense of professionalization concerning ministry. When this idea becomes lodged in the minds of our congregations, we are afield from the New Testament idea.

I have been on the staff of two different churches and am well acquainted with the staff dynamics of a dozen more. One of these churches devoted more than a year to the creation of a mission statement, the point of which was that the members of the congregation are the "ministers" and the pastoral staff the "enablers." After devoting so much time and energy to the creation of just the right statement, with months spent haggling over terminology, the members of the church were exhausted.

But their mission statement is no closer to coming true than the day it was conceived. Many in the church continue to think of the pastoral staff as their "paid help," whose job it is to do the work of ministry. This provides us with a critical lesson, which is, quite simply, never to be content with right doctrine. James implores us to combine right practice with right belief. We must find ways to teach and train our members in Christian community responsibility.

The New Testament model is different from the one operative in many evangelical churches. In his insightful book *Paul's Idea of Community*,[4] Robert Banks points out that Paul seems to have made no distinction between clergy and laity, but rather entrusted to the entire church, not just elders, virtually

---

4. Robert Banks, *Paul's Idea of Community* (Exeter: Paternoster, 1980).

all the responsibilities within the body. He notes that we are all free in Christ (2 Cor. 3:17), and that this freedom is a freedom to live in interdependence.[5] In fact, in matters of organization,[6] corporate welfare,[7] discipline,[8] and growth,[9] Paul assigns responsibility not to a specific group with the body, but to the body as a whole.[10] For Paul the functions of official priesthood, that is, to mediate between God and human beings, are shared by the entire Christian community. He never says that these responsibilities belong to any one person or group.[11]

James offers a remarkably similar picture. With few exceptions (such as the prayer for healing in 5:13) James stresses persons in leadership roles *only* when he is referring to *false* teaching and practice. His entire letter is an appeal to the Christian community *at large*, not simply to its leaders. His instructions concerning prayer, doctrine, divisions within the church are, with few exceptions, instructions to the entire community. We are called, then, to seek ways to be faithful to this teaching.

JAMES HERE PLACES before us two responsibilities: to teach and practice a biblical model of Christian community, and to balance discipline with mercy. To these we now turn.

Christian community. The New Testament conceives of the Christian community in ways that are often alarmingly dissimilar to our own patterns of organization. This is not to say that having pastors with specific job descriptions is wrong, because the New Testament offers no one pattern of church leadership. But it is to say that we have a responsibility to and for each other as the local body of Christ, and these responsibilities often involve matters of church order, discipline, teaching, and welfare. It is the responsibility of pastors to teach this as a matter of New Testament theology.

For this to take place our pastors need to allow others in the congregation to step forward and develop the gifts God has given to them. This requires a

---

5. Ibid., 32.

6. In 1 Cor. 11:33–34, for instance, Paul instructs the entire congregation concerning the Eucharist; he does not give directions to the "elders" (see also 14:39–40; 16:2–3).

7. Paul instructs the entire congregation to "carry each other's burdens" (Gal. 6:2) and to "encourage one another and build each other up" (1 Thess. 5:11).

8. Paul says that when one member has a grievance against another, it should be taken to the members of the congregation, not the church leaders (1 Cor. 6:1–6).

9. In Rom. 15:14 Paul says, "I myself am convinced, my brothers, that you yourselves are full of goodness, complete in knowledge and competent to instruct one another."

10. Robert Banks, *Paul's Idea of Community*, 139–41.

11. Ibid., 133.

certain humility on the part of pastors. Well do I remember my first experience in youth ministry. I was one month out of college, and 113 high school students had signed up to go water skiing. I was placed in charge of the event. I faced the task with some trepidation, for although I grew up in California, I had never tried water skiing. Nevertheless, I took my assignment seriously. I planned and taught every Bible study. I kept the roster of when each student got to ski in which of our six boats. I decided when we got up and when it was time for the all-quiet to be sounded at night. In short, apart from the actual cooking of the meals, I had reserved for myself each and every "official" decision made on the trip. As a result, I not only deprived the other counselors of opportunities to develop their gifts and skill, I also booked myself so solid that I had no time to spend with the students. I was an abysmal role model on all counts. I learned that weekend that as pastor I had a responsibility to allow others to gain experience in ministry, and that I could not do everything myself.

We need to seek ways to help the members of our congregation discover their gifts for ministry and to engage in responsible Christian service along the general pattern outlined in the New Testament. This can be accomplished in a variety of ways, including offering spiritual gift surveys, schools of prayer, concerts of prayer, and training in Stephen Ministry. However it is accomplished, as evangelicals we need to allow our fellow believers to shoulder the burdens and responsibilities that attend to church membership. We are not true to either our members or ourselves if we fail in this regard.

Forgiveness and discipline. At a number of points in his letter James indicates that he is in touch with the Jesus tradition, perhaps even portions of the tradition more rudimentary than those related in the Gospels. His teaching here is another case and bears similarity to the Matthean teaching on community discipline and forgiveness.[12]

Matthew 18:1–35 manifests a clear tension between rigor and mercy, which is also evident in James. The members of the community are expected to grow to maturity and even perfection (James 1:4). Yet the community is also called on to follow what Richard Hays calls "the hermeneutic of mercy."[13] Both James and Matthew instruct members of the community to attempt to turn those who are wandering back to the truth. Both make clear that the case of an unrepentant sinner is serious, because righteousness must be taken seriously. In Matthew Jesus counsels the expulsion of an unrepentant sinner and instructs the community to treat such a sinner as "a pagan or a tax collector" (Matt. 18:17)—that is, as a person who becomes the object of the

12. On this matter see Richard B. Hays, *The Moral Vision of the New Testament: Community, Cross, New Creation; A Contemporary Introduction to New Testament Ethics* (San Francisco: Harper, 1996), 101–4.

13. Ibid., 101.

missionary interests and efforts of the church. With James the situation is no different. The one who wanders needs to become the object of the reconciliation of the church. His or her sin has placed them outside the community. Jesus and James both argue that the entire community of faith must be about this task and make the relevant decisions (cf. Matt. 18:17–19).

The teaching of James throughout his letter is often harsh and even rigid. But then, so was the mandate given by Jesus. But here at the end of his letter James allows the note of grace. The note that has sounded in *pianissimo* through most of the letter here rings out loud and true. Forgiveness must be offered, but it must be balanced with faith that is active, faith that has captured mind and heart and body.

This tension is enormously difficult to live out. On the one hand, we must not fall victim to the siren song of lassitude. Far too often the church of Jesus Christ has, chameleon-like and with dulled senses, adapted its moral vision to fit in with the surrounding culture. Ron Sider reminds us that Jesus spoke some extraordinarily harsh words concerning the corrosive power of money,[14] but American evangelicals easily choose to ignore these words.

Recent years have seen the growing acceptance of women in ministry within evangelical circles, and some say that in like fashion homosexual practice will come to be accepted. The disturbing aspect of this statement is that concession to culture is presumed to be natural, inevitable, and *good*. As evangelicals we are committed to Scripture as our guide, not the capricious winds of social fashion. We do no one any favors when we tell them that attitudes and behaviors that the Bible calls sinful are, instead, lifestyle choices that God actually blesses.

But there is a grave danger on the other side. We need to be honest with ourselves, certain that today's sinners (and this includes you and me) ought to receive the same unconditional love from us as those of first-century Palestine did from Jesus. It is all too easy to maintain an attitude and practical posture of moral superiority that excludes persons on whom Jesus would shower his unconditional love. Hannah More put it well:

> We contrive to make revenge itself look like religion. We call down thunder on many a head under the pretense that those on whom we invoke it are God's enemies, when perhaps we invoke it because they are ours.[15]

---

14. Ronald J. Sider, *Rich Christians in an Age of Hunger: A Biblical Study* (New York: Paulist, 1977).

15. Hannah More, *Religion of the Heart*, ed. Hal M. Helms (Orleans, Miss.: Paraclete 1993), 205.

James calls us to recognize sin *and* to forgive the sinner with warm welcome. To fail at the first is to take sin too lightly. To excuse sin, whether as a harmless quirk or a lifestyle choice, is to deny both the seriousness of the offense and the responsibility of the offender. To this James offers the sternest warning at his command: The result is death. To fail at the second, however, is to fall prey to sterile doctrine and to miss the forgiving spirit at the core of Jesus' ministry. Both are needful.

This tension between righteousness and mercy is a difficult one to negotiate properly. We rarely do it well, as even a cursory investigation of popular conceptions of the Christian faith reveals. This confusion concerning the tension between morality and rigor demonstrates that the Christian community has not consistently understood or practiced the balance as both Jesus and James have expressed it.

James calls us to moral purity and to maintaining a heart of forgiveness. When we do so, we are the true children of God, combining both faith and actions in the fashion that James has taught. It is a call true to the Lord that James served, and to whom we owe ultimate allegiance. But James is not merely the standard bearer of a sterile and impersonal code of conduct. Rather, he writes from an experience of the living Christ, who animates this standard, giving breath and vitality to what can otherwise become a barren and shallow code. He invites us to enter into this love relationship with God and to learn what it means to live in the Spirit. George Caird put it well when he said:

> To follow Jesus or to follow his example turns out to be, as popular tradition has held, the higher road, that particular morality which the gospel imposes on the Christian. But such morality does not consist in conformity to any stereotyped pattern; it consists rather in learning from Jesus an attitude of mind which comprises sensitivity to the presence of God and to the will of God which is the only authority, a constant submission of personal interest to the pursuit of that will in the well-being of others, and a confidence that, whatever the immediate consequences may appear to be, the outcome can safely be left in God's hands.[16]

---

16. G. B. Caird and L. D. Hurst, *New Testament Theology* (Oxford: Clarendon 1994), 204.

Scripture Index

Scripture Index

Subject Index

Abraham, example of, 153–55

adultery, 84

adversity, joy in, 310–12; perseverance through, 296; source of, 22; times of, 300; virtues of, 27. *See also* affliction, suffering

affliction, used by God, 309, 311, 313

ambition, 205–6

angels, as friendly guardians, 83

anger, 61, 104–7; prayers offered in, 222; speaking without, 89–92

anointing, of the sick, 303–6

antinomianism, 179, 181, 318

apostolic authority, 46

apotelestheisa, 74

astheneo, 304

atonement, 235

authority, 40–43, 46, 247; of judging, 257; over all the earth, 184–85; and wisdom, 205. *See also* power, political power

belief, meaning of, 160

Benedict of Nursia, 296

Bible, world of, 9

boasting, 250–54, 261

Bonhoeffer, Dietrich, 163–64, 193

brothers, as a term, 248, 250; use of, 46–47, 55, 298

Caird, G. B., 87, 325

Catherine of Genoa, 294–96

charity, relation to wealth, 112

Christian community, 90, 92, 195; creation of, 16; division of, 223; egalitarian, 117; and false teaching, 319–20; and favoritism, 113; idea of, 321–22; and mercy, 323; model of, 140–45; of mutual care, 28; and the rich, 55; and the world, 226. *See also* church, community

Christology, 285, 306; of James, 24–25, 120

church, control of, 176; discord in, 209; favoritism in, 114–17, 119; judgment within, 255; leadership in, 42–44, 184, 259; slander within, 258; and state, 244; as successor to Judaism, 39; and truth, 46; of twentieth century, 197; and the world of evil, 189. *See also* Christian community, community

church architecture, 135

Churchill, Winston, 198–200

Church of Christ, 195

Clinton, Bill, 201

commands, of God, 101

communism, 80

community, call to, 243; confession and, 315; idea of, 44; marked by mutual care, 15; and the poor, 147; practice of, 68; and sacrifice, 233, 236; and status, 22. *See also* Christian community, church

compassion, 101; community of, 141, 143; for one another, 84–86

complaining, avoidance of, 286–87

compromise, bane of, 226

confession, 318; and community, 315

consumerism, 134–35

contrition, 230

conversion, 319

covenant, with God, 233

creation, 77

crown of life, 71–72, 81

culture, captivated with wealth, 261; and Christianity, 241; sick and dangerous, 132–39; standards of, 131. *See also* world

cursing, question of, 181